THE
GRIMÀLDIS
OF
MONACO

BOOKS BY ANNE EDWARDS

BIOGRAPHY

Sonya: The Life of Countess Tolstoy

Vivien Leigh: A Biography

Judy Garland: A Biography

Road to Tara: The Life of Margaret Mitchell

Matriarch: Queen Mary and the House of Windsor

A Remarkable Woman: A Biography of Katharine Hepburn

Early Reagan: The Rise to Power

Shirley Temple: American Princess

The DeMilles: An American Family

Royal Sisters: Queen Elizabeth and Princess Margaret

The Grimaldis of Monaco

NOVELS

The Survivors

Shadow of a Lion

Haunted Summer

Miklos Alexandrovitch Is Missing

The Hesitant Heart

Child of Night

Wallis: The Novel

AUTOBIOGRAPHY

The Inn and Us (with Stephen Citron)

CHILDREN'S BOOKS

P. T. Barnum

The Great Houdini

A Child's Bible

THE
GRIMALDIS
OF
MONACO

ANNE EDWARDS

WILLIAM MORROW AND COMPANY, INC.
New York

Library of Congress Cataloging-in-Publication Data

Edwards, Anna, 1927–
    The Grimaldis of Monaco / Anne Edwards.
        p.   cm.
    Includes bibliographical references and index.
    ISBN 0-688-08837-6
    1. Grimaldi family.   2. Monaco—Princes and princesses—Biography.
3. Rainier III, Prince of Monaco, 1923–   —Family.   I. Title.
DC943.A1G754   1992
944′.949′0099—dc20   92-6734
    [B]   CIP

Printed in the United States of America

First Edition

1   2   3   4   5   6   7   8   9   10

BOOK DESIGN BY MICHAEL MENDELSOHN

MAPS BY ARLENE SCHLEIFER GOLDBERG

For Polly Brown
With Love and Gratitude

ACKNOWLEDGMENTS

In most works of nonfiction the author's family is mentioned with gratitude in the closing paragraph of the Acknowledgments. I have been fortunate in the writing of this book to have had the assistance of many fine archivists, librarians and authorities in French and Monégasque history. But my greatest debt is to my husband, Stephen Citron, who—although he has his own demanding career as an author and musicologist—has helped me in every step of the progress of this project, as he has in all my past endeavors. On this book he has been my companion, able translator, research assistant and editorial adviser, taking months away from his own work to travel with me to various European archives to help me in the difficult task of re-creating with accuracy the history of Monaco and the lives of the Grimaldis, reading journals, documents and letters of the far past, handwritten in French and Italian, and translating the contents for me. And this was just part of his contribution to this work. In addition, he provided encouragement, keen critical insight and even supplied computer expertise when I seemed to be losing my battle (and perhaps a chapter of hard work) to that mechanical monster—and always with gracious forbearance.

I benefited greatly from the considerable help of two other members of my extraordinary family: my stepson, Alexander Citron, whose English translations from French of archival letters and papers were an immense aid, and Polly Brown (to whom this book is dedicated), my Washington researcher and much-loved daughter-in-law.

I owe a large debt to H.S.H. Prince Rainier for my access to the Archives du Palais Princier de Monaco, and for the right to use many of the photographs from the archives for this book. I am most grateful to Monsieur Régis Lécuyer, Conservateur adjoint of the Archives du Palais Princier, who not only helped me to locate the material most relevant to my book, but read through several chapters to assure that they were accurate in all historical detail and answered all my questions (and there were many) with much kindness and consideration. My appreciation, as well, to the members of M. Lécuyer's staff who were so generous with their time while I researched in their archives. Among the many other people in Monaco to whom I am indebted, I must thank especially Madame Nadia Lacoste, Attaché de Presse du Société des Bains de Mer; Mlle. Judith Mann, Secretary to Princesse Caroline; M. George Sandulescu, Director, Princesse Grace Library; Comtesse Elizabeth Prince de Ramel; Mlle. Maguy Maccario, Promotional and Marketing Manager, Monaco Government Office; and Ms. Brigette Charles, Monaco Tourist & Convention Office, London.

I am grateful for the assistance of the staff members of the Greater Manchester Library in my research there; Charles S. Longley, Curator of Microtexts and Newspapers, Boston Public Library; Nicholas Aldridge, Summerfields, Oxford; Christopher Atkinson, Stowe School, Buckingham; Charles Israel, University of North Carolina Library; Brenda Gallaway, Urban Archives, Temple University, Philadelphia, Pennsylvania; Jody Davis, Park County Historical Society, Cody, Wyoming; Elizabeth Holmes, Buffalo Bill Historical Center, Cody, Wyoming, and Andrea Ducros, New Orleans Public Library.

I am especially thankful to Mrs. Phyllis W. Johnson who was so resourceful in checking New Orleans birth and census records regarding the Heine family; Zuma Y. Salaun, Historical Nuggets, New Orleans; Mary Gehman, New Orleans, and to George Gagnet, also of that city and a cousin to the first American woman to become a Princesse de Monaco, Alice Heine.

I have been fortunate to have two extraordinary English editors, Richard Johnson and Robert Lacey of Harper-Collins, whose careful attention to my manuscript has been tremendously helpful. This is the sixth book on which Harvey Ginsberg has been my editor at William Morrow and it has been a collaboration that, in my long association with publishers, I know to be unique. Among the other people at Morrow to whom I am deeply indebted are Lisa Queen, who has been a tower of strength in her belief in my work; my excellent copy editor, Joan Amico; the enthusiastic and talented Robert Aulicino, who designed the cover; Frank Mount and Scott Manning.

Few authors have the valued advice of two extraordinary agents. For twenty-five years my English agent, Hilary Rubinstein, has been an encouraging constant in my life. If I have never told him how much this has meant to me, let me do it now, along with my deepest gratitude to Clarissa Rushdie and Linda Shaughnessy of the A. P. Watt, Ltd., office. At I.C.M. in New York, Mitchell Douglas, who has represented me for seventeen years, always has given me good counsel, been there when I needed him and offered his enthusiasm at every turn. My added gratitude to Peter Napolitano, whose cheerful help has been enormous.

Lastly, to my able assistant in London, Sally Slaney, whose keen eyes, good instinct and tremendous stick-to-itiveness have been invaluable assets, my sincere admiration and appreciation.

CONTENTS

11

OCTOBER
1990

1

Speedboat racing was Stefano Casiraghi's passion, and although Princesse Caroline feared the dangers of the sport, she was confident of her husband's ability and knew how much retaining the world offshore powerboat championship, which he had won the previous year, meant to him. She had remained in Paris with their three children while he competed in his speedboat, the Pinôt di Pinôt. On the morning of October 3, 1990, she had spoken to him as he was leaving for the race, and his high spirits had been contagious.

Under normal circumstances, she would have been in Monaco cheering Stefano on. However, after ten years she had finally arranged a meeting in Paris with Philippe Junot, her first husband, to solicit his help in having their short, disastrous and childless marriage annulled so that her union with Stefano would be recognized by the Roman Catholic Church and their children legitimized. Despite the fact that over half of Monaco's citizens had signed a petition to the Pope supporting Caroline's wish, the Roman Church remained obdurate. She now planned to appeal personally to Junot for his cooperation. Although stubbornly unhelpful in the past, Junot had recently remarried and the new Mrs. Junot had given birth to their child. Caroline was, therefore, optimistic that he could be persuaded to back her plea for a Church annulment of their marriage so that he could legitimize his own child.

Caroline did not need her father's constant reminder that if she failed with Junot the succession of the Grimaldis was seriously threatened. Monaco had an heir to the throne in her younger, unmarried brother, Albert. Should he remain single, or die before fathering a child, their father, Prince Rainier III, had it in his power to designate Caroline as his successor. But as things stood the Grimaldi line could end there, for in order

15

for the Principality to pass to her son with Casiraghi, the legit-imacy of her remarriage and of the boy's birth had to be es-tablished. Because of a Franco-Monégasque agreement made in 1911, if there were no direct Grimaldi heir either by birth or adoption, Monaco would cede to France. Junot, therefore, must be persuaded to supply the Vatican with the necessary information (corroboration that the marriage had either not been consummated or had been entered into under false prem-ises) to obtain the vital Decree of Nullity.

Caroline's romantic exploits once had been front-page news. Her first marriage, in June 1978, at twenty-one, to Junot had lasted only twenty-eight months, and when—after obtaining a civil divorce from Junot, she wed Stefano in a civil ceremony on December 29, 1983, she had been four months pregnant. Since then she had worked diligently to maintain a sober image. "When you're young," Caroline had recently told a reporter in the pronounced American accent that always surprised people, "you make mistakes of course. If you're anybody else [but a royal princess] you have time to sort it out for yourself."

She carried herself with regal pride and was far more stun-ning in person than photographs suggested. She had amazing navy-blue eyes, dark, arched brows, a full, sensuous mouth and a rich brown mane of hair framing her well-boned face. Her carriage and demeanor (always courteous but somewhat dis-tant), her unexpected intelligence and sharp wit, gave her added presence. Since her mother's death in 1982, Caroline had be-come Monaco's First Lady and had quickly shed her old image as a royal rebel.

Her hair was being styled by the proprietor of a Parisian salon when her good friend, former Chanel model Ines de la Fressange, suddenly appeared, her almond-shaped eyes even darker than usual. Nervously she began to speak. There had been an accident, she told Caroline. Stefano's boat had capsized.

"Stefano?" Caroline asked, her voice a brittle whisper.

Ines de la Fressange placed her hand comfortingly on Car-oline's shoulder. "Dead," she whispered. They left the salon by limousine a short time later. Caroline's planned meeting with Junot was canceled. In a matter of hours Caroline, having now been told the full story of her husband's death, would be back in Monaco with her three children.

16

The Pinôt di Pinôt had flipped over near Saint-Jean-Cap-Ferrat. Stefano's copilot, Patrice Innocenti, had been ejected and thrown clear but Stefano had remained strapped to his seat and had borne the full impact of the two-engine, five-ton boat as it smashed into a wave at ninety-three miles per hour. Trapped beneath the hull, Stefano had died instantly. The two men had been trying to make up for time they had lost earlier in the race when they had stopped to rescue a pilot whose vessel had caught fire.

Caroline's plane swerved, circled and landed in Nice, the nearest major airport to Monaco. Eight years earlier, when her mother died, she had also returned home from Paris to bury a loved one. Then, her father had leaned on her. Now, she turned to him for support and he did not disappoint her.

She had been unable to tell the children that their father was dead, perhaps because she could not yet bring herself to believe it. Not until she saw Prince Rainier's ravaged face did she break down and cry. Since her mother's death father and daughter had become extremely close. He had fought the Church on her behalf and had wholeheartedly welcomed Stefano into the family. Now, he was the one to sit down with his young grandchildren—Andrea, Charlotte and Pierre—and tell them of their terrible loss.

Monaco, the smallest principality in the world, the size of Hyde Park in London and Central Park in New York, is a rocky and fortified promontory that stretches out into the deep blue waters of the Mediterranean. It seems to stand apart from the rest of the Côte d'Azur, and not to belong to the present order of things. An air of mystery has hung over it since the fourteenth century, when people spoke of it as "a nest of robbers." Even its Casino, which opened in the mid-nineteenth century and became its greatest attraction, was said to be haunted by an evil spirit that lured men to their ruin.

More recently, Monaco's glamorous city, Monte Carlo, had become the sun and fun spot of the rich and famous and of those who were desperate to be so. Prince Rainier's reign had brought the diminutive Principality great notoriety and prosperity, in part because of his marriage to the American film star Grace Kelly. Caroline had great pride in her parentage and in her lineage. Monaco may only have covered 1.95 square kilo-

17

meters, but it had survived centuries of wars, tragedy and an uncompromising sea, and had remained independent despite being almost entirely surrounded by much larger countries.

Since François Grimaldi had first seized Monaco from the Genoese in 1297 the line of succession had been unbroken, although their rule had been interrupted several times. There was a great deal more to Monaco than Monte Carlo, which was often disparagingly called Las Vegas-*sur-plage*. The world might believe that gambling had saved the Principality from financial ruin, but Caroline contended that it was the great independent spirit of the Princes of Monaco and, especially, of certain of their wives that had kept the country from going under, or being lost to France.

Caroline had led an international life. Her mother, after all, was American, she was educated in England and France, married first to a Frenchman, then to an Italian, had divided her time between Paris and Monaco for years, and could speak six languages. Yet she felt Monégasque through and through.

The sea was calm on the day of Stefano's funeral. The heavy gold cross Caroline wore around the neck of her stark black dress glittered in the bright sun. A thick black lace shawl covered her head and fell over her shoulders. Black stockings, shoes and gloves and large dark sunglasses completed her mourning outfit. Her father and brother flanked her; her sister, Stephanie, stood directly behind her as the grieving family waited at the foot of the steps of Monaco's five-centuries-old Cathedral for the mahogany coffin to be lifted out of the silver Mercedes hearse by the pallbearers. As it appeared, Caroline faltered. Her father tightened his grip on her arm and Stephanie moved closer to her.

She immediately straightened, and together the Grimaldis started up the steps of the Cathedral, hundreds of floral wreaths lining the way. Fourteen members of the Carabinieri, the Palace Guard, dressed in white ceremonial uniforms, mounted a guard of honor as the coffin was borne into the Cathedral, which was filled with over seven hundred mourners, among them Madame Danielle Mitterrand, wife of the French president, the actor Alain Delon, Caroline's close friend, the designer Karl Lagerfeld and Prince Fuad of Egypt. The Grimaldis occupied the first pew. The scent of burning candles pervaded the vaulted interior as the Requiem Mass was celebrated by Monsignor Joseph Sardou, Archbishop of Monaco.

Stephanie wept throughout, and at one stage had to be taken by her brother to the chancel, returning just as the Archbishop ended the Mass. But Caroline sat erect, her head lowering only in prayer. If she shed tears behind the dark glasses they could not be seen. No one inside the Cathedral could help but note the queenliness of her bearing or the close attention paid to her by her father.

The actual burial service took place at the Chapelle de la Paix a few hundred yards from the Clos Saint Pierre, Caroline's pale-pink villa that she and Stefano had decorated together and where they had spent some of their happiest days in the eight short years of their marriage. Only the intimate family were present to see Stefano laid to rest in his red and white pilot's suit. It was twelve noon, and in tribute the Hôtel de Paris in Monte Carlo did not serve lunch in its three-star restaurant, the day's speedboat race was canceled, and a wreath was lowered onto the glistening patch of sea where Stefano Casiraghi had perished.

Days and weeks passed, and Caroline remained cloistered at Clos Saint Pierre. She refused to go to her office in the Palace, but she did walk twice a day across the ancient cobblestones to where Stefano was entombed. Added to her grief was a terrible and growing anger. Stefano had died with their children still marked illegitimate; her father's withholding of the four million five hundred thousand francs he gave annually to the Catholic Church had not managed to budge the Church authorities.

Still, at heart, Caroline was a true Grimaldi, and was not about to give up the fight. The Grimaldis had a history of tenacity. They had endured longer than any other European monarchy including those of Great Britain, France and Russia. Keeping the Grimaldi line intact was of the utmost importance. They were the last of a vanishing breed, an endangered species who had fought against the most staggering odds to survive. Often, this had been achieved through the women belonging to the House of Grimaldi or to whom the Grimaldi men had been married. But the chain remained unbroken.

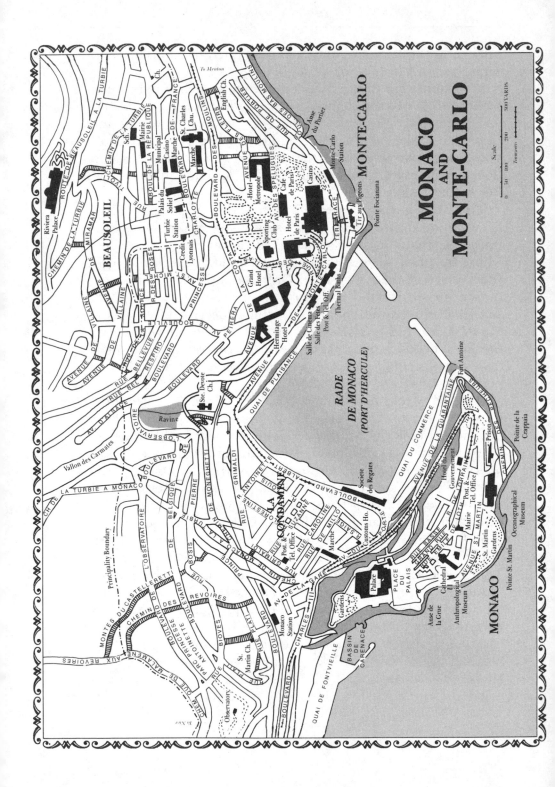

A ROMANTIC
PAST
1215–1795

2

THE EARLY HISTORY of the Grimaldis, "an ambitious, hot-blooded, unscrupulous race, keen to plunder, swift to revenge and furious in battle," is entangled from the thirteenth to the sixteenth centuries not only with the wars of the Genoese but with the quarrels and hatreds, the conquests and stratagems of other Italian republics. Whenever there was fighting to be done, it seemed, a Grimaldi laid his hand upon a sword and led his followers into battle.

Monaco's position was exactly suited for the role which its successive rulers were to play. A huge, bare rock with precipitous sides, it was connected to the mainland by the narrowest strip of ground; and its strategic location, jutting out into the Mediterranean, and its natural defenses made it a place of much importance. The tremendous cliffs of the Southern Alps guarded it from danger on the north, a restless sea almost encompassed it, and its inhabitants—however small in number—were cunning providers, skilled in all the arts of defense. If their territory did not produce corn and wine, these rovers knew where to find such supplies without paying for them. Free trade was their rule, and they never paid import duties.

Centuries before the Grimaldis took possession of Monaco, the Carthaginian general Hannibal used its port for his fleets in 221 B.C. during his struggle with the Romans. In his conflict with Pompey in 69 B.C., Julius Caesar anchored his ships there. After the fall of the Roman Empire in 476, it was ruled by the Lombards, an ancient Germanic people. When they were driven out by Charlemagne in 774, it became a prey to the Muslim tribes of Saracens who originated in northwest Arabia, and in subsequent years it was a vital fortress in the constant conflicts between the Guelf and the Ghibelline parties, the opposing political factions in Italy and Germany. In 1190, the Holy

Roman Emperor Henry VI, crowned King of Germany and Italy, gave Monaco to Genoa on condition that its fortifications should be reserved for the service of the Holy Roman Empire.

Throughout this time Monaco appears to have been any warring country's refuge. When first heard of in about 200 B.C., it was an uninhabited rock at the foot of which sailors who voyaged along the coast of Liguria (which we now know as the Italian Riviera) and of Provence came to seek shelter from tempest and attack. Greek and Roman geographers called it "Portus Monachus" or "Portus Monachi" because there was said to have been, in more ancient times, at the extremity of this promontory, a temple dedicated to Hercules and served by a single priest, the monk Monachus. But the men who sailed their ships into the port referred to it most commonly as "the Rock."

Monaco was still a wild, uninhabited place, without bounds and without jurisdiction, when on August 16, 1174, the powerful Genoese drew up a charter granting themselves the right to construct a castle on the Rock to defend the adjacent coast.

The Genoese, who were interested in Monaco strictly for maritime usage, intended the castle to be "for the defence of the Christians against the Saracens and for the use of imperial troops in case of war between the [Holy Roman] Empire and the Provençals." Construction was begun and the Genoese kept a small contingent of soldiers to protect their interests.

The Grimaldis were not yet connected with Monaco. Their first known ancestor, Otto Canella, was a consul of Genoa in 1133. The youngest of his three sons, Grimaldo, was also active in the affairs of the Genoese republic, and it was he who gave his name to the family. They were an ambitious tribe, greedy for power within Genoa, always with an eye toward their own enrichment. The family, who were Ghibellines in the long struggle between the popes (Guelfs) and the emperors (Ghibellines), were pitted against the Doria and Spinola families on the Guelf side.

By the late thirteenth century, during the years when Marco Polo was journeying throughout the Orient, Rainier Grimaldi, a wealthy sea trader, became the head of the family. He was an elegant, darkly handsome man, and a bold sailor who commanded ships in the service of Charles II, King of Naples. Respected and feared both by his family and his enemies, he

24

brought the name of Grimaldi into prominence. His home in Genoa was a palace equal to the king's and he ruled his kinsmen with a just but iron hand.

One who envied Rainier's wealth and resented his power was his nephew François Grimaldi, nicknamed The Spiteful. Perhaps in a bid to strengthen his position in the family, in 1295 François successfully commanded an army of Ghibellines in Liguria against his uncle's enemies, the Genoese Guelfs, forcing them to flee and take refuge on the Rock, where in 1215 the Genoese had built a fortress. François waited two long years for his chance to attack. On the dark, cold night of January 8, 1297, a near-gale wind blowing, the sea lashing against the base of the Rock, he led a small band of followers up the precipitous side of the cliff to the fortress. While his men were pressed against the stone walls, well hidden by the darkness, François—disguised as a Franciscan monk—knocked on the postern gate and asked for hospitality for the night.

The modest detachment of half-asleep Genoese soldiers who manned the fortress let him in. Once inside, François drew his sword from beneath his friar's robes and shouted to his waiting companions, who burst through the door to assist him in overcoming and killing all of the surprised Genoese.

Monaco was for the first time under the rule of a Grimaldi. But cunning as François was, he did not have the army or the funds to resist the continuing attacks of the Genoese, and only four years later he was forced to flee Monaco. The family, their fortunes increased by sea trade, did not give up in their efforts to regain it, and in 1338 Charles Grimaldi, the son of Rainier, through purchase from Genoa, which held title to the Rock, became sole lord of Monaco, which consisted of a fortress and some narrow rows of simple houses that were home to the two hundred or so Monégasques.

Along with dreams of expansion, Charles envisioned a great castle being constructed on the crest of the Rock. These aspirations were set aside when the dynastic quarrel between Philip VI of France and Edward III of England erupted into what was to become known as the Hundred Years' War. Edward invaded France in 1349 and Charles went off to fight in the service of Philip as Admiral of the French fleet.

During his long absence the aggressive character of the Monégasques exhibited itself in acts of relentless piracy. From the craggy height and vantage point of the Rock, they could sight approaching ships early enough to man their own craft and take the alien vessels by surprise. Monaco, because of its impregnability, became the home of bankrupts and the refuge of criminals and pirates who ravaged the coasts of Liguria, ruining commerce and showing no mercy for their victims.

When Charles finally returned after a decade's absence, he put an end to piracy in the waters surrounding Monaco, and having been rewarded handsomely by Philip VI for his wartime service, he bought the small neighboring villages and farmlands of Roccabruna and Mentone (later Roquebrune and Menton). A township soon grew in the shadow of the fortress, and within thirty years Charles Grimaldi had become the richest of the feudal lords, or seigneurs, along the Riviera. But the Genoese republic, now fearing Monaco's alliance with France, in 1355 attacked by sea and land with four thousand troops. With an army only one-tenth that size, unable to resist such a superior force, Charles Grimaldi surrendered, his fortunes lost. Shortly after the last battle in 1357 he died, and his son Rainier II was forced to flee and never returned. Yet once again the resilient Grimaldis accumulated great wealth through sea trade, and in 1419 Rainier II's three sons—Ambroise, Antoine and Jean— purchased Monaco in the name of Grimaldi from its current owner, Queen Yolande of Aragon. The citadel of Monaco had been embroiled for centuries in battles for its limited land and had flown more flags than any Mediterranean neighbor. The Grimaldis had recovered their Rock and the three brothers ruled their small dominion in yearly rotation.

Jean was the last to die and it was his will and testament, written in 1454 in Italian (which was the official language of Monaco), that would regulate the succession of the Grimaldis down to the present. The eldest son would inherit, and if there was no male issue, the eldest daughter would succeed on condition that her husband assumed the name and arms of Grimaldi. In 1487 Lambert Grimaldi amended the laws of succession to exclude those family members who had entered the Church.

Over the next two centuries four seigneurs of Monaco died violently; this was, after all, a time when Italian princes poisoned each other, the Spanish Inquisition burned its prisoners at the stake, and England's Henry VIII had two of his wives beheaded. The lust for power and the power of lust were not limited to the great states and their popes and monarchs. Even rulers whose small empire was a rock with under a thousand subjects were vulnerable. In 1505 Jean II was murdered by, and then succeeded by, his brother Lucien, who in turn, along with Augustin, another brother, was assassinated by his nephew François. In 1604, after reigning for fifteen years, Lucien's grandson Hercule (infamous for his debauchery) was stabbed to death in a narrow, dark alley in Monaco by a group of Monégasque men whose daughters he had defiled. His body was thrown over the cliff into the sea.

The Grimaldis survived these incursions on family unity and good name. But they became wary. Hercule had left a seven-year-old son as heir. Fearing that the boy, who was now Honoré II, and his younger sister, Jeanne, might be murdered by the same men who had killed their father, family retainers hid the children in the vaults beneath the castle until their maternal uncle Federico Landi, Prince de Valdetare, a Milanese, arrived with his wife and was declared Regent. He saw that Honoré received the oath of loyalty, instituted criminal proceedings against Hercule's murderers and then—leaving the children in his wife's care—returned to Milan, where he signed an agreement with the Spanish government to allow its troops to garrison in Monaco. A few months later, the Spanish regiment installed, he went back to Monaco. After a week's stay he set out again for Milan—this time with Honoré. The boy remained in Milan with his uncle for the next ten years.

Milan was under Spanish domination after having flourished for years as one of Italy's most important duchies, and the proud, arrogant Milanese bridled with resentment. Prince de Valdetare was most conscious of rank, and was determined to have his nephew assume the title of Prince de Monaco. To this end, in 1612, in a document requiring Honoré's signature, he inserted the words: "Honoré II, regnant, *prince* and seigneur by the grace of God of Monaco, Mentone, and Roquebrune." The Spanish government let this pass, and thus Monaco became known as a principality.

Honoré II, now designated first Prince de Monaco, returned

to his Principality in 1615, shortly before his twentieth birthday. The shock must have been tremendous. He had left the sophistication and culture of Milan for life on a rock with no roads for fine carriages, nor castles for balls, nor beautiful ladies to dance with or from whom to find a suitable bride. His sister, Jeanne, now married, had remained in Monaco while he was in Milan. Fortunately her husband had a fifteen-year-old sister—demure, slim, dark-haired, a potential beauty, raised by nuns in a nearby convent. Named Hippolyte, she proved to be Honoré's salvation. They married a few months after his return and settled down to live in Monaco. Well-educated, his appearance refined and urbane, and with none of the lustiness that had marked his ancestors, Honoré occupied his time extending and refurbishing the castle in the style of the Milanese splendor of his youth.

Despite this idyllic existence, and his happy marriage, Honoré considered himself a prisoner of the Spanish. He had no real power in his small principality as long as Spanish soldiers occupied the garrison. And with so few other men on the Rock, Monégasque women were marrying Spaniards. Honoré's one aim was to disengage Monaco from Spain, and the only country powerful enough to help him succeed was France. He turned to Cardinal Richelieu, head of the Roman Catholic Church and chief minister to Louis XIII. (Earlier that year, 1630, Richelieu, had gained full control of the French government.) But what did Monaco have to offer in exchange?

For one thing, it occupied a position between French- and Spanish-held territory. For another, it would be a viable port in time of war. Nonetheless, five years were to pass before a treaty was drawn up by the Cardinal and signed by Louis XIII which assured Honoré II and Monaco the protection of France. The treaty then had to be put into effect and the Spanish made to leave the Principality. But French troops were pledged to help Sweden's King Gustavus II when he entered into the vast conflict, later called the Thirty Years' War, against Germany. In 1635, France entered openly into the battle which had spread to include most of Europe. Despite their treaty, the French could not concern themselves with Monaco's trials, and the Principality was no better off than before.

A plan for the small Monégasque army to infiltrate and overpower the Spanish garrison failed and Honoré found himself in desperate straits. Monaco was an occupied zone and Honoré's letters imploring Richelieu's assistance were ignored. This situation lasted for a decade. Finally, on the evening of November 17, 1641, the wind at hurricane velocity, Honoré commanded a loyal band of Monégasques in an attack on the Spanish garrison and eventually overpowered it. The victory was much admired by Louis XIII, who sent Honoré a royal command for an audience. This, Honoré knew, was his chance to achieve from France the protection that had been pledged by Richelieu.

Because no roads yet connected Monaco with France, on April 25, 1642, Honoré traveled by sea to Marseilles and then on to the royal field headquarters near Perpignan, where he was met by a company of a hundred French soldiers. Two leagues farther on, a royal coach waited; one league more, and a guard of honor presented arms and Honoré was welcomed by the King and invested with the Order of the Saint Esprit. The two men took an immediate liking to each other. At Narbonne, on his return journey, Honoré received letters from Louis XIII creating him duke and peer of the realm, with title to the duchy of the Valentinois (in Provence and ten times the area of Monaco) and its revenues.

It was one thing to hold the title of Prince de Monaco; quite another also to be the Duc de Valentinois, recognized by the French Court with all the additional rights and privileges of such a high and esteemed peerage. Honoré immediately set forth on a campaign to upgrade his image and style of life to suit his new prestige. He funded a ballet company, hung Gobelin tapestries in his palace alongside paintings by Titian, Rubens, Raphael and Dürer, and encouraged and bought work from local artists. He also inaugurated colorful religious festivals that united his own family with his people in worship.

But with the deaths of Cardinal Richelieu in 1642 and Louis XIII a year later, and the expense of Honoré's refurbishments and acquisitions, Monaco needed money and a vital connection with the new Court of Louis XIV.

Honoré's only son died in 1651, making his grandson, Louis, godson and namesake of Louis XIII, his heir at the age of nine. The young man had spent a happy childhood on the Rock, adored by his grandfather and the Monégasques. To strengthen his sense of dedication to Monaco, Honoré had permitted him to travel abroad. Now Honoré was aging and the time was right for the future Prince de Monaco to marry a rich bride with close ties to the French monarchy. One of Honoré's last acts was to find for Louis a prestigious wife, the daughter of a high noble in the French Court.

Although a principality as inconsequential as Monaco to the power balance of Europe might not have seemed the greatest bait with which to catch a wealthy, well-connected bride, there were many advantages in such an alliance. First, French nobility was passed on only in the male line. This meant that noblemen wishing their daughters to marry into their rank had to pay huge dowries even if it meant going heavily into debt. The higher the rank of the prospective son-in-law, the larger the dowry. And a foreign sovereign prince with rank and peerage in the Court was close to the top of the social scale.

The French Court was hierarchically arranged. On top of the pyramid was the King. Then came the Queen and the immediate heir to the Crown; next the legitimate descendants in the male line of the present or former kings of France, followed by the princes of royal blood (comprising all those who descended from former French kings other than those of the present line), and—after them—the so-called foreign princes, whose title was that of *ducs et pairs étrangers,* who were recognized by the Crown and who were deemed to owe a special loyalty to France. At this time there were only seven: Bouillon, Rohan (Brittany), Lorraine, Soissons (Savoy), Gonzaga-Nevers (Mantua), La Tremoille (Neuchâtel) and Grimaldi (Monaco).

As Honoré's first loyalty had always been to his Principality, he had never spent time in the French Court, where the foreign princes were accorded extra privileges and took precedence over all other *ducs et pairs:* the descendants of families which from the dawn of the French monarchy had held hereditary fiefs. The foreign princes walked immediately behind the princes of royal blood in all processions such as Te Deums and royal marriages and funerals, and their wives were entitled to bring two carriages into the royal courtyard, one for themselves and another for their entourage, and to be seated on *tabourets* in the presence of the Queen.

By marrying Louis, a nobleman's daughter would thus be

assured of social, economic and Court preeminence as well as of retaining the guarantees of the aristocracy: the right to be heard in a high court of law, to be exempt from corporal punishment, to be beheaded rather than hanged if found guilty of a capital offense. At this time, nobles also had total immunity from direct taxation—an inadequate tradeoff, for nobles were debarred from increasing their wealth through manufacturing or business, and their lands and a life at Court were expensive to maintain. Many of them were impoverished and the real income of nearly all was declining, which would prompt France's great statesman and diplomat Charles Talleyrand later to write: "A Court is an assembly of noble and distinguished beggars."

Nonetheless, the advantages of life as a courtier seemed to outweigh all other considerations. The King moved from the Palais Royal in Paris to Fontainebleau and then to Versailles, the center for the arts and fashion. There were about ten thousand members of the Court (which included the nobles and their entourages) as well as fifteen thousand members of the King's staff and servants. Most of the courtiers had their own homes and estates. Since proximity to the King had real advantages, they did not want to be left behind and had to be housed at the royal palaces, where the best accommodations were allocated to the highest-ranking members.

Understandably, a nobleman would overlook a great deal in a prospective son-in-law to see that his daughter not only remained part of the Court but was married to a *duc et pair étranger*. Honoré had a good chance, therefore, of finding a suitable wife for Louis. His own marriage had been happy and his life had centered around his family and the Principality. If Louis married into the French aristocracy, he would have to spend most of his time at the French Court. But in the interest of the future security of Monaco, this seemed a small enough sacrifice.

The aging Prince sat down with several of his advisers and went through the list of French aristocrats with marriageable daughters. At last they agreed that Charlotte-Catherine de Gramont, daughter of the influential Maréchal (Duc) de Gramont and grandniece of the late Cardinal Richelieu, perfectly fitted the bill. Gramont's elevated position as Maréchal (Grand Marshal of Lodgings, who allocated rooms wherever the King took his Court) brought him into close contact with the King, and his daughter was said to be not only beautiful but also witty and intelligent. True, Louis was only seventeen, and she was twenty, but it was understood that she was unmarried because she had been passionately in love with a cousin whom her father refused to allow her to wed. Honoré had been assured the affair was over. All the more reason, the wise men of Monaco concurred, for the Duc de Gramont to accede to their request on behalf of young Louis.

They were proved right. But what they had not anticipated was the young woman's tempestuous nature.

3

WHEN LOUIS AND CHARLOTTE-CATHERINE first came face to face, they were to be married in March, 1660. He saw a sophisticated young woman of twenty with piercingly direct dark eyes, aristocratic nose, a mocking smile, flawless white skin and a voluptuous figure swathed in an expensive gold silk décolleté gown that framed the soft curves of her body and set off the magnificent diamond and pearl necklace that caressed her long, graceful neck. She held her head in an arrogant manner, and even a young man far less sensitive than Louis could have seen that she was a willful, defiant woman, spoiled and disdainful of those who did not arouse her interest. She had been educated at the fashionable Convent of the Visitation de Faubourg Saint-Jacques in Paris, which was attended by many aristocratic young women, most of whom resented the restrictive rules and the unattractive habits they were made to wear. Queen Christina of Sweden had recently visited France, and Charlotte-Catherine had been much impressed with her flamboyant personality and her philosophy that "the more passions and desires one has, the more ways one has of being happy."

Considered a rebel even by her peers, Charlotte-Catherine had a taste for adventure and was of a highly sensual nature. The inexperienced youth of seventeen, hair not yet grown on his face, who was her prospective bridegroom did not win her heart. And although he possessed a gentle manner, a soft, sensitive smile and wistful green eyes, he was unfamiliar with the gallantry, wit and fashion of the French Court.

Charlotte-Catherine's family lived on a royal scale, but like many of the aristocrats of the time, her father was short of funds and had been forced to borrow 100,000 livres from Cardinal Mazarin and another 200,000 from the royal treasury for her dowry. Furthermore, the King had approved the wedding contract and his generous wedding gift to the groom had been the Duchy of Valentinois in Dauphiné, the Duchy of Carladez in Lyonnaise, the Marquisate of Baux and the Lordship of Buis in Provence, with an income of 75,000 livres annually from rents.

True, Louis's principality was the smallest in Europe and could not increase its territories because it was hemmed in by France. Still, Charlotte-Catherine would be married to a *duc et pair étranger* and would be the Duchesse de Valentinois, and after the death of her bridegroom's grandfather, she would become Princesse de Monaco. And her father had assured her that at least while Honoré II was alive, she and her husband would not have to move to Monaco. However, her cousin, Antonin Nompar, Marquis de Puyguilheim, Captain of the King's Household Troops and a man with a notorious romantic reputation, also lived in Paris and despite her father's opposition was still her lover.

Louis, with his unworldly past (for it was he, not his bride, who was entering this union as a virgin), was unprepared for what he would encounter once wed to this astonishing young woman. He only knew that he had never seen anyone quite like her, and was satisfied with the choice his grandfather had made for him.

Charlotte-Catherine had tried her best to avoid this marriage. But her father had been determined, Puyguilheim was unwilling to incur the King's wrath and the consequences if they eloped, and the King was too distraught over his own marriage arrangements to be sympathetic to the romantic complications of a nobleman's headstrong daughter—even though he was not without understanding.

Only twenty-one years old himself, the King had been desperately in love for several years with Cardinal Mazarin's niece Marie Mancini. He had just been informed that for political, dynastic and economic reasons (the dowry was to be 500,000 gold écus) he must marry his first cousin, Marie Thérèse, daughter of Philip IV, King of Spain. Brokenhearted but dutiful, he had said good-bye to his great love only a few days before the Duc de Gramont asked permission for Charlotte-Catherine to marry.

They were wed at the Gramonts' Château de Pau in the Pyrenees. "The whole house is among the most lavish and festive in the region," wrote a wedding guest. "The palm court, the amount of marble all gave the place a very lavish feeling . . . the King's Chamber, former bedroom of the Kings of Navarre, had been reserved for the [bridegroom] and the walls had been decorated with fine tapestries." The newlyweds remained at Pau for the month of April and then left for Paris, where they occupied the second floor of the Gramonts' magnificent town house on the rue de l'Autriche. Having spent all his life in the provincial atmosphere of the Rock, Louis had difficulty adjusting to the dramatic change in his social position and life at Court.

The King was married less than three months later and to counteract the dolorous effect of Marie Thérèse's ponderous Spanish piety, the summer of 1660 was filled with Court balls, ballets and gambling, either at cards or at *hoca*, a forerunner of roulette, played for exceptionally high stakes.

Louis was overwhelmed by the King's tremendous public presence, so unlike the homespun warmth of his grandfather. The French King had only to enter a room and all the chattering courtiers instantly fell silent. There was a grace about all his movements—even the way he took off his hat to a lady. As a young man he had studied ballet to give him command of his body. In 1653, when he was fourteen, he had been costumed as the Sun in a Court ballet, an appearance that was responsible for his becoming known as the Sun King. The training in ballet had been invaluable for one whose *métier* included making an entrance, assuming a mask for his public persona, and controlling his demeanor at all times when he was on view. Above average height, broad-shouldered and muscular, the King was a striking figure. He loved women, and once he had overcome the grief of his first lost love and accepted the idea that having a mistress did not diminish his ability to be a good husband, he found that beautiful women gave themselves quite willingly to him.

Within a year the King was desperately in love with the fair, blue-eyed Louise de La Vallière, whose artistic temperament and cultural interests influenced the Court. But opera, poetry and plays (including the works of Molière, which Louise encouraged and had presented at Fontainebleau) were all too

35

strange to Louis Grimaldi. Nor would he be drawn into Court intrigues or don costume for the popular masquerades. He was awkward and unsure, uncomfortable in a Court where men wore satin and brocade, bought jewels, rode about in gilded carriages, gave glittering parties and gambled for high stakes.

Charlotte-Catherine gave birth to a son, Antoine, on January 25, 1661. Honoré II died in 1662 at the age of sixty-five and the new Prince and Princesse de Monaco (Charlotte-Catherine under great protest) and their child left Paris and the glamour of the Court to take up rule of the Rock. The Princesse cried for the whole length of the journey. Her lover, Puyguilheim, according to a contemporary diarist, "followed her coach now disguised as a merchant, now as a postilion, or in any travesty, which would render him unrecognizable to her attendants [and her husband]."

Whatever little Charlotte-Catherine expected of Monaco, what she found was a tremendous shock to her. The town comprised just three narrow parallel streets rimming the rocky plateau and ending by the old castle in a square about eighty yards wide. Ramparts protected any access from the harbor, and the roads could not accommodate a proper carriage. There were no fine houses apart from the castle, and the Court consisted of Grimaldi relatives and a lackluster group of ministers and army officers.

Although the exterior of the castle was severe and the garrison occupied the main building, which had the view of the sea, the interior, which had been entrusted to Italian artists during the reign of Honoré I (1532–1581) and refurbished so magnificently by Honoré II, was quite impressive. Along with the great tapestries and paintings, there was a splendid hall, fine mythical frescoes in the Hercules Gallery and a great staircase built to resemble the more famous one at Fontainebleau.

Charlotte-Catherine's apartments in the Royal Quarter were quite pleasant and commodious, and there was also the lovely small Palatine Chapel. But Monaco still remained little more than a garrison. The artists and intellectuals whom Honoré II had gathered around him had departed with his death, leaving the wives and daughters of the soldiers, the townspeople and the palace staff. There were none of the glamorous courtiers and aristocratic foreign visitors of the French Court. Charlotte-

Catherine had no one at all to confide in or to share her interests.

Within three years she gave birth to as many daughters and then, leaving Louis and their children, returned to Paris. The story circulated that she had gone for a carriage ride and simply continued on to Paris (via Menton and Nice) without giving any notice to her husband. On her return to the French Court she was taken in by the King's sister-in-law, Henriette, Duchesse d'Orléans, daughter of Charles I of England and his exiled Queen, Henrietta of France.

Rumor persisted that Charlotte-Catherine ("a little cocky, proud of her rank and beauty") and the Duchesse d'Orléans were romantically involved. Obviously the Princesse de Monaco enjoyed the exhilaration of *liaisons dangereux,* for she resumed her affair with Puyguilheim, and only a few months were to pass before she became the King's mistress (although Louise de La Vallière remained his *maîtresse en titre*), making objections on her husband's part almost impossible because of his allegiance to France. The King ordered Puyguilheim out of Paris on a pretext; and when Puyguilheim refused the royal command, Louis XIV sent him to the Bastille for six months. By the time he was released, the King's affair with Charlotte-Catherine was over. Court gossip had it that one night the King did not find the key to her room in its usual place, as it had been taken by another admirer. But the King also had fallen in love with Madame de Montespan, his mistress for the next fifteen years. Puyguilheim bitterly blamed his imprisonment and lost esteem on his former lover and humiliated her in the presence of the King and the Court. The King described the incident in a letter to his envoy at The Hague, where Louis had gone to consult with Charlotte-Catherine's brother Armand, Comte de Guiche:

"Last Monday at Versailles a trinket worth twelve hundred *pistoles* was being played for in the salon, and the ladies had sat down on the floor itself to be all the cooler. I was standing up and watching the play with some interest to see who would win. It happened that as I stepped back a couple of paces to have a better view, those who were between me and the wall were obliged to move. Among them was Puyguilheim, and in his haste to make way for me he accidentally stepped hard on one of the Princesse de Monaco's hands; she was propping herself on it as she sat on the floor, as I said, but it was covered by her skirt so no one could see it even, and that makes what happened next most remarkable.

"The Princesse looked at her fingers for a while and showed them to the ladies near her, complaining that they hurt, and then suddenly, having raised her voice and having seen that it was Puyguilheim who had stepped on her hand, she began to cry, got up from the floor, angrily throwing down a book she was holding, and withdrew into another room where she wept for some time, while several persons tried in vain to comfort her."

Fearing a duel between either Louis or de Guiche and Puyguilheim, which would create additional scandal about his own relations with Charlotte-Catherine, the King was doing his best to make the attack (which he actually believed to be spiteful) seem an accident. Louis, caught between his own unfortunate royal cuckolding and his fear that gallantry on his part could cost him the friendship of the King, backed down.

Instead of returning directly to Monaco, he joined de Guiche, his wife's flamboyant, arrogant and profligate brother, who was in the service of the Dutch Navy, aboard *Duevenvoorde*, which was headed for Dunkirk to engage the enemy English fleets in a conflict precipitated by the seizure of Dutch merchant ships by England. Once arrived at the scene of battle, "[de] Guiche and Louis fought bravely; their ship was set on fire and they refused to leave her, but the flames reached the gun-room. Clad only in their underdrawers, the two young men were about to jump overboard when they were taken off by the *Petite Hollande* and in a state of undress fought the English alongside the ship's crew until she, too, went down. Again they were rescued by a Dutch vessel, taken before the admiral, who congratulated them and had fresh clothing given them."

Word of their Prince's bravery in battle instilled pride in the Monégasques and evoked appreciation from the Dutch. Back home, he instantly raised his own regiment, the Monaco Cavalry, and took part in the beginning of French hostilities against Spain in the War of Devolution. From March 1667 to May 1669 when a treaty between France and Spain was signed at Aix-la-Chapelle, he distinguished himself at the head of his regiment. His principality appears to have accepted his long absences with the French Army as part of the price of France's protection.

Louis's military career kept him from becoming despondent over his wife's love affairs and the intrigues they gave rise to. The Princesse de Monaco had remained at Court while her husband was fighting the Spanish. Her numerous romantic liaisons were scandalous. She had become embroiled in an affair with the Chevalier de Lorraine, "a coldly vicious mignon . . . beautiful as an angel," who, unfortunately, was also the lover of Philippe, Duc d'Orléans, younger brother of the King ("a funny little fellow, gay and slightly mad," who wore scent and dressed as a girl at masquerades and had "dallied" with Charlotte-Catherine). Even her former good friend, lover and protector, Henriette, Duchesse d'Orléans (who, in view of her own sexual proclivities, did not find her husband's a problem), was appalled by Charlotte-Catherine's poor choice and turned against her.

Because Henriette was extremely powerful at Court, Charlotte-Catherine swiftly became a social outcast. Louis collected her from Paris, and for the next four years, her behavior tempered by recent changes in the French Court, she remained the dutiful wife in Monaco. The Duchesse d'Orléans had died suddenly (believed to have been murdered by one of her husband's lovers). The King had grown more intensely involved with Madame de Montespan. The Chevalier de Lorraine languished in exile in Italy (perhaps as a suspect in the death of the Duchesse d'Orléans), and Puyguilheim had married. (He was to rise to fame when he brought the family of King James II to safety in France after the Glorious Revolution of 1688, and a year later unsuccessfully commanded the Irish expedition to restore James. He was created Duc de Lauzun in 1692.)

In the spring of 1672 France went to war against the Dutch who had put an embargo on imports of French wine and brandy, the tariffs from which France desperately needed to strengthen its currency. Louis joined the army in the field. Charlotte-Catherine, another child on the way, left her children behind and returned to Paris to live at the Palais Royal as first Lady-in-Waiting to Françoise, Madame de Montespan (usually known as Athénaïs because of her intellectual leanings), who had kindly offered her home and protection.

It was easy to see why Charlotte-Catherine was drawn to

Athénaïs. The King's new mistress not only belonged to one of the oldest families in France, she was "sophisticated, witty, sure of herself, voluptuous, experienced, one of those women who knew that the best shop for beauty spots was 'A la Perle des Mocher' in Rue St. Denis and knew exactly how to place them: a *passionée*, near the eye, a *baiseuse* at the corner of the mouth; knew the smart names for a lady's three petticoats: the *fripon*, the *modeste* and the *secret*; knew that for a perfect glove the skin must be prepared in Spain, cut in France and sewn in England, while its scent should be ambergris or musk." Charlotte-Catherine had much to learn from Athénaïs about being seductive and at the same time a woman of style.

For her part, Athénaïs needed a wily and knowledgeable confidante, as she was extravagant but not well off and a heavy gambler whose jewels were forever in and out of pawn. Unlike Louise de La Vallière, Athénaïs was a married woman. Adultery in a king could be condoned, but double adultery was a different matter. Moreover, the Marquis de Montespan was not at all anxious to divorce his wife. Athénaïs, who by now had two children with the King, was in a terrible quandary, and Charlotte-Catherine, if somewhat headstrong, was a woman who would understand and could discuss with her the difficulties of the situation.

Seven months after Charlotte-Catherine returned to Paris, she bore Louis another son, François. Room was made in the Montespan household, but in 1673 Athénaïs obtained a legal separation from her husband and took apartments close to the King. Charlotte-Catherine was given a house in Saint-Germain. She died six years later at the age of thirty-nine, after a long and painful illness (most likely cancer), having never seen her husband or Monaco in the last six years of her life. Louis displayed no grief. "It's very understandable," one of his wife's former friends wrote to another, "that he should show so little regret at losing someone who had left him of her own accord."

He returned to Paris to take charge of his young son François, who had been in the care of the Gramonts. Monaco was in a stable situation and his ministers appeared to be reliable men. In truth, Louis seemed relieved to be back in Paris. His short time at Court after his marriage had given him an appetite for a more stimulating life than could be found on the Rock. During his six-year separation from Charlotte-Catherine, he was known to have had one great affair. He had fallen in love with and pursued Hortense Mancini, Duchesse de Mazarin, whom he had met on a trip to Rome. He followed her to England where he became Charles II's rival for her favors. She had arrived in England somewhat short of money after abandoning a husband insufficiently exciting for her tastes.

A mature woman of thirty, Hortense possessed a reckless, passionate personality. A stunning beauty with a Junoesque figure, jet-black hair and jade eyes, she loved to gamble, shoot and swim, and had a remarkable appetite. King Charles was besotted with her at first meeting and set her up in apartments at St. James's Palace, gave her a thousand pounds from the English treasury to tide her over and agreed to a four-thousand pound yearly allowance.

The Duchesse was more concerned with passion and fun than with money, and Louis's flattering attention amused her. King Charles's longtime mistress, Nell Gwyn ("the merciless Nell" as she was called), told him of Hortense's other amour. In a fit of pique the English King withdrew his allowance. Louis immediately granted her an equal amount to become his mistress, which infuriated King Charles, who upped the ante, took the Duchesse back and then avoided her whenever possible. Louis departed England but his magnanimity to the redoubtable lady did not help his or Monaco's relations with King Charles.

As for Louis's children, his eldest daughter, Jeanne-Marie, had entered a convent at sixteen, and her younger sister Thérèse had died at the age of twelve. François was a quiet, religious boy who would later become Archbishop of Besançon. Antoine, Monaco's heir, came of age in 1682 and established his own household. In the years after Charlotte-Catherine's death, Louis lived a simple life with the one daughter left to him, his youngest, Anne-Hippolyte, with whom he remained close until she was in her thirties, when she married the seventeen-year-old Duc d'Uzès. She died in childbirth two years later.

From that time Louis lived mainly at Versailles, where he had a home which he called his "pavilion" near the royal stable buildings. Louis XIV's château of Versailles was a massive complex of brick and gray stone. The main building was a third of

41

a mile long and it was in this block that Court was held when the King was in residence. Originally Versailles had been a royal hunting lodge and the huge stables still held the finest horses in the land. The King rode to hounds several times a week, and the trees echoed to the *trompe de chasse* as he and his suite galloped wildly through the forests after their prey.

The Prince de Monaco's pavilion had begun life as a building in which the ladies could wait for the hunters to return for lunch before setting off again for the afternoon's sport. As Versailles grew, there was a need for a larger pavilion. The King had given the old structure to Charlotte-Catherine when the new one was built at the time of their short affair. Louis had inherited this upon her death, along with the house in Saint-Germain, in which she had spent her last years.

The King had fought in the field during the Dutch War of 1672–1678. When peace was finally concluded, he became a willing slave to Versailles, where much new construction, refurbishment and extensive embellishments of the gardens were taking place. During the fifteen years that Athénaïs was the King's mistress, sensuousness and vigor reigned in the Court, as was evident not only in the new statuary on the grounds but in the constant procession of *fêtes,* in the poetry and music of the tragicomedies performed, in the brilliant and lavish firework displays that ravished the night skies, and in the carousels which perpetuated the ceremonial of chivalry.

Louis appears almost to have forgotten that he was Prince de Monaco. His ambitions were turned to the King and the Court. He wanted desperately to wear the blue coat that proclaimed to one and all that he was a companion of the King. Although he received his due as *duc et pair étranger,* the fact that he had never become an important member of the King's close circle nettled him.

Even though Louis had used up a sizable portion of his dead wife's fortune over the years, he was determined to remain in Paris near the King, ambitious for a prestigious ambassadorial appointment and the recognition at Court for which he hungered. The difficulties he had endured during his life had given his face the strength of character it had lacked in his youth. Still he did not have the élan, the intelligence, the wit or the athletic prowess to catch the educated, sophisticated eye of the

King. He was unfortunately inclined to excess in his eating habits, and was now a man of considerable girth who suffered painfully from gout.

For ten years he persevered in his efforts to find a means of aggrandizing his position in the French Court, leaving his own principality to be run by appointed officials. His ambition was not entirely due to vanity. He was more than aware that Monaco needed the full support of a powerful Court if it was to survive, and all his cards were in the hands of Louis XIV. With Antoine, his heir, still unmarried, he was pressed to find him a wife as soon as possible. But the Duc de Valentinois had no wish to settle down. Finally, in the spring of 1688, a marriage was arranged between Antoine and Marie de Lorraine, daughter of the Comte d'Armagnac.

One wonders what influenced the Prince de Monaco to agree, for Marie's dowry (her family having lived for years above their means) was quite meager. Barely sixteen, spoiled by her parents' fondness for her and very much under her haughty and ambitious mother's thumb, Marie did possess a saucy beauty that was very appealing. She was high-spirited, loved *fêtes*, balls and theatricals, and dressed with unusual flair and sometimes rather shockingly; her neckline was scandalously low. She had lively dark eyes and a magnificent mane of chestnut hair that she often styled with jeweled combs in the Spanish fashion. After Louis's difficulties with the similarly high-spirited Charlotte-Catherine, one would think he might have been wary of Marie de Lorraine as a wife for Antoine. But the prospective bridegroom, who enjoyed the favors of many of the female singers at the Paris Opéra and considered himself a connoisseur of Parisian beauties, was dazzled by her. The Comte d'Armagnac was in the King's inner circle and the match was approved by Louis.

Also, Queen Marie Thérèse had died in 1683 and Françoise, Madame de Maintenon,[1] a widow of forty-five but still a sultry beauty, had recently become the King's morganatic wife. She had led a clouded life. Her father had been infamous: he had counterfeited money, killed his wife's lover, and finally been imprisoned for having joined a conspiracy to put Louis XIII's

---

[1]Françoise Scarron, born d'Aubigne and created Marquise de Maintenon by Louis XIV.

younger brother, Gascon d'Orléans, on the throne. He married the daughter of the prison governor (having divorced his first, unfaithful wife), and their daughter Françoise was born in the prison precincts. She was brought up by Ursuline nuns and at the age of sixteen married the poet Paul Scarron, twenty-five years her senior and almost entirely paralyzed from the neck down. Eight years later, after Scarron died, she lived as a boarder in a Paris convent and, when Athénaïs had her first child with the King, became nurse and governess to this and the five other children they had together.

The King was drawn to Françoise, and after Athénaïs was found to be involved with black magic (hoping to rid herself of any competition for the King's favors), he turned to this warm and amusing woman. "Madame de Maintenon knows how to love," he was once heard to say. "There would be great pleasure in being loved by her."

The King had become so reliant on Madame de Maintenon that he called ministers to her apartments for discussions and drafting of dispatches while she sat listening and doing her needlepoint. A letter she wrote at this time boasted that the King frequently demanded two *bonnes bouches* (her euphemism for sexual intercourse) before his *coucher,* the formal and public ritual where a hundred or so courtiers watched and often assisted the King's valets in undressing him and seeing that he was secure in bed. Now approaching menopause, she was anxious that the King take no more *maîtresses en titre,* and Marie de Lorraine had already caught his eye.

Antoine married Marie de Lorraine on June 13, 1688, with Madame de Maintenon's approval, the King's blessing and the generous gift of a château just outside Paris. While this was being refurbished, the newly married couple lived with the bride's parents.

It was not long before Marie, marriage seeming to add to her allure, began enjoying the attentions of the courtiers and the glittering young men who frequented the d'Armagnac house, which was always open day and night. ("More of an elegant flirt than all the ladies of the Kingdom put together" was how one member of the Court, the famous diarist Madame de Sévigné, described her.) Louis had learned by bitter experience the demeaning nature of scandal, and he did all he could to quiet the gossip about his daughter-in-law and his son, who divided his time between the singers' dressing rooms backstage at the Opéra and on the battlefield in the King's service.

"I still think excuses should be made for your young wife," Louis wrote to Antoine in a letter dated June 29, 1690, "because she is so young and that is also why you should bear with her to some extent. I trust that with time, she will act better towards you and will realize more than she does at present where her true and chief interest lies. Your misfortune is entirely due to the fact that you haven't gained the favor of your mother-in-law, Madame d'Armagnac. She's the stumbling block . . . as long as you and she don't get on together, you can't expect much tenderness from the daughter." But since Marie's flirtations were well known in the Court by now, Louis feared a repetition of his own sad marital history.

With Louis's prodding, the King wrote to Marie that as Antoine was off with his regiment, "the air of the Mediterranean would do her good." She could do little but comply with what was really a royal command, however gently stated. Accompanied by her father-in-law, Marie went by coach and sea to Monaco, where they received word that Antoine had been seriously wounded at Namur, a battle conducted personally by the King. The estranged couple were reunited when Antoine returned to the Rock to recuperate.

An English visitor to the Court and to Monaco records that Marie was very "*grand* and enjoyed as it were the sovereignty of a rock, beyond whose narrow limits anybody might spit, so to speak whilst standing in the middle. But the Duchesse soon found that her family had *bought* the title very dear.

"Her husband was diffident, his face and figure had acquired for him the name of Goliath. He suffered for a long time the haughtiness and the disdain of his wife and her family. At last he and his father grew tired [of her]." Antoine announced that he would rejoin the army. Marie (acting "as if she had been carried off to the Indies") begged to be allowed to go back to Paris, making "all kinds of promises." Once there she spread the story that her father-in-law had attempted to rape her.

"I know not who counselled her," the diarist continues, "but without changing her conduct she thought only how to prevent to return to Monaco and to insure herself against this, she accused her father-in-law of having made *vile* proposals to her, and of attempting to take her by force.

"Monsieur de Monaco [Louis] had always been known as a kind man although he had a huge pointed billy [beard] which absolutely excited fear it puffed out so far."

When Antoine heard the scurrilous story being spread by his wife, he was furious, and on returning to Paris he took up private residence in his château on the outskirts of the city. The marital impasse between the equally headstrong Duc and Duchesse de Valentinois lasted six years, during which time Marie openly engaged in numerous affairs, many of them unwisely and indiscreetly chosen. In the end it was Louis XIV who intervened and brought about a reconciliation. "The King is going to request Monsieur d'Aumont to deal with your troubles," Louis wrote to Antoine from Paris in December 1690. "They are being gossiped about here in the oddest way, and Madame d'Armagnac is loud in naming her conditions for agreeing to let her daughter go back to you. [It had been rumored that Antoine had found Marie unappealing. Madame d'Armagnac wanted to be assured that her daughter would soon bear an heir to Monaco.] It would be a good thing if you made the best of them."

Antoine was cavalier about sex, preferring an evening's romp to a long-term mistress. He had a leonine appearance, a large head framed by masses of dark hair, a prominent nose, fierce eyebrows and a deeply cleft chin. He was a valiant soldier, injured more than once in battle, a hard man who possessed a sadistic streak that often flashed to the surface.

Marie's situation was made worse by a story circulating in the Court that Antoine had acquainted himself successively with the names of all her lovers and had hung them in effigy, dressed in full Court costume, in the courtyard of his château. "Not even is this measure retrospective," wrote Madame de Sévigné, "but folk amuse themselves by informing [Antoine] of what is now going on. The consequence is that the gibbets have to be put closer together and more than half of the courtiers are now dangling in effigy . . . I can assure you that I have had many a laugh over this, and others as well. The King himself laughs at it. This frenzy of hangings passes all belief." (Alexandre Dumas,

46

the son, wrote a novel several decades later titled *La Princesse de Monaco*, which dredged up the old scandal.)

The King's humor soured when Antoine's gruesome charade continued, and he sent word to him to be more merciful. Antoine replied that his wife's lovers ought to be thankful that he contented himself with hanging only men made of straw.

Eventually he took Marie back. "Madame d'Armagnac accompanied by her son . . . took her daughter to the Paris house of the Duc de Valentinois [Antoine]. Madame d'Armagnac had dinner there, slept there, and what was worse, stayed there," wrote Madame de Sévigné, adding that Antoine made his adulterous wife pass beneath the effigies of her lovers before she was allowed to enter the château, and that she was then forced to attend a great bonfire in which they were all burned.

The imposed reconciliation was shaky at first. Nonetheless, on November 10, 1697, a girl, Louise-Hippolyte, was born to them. In 1698 Louis finally realized his ambition and was appointed as the King's Ambassador Extraordinary to the Holy See, at that time a very delicate and important mission. The question of the succession of Spain was on the eve of being raised. Louis XIV had declared himself heir in the rights of his Spanish Queen, Marie Thérèse, notwithstanding his having signed an act of renunciation upon their marriage. This claim to the Crown of Spain was that Spain had failed to pay Marie Thérèse's dowry, which was to have been compensation for her renouncing her claims to the Crown. The French King did not really want to extend his rule to include Spain, but to ensure the throne for his grandson, the newly crowned Philip V of Spain, formerly Duc d'Anjou, grandnephew and heir to the late, childless Charles II of Spain.

Rome would necessarily have a voice in the matter, and Austria was also keen to take possession of Spain and had its representative at the Holy See. The King and his advisers believed that an envoy with the Prince de Monaco's Italian connections would be better received than a Frenchman.

Louis's years at Court had developed his appetite for grandeur, and his entry into Rome was accompanied by an extravagant display of pomp. He had waited a long time for this moment of glory, and he spent enormous amounts, very nearly ruining Monaco, which had to pay the bills, to maintain his image. His carriage horses were shod in silver, the vehicle they drew trimmed in gold. His clothes were made by the King's tailors, and his parties were as opulent as any in the French Court. Funds failing, he exercised his absolute power in Monaco and forced the communes to turn over all taxes for his personal use. He also demanded the title of Highness. A contemporary comments: "It is difficult to comprehend why the King permitted such a man to remain as his representative." Contrary to instructions from the King that he should act as a French *duc et pair* on a diplomatic mission, Louis had chosen to behave as a sovereign ruler. An already difficult situation was reduced to hopeless immobility.

Louis died, nearly blind and crippled from gout, in Rome in 1701 at the age of sixty-nine, his mission never completed. Antoine and Marie returned to the Rock where they lived together, if not happily, then at least without further public scandal. It does not seem that Antoine ever returned to her bed. He had numerous mistresses and five more children by them, three of whom he acknowledged. One of these, a son, Chevalier de Grimaldi, was closest to his father, but to Antoine's despair, he could not succeed him because of his illegitimacy. Thus the ruling House of Grimaldi—Marie's childbearing days over—was without a male heir.

4

MONACO WAS VIRTUALLY UNCHANGED since the sixteenth century. By 1700, its three townships remained little more than a garrison and two villages. To see the Rock at its best one had to climb for four or five hundred yards through olive gardens that skirted the sides of Tête du Chien, a mountain named for its fancied resemblance to a dog's head. From this elevation the solid gray rocks made a striking contrast to the lustrous, uneasy azure sea, which even in the calmest weather fringed the dark headlands with a ruff of pearly foam. To the east were Menton and Roquebrune, their dense olive groves a rich green against the unusual angular mountains behind them.

A visitor in 1705 recorded that the garrison at Monaco consisted of "five hundred men, paid and officered by the French King. The officer that show'd me the Palace, said with a great deal of gravity that his master and the King of France, amidst all the confusions of Europe, had ever been good friends and allies. The Palace has handsome apartments . . . many of them hung with pictures of the reigning Beauties in the Court of France. But the rest of the furniture was at Rome, where the [late Louis] Prince of Monaco resided [as] Ambassador."

The Court consisted of fewer than twenty members and their families, all directly related to the Prince and Princesse. Marie had brought her sister-in-law from Paris as Lady-in-Waiting and also her mother ("How can so much rain fall on so small a principality?" she was heard to complain). For Marie, life on the Rock must have seemed a penitence for her adulterous past. Besides her three surviving daughters, Louise-Hippolyte "Coco," Marguerite-Camille "Poupon," and Marie-Pelline "Chabeuil," all she had for entertainment was her needlework and the refurbishment of the Palace—it having been stripped of

49

most items of value to cover her father-in-law's Roman extravagances. There were few outsiders.

Antoine had acknowledged a woman from Provence, Elizabeth Dufort, as his mistress, and had established her in a villa only a few steps away from a summerhouse called "the Desert," where Marie spent much of her time in good weather. The leg wound he had received at Namur had never properly healed, and by 1710 it had made him a semi-invalid. He turned his back on France and settled down for the remainder of his life in Monaco, installing "a kind of lift" between the ground and first floors of the palace, enjoying the total dependence the Monégasques, his family and mistress had upon him. Life became more pleasant after the death of his acerbic mother-in-law, but he remained a difficult man, hard to please, easy to arouse to anger.

He had never lost his taste for beautiful opera singers or their music; and with the help of Destouches, the manager of the Paris Opéra, he brought singers, dancers and musicians from Paris and converted a large room of the palace into a concert hall with a stage where programs were conducted, often under his own baton.

As his daughters matured, his greatest concern was the future of the House of Grimaldi. Because Marie had given him no male heir, his daughter Louise-Hippolyte could succeed only if she either married a Grimaldi or her husband changed his name and arms to take on those of the Grimaldis. The legitimate heir to the Principality at this time was Antoine's younger brother, François-Honoré, Monsieur l'Abbé de Monaco, who—because of his Church affiliations—could be expected to renounce his rights. (He did agree to do so for a price, to be paid by Louise-Hippolyte's future husband.)

Finding the proper husband for Antoine's beloved Coco was not an easy task. The man had to be rich enough to pay all of Monaco's debts, those left by Louis as well as those incurred by Antoine, and to supply dowries for his bride's two younger sisters. Also, Antoine's father-in-law, the Comte d'Armagnac, insisted on having his say in the choice of a husband for his granddaughter and had even ventured the bizarre idea of having his own son, Charles de Lorraine (who was her uncle), marry Louise-Hippolyte.

Many candidates were drawn by the prospect of one day becoming Prince de Monaco, and so *duc et pair étranger* at Court. The field finally narrowed down to two aspirants: the Comte de Roye, a dashing young officer and member of the prestigious Rouchefoucauld family, who was Antoine's choice, and who would agree to marry Louise-Hippolyte only if he were to receive the lucrative estate of Valentinois, and the Comte de Lux, the sixteen-year-old son of the Duc de Châtillon, a member of the distinguished Montmorency family, sponsored by Louise-Hippolyte's grandfather, the Comte d'Armagnac. On December 12, 1712, d'Armagnac wrote Antoine a scalding letter about the situation.

"Since you twist everything I write to suit yourself, I must use the kind of language that leaves no room for mistake. It is not fitting that you, as the father of Mademoiselle de Monaco should choose a husband for her other than one whose rank is not lower than her own by birth. What are you thinking of, to want to strip yourself of the duchy of Valentinois in order to get yourself a son-in-law whom you will honor by giving him the hand of my grand-daughter? This son-in-law must have a high rank, be possessed of a good fortune in land and property, with no debts attached, but I can see only beggary in the marriage proposed by you, the young man is known as a rascal and to be always in want of money. What kind of marriage are you being pushed into? I had thought that by referring indirectly to the matter you would see it clearly for what it is, but as you did not, I must talk straight.

". . . The Duc de Châtillon has a title and honors and safe possessions in a family that is one of the highest in the land. I do not see any comparison between the two. I'm telling you just what I think, for your honor is involved; and I know that mine is. Think all this over carefully. I warn you that the blame will be yours alone, and that I shall oppose anything detrimental to the honor of a grand-daughter of a man like myself, to whom you owe some consideration, I think."

Antoine would not be compromised by his father-in-law and after many months the impasse remained. Marie's refusal to sign the marriage contract for her daughter to marry the Comte de Roye was strongly supported by her father, who wrote to her from Versailles, "When you have a good case, stick to it," adding ". . . do not sign anything whatever unless I or one of your brothers writes personally to say so."

These quarrels continued over the next two years, to the great displeasure of Louis XIV. Finally Comte de Roucy, the father of Antoine's candidate, with an eye to the King's disapproval of the standstill, released the Prince de Monaco from his agreement. In the end the Comte d'Armagnac abandoned his support of the Comte de Lux.

For two years, Louise-Hippolyte had been in the care of the nuns at the Convent of the Visitation at Aix-en-Provence, placed there against her will by her father until her marriage was settled. Marie now took matters into her own hands. Leaving Monaco secretly, under cover of night, she joined her father in Paris and between them they decided on the next candidate, a young man of twenty-five, Jacques de Matignon, Comte de Thorigny, the rich scion and only son of the Comte de Matignon, at the time Lieutenant-Governor of Normandy.

Aware that Antoine would reject any name they put forward, Marie and her father enlisted the Duchesse de Lude, widow of the Comte de Guiche (Antoine's great-uncle), to act as mediator. The Duchesse presented de Matignon's name to Antoine as her own suggestion. Not suspecting the duplicity involved, and still smarting over Marie's defection, Antoine secured the Duchesse de Lude's promise that the young man's name would be kept secret from his wife and her father. He then insisted that they agree in advance to the "unknown" future son-in-law he had chosen.

On Christmas Eve, 1714, the Comte d'Armagnac (who must have been privately triumphant at his clever deception) wrote to Antoine: "It gives me great pleasure and I greeted your representative as though he were bringing an olive branch from you. Although he did not explain about the choice you have made, I don't doubt it is a good one."

Believing he had outwitted his wife, Antoine got de Matignon to agree to sacrifice his name and coat of arms to obtain a duchy of his own if he married Louise-Hippolyte. He then wrote to Marie to tell her that, providing they obtained the King's consent (necessary for peers of the Court), the selection of a husband for their oldest daughter had been made. She wrote back congratulating him on a brilliant choice and asked if she could now return home:

"Forgive me, Sir, if I have done something wrong, for the sake of my respect and obedience towards you and of my love for my children . . . I ask your pardon, Sir, and to be allowed to come and tell you myself, more strongly than I can ever do by letter, how willingly I shall meet your wishes for the rest of my life."

He replied condescendingly: "I shall see whether [your apology] is followed up by the obedience you promise me, that I dare to say you owe me, and I am prepared to believe you are ashamed for having cut yourself off from it in such a scandalous manner. I have no desire at all to go over the past, you know there would be far too much for me to say. I draw a curtain over a sad picture, so as to start a peaceful life with you and the children again."

The time for action had come. The marriage contract had to be negotiated and Louis XIV's consent obtained. After protracted dealings the wealthy de Matignon agreed to pay Antoine 700,000 livres to cover all of Monaco's debts and to give an additional 600,000 livres as dowries for his bride's younger sisters, as well as to pay their uncle François-Honoré 200,000 livres to renounce all his rights.

It remained for the marriage contract to be signed by the King, but in August 1715, Louis XIV was on his deathbed in his magnificent white-and gold paneled bedroom in Versailles. Gangrene had blackened one entire leg and he was in excruciating pain. What conscious moments were left to him he used to prepare himself, his Court, his country and his young heir—his great-grandson, four-year-old Louis, Duc d'Anjou—for his impending demise. (Louis XIV had six children with Queen Marie Thérèse. Only one, Louis, Dauphin of France, survived childhood but predeceased his father. The Dauphin's son had died suspiciously in 1712, as had his wife and their oldest surviving son. This brought the late Dauphin's youngest grandson, the Duc d'Anjou, into the direct line as heir to the throne.)

"Soon," Louis told the boy when he was brought to his bedside, "you will be King of a great kingdom. I urge you never forget your obligations to God; remember that you owe Him everything. Try to remain at peace with your neighbors. I have loved war too much. Do not copy me in that, or in my over-spending. Take advice in everything; try to find out the best course and always follow it. Lighten your people's burden as soon as possible, and do what I have had the misfortune not to do myself."

Louis XIV, who had been a very good friend to Antoine and to Monaco, died on September 1, 1715, four days short of his seventy-seventh birthday and having reigned for over seventy-two years. The Duc d'Anjou was now Louis XV, and until his majority he would be controlled by the Regent, Philippe, Duc d'Orléans, son of the late king's effeminate brother and his second wife, Elizabeth of Bavaria. Both the child-king and his Regent signed de Matignon and Louise-Hippolyte's marriage contract on September 5, their first official signatures of the new reign. The wedding took place on October 20. Antoine and Marie, although never reconciled, did establish a *modus vivendi*. Once Antoine learned that he had been outfoxed in the matter of his son-in-law, relations between them again be-came unpleasant so much so that the newly married couple (who had lost a child during their first year together) moved to Paris to be away from his oppressive outbreaks of temper and tyrannical control.

Despite being surrounded by acquisitive countries at a time when they were at constant war with each other, the Principality managed to survive, thanks to the protection of France. Without the reinforcement of French troops, Monaco's small garrison could not have withstood an outside attack.

The simple fact was that what could be gained by capturing Monaco was not worth retaliation from the French. Monaco was ostensibly a poor and backward principality with no lucrative products and little land for expansion. Not until 1730 did An-toine finally have a carriage road constructed between the Rock and Menton. Before then the only link was ten kilometers over precipitous, rock-strewn paths, which deterred commerce even within the Principality.

The odds were against the small country producing a great philosopher, scientist, poet or artist. During Antoine's long res-idence on the Rock, he had commissioned several operas, but had brought few other distinctions to Monaco. The Grimaldis were reliant upon their wives' or daughters' dowries to keep things running. There were no big landowners to tax, no customs duties to collect from a busy port. The Grimaldis had increased their prestige and rank at the French Court through marriage. None of them had cared much about Monaco or wished to visit it.

Like his father before him, Antoine had looked for his glory in the service of Louis XIV, an absolute monarch, whose power was not shared by any individual or institution. Even a few days before the French King's death, Council was still held from his bed. There was no deviation from ritual. The Court and the government had to revolve around the King. And Antoine, who greatly admired Louis XIV, preferred to be in the service of such an omnipotent monarch rather than affirming his own power and bringing any improvements to Monaco. The harvest of fruit and fishing were the chief sources of income to the people.

Marie died in 1724, at the age of fifty-seven, and Antoine did not mourn her death any more than his father had grieved for his mother. Marie's possessions and a sizable inheritance were to pass to her oldest child, a stipulation set forth in her original marriage contract, making Louise-Hippolyte her heir. But Antoine, in difficult financial straits and in view of his son-in-law's affluence, pressed a claim in the French courts on his own behalf for control of his late wife's estate. An acrimonious lawsuit ensued which lasted for several years, by the end of which time Antoine had run out of both cash and credit. He then appealed directly to his son-in-law, to whom he had been cold and uncivil throughout the legal battle.

"You mention the state of your affairs," the Duc de Valentinois wrote back, "as though you wish me to do all I can to ease your situation. I will willingly help . . . on condition, if you please, that you take no steps to prejudice the future interests of your grandson [who stood to inherit from his mother] . . . He is such a [good-natured] boy that nobody could think of playing a dirty trick on him."

The Duc de Valentinois was, in effect, offering Antoine a loan on condition that he withdraw his lawsuit. Antoine was furious. His brother, François, who was once again in his good graces, wrote to tell him that he had been invited to visit the de Valentinoises in Paris, to which Antoine angrily replied: "What it all amounts to is this—[those two] are following the fine system they adopted right after [Marie's] death which is to see me die with rage in my heart because, thanks to them, my situation is no brighter . . .

"So I leave you to judge for yourself, my dear brother, whether in all decency you can accept their offer of hospitality, considering how my relations with them are, and are bound to be . . ."

By 1730 the litigation over Marie's will had not been settled. Antoine's health, never good, was failing. Louise-Hippolyte, with her younger son, the Comte de Carladez, then eight years old, made the journey to Monaco to see him, and during their six-week visit father and daughter were reconciled. Antoine died on February 20, 1731, leaving an affectionate unsigned letter to his daughter, which was sent on to her by his doctor "with an account of the Prince's last hours."

Louise-Hippolyte had always been a retiring woman, and had been much marked in youth by the angry quarrels between her parents and her enforced two-year convent confinement before her marriage. Her marital life had seemed happy. Her husband was rich. She had homes in Normandy and in Paris. And the Duc de Valentinois—rare among his class at that time—had been a faithful family man. What happened next was, therefore, a shock to all who knew her.

Returning to Monaco, this time alone, she took the oath of loyalty and was immediately made Princesse de Monaco without any mention of her husband, who—since he had legally changed his name to Grimaldi—should have ruled with her as Jacques I, Prince de Monaco. But Louise-Hippolyte decreed that she would reign alone; all documents were to be in her name only, and her children and husband would remain in France.

Historians are divided as to what could have been behind her unexpected behavior. One view was that Antoine had convinced his daughter with his dying breath to deny her husband his position and title at her side as a last revenge. The English historian Pemberton sets forth a case against Antoine's auditor-general, a man named Bernardoni, whom he suspects of stepping in to control the new Princesse de Monaco, wishing to supplant her husband's influence with his own.

Bernardoni did, indeed, speak out against the Duc de Valentinois, but it seems unlikely that Louise-Hippolyte would have rejected the faithful husband and father of her six surviving children, a man with whom she had lived for fifteen years in apparent harmony, either to appease the vengeance of a dead father or to satisfy the avarice of an auditor-general. Another argument against the latter is that she replaced Bernardoni within six months of her accession.

It is far more likely that she was not truly happy in her marriage. When her husband (having been denied the title of Prince of Monaco) joined her with their children on the Rock several weeks after she had taken the oath of loyalty, he remained only a short time before returning alone to Paris.

In October of that year, Madame de Simiane, a granddaughter of Madame de Sévigné, wrote: "It is said that there has been a quarrel between Monsieur and Madame de Monaco, because he wished to be named with his wife in the proclamation of accession, and she did not wish it; and that they have separated . . ."

Louise-Hippolyte's rush to have herself pronounced Princesse de Monaco could also have been motivated by her fear that the second Marquis de Cagnes, who was six years old at the time and a direct descendant of Gaspard Grimaldi, first Marquis de Cagnes, a great-grandson of Honoré I, might lay claim to the throne. But the young Marquis's father was dead and no one on his maternal side bothered to put his name forward to contest the Princesse de Monaco's claim.

Louise-Hippolyte's new power appears to have given her the personal strength and sense of independence she had lacked during the years of her father's tyranny and her husband's loving but strong hand. Having successfully removed the yoke of male domination from around her neck on December 3, in the Throne Room of the palace, she received the investiture alone, standing erect and regal, a handsome, dark-haired woman of thirty-four, her figure still trim despite her years of childbearing. A portrait executed at that time shows a surprisingly winsome young woman, elegantly gowned, far more determined than her biographers have portrayed her. The Rock with its palace and curving stone walls are pictured behind her, and in her graceful hand she holds a full-sized black mask—not the sort that a woman of that time would wear to a masquerade but more suggestive of a means (reminiscent of Dumas's *The Man in the Iron Mask*) of concealing identity. Perhaps the artist, J. B. Van Loo, was suggesting that she had suddenly revealed her true self.

One would like to believe that this one shining act of self-liberation was enough to satisfy Louise-Hippolyte, for a small-pox epidemic swept the entire Mediterranean coast during the weeks before Christmas, 1731, and on December 29, having known sovereignty for only seven months, she died of the dread disease. With her demise the House of Grimaldi became extinguished and that of Matignon (her husband, and thus her son) succeeded. In appearance, the fair-haired eleven-year-old Honoré III, his features touched with arrogance, resembled the Matignons. The fierce strength of face that so identified Antoine and had shown through at the end in his daughter was not evident. Only in his quick temper could Honoré's Grimaldi heritage be discerned.

The Duc de Valentinois, now his son's legal guardian, left immediately for the Principality and, after meeting with its jurists (a small body of five men elected by Monaco's leading citizens and established at the time that Menton and Roquebrune had been acquired), convinced them that he should rule as Prince de Monaco until Honoré reached the age of twenty-five and, further, that his son "should abdicate [at that time] in favor of his father and thus follow the example of those who relinquished to their father the command of their fiefs inherited through the mother."

The Duc's action validates the theory that Louise-Hippolyte had a good idea of her husband's true ambitions and had acted as she did in order to protect her own and her son's interests. However, the Duc de Valentinois's aspirations were quickly thwarted. Cardinal Fleury—who, with the recent death of the French Regent and his own new position as chief minister to the young King, was the most powerful man in France—sent letters of condemnation which indicated serious sanctions would be imposed if the Duc did not withdraw. Under the circumstances the Duc accepted his position as legal administrator to his son, who would be rightfully named Honoré III, Prince de Monaco.

On May 20, 1732, the Duc signed a document as Jacques I appointing Antoine's favorite son, the illegitimate Chevalier de Grimaldi, as Governor-General of the Principality with wide powers. The Duc then returned to Paris, but it was not until November 7, 1733, that he signed a formal abdication, though retaining the regency until Honoré III had reached his majority. He returned to Monaco with Honoré for him to take his oath of loyalty in May 1734. Then father and son left Monaco, the former never to return; the latter to remain abroad for fifteen years.

For the next half century, even after Honoré III's return, the Chevalier de Grimaldi governed Monaco. It could be argued that the Chevalier, although he would never be recognized as Antoine II, was more the Prince de Monaco during his lifetime than Honoré III who, when he reached his majority, gave his first priority to France. The Chevalier did well by Monaco in that peace, if not prosperity, reigned.

Though Honoré was a rich man through the inheritances of his grandmother and his mother, none of his wealth was used to improve conditions in his principality. His father placed his education in the hands of Jesuits until he was fifteen, when he became a musketeer in the King's Guard. The Duc's ambitions for him became concentrated on his army career, which did not advance as fast as the father would wish.

"He [Honoré III] has now been a musketeer for nearly two years, and this seems a long time to me," he wrote to his late wife's uncle François, now a retired archbishop. "I've spoken and written to Cardinal Fleury about having a cavalry regiment for him, but I've only received vague replies. If it were a request on my own account I should not have been at all surprised . . . after the fine services that rascal Bernardoni did me with His Eminence . . . but it concerns my son, who ought not to be made to suffer because of alleged faults of his father. I wrote to tell the cardinal that if he should not be favored among those wishing for a regiment he would be obliged to remain in his natural position, which is that of a sovereign prince who will one day have an income of a hundred thousand écus; to judge by His Eminence's reply, he is not used to receiving such pressing applications. He ought also to have considered . . . that the one man of France most able to dispense with favors from the Court is Monsieur de Monaco. I've decided to say no more to him on the matter, so I have the honor of writing to ask you to try and find out what his intentions are . . ."

France was a different country after the death of Louis XIV. Although Cardinal Fleury, an astute diplomat and clever at foreign policy, had done his best to maintain his country's prestige, it had lost much of its predominance in continental Europe and was plagued by serious financial crises. Fleury's power was enormous; and even after Louis XV reached his majority in 1735, he retained his control. The young King, who had lost both his parents at the age of two, had grown up without affection. Shy, and more comfortable with women and animals than with men, he was "happier choosing a dress for his mistress than drafting an edict for his people." He relied almost entirely on the Cardinal, who had once been his tutor, to carry out the country's administration. It was, therefore, not the King but Fleury who must be won over when favors such as the Duc de Valentinois's request were sought by the nobility.

Finally, after two years of prodding by intermediaries, on payment of fifty-five thousand livres, Honoré III was made a lieutenant and given an infantry regiment. This accomplished, his father concentrated his efforts on finding his son a bride. Negotiations were not easy, for Honoré would not cooperate. After he had twice refused to sign prestigious marriage contracts with the daughters of powerful noblemen, his frustrated father obtained a *lettre de cachet* from Louis XV and had his son confined to Arras Fortress as punishment. When Honoré was released several months later, he had naturally enough formed a bitter resentment toward his father.

This was a period of much trial for the French armies. The great power held by France during the long reign of Louis XIV had dwindled in the last two decades and been dispersed among several of its neighbors. Although still a significant military force, Spain had been shorn of her European possessions and had lost the primacy she had previously enjoyed. The prestige of Prussia had risen meteorically, and the Prussian Army had become the mightiest on the Continent.

With Prussia's invasion of the Austrian-Hapsburg province

of Silesia in December 1740, the complex War of the Austrian Succession was set in motion and had all Europe in arms. A year later, yielding to his military advisers and his mistress Madame de Châteauroux (one of the three sisters who became Louis XV's mistresses and the one he claimed was the only woman he ever loved), who wanted him to "play Mars to her Venus," Louis plunged France into the war. First Prussia was allied with France against Austria and England and then with England against Austria, France and Russia. France's allies changed constantly as the war progressed in different stages and other countries—the Netherlands, Sardinia, Spain and Bavaria—were drawn in.

With all Europe at war, the echoes of cannon resounded in the mountains that shelter Monaco. Honoré was sent to join Marshal de Saxe, whose armies had been victorious against the British and their allies in Belgium. The regiment of Monaco, under Honoré's command, displayed immense courage at the memorable battle of Fontenoy, where Honoré's younger brother, the handsome Chevalier de Monaco, was shot through the thigh.

The orders issued by Marshal de Saxe on the eve of the battle were: "Whether the attack is successful or not, the troops will remain in the position that night overtakes them in, to recommence the attack on the enemy [with daylight]."

Despite de Saxe's orders, the French retreated at night—leaving hundreds of their dead behind as terrible proof of the losses they had sustained. During the siege of Veroux, Honoré was seriously wounded but recovered sufficiently to take up arms again in the battle of Lauffeld, where his horse was shot from under him. Then he participated at the sieges of Bergen-op-Zoom and Maastricht which brought the war to a conclusion.

Though Honoré and his brother both fought for France, Monaco remained neutral in the war. Once the Monégasques gave help to a distressed British ship; and in 1746, a British admiral seized a Monégasque vessel which he said infringed the laws of neutrality. Monaco's fleet had long ceased to be a power, though the Principality retained its ancient right to chase and loot any Turkish ship which appeared in the Mediterranean.

On the tenth of May 1748, only twenty-eight years of age,

Honoré was made a brigadier-general by royal warrant and returned to Paris to recuperate before rejoining his regiment. Once again he came up against his father, the determined Duc de Valentinois. The King, influenced by Madame de Pompadour, who had become his mistress shortly after Madame de Châteauroux's sudden death,[1] agreed with the Duc upon the daughter of the Duc de La Vallière as a bride for Honoré. For a third time, Honoré obstinately refused to marry someone chosen for him, and because of his insolence was thrown into the Bastille for three months.

During this period Monaco came under repeated threat. In winter 1746, the War of the Austrian Succession still two years from its end, the French suffered a stunning defeat in Italy and Menton was nearly invaded. Then, in the spring of 1747, when France resolved to take Nice from the Italians and to win back what they had lost in Italy, Monaco again narrowly escaped attack.

By the time Honoré was released from the Bastille, peace had been agreed at Aix-la-Chapelle. He resigned his commission and went to Monaco, but he did not stay long. The Principality was content under the governorship of the Chevalier de Grimaldi, and Honoré felt no close bond, other than his inheritance, to the Rock. Unlike his grandfather, Antoine I, who had spent his childhood in Monaco and who had returned with a wife, family and an established mistress to take up his rule, Honoré was a bachelor without any attachments. He had grown up between his father's mansion in Paris with all the entertainments and advantages of a family in Court favor and on the vast Matignon estate in Normandy, with its nine thousand acres of splendid hunting grounds (far larger than all of Monaco) and successful stud farm.

Although he was not keen on life at Court, Honoré had a great love for its culture of horseflesh and hunting. He appeared to suffer little guilt about leaving the Chevalier in charge

[1]Louis was married to Marie Leczinska, daughter of Stanislas, a Polish nobleman elected King of Poland in 1704 and subsequently deposed. She was older, unattractive and dressed "in queer-looking furs and peacock plumes," which did not help to win her husband's love. The night the Duchesse de Châteauroux died, the Queen lay awake thinking each sound was her ghost. Finally, her maid said, "Even if she did come back, would it be *your* room she'd come to?"

of his country. The importance of Monaco as a possible stronghold during the French and Italian conflict had diminished by the end of the war and France's repossession of Nice. Monaco was fairly isolated from the problems that faced the rest of Europe, for the political axis had now shifted from the Mediterranean to Austria and Prussia.

Honoré was thirty when he met the alluring Anne, Marquise de Brignole-Sale, at a gala ball at Versailles, and fell in love for what seems to have been the first time. The Marquise was ten years his senior, a handsome, passionate woman from a powerful Genoese family, the Balhis. She was married to the immensely rich Marquis de Brignole-Sale, a dull, cadaverously thin, punctilious man who was no match for his vital, intelligent wife. The socially ambitious Marquise took her eleven-year-old daughter, Marie-Catherine, with her and left the Palazzo Rosso, her husband's ornate estate, for Paris, where her forceful personality, great wealth and beauty brought her instant success at Court.

With Madame de Pompadour *in situ* as the mistress of Versailles, the French aristocracy during the mid-eighteenth century was at the height of a period for provocative liaisons. For an older woman to take a young lover was not considered daring by any means. The Marquise de Brignole-Sale fell deeply and passionately in love with Honoré almost at first sight. His motherless childhood and his difficult youth, the painful years of war, and the bitterness of his imprisonment had given him a suspicious character, and he was inclined to swift mood swings. He was sharp and sensual, and gave the impression of being an injured boy in a man's body, just the sort of personality to capture the heart of an older woman who could be both mother and mistress.

The affair remained passionate for several years, and in 1754 Honoré, flagrantly cuckolding his paramour's husband, spent three months in Genoa at the Palazzo Rosso. By now the Marquise's daughter, Marie-Catherine, was a well-developed beauty of fifteen with a handsome widow's peak, wide, dark eyes, a bewitching smile, a full bosom and slim waist. Under the gaze of his aging mistress, Honoré began to court her daughter. The situation grew tense and Honoré was asked to leave in straightforward terms—which he did, but only after deciding that he would marry Marie-Catherine. His feelings were obviously reciprocated, for she sent a letter to Honoré upon his return to Paris stating: "I, the undersigned, declare and promise to the Prince de Monaco never to marry anyone but him, whatever may happen and never to listen to any proposal that might tend to release me."

5

THE MARQUIS DE BRIGNOLE-SALE, whose consent had to be obtained, was not at all pleased with his daughter's wish to marry the man who had so recently been his wife's lover. Honoré pressed his case for seventeen months to no avail; the Marquis would not acquiesce. To Marie-Catherine's chagrin, Honoré did not persist. Instead, he reopened discussions with the Duc de La Vallière for the hand of his younger daughter. In view of the fact that five years earlier Honoré had refused to marry her sister, it was an audacious move. Also, he had never set eyes upon the young woman and was still in love with Marie-Catherine. But he was determined to marry and start a family and the Marquis's opposition appeared to be impossible to overcome. Mademoiselle de La Vallière and her family were much in favor at Court and in a position for the Grimaldis to regain the French rank and honors lost when Antoine I became the last of the male line. According to the treaty made between Honoré II and Louis XIII in 1642, the duchy of Valentinois could descend to either male or female issue, but the peerage and recognition at Court became extinct if a woman inherited it.

Honoré's petition was placed before the King, who was much dominated in such matters (and most others as well) by Madame de Pompadour. With her approval, a royal announcement sanctioning the marriage and the restoration of the rank and style of foreign prince was made on July 8, 1756. This caused an angry outcry at Court from the extremely self-righteous aristocracy who had been "scandalized" by Honoré's recent liaisons with the Marquise and her daughter. It seems more likely that jealousy rather than affronted propriety raged in their breasts, for Honoré had always been considered an outsider at Court.

In the face of such strong protest, the King withdrew his

endorsement. Honoré, hoping to force the royal hand, wrote to Louis XV threatening that unless the marriage contract went through, he would, on Monaco's behalf, "make no proposal for any closer agreement with you beyond that existing between us," apparently meaning that the Principality would not take up arms in defense of France.

The King was unimpressed and remained adamant. On July 30 he wrote to the Duc de La Vallière: "Cousin [in the French Court one entitlement of being a *duc et pair* was to have the King address you as *cousin*], I came to my decision after examining all the communications from Monsieur de Monaco, and I do not wish to change at all. I shall be grieved if this causes the marriage to fall through, but you will lose none of your rights nor any of my kindness towards you." Immediately thereafter, the marriage negotiations came to an end.

Reenter the vengeful Anne, Marquise de Brignole-Sale, who sent her former lover a scathing letter charging him with vile behavior toward her daughter and herself and with creating havoc in her marriage and her family. "You accuse me of so many dreadful things that I'm obliged to defend myself," he replied at the start of a thirty-two-page letter. "I may even find good reason for attacking you," he added before recounting, point by point, his honorable petition for her daughter's hand, adding that "my respect for the mother is reflected in the choice."

Honoré's letter touched a sympathetic nerve in the Marquise, and she suddenly did an about-face and attempted to obtain her husband's consent to the marriage. For several months she was unrelenting in her crusade. Finally, at the end of October 1756, he capitulated. Still, one more battle had to be fought for he drew up a decree that forbade Marie-Catherine to transfer her large inherited wealth outside the Genoese republic. This was unacceptable to Honoré, and it took the Marquise four more months to persuade her husband to withdraw the decree.

Finally, by June, this restriction was removed and the contract was signed. Honoré sent his fiancée, who was half his age, his mother's jewels as an engagement present, which she acknowledged as "of perfect splendour . . . Although mama must have sent you my thanks for your beautiful presents, I cannot allow myself not to repeat them . . ."

Bound by royal protocol, Honoré could not travel to his bride to exchange marriage vows, and as the Marquise would not allow her daughter to go to Monaco before the ceremony, the couple were married by proxy in Genoa on June 15, 1757. Marie-Catherine had not seen Honoré for two years. Despite his absence from the ritual she appeared to be in a romantic daze as she said her vows and then with her mother and relations boarded a splendidly decorated galley. Genoese ships, their flags undulating in the soft summer breeze, escorted it ceremoniously as far as the territorial waters of Monaco.

Honoré stood on the landing stage in Court costume, backed by Monaco's full contingent of soldiers in their dress uniforms. As his bride's ship pulled into the harbor, the sky and the Mediterranean were a brilliant azure and the sun so dazzling that the Rock glistened. The ship came to a halt. The gangplank was lowered. Honoré waited nearly a quarter of an hour, but his bride did not appear. Finally, a messenger disembarked and presented him with a letter from the Marquise, now his mother-in-law, informing him that "conscious of her birth and rank," Honoré should board the Genoese ship to greet his wife.

Honoré was indignant. As a sovereign prince, his rank was higher than Marie-Catherine's and therefore he insisted that she must be the one to advance first. The Marquise refused and the gangplank was raised. A member of Honoré's regiment wrote some days later:

> The Genoese boat had dropped back to outside our waters, taking the precious charge, the object of our regrets with it. These proud republicans still persisted in wanting the Prince to go and collect his Princess from the boat, and the Prince remained unshakable in his determination to do nothing of the kind. After six days of useless negotiations, of letters and messengers being sent back and forth . . . arrangement over the final expedient [was] proposed by the Genoese. This was to make a bridge out from the Condamine landing-stage to join one let down from their boat. The next day . . . a general post was sounded, we all took up our positions for the great event, the fleet arrived in the harbor, the palace guns fired a salute, the galley drew near our bridge and started to lower another, as had been agreed. The Prince grew tired of waiting for the end of what seemed a long job, and became impatient to embrace his darling bride. He

67

jumped into a boat, followed by his most intrepid courtiers, and in spite of the fuss reached the galley's ladder. He had scarcely put foot on it when the Princess came down followed by her mother, three uncles and a cousin. The flags and banners were hoisted, the galley-slaves saluted, the guns thundered and the people shouted with joy.

They're now at the Prince's summer-house at Carnolès [Menton] . . . There are six or seven officers, Monsieur le Chevalier de Grimaldi, a lady-in-waiting, some gentlemen and myself, among the elect. The bride's family has gone back to Genoa, except for the Marquise de Brignole-Sale, who is a woman of great spirit and merit. The bride is charming, kind and lovely, and she is making her husband happy.

The Palais Carnolès, with its beautiful gardens and spectacular vista of Cap Martin and the sea, had been built by Honoré II early in the seventeenth century on the site of the ancient Franciscan L'Église de Notre-Dame-de-Carnolès. Honoré II had engaged two leading Paris architects to design his summer palace and it appears to be the forerunner of Jacques-Ange Gabriel's Petit Trianon, the small château at Versailles that became the favorite residence of Marie Antoinette and later the Empress Eugénie. Although palatial, with its grand salon, ceiling murals and Greek columns, the ambiance and privacy Carnolès afforded made it an ideal setting for a honeymoon.

Marie-Catherine was a highly emotional woman filled with a sense of fantasy, and she appeared to be euphorically happy. It is difficult to know if she was aware that her mother and her husband had once been passionate lovers. But in the beginning, she did encompass Honoré in a romantic aura. He was the older, experienced man, and she looked up to him with wide, awe-filled eyes.

On May 17, 1758, eleven months after their marriage, she gave birth to a son who was named after his father. But once having captured the heart of his young wife, removed her from her mother's control and then domesticated her, Honoré grew restless. The Chevalier de Grimaldi still held the administration of Monaco in his hands. Marie-Catherine was occupied with his son, on whom she lavished attention. There was no good hunting in Monaco; no old friends; none of the pleasures of Paris and his family's estate in Normandy. And so in the summer of 1760, Honoré left his wife and his Principality for an extended visit to France with a promise to Marie-Catherine that she could join him soon.

The Paris and the Court to which he returned were much altered from those he had left a few years earlier. Due to Madame de Pompadour's influence, France was having to fight simultaneously a war with England and a Continental war as an ally of Austria against Prussia (the Seven Years' War, 1756–1763) and simply was not equal to such a contest. The effects had been profound. Not only did trade decline, inflation spiral and taxes soar, France lost its empire in India and North America. Pompadour was hated within the Court and her extravagances at a time of such poverty among the unprivileged had cost the King the sympathy of his subjects. Ominous rumblings could be heard beyond Versailles, "[p]articularly from Paris, where the King did not dare set foot, even for a day."

Morale was low at Court despite the usual round of galas, balls and masquerades. The King tried unsuccessfully to ward off depression. "Hiding his identity under the name of a Polish count and fortified by a mixture known as 'General Lamotte's drops,' he would slink off to his private brothel in the Parc aux Cerfs [in the village of Versailles]. Returning at dawn, he would grind and prepare himself a cup of strong coffee. 'What would the world be without coffee?' he would sigh. And then, sadly add: 'After all, what *is* the world—with coffee?' "

To add to the gloom, his son the Dauphin died in October 1765 at the age of thirty-six. "Poor France!" Louis cried. "A King of fifty-five and a Dauphin of eleven!" This was the new heir, his grandson, the Duc de Berry—the future Louis XVI.

Honoré found himself in a Court divided between Pompadour's supporters and the conservatives who opposed her. The intrigue was beyond Honoré's grasp and he remained in Paris, which was cloaked in dismal vapors. Soon, loneliness set in and he wrote to Marie-Catherine admitting how greatly he missed her. "My dear love," she replied, "I swear I feel as deeply as you how cruel it is to be separated from the one you love most in the world. My sorrow is ever with me. I'm only truly happy when dreaming, for then I've always the feeling of being with you . . . and I'm always happy to see you respond affectionately to the signs I give of my tenderness for you; but waking up is cruel for however much I look I don't find you . . ."

She joined Honoré in Paris that December, having left her son in Monaco in the care of her parents. The reunion was marred when, on January 12, 1761, the Marquis Sauveur Gaspard, a son of the late Marquis de Cagnes (who had been the direct male heir to Monaco at the time of Antoine's death) addressed to the Court of France a protest against what he called the usurpation by the family of the Comtes de Matignon of his father's right to the succession of the Principality of Monaco. A petition was entered claiming the title of Prince de Monaco. It appears to have been tabled and ignored, but Honoré would never again be easy about the matter.[1]

Marie-Catherine remained in Paris with Honoré for two years, and then, finding herself pregnant, decided to return to Monaco and the son she had not seen since her departure. "Our son . . . did not know me," she wrote in a letter to her husband. "He's got amazing strength and vigour, he's big and a lovely child, with the eyes, forehead and nose of his papa, and the mouth and chin of his mama. I found my mama has got fat and Papa is still as thin as ever. Goodbye dear love, with my fondest kisses . . ."

She suffered a miscarriage in her fifth month and Honoré returned to Monaco, remaining just long enough to collect her and bring her back to Paris with him. There he left her to recuperate in the care of his brother and sister-in-law while he went off to Fontainebleau. It was at this time that the first signs of disharmony in their marriage can be detected.

"You are forgetting about me, dear love," she wrote in May 1763. "The pleasures of Fontainebleau take up all your time. This is the third letter I've written to you and I've only had one

---

[1]Thirteen years later, in 1774, Marquis Sauveur Gaspard renewed this protest before the Vienna High Council. By all evidence in this hearing, the fiefs of Monaco, Menton and Roquebrune constituted imperial fiefs. The French Revolution, fifteen years later, prevented any further attention being given to this matter. But on January 21, 1841, the Marquis Charles Philippe Auguste de Cagnes, a retired general, revived the pretensions which had never been renounced and demanded suspension of the enfeoffment. The petition was ignored by the French Court.

from you. That's not very nice, make up for your mistake promptly by sending me your news . . ."

She was pregnant once again, but her request sent Honoré even farther away, to Normandy, where he spent his time exercising his yearlings on the grounds of his family's estate. He ignored all her entreaties for him to return to Paris, and was still in Normandy on September 10, when she gave birth to another son, Joseph-Marie-Jérôme. This good news did not bring Honoré rushing back to her side. Over the next two years he was to visit her only three or four times in Paris, and his stays there were brief. Each time he left, his attitude toward her grew more distant.

Honoré's younger brother, Charles-Maurice, the Comte de Valentinois, and his wife, Marie-Christine, Comtesse de Valentinois, shared the Matignon Paris mansion with Marie-Catherine, and the sisters-in-law did not get on well. The Comtesse was a Saint-Simon, a descendant of the famous chronicler of Louis XIV's reign and a member of a family long associated with the Kings of France. She was envious of her younger, richer sister-in-law, although she was contemptuous of her provincial manners and style.

Versailles remained the center of noble society. Pompadour had died in 1764, and the following year, the King took as his *maîtresse en titre* Madame Du Barry, a striking beauty, although a pale reflection of her predecessor. Born Jeanne Bécu to an impoverished mother and an unknown father, she had been a prostitute in Paris, eventually becoming the mistress of a dissolute nobleman, the Comte Du Barry, who was a well-known procurer in the Court. The office of *maîtresse en titre* could go only to a nobleman's wife. Therefore, when Jeanne won the King's favor, she was swiftly married to Du Barry's obliging brother. She lacked Pompadour's political power but was responsible for the dismissal and eclipse of most of the King's former close advisers. His prestige was diminished and the royal treasury became more depleted.

Du Barry was, to say the least, unpopular. "What do you see in her?" the Duc de Richelieu asked the King. "Only this," Louis replied. "She makes me forget I will soon be sixty." (Richelieu had been one of Pompadour's favored courtiers. A procurer for the Court himself, he was much given to the grand luxuries of milk baths and wearing silver heels on his shoes.)

Du Barry was even more excessively extravagant than Pompadour. She redesigned fifty rooms at Versailles for the King's private apartments and filled her own with the finest porcelain, ebony-encrusted furniture, costly ivory and leather-bound volumes of erotica. She rode in the most sumptuous carriage yet seen by the Court; painted by Vallée with cupids, hearts and beds of roses, it was decorated with the arms and motto of the Barrymores of Ireland, to whom she claimed the Du Barrys of Gascony were related. To pique the King's jaded appetite she dressed as a curly-haired boy and played the guitar.

While taxes for the people skyrocketed ever higher, the Court at Versailles continued its grand balls, operas, hunts and receptions. On ball nights the great château blazed with light, the hundreds of flaming candles in the massive crystal chandeliers reflecting in the towering mirrors that lined the walls. Men wore powdered wigs, heavily embroidered satin and brocade suits, silk stockings and shoes with jeweled buckles that sparkled as they moved to the music, their jeweled swords lashed at the hip. Diamonds blazed as the ladies, their décolleté silk or brocade ball gowns stretched wide over panniers, tried to gracefully navigate the dance floor with their trains, the lengths varying according to their rank. Also required was a perfectly round patch of bright rouge, worn on each cheek, precisely three inches in diameter.

Marie-Catherine would have none of this. She used no color on her face and refused to wear a train. She sat out most dances with the older women. Her sister-in-law, a robust woman who had to be laced tightly into her clothes, was constantly critical of her. In contrast, according to the highly romantic Lady Sarah Lennox, daughter of England's Duke of Richmond, who visited Paris in June 1765, the Princesse de Monaco had "a round face with a sweet and charming expression. Her complexion is lovely and she's got the best figure of any woman I know. She is the only one here not to paint her face, all the others dab rouge on in a horrible manner."

Lady Sarah was not the only one that summer to take particular notice of Marie-Catherine. The youthful, extremely attractive widowed Prince de Condé (descendant of Athénaïs

Montespan and Louis XIV and owner of the magnificent Château de Chantilly) began to pay her considerable attention. She appears to have regarded him as a kind friend; being something of a recluse, she had few others. He often stopped by in the afternoon to see her and frequently sat with her at a ball. The Comtesse de Valentinois wrote to Honoré of the Prince de Condé's attentions to his wife, commenting in a spiteful tone that Marie-Catherine "enjoys these 'overtures' and does nothing to discourage the Prince's admiration."

Honoré left his mistress in Normandy and descended on his wife in Paris in a jealous rage; after shocking her with his accusations, he departed in a fury. Two months later, her letters reveal the coolness that now existed between them. "As you say nothing about your return," she wrote, "I don't know when you will be back here . . . [but] I am most grateful for the kindness you showed in enquiring about my health."

A year passed without his return to Paris. The Prince de Condé continued his attentions and Marie-Catherine did not turn him away.

The twenty-eight-year-old Duke of York, brother of George III of England, was traveling through France in August 1767. He was on his way from Paris to Genoa to see a young woman with whom he was passionately in love. When the Duke and his entourage reached Toulon, the governor of Provence, the Duc de Villars, gave a ball in his honor. "H.R.H. had danced rather too much," the *London Gazette* later recorded, "and this not only fatigued him but occasioned a very strong perspiration; as soon as the ball was finished the Duke of York gave orders for his carriages to be got ready. . . . The gentleman of the train, Colonel de Morison, represented to H.R.H. the necessity of remaining where he was [and confining himself to bed]. . . .

"The Duke of York declared there was no actual occasion for such caution, that he would wrap himself up in his cloak, and that would be sufficient. He did so and stepped into his carriage. This was on the 29th of August.

"Imprudently H.R.H. attended theatre the next evening in Toulon and had to return to his apartments with a terrible chill. The members of his suite tried to convince him that he should remain in Toulon until he was fully recovered. But he would not be delayed." His original plan to continue by sea to Genoa seemed unwise in view of his ill-health. Thus it was decided that he should continue the rest of the way by land and that he would stop in Monaco en route. Such high-ranking guests were infrequent on the Rock and so, although Honoré was in Normandy when he received word of the royal visit, he hurried back to Monaco to prepare a proper welcome.

"He arrived at Monaco in good spirits," the *London Gazette* continues, "a handsome figure in his rear admiral's uniform. The weather was uncommonly hot and as he stood in the sun taking the salute from Monaco's small, gleaming honor guard, he grew quite feverish."

Honoré had been placed in a difficult situation. His royal guest "took to his bed entirely." Great diplomacy was now required. Monaco did not have the medical resources of London or Paris, and the Duke of York's condition worsened rapidly. The local physicians and those brought from Nice were unable to reverse the downward slide. Honoré wanted to notify King George, but the Duke of York refused to allow him to send the message.

After taking affectionate leave of all those who had traveled with him and thanking Honoré for his kindness, the Duke died on September 17, a fortnight after his arrival in Monaco. Honoré ordered a cannon to be fired every half hour and had the Duke of York placed upon his own bed for the lying in state. In accordance with the custom of England for royal deaths, the walls of the room were hung with black, and a huge canopy of black and silver with a representation of a coffin upon its dome was placed in the middle of the room. The bed had been raised onto a platform reached by six steps covered in black and rimmed with lighted tapers in large gold and silver candlesticks.

A gun salute sounded as the procession made its way to the frigate which was to carry the Duke of York's body back to England. Honoré waited by the landing until the coffin and all the royal suite were aboard the *Montreal* and the royal standard was lowered to half-mast. He then gave the command for two rounds of cannon to be fired, to be followed by his regiment shooting two additional rounds.

It was, perhaps, Honoré's greatest moment. He made sure that every rule of protocol that covered the death of a King of

England's brother was followed to the letter. For his efforts, George III sent Honoré two of the Duke of York's finest race horses and invited him to London as his guest, an invitation that was too prestigious for Honoré to refuse.

He returned to Paris and outfitted himself grandly. Although Marie-Catherine begged to join him, he left for London without her on March 26, 1768. The King received him with suitable ceremony, and he was entertained by many members of the royal family. He went on a tour of Cambridge, visited the races at Newmarket ("accompanied by a gentleman and two servants") and was the guest of honor at a ball attended by the Dukes of Northumberland, Grafton, Gloucester and Cumberland but—to his tremendous disappointment—not the King.

If Honoré thought that his visit would create stronger ties with England, or that the accident of the Duke of York's having died in his Principality would bring him special recognition from George III, he had misjudged. The royal brothers, who were only one year apart, had been exceedingly close as children. But by the time they were young men, the Duke of York's foppish ways, his love of dancing and his extravagant tastes had alienated his more sober, domesticated brother. At York's death, Horace Walpole was moved to write, "Thus ended his silly, good-humoured, troublesome career in a pitious manner." The King made no public comment on his feelings, but to Honoré, in whose care his brother had died, he was politely appreciative and little more.

On the bright morning of June 4, eight weeks after his arrival in England, Honoré embarked at Dover for Calais, his royal journey having amounted to rather less than he had hoped for. Back in Paris, he was confronted by his sister-in-law with malicious gossip about Marie-Catherine and the Prince de Condé. Husband and wife became quickly estranged. In behavior that contrasted sharply with his usual reserve, Honoré flaunted his various mistresses, and in July 1769 Marie-Catherine left their Paris home for a retreat in a nearby convent before going on to the Convent of the Visitation at Le Mans, where the Bishop was a Grimaldi relative. The Marquise de Brignole-Sale now intervened, hoping to arrange a reconciliation.

"My daughter is by no means fickle, and she loves you steadfastly," she wrote to her son-in-law. "Open your heart to me; if you think there is something about her conduct that can be improved, let me know. But have you nothing to reproach yourself for? What you write to tell me pierces me to the heart . . . Don't embitter the little time I still have to live!"

Honoré and Marie-Catherine publicly reconciled but the animosity between them remained. Her father, the Marquis, had recently died and left her a sizable inheritance with the stipulation that Honoré have no rights in it and no power of attorney. Furious over this slight, Honoré petitioned the Genoese Senate to give him control of his wife's assets. He was outraged when this claim was rejected, and he threatened to send her back to Monaco alone while he stayed in Paris. She had by this time returned to the Matignon town house, but Honoré's action compelled her to once again take refuge in the convent.

The Prince de Condé, still very much in love with Marie-Catherine, exerted his influence and on January 9, 1771, she was granted a legal separation and total control of her inheritance. A few days later she moved into the Prince's magnificent Château de Chantilly. Honoré, much disconcerted by this, wrote to the Marquise de Brignole-Sale: "My legal advisors wanted me to pass an act at Monaco recalling her to her duties. I do not flatter myself that would turn her from the bad path she has taken."

To his beleaguered wife's relief he did not do this and she bought the elegant Château de Betz, close to Chantilly, where Honoré, relenting, allowed her sons to visit. Her love for the Prince de Condé deepened and in time Honoré came to accept it.[2]

Honoré's life in Paris had become difficult. Everywhere there were signs of discord. On April 27, 1774, the King took mortally ill. Asked to pray for their monarch, Parisians quipped: "Our father who art in Versailles, hallowed be thy name; thy will is done neither on earth nor in heaven . . ." On May 9, ". . . motionless, his mouth open, his face neither deformed nor showing

[2]Marie-Catherine and the Prince de Condé went into exile in England at the time of the Revolution. She gave over her vast fortune to assist the royalist forces. She married the Prince some years after Honoré's death in 1795. She herself died in England on March 8, 1813, at the age of seventy-four, her money entirely gone. The English royal family paid for her burial in England.

any sign of agitation, but towards the end swollen and copper-coloured," he received extreme unction.

It had been arranged that a candle would be extinguished in the window of the sick room when the elderly King drew his last breath. His grandson and heir, the twenty-year-old Duc de Berry, and his nineteen-year-old wife, Marie Antoinette of Austria, sat vigil watching the flickering flame, which was blown out at 3:15 in the morning of May 10. The Duc de Berry was now Louis XVI, King of France.

The last years of Louis XV's reign had left Honoré with great bitterness, disgust and a certain amount of fear. Monaco was dependent for its protection upon France, which was still the biggest state in Europe, with a population of twenty-five million people, but it was now a divided land. Honoré's behavior shows that he was concerned about what this meant to his little Principality. He decided that Monaco must prosper if it was to prevail. His course of action was to set about to marry his elder son, who would succeed him, to a wife with a vast fortune and a marriage contract that would guarantee her husband, and ultimately himself, control over it.

6

IN THE SUMMER of 1785, Louis XVI was returning to Versailles after a visit to the port of Cherbourg, when a peasant approached his carriage and sang a song in his praise.

"I like your song," said Louis. "Who wrote it?"

"I did, my lord."

"You did! *Bis, bis!*"

"*Bis?*"

"That means sing it again."

The man complied and when he had finished was rewarded with some gold coins.

"*Bis, Sire, bis,*" he said and thrust his other hand forward.

The King laughed and ordered more louis d'ors be given the man.

Such personal generosity might appease a single peasant, but France's basic problems—the slow growth of national wealth and the misery of the poor—would not be solved so easily.

The French Revolution was moving into its first phase. The storming of the Bastille was still four years away, but already Monaco was feeling the effects of the brewing revolution, the growing unrest in Nice spilling over the border. The Chevalier de Grimaldi who had maintained peace and a sense of continuity for the Monégasques throughout his long control of the government, had died the previous year. Honoré returned from France, but he brought with him his French aristocratic attitudes and was concerned more with the safety of his properties in France than with the signs of discontent in his Principality. A group had organized in Menton and were demanding lower taxation and the right to elect representatives to the government.

With Marie-Catherine's fortune no longer in his command and his French revenues threatened, Honoré ill-advisedly raised taxes, promising only future roadworks to enable farmers to market their produce and export them abroad. Clearly, he underestimated the great dissatisfaction that pervaded the Principality. Of its three towns—Monaco, Menton and Roquebrune—only Monaco felt a strong allegiance to the Grimaldis.

The people of Menton and Roquebrune had not been liberated from an oppressive country. Nor did they have a history of monarchy. They had been bought and sold along with their lands from one feudal lord to another, and their heritage and geographical situation gave them closer ties to Genoa, Sardinia and Naples than to France. They grew olive trees and grapes on their rugged, rocky terrain and ate bountifully from the nearby sea. They were poor but not starving, and the combined population (about 1,280 at this time) was made up of small individual landowners rather than feudal lords and serfs. Therefore, they keenly felt Honoré's heavy taxation which took nearly 70 percent of their earned income, it being a true yoke about their necks.

The French were leading the way for them, and they presented a petition that demanded of Honoré reforms, representation, lower taxes, and roads to allow them better access over the mountains and to the ports in Monaco and Nice. The list made evident the Monégasques' discontent, and the tone of the petition—a demand really—presented the possibility that they might well be moved to do something about it.

Honoré, sensing the danger but not the immensity of it, made his own compromise by permitting each town to form its own council while he ignored all their other demands. This, following the dramatic move of the French people in storming the Bastille on July 14, 1789, was not enough to appease the growing dissent.

Honoré's world was shifting beneath his feet. Along with his troubles in Monaco, the new French National Assembly which had been formed in hopes of breaking the deadlock that was preventing emergency action to relieve the suffering of a hungry populace, had abolished all feudal rights and revenues. On September 4, 1790, Honoré protested to the Assembly that the taxes received from the duchy of Valentinois "were in accordance with the terms of the Treaty of Péronne [forced on Louis XI in 1468 when he was defeated in that city in a war with

Charles of Burgundy], compensation for the loss of the states in the Kingdom of Naples." The issue was tabled while the Revolution moved inexorably on. The momentum and the seriousness of the growing rebellion eluded Honoré, although the rest of Europe's monarchs and aristocrats had been stunned out of their apathy by the formation of the French National Assembly and the overthrow of the Bastille.

Money was Honoré's solution to the increasing restiveness of the Monégasques, money in sufficient quantities to enable him to put their demands into effect and to hire troops to protect his threatened interests. How he could raise it was another matter. With Monaco's long association with France, he could not expect to be helped by another nation. To solicit help from Austria because of Marie Antoinette's connections would be considered traitorous by the French Assembly and would make it impossible for him to return to France, at least until the rebellion had been suppressed, which was what he expected to happen in the end.

He had arranged what he had believed to be a brilliant match for his older son, Honoré, by marrying him in 1777 at the age of nineteen to Louise-Félicité d'Aumont, heiress through her mother to the considerable fortune of Cardinal Mazarin and, ironically, the great-granddaughter of the infamous Hortense Mancini, erstwhile mistress of England's Charles II and of Prince Louis of Monaco. Expecting a huge dowry from the bride's family, Honoré had transferred the dukedom and peerage of Valentinois to his son and heir in order to seal the contract, thus severing his own links with the French Court. An even greater inducement than the money in the bride's dowry had been the vast lands and possessions of the Mazarin-d'Aumonts which were to pass into his hands in 1781, upon the bride's coming of age, as part of the wedding contract.

Confident that he had engineered a splendid marriage for his son while filling his own coffers, Honoré had lived ever more extravagantly, only to be faced in 1788 with the shocking knowledge that the Mazarin-d'Aumont "fortune" was uncollectable since it was encumbered by huge mortgages and numerous lawsuits. The debts had increased as the young Grimaldis lived high on borrowed money, Louise-Félicité running up vast bills with gambling losses, jewels and clothes. By May 1789, the liens against the bride's dowry amounted to 1,390,000 livres— exceeding its actual worth. Not only was there no money to help Monaco's woes, Honoré had to look elsewhere if he was to save his own estates.

In April 1790, he left Monaco in the hands of his self-appointed officials, none of them up to the task before them, and went to Paris where, after his petition had been rejected, he battled the Assembly for over a year for recognition of his claim to the revenues of his estates. Finally, in September 1791, it issued a decree allowing him an indemnity and charging the King's government to pay over to him the amount of 273,766 francs. This was a farce, for three months earlier the Assembly had suspended the King from his royal functions. Louis XVI, Marie Antoinette and their children were prisoners in the Tuileries while outside the gates of their palace-prison crowds shouted, "Austrian-whore [the Queen]!" Honoré stood no chance of collecting from the government of an imprisoned monarch.

There remained some hope that the struggle of the conservatives, led by Mirabeau, to make France a constitutional monarchy would succeed. The left wing demanded the abolition of the monarchy, but a majority in the Assembly prevailed. Despite this, nothing had changed for the royal family: they remained virtual prisoners.

The Paris to which Honoré had returned was in turmoil. Of the 650,000 people crowded into the city, over half were unemployed, roaming aimlessly through the narrow, winding, muddy streets of the still largely medieval city, their anger rising as their stomachs growled with increasing hunger. Even for those with a few sous in their pockets, bread was short, for there had been severe storms that winter and the wheat harvest had been nearly ruined. To add to the discontent of the French workers who, after the storming of the Bastille, had believed revolutions in other countries would help their cause, Europe did not follow their lead.

The frustration and inconclusiveness of their situation—the King unable to act and the Assembly playing a waiting game— enraged them further. During the harsh winter of 1792 when crops once again were sparse and the price of a loaf of bread exorbitant, calls for bloodshed "rose like a mad man's shriek."

In April 1792, against the King's judgment, the French Assembly declared war against Austria, which had announced itself ready to restore the King "to a situation in which he would be free to strengthen the foundations of monarchical government . . ."

The effect of this devastating war was not only that the Queen, Marie Antoinette, became an enemy alien (she was Austrian by birth), but that the country was now forced to feed, clothe, equip and shelter an army of 400,000 men.

Honoré remained in Paris, not knowing where to turn, for on January 13, 1793, the People's Councils of Monaco, Menton and Roquebrune formed a Conventional Assembly, declared the end of Honoré's reign and voted to ask for union with France, the first foreign land to do so. General Brunet, the commander of the French troops who were at the time engaged in hostilities in Sardinia, conveyed this request to the Assembly in Paris. It arrived and was acted upon only hours after a French tribunal of 749 members voted by a majority of 53 that the King, now a prisoner at Temple Prison, be condemned to death on the guillotine.[1]

The dangers on the streets of Paris were always present. However, having given his horses and carriages to the military and donated to the populist cause, Honoré III remained miraculously unharmed. His son, Honoré, in poor health and now separated from his wife, had come to live with him. His younger son, Joseph, who had married the beautiful Françoise-Thérèse de Choiseul-Stainville in 1782, traveled abroad trying to raise funds to extricate his family from their problems. This brought

---

[1]There was only one English-speaking member of the Convention, Thomas Paine of Pennsylvania, then a deputy for the Pas de Calais, who voted aginst the death penalty. "Paine stood silent on the rostrum, while a secretary read a French translation of his speech. After the first few sentences Marat [Jean Paul, revolutionary leader] broke in: 'Thomas Paine mayn't vote on this. He's a Quaker; his religious principles are opposed to the death sentence.' . . . Paine continued through his interpreter: 'The man you have condemned to death is regarded by the people of the United States as their best friend, the founder of their freedom. [Louis XVI had sent money and men to the aid of American revolutionaries in their war against England, placing his own country in financial jeopardy at the time.] That people is today your only ally; well, then, it comes in my person to ask you to suspend the sentence you have decreed. Do not give the despot of England [George III] the pleasure of seeing on the scaffold the man who delivered our brothers in America from tyranny." [Cronin, *Louis and Antoinette,* page 369]

him under suspicion as a suspected enemy of the people and so he was forced to remain with his wife out of France, having left their two daughters in the care of a governess.

The King was executed on January 21, 1793, and on March 4, 1793, Monaco officially became part of the French Alpes-Maritimes *département,* which included Nice. Lazare Carnot, considered to be the military genius of the Revolution, stated that since "it appears that the ex-prince did not declare himself an enemy of France during the Revolution, and since he has always claimed her protection as a friend and ally, the committee is of the opinion that in abolishing his honorific and feudal revenues you ought to accord him protection and safeguard for what he may possess as an ordinary citizen." This seemed to indicate that if Honoré did return to Monaco his life would not be in jeopardy. Jean-Michel Alexandre de Millo, seventy-three years of age and a former associate and friend of Honoré's, was elected mayor on March 24. Only days later he was removed from office.

A revolutionary group called the Société Populaire came into control, and anyone unsympathetic to the cause was either banished or imprisoned. (Although deaths occurred, there is no official record of executions having been carried out.) There was a move to "dechristianization." The sounding of church chimes was forbidden, as were any religious ceremonies not held in churches, which were closed at night, and priests were forbidden to celebrate midnight mass or hear confessions. Nonetheless, the Revolution in Monaco was at best a small replica of that in France. Since the Principality had never had an aristocratic or affluent society other than the Grimaldis, life simply became bleaker than before, and the people suffered deprivation but not the hunger (for farming continued) nor the fear that consumed France.

Severe storms sent massive waves crashing against the sides of the Rock on March 3, 1793, forcing a French ship with two commissars of the French Republic to wait until a day later to make the decree public. There are no reports existing that any great cheering was heard as the Grimaldi standard was taken down from the Palace. There was, however, tremendous pillaging of the art, silver and other treasures inside, perhaps by the

French before they sailed. A meticulous inventory was then done of every room in the Palace; and it appears that after that day, nothing further was ever removed.

In September the ex-Prince, his ailing older son and his estranged wife, Louise-Félicité, and their younger son, eight-year-old Florestan, were imprisoned in the barracks of the rue de Sèvres as enemies of the people. The child and his mother were rescued by the Grimaldis' friend and family doctor, a man named Desormeaux, who forged a release order and then hid them in his home until the end of the Reign of Terror.[2] Françoise-Thérèse, the wife of Honoré's younger son, Joseph, was not so fortunate. Unable to bear being apart from her daughters during this horrifying time, she had returned to Paris in November 1792, and was immediately arrested. Despite his imprisonment Honoré managed to secure funds on her behalf, and she was released against surety.

Honoré was very fond of Françoise-Thérèse, who, with Joseph, had spent several months at Carnolès with him when they were first married. She was a delicate girl, fair-skinned, with pale hair set off by violet eyes, and had a charming manner. When she was arrested again in September 1793, Honoré was also incarcerated and could not help her. Since Joseph was under high suspicion of being an enemy of the people (the reason for Honoré's arrest), she feared the worst. Claiming to be ill, she was allowed to go into an anteroom to lie down while the charges against her were put before the magistrate. Somehow she managed to slip past a guard and onto the street. Eventually, she made her way to a convent in the rue de Bellechasse. The few remaining nuns took her in. Three months later, the convent was raided and Françoise-Thérèse was arrested for the third time.

In prison, Honoré appealed through every channel open to him for the safety of his family. A delegate from the People's Union in Thorigny (the governing body where Honoré's estate

[2]The Reign of Terror was the period between 1793 and 1794 when the Committee of Public Safety, operating as a war dictatorship, was instituted to rule the country. Maximilien Robespierre was the dominant member. Their aim was to eliminate all counterrevolutionaries, to raise new armies and to regulate the national economy. During this time thousands of victims were guillotined or arrested. Many more were the victims of mass drownings called *noyades*. Robespierre was overthrown on July 27, 1794, and executed.

was located) reported to the Convention on December 1, 1793: "Citizen Grimaldi . . . very different from other seigneurs of the old order . . . has always shown himself kind, just, and understanding . . . always affable, sympathetic and generous [to the people]; mindful of the farms, he never went hunting or shooting over them except when no harm could be caused. He had fines imposed under the game laws refunded, he allowed poor people to gather wood from his park, had 900 loaves sent every week to families in want, and gave a number of other doles, pensions and help in kind." In the end, the local council and People's Union of Thorigny asked for his release and that he should receive safe passage to Thorigny (which was far more peaceful than Paris), where they would be responsible for him.

The plea was rejected and Honoré, his two sons and his daughter-in-law remained in prison. On July 25, 1794, Françoise-Thérèse received an order to appear before the Revolutionary Tribunal at ten o'clock the next morning. "She showed not the slightest sign of emotion," one of her fellow inmates recorded. "She . . . kissed her maid, and took leave of us just as though parting from fellow travellers whose company had been pleasant and agreeable during a long journey."

The sound of the guillotine was an ever-present daily terror at this time. Françoise-Thérèse, wife of Grimaldi-Monaco, aged twenty-six, was to be victim number 28 on July 26, condemned to die as an enemy of the people. Although frail even before her harsh imprisonment, Françoise-Thérèse stood erect when the verdict was delivered. She was then led to the records office, only a few steps from the place of execution. She had been advised by other prisoners to claim to be pregnant, which would give her time at least to try for an appeal, since pregnant women could claim exemption from execution until after the birth of their child, or proof that they had miscarried or lied. It meant confessing to have conceived adulterously as she and Honoré had not lived together for two years. There and then—the numbers 18 and 19 having been called—she announced she was pregnant, naming a dead prisoner as the father, and was promptly returned to a cell where she was left alone.

With her shoe she carefully broke a pane of glass in a narrow slit of a window and cut off two locks of her long fair hair. She then enclosed them in letters, one addressed to her daughters, the other to their governess, Madame Chevenoy. This accomplished, she wrote a note in a firm hand to the Public Prosecutor, Fouquier-Tinville: "I should be obliged if Citizen Fouquier-Tinville would come and see me here for a moment. I earnestly ask him not to refuse this request." She covered her head with her shawl, gave the note to the guard on duty and waited.

When no one had appeared by the following morning, she wrote a second note: "I give you notice, Citizen, that I am not with child. I wanted to tell you [in person] and now, having no hope of you coming, I inform you in writing. I did not soil my lips with this lie for fear of death nor to avoid it, but to give myself one more day so that I could cut my hair myself instead of having it cut by the executioner. This is all I could leave to my children; it had at least to be clean."

With rouge on her cheeks so as not to appear frightened, she waited once more in the records office. Forty-two heads were to fall that day. Françoise-Thérèse was the last to mount the guillotine. It was five in the afternoon and the sun had lowered beyond the wall of the prison when she died. The following day, Robespierre, whose key words had been "punish," "terror," "victim" and "blood," had been overthrown by the Convention and the Reign of Terror had ended.[3] He was to follow Françoise-Thérèse to the guillotine, preceded by the Public Prosecutor, Fouquier-Tinville a short time later. Had she waited twenty-four hours to send her note, Françoise-Thérèse need not have died.

Although he was released from prison in October 1794 and was living once again in his Paris town house—stripped of all its former furnishings and art and silver—the strain had been too much for Honoré. He was never to regain his strength. He died at the age of seventy-five on May 12, 1795. His elder son was now officially Honoré IV, but he did not have the right to be called Prince de Monaco. His health broken, he nonetheless succeeded in regaining control of his father's estates. As he was not well enough to conduct his own affairs, he placed them in the capable hands of his brother Joseph, who returned to France at the end of 1795 exonerated from all charges, a few months

[3]Thomas Paine had also been imprisoned and was marked for execution, but a feverish illness kept him semiconscious for a month. Then, the end of the Reign of Terror having come, his life was saved. Madame Du Barry had not been that fortunate.

after the death of Louis XVI's ten-year-old son, and heir.

Monaco's former ruling family did at least have a direct male heir, and he had two sons, Honoré-Gabriel and Florestan. But Monaco was no longer a principality. It had even been renamed L'Hercule. So it seemed just as unlikely that the Grimaldis would occupy their Palace again as that a Bourbon king would sit on the throne of France.

A FIGHT TO
SURVIVE
1796–1856

7

THE WORLD Honoré IV awoke to after the Revolution was one of decreasing familiarity. Cut off entirely from Monaco, his family properties in Normandy in desperate straits after their mismanagement under sequestration, his château in Thorigny in disrepair, the Paris town house divested of its former glory and his mother's great fortune gone with the defeat of the royalists, he was a man teetering on bankruptcy with nowhere to borrow and no talent for making money. He turned to his brother, Joseph, to help him out of his predicament, a decision that created quarrels with his two sons, who were torn between the erratic highs and lows of their divorced mother and the misanthropic attitude of their father.

His chronic ill-health (he had suffered from a severe stomach disorder most of his life) kept him out of the French Army for the first few years following the Revolution. Then, miraculously—or perhaps because of the imposed limitation of diet he had endured during his imprisonment and immediately thereafter—his health improved. With no other satisfactory alternative, he joined the French Army in 1806 and was appointed aide-de-camp to the brilliant and dashing military leader Joachim Murat, who had fought under Napoleon in Egypt in 1798 and married his sister Caroline in 1800. (Murat, by Napoleon's decree, was to become King of Naples just two years after his army association with Honoré. In 1815, following Napoleon's fall from power, he was arrested and executed in an attempt to regain the throne of Naples.)

Severely wounded at Friedland during Napoleon's campaign in Russia, Honoré was awarded the Legion of Honor. Despite the almost total disability of one arm, he fought with Murat in Spain when the French Army marched through it to cross the frontier of Portugal; but because of his ill-health he was sent back to Paris. He never recovered from his war injuries, nor did he receive a just pension from the army.

Napoleon was crowned Emperor by his own hand on December 2, 1804, in the Cathedral of Notre Dame. Post-Revolution French society consisted of *parvenus* who had come to power through political or military achievement and had grown rich through speculation. As a model they had only the society they had just destroyed, the extravagant aristocrats of Versailles, which was now silent and deserted. The opulence of the new Court, which moved from Empress Josephine's luxurious Palace of Malmaison to the Tuileries was no less glittering than the old, but it was outstandingly vulgar.[1] To inject a grander tone of manners and etiquette, the new Emperor brought more and more of the old aristocrats into his Court. Some adapted themselves to the new order; others—like Honoré—remained outsiders and were swiftly passed over.

It does not seem that Honoré attended many, if any, of the salons, *fêtes* or celebrations that filled the Court calendar. Members of the Bonaparte family were given princely titles and the style of Imperial Highness. According to the Duchesse d'Abrantès, one of Josephine's good friends, "Balls, suppers and other court entertainments were revived. Unfortunately, neither the Emperor nor his courtiers quite knew how to go about it all, so the ceremonies were stiff, and the atmosphere was one of paralysing dullness. Napoleon himself was no help. He was given to walking rapidly up and down the two lines of his courtiers, stopping to tell the women they looked old, or overdressed, or underdressed, or blaming the men for shortcomings and occasionally flying into a rage. . . . In the houses of the nobility, many a snicker could be heard about the lack of manners at the new court. Napoleon knew all about that; and few things annoyed him more."

---

[1]The Empress Josephine (1763–1814) was born Marie Joséphine Rose Tascher de La Pagerie in Martinique. She married Alexandre de Beauharnais (an ancestor of a future Princesse de Monaco, Lady Mary Douglas-Hamilton, wife of Albert I). Two children were born to this union: Eugène (later Viceroy of Italy) and Hortense (later Queen of Holland). Beauharnais was guillotined in 1794. Josephine married Napoleon in 1796. The marriage was annulled in 1809 on the grounds of her infertility and Napoleon married Marie Louise, daughter of the Austrian Emperor Francis I.

Honoré withdrew, unmissed, from this society. His financial situation was increasingly bleak. The great house in Paris had been sold in 1804 by Joseph (who by nature, if not by breeding, fitted well into the *parvenu* society) to an English speculator for 195,000 francs, which only covered the debts from taxes and repairs owing to it. (The following year it was resold to Talleyrand, who sold it to Napoleon in 1812 for 1,280,000 francs. In the twentieth century it became the official residence of the French president.) Next, Honoré's estates in Valmont and Thorigny were put up for auction. Placed in the hands of dishonest agents who took a large amount "under the table" for their commissions, the sale did not raise sufficient money to pay off the encumbrances. Honoré, his war wounds now causing grievous discomfort and increasing his immobility, rented a small house at 763 rue d'Enfer. He was supported by his resentful older son, Honoré-Gabriel, who wrote to him in January 1808: "You say your brother is unable to help you, and I must admit that remark surprises me. You can't be unaware that the sums paid over to you come from my account and not from my uncle's . . ."

Looking back half a century later on the years of Napoleon's reign, Victor Hugo placed these words into the mouth of an old revolutionary in his epic novel *Les Misérables:* "We overturned the old world, we revolutionaries, and it was like the overthrow of a hothouse; from being a forcing-house of misery the world became a vessel of joy . . . You may call it uncertain joy, and now, after the fateful return of the past that is called the Restoration, vanished joy. Our work, alas, was not completed. We destroyed the structure of the *ancien régime,* but we could not wholly destroy its thought. It is not enough to abolish abuses; custom must also be transformed. The mill was pulled down, *but the wind still blows.*"

And indeed it did. For the very people of France who had mounted the barricades were now half starved under an equally oppressive government. Each successive year Napoleon's foreign campaigns, the living conditions of the poor (which had seemed intolerable under King Louis XVI) worsened. By the time of the Emperor's retreat from Russia in 1812—his *Grande Armée,* some 500,000 strong, reduced to a fifth of its original

93

strength—many Frenchmen were beginning to feel almost nostalgic for the days of the Bourbon Kings.

In 1813, Great Britain and Sweden joined with Spain and Austria in the War of Liberation against France. Paris fell to the allies on March 31, 1814. Napoleon abdicated, first in favor of his young son (child of his marriage to Marie Louise of Austria), and then unconditionally, and was exiled to the island of Elba off the coast of central Italy. Napoleon's defeat brought about an affirmation of solidarity among the European monarchies and the same year the return (cheered tumultuously by the people) of a Bourbon King—Louis XVIII, brother of Louis XVI—to the throne of France.

Hugo writes: "Dictatorship was ended . . . the Napoleonic empire dissolved in a darkness resembling the last days of Rome, and chaos loomed as in the time of the barbarians. But the barbarism of 1815, which must be called by its proper name of counter-revolution, was short-winded and soon stooped for lack of breath. . . ."

The last years of Napoleon's reign had been unduly harsh on the people of Monaco, whose exports were reduced by the allied blockades and who received little help from the Alpes-Maritimes *département* into which they had been incorporated. But Joseph Grimaldi had never lost contact with former family supporters; and almost immediately upon Louis XVIII's ascent to the throne in 1814, he petitioned the King in the name of the Grimaldi family to "allow them of his gracious kindness to enter into their rights and possessions again and to deign to take the Principality of Monaco under his powerful protection." Talleyrand, the King's foreign minister, negotiated the First Treaty of Paris, which returned France to the borders that had existed in 1792. He now resurrected the Principality of Monaco (including the return of its name) by adding a paragraph to the Treaty which renounced all France's sovereign rights over territories outside the frontiers fixed for her. The way was cleared for the Grimaldis to return to power in Monaco. But *which* Grimaldi was the key question

Honoré IV's physical condition had worsened—he was paralyzed now on one entire side of his body. Joseph came to see him on the rue d'Enfer and persuaded him to renounce the duchy of Valentinois and the peerage in favor of Honoré-Gabriel, while delegating full powers in the Principality to him. To the twenty-eight-year-old Honoré-Gabriel's rage and shock, his uncle Joseph took over the position that should have been rightfully his—and it was only the hope of finally attaining that position that had enabled him to survive a difficult life.

Born eleven years before the storming of the Bastille, he had known fear when his aunt had died on the guillotine and many other members of his family had been imprisoned. Before that time he had been tossed back and forth between an ineffectual father and a shrewish, wildly emotional mother who hated each other. Seven years older than his brother Florestan, and ten when his parents were divorced, he had always borne the responsibility that being an older son in a fatherless household entailed—but seldom with good grace.

His early years in Paris had been hard. The family was near bankruptcy. He rented a small apartment in 1805 and then, unable to find anything else to do, joined Napoleon's élite guard, rapidly rising to the rank of captain. Nevertheless, he was bitter that after serving well in Germany and Poland and then with Murat in Spain (where his ailing father was his superior officer) he had not risen higher. He returned to Paris in 1808 and was made an equerry to the Empress Josephine at Malmaison, proudly wearing his scarlet uniform. When Napoleon annulled his marriage to Josephine in 1809, Honoré-Gabriel remained with her. His job was to budget the household, and it was not an easy one.

His own life had become a daily financial struggle to make ends meet. He received 15,000 francs annually in his position, which meant he could afford few luxuries. Whatever outside money he acquired came from his mother's inheritance, and she never gave a penny without expecting a return. In the case of her sons, this meant that they would be available when she felt the need for their attention and that they would not go against her wishes. Her approval (which he constantly sought) did not come easily. She repeatedly threatened to cut him out of her will if he displeased her, and she had not been happy about the illegitimate son he had fathered in 1814, born in Paris and delivered by the Grimaldis' discreet friend Doctor

95

Desormeaux. The child was named Oscar, but the mother's identity was not (and never has been) revealed on the birth records.[2]

Honoré-Gabriel's uncle Joseph had lived by his brains for his entire life, managing to escape the ordeals suffered through the Revolution by his father, his brother, and his tragic first wife, Françoise-Thérèse, remarrying a rich widow and cleverly shifting allegiances as rulers came in and out of power. He had squandered his second wife's inheritance in the eight years since her death. He now looked to Monaco for his income. His first action was to repeal the existing laws to reestablish the status quo prevailing before January 1, 1792, which meant the Palace and all its contents would be turned over to the Grimaldis and, once again, taxes paid directly to them. It also reinstated Italian, which had been banned since the Revolution, as the official language. This caused great chaos for any Monégasques under twenty-five, who had been speaking French all their lives. An uncommonly cold winter greeted Joseph's arrival in Monaco, further depressing the economic situation and the Monégasques refused to pay their taxes. In January 1815 Joseph hurried back to Paris in the hope of raising funds there. This threw the Monégasques into greater upheaval for, with the French garrison gone and the provisional government dismissed, there was no one to restore order to what was, in effect, a principality without a prince.

By now, however, Honoré-Gabriel had rallied his forces. Through the Duc d'Aumont, his mother's cousin and a confidant of the King, he petitioned Louis XVIII to rescind his uncle's usurpation of his inherited rights, on the grounds that his father was mentally incapable of knowing what he was signing when he put his name to the document. Within a matter of days, unable to borrow the money he needed to return to Monaco, Joseph capitulated, writing to his brother: "I have consulted with your friends d'Aumont and d'Esclignac [a nephew of Talleyrand] and together we have drawn up the document

[2]His son was recognized by Honoré and on November 28, 1814, was legalized as Louis-Gabriel-Oscar Grimaldi, Marquis des Beaux (1814–1894). A letter to Charles III (Florestan's son) dated March 17, 1870, alludes to a legacy of 300,000 francs from the Marquise d'Herecy to the Marquis des Beaux. The Herecys were a Normandy family, and the Marquise was the wife of Honoré's closest childhood friend.

I am submitting to you; by it, your son will be bound in such a way, and in accord with the family council, that I do not think he will be able to deviate from these agreements. By this means there will be peace in our family again, and you will have sufficient income on which to live comfortably. Say whether you're agreeable to it; I did nothing without d'Aumont's consent, and you know of his friendship for you."

In what Joseph considered a final act of goodwill toward his brother, he agreed to renounce any claim he might have on Monaco with the promise that Honoré-Gabriel would care for his father (he also requested that his own interests would be looked after). A document was thus signed by Honoré IV revoking the first document and assigning all sovereign rights to his elder son. Upon its execution on February 23, 1815, Honoré-Gabriel (now Honoré V) set off for Monaco.

While Honoré V and his entourage traveled by coach through France, Napoleon, with a handful of followers, had escaped from Elba, landing in Cannes on March 1, 1815. On that very afternoon, as Honoré V's carriage passed through Cannes, he was halted by soldiers. To his dismay, he learned they were Napoleon's advance guard. To ensure the former Emperor's safe passage on his way to Paris, all travelers were being stopped and detained until he had moved farther along on his journey. Honoré recognized the leading officer, a general he had served under while a captain in the élite guard during Napoleon's campaigns of 1806 and 1807 in Germany and Poland. The general thought Napoleon might want to exchange a few words with Honoré in order to hear the news from Paris.

Honoré was led on foot through an olive wood for some little distance. In a small clearing, Napoleon was sitting over a bivouac fire. Napoleon's valet, Marchand, was later to record, ". . . the Emperor met with the Prince de Monaco, who was embarrassed at first, but ceased to be when he found himself greeted like someone the Emperor knew . . . a big fire was lit, and he and the Emperor went and stood near it. All the while they were speaking together, the Prince kept his hat in his hand. The Emperor wished him a happy journey as they parted. The Prince did not hide from the Emperor how risky such an expedition was. The fairly wide circle we had formed around the two prevented us from hearing what they said yet the Emperor's good spirits gave cause for thinking he was satisfied with the details he got about Paris and the state of mind in France. The Prince had given him the opinions of the drawing-rooms. . . ."[3]

To his annoyance, as his rank was now above the ex-emperor's, Honoré was not permitted to continue on his journey for an hour after Napoleon had gone on his way. He had never been a great admirer of Bonaparte, whom he considered largely responsible for his impecunious past, and he found it difficult to forgive his callous treatment of the Empress Josephine. One still could not dismiss Napoleon's charisma or his military genius, but Napoleon's ignorance in many areas was remarkable, and he spoke French very badly, frequently committing the most illiterate mistakes, which brought out Honoré's snobbishness. The moment he was permitted to continue on his journey he did so, pausing in Nice to inform the Sardinian authorities (who now controlled the city) of Napoleon's return, an act of spite.[4]

After this meeting, Napoleon marched triumphantly northward, rallying the people once more behind him. He entered Paris twenty days later. Louis XVIII was quickly transported out of France by the royalists, and Bonaparte began his "ephemeral rule" of the Hundred Days. Then the allies again advanced into states controlled by France. Napoleon was utterly crushed at Waterloo, in central Belgium, his army suffering huge losses. On June 18, 1815, he surrendered to a British warship, the *Bellerophon*, in the hope of being given asylum in England. Instead, he was sent as a prisoner of war to the island of Saint Helena in the South Atlantic Ocean, twelve hundred miles west of Africa, and Louis XVIII returned to Paris and to his throne.

Honoré V had, meanwhile, established his authority in Monaco. As he had left his Principality at the age of four, the task before him was not easy. An entire generation had grown up

[3]Alexandre Dumas, père, published an account of this meeting twenty-five years later which so enraged Honoré V (Honoré-Gabriel) that he demanded a retraction, informing Dumas: "Sir, I have a painful duty to perform . . . but the conversation you give as having taken place between the Emperor and myself is a travesty of the truth. He did not keep saying to me: 'Good morning, Monaco,' he never asked me to follow him, and I did not reply that I awaited his orders." In fact, the day following his meeting with Napoleon, Honoré V had dispatched a letter to the French minister for war, Marshal Soult, giving a detailed report of the encounter.
[4]Sardinia was the name given to the possessions of the House of Savoy. The Kingdom included Piedmont (northwest Italy), Nice, Liguria and Genoa.

with little or no knowledge of the Grimaldi family and had then endured his uncle's mismanagement (or rather, lack of management). Monaco remained as isolated as it had been before the Revolution. The most direct access by land was still a road too narrow for a carriage to pass, which wound precipitously down from the ancient Roman ruins of La Turbie through pine forests and olive plantations. And so Honoré V approached the Rock on horseback, having left his carriage at La Turbie. Menton, which was joined to the Rock by a carriage road, was more accessible but farther away and either he wished to arrive as soon as possible or he rather liked the image of the returning Prince on a charger.

Honoré's prime objective was to reclaim the Principality for the Grimaldis and to ensure that whatever monies could be found in the treasury would be transferred directly to him. He belonged to that class of Frenchmen (and he had been born in France and lived his life there until this time) who was not accepted by the true aristocrats, yet who did not himself accept the *parvenus*. Arrogant above all else, he was also an angry, self-important and embittered man. He possessed a waspish tongue, a quick, cruel wit and an air of condescension. With his dark, lean good looks—piercing eyes beneath well-arched brows, aquiline nose, gracefully bowed mouth, narrow clefted chin—he cut a dashing figure which his penchant for scarlet uniforms and gold braid enhanced.

Upon his arrival the Monégasques had greeted their thirty-six-year-old Prince warmly, and with some hope that he would aid them in their difficulties. They quickly found they were welcoming a despot who, although outwardly a perfect gentleman, had little sympathy for the grievances of his people. Honoré was appalled at the state of his Palace, now little more than a shell, and a dirty shell at that, for it had been used as a poorhouse for a decade. The silver, porcelain, tapestries and paintings were gone, and the treasury of Monaco was almost empty.

The taxes raised on olives, fruit for export and the manufacture of bread brought in a revenue of 45,000 francs, but this was entirely swallowed up in salaries and administrative expenses. Honoré's initial edict on March 12, 1815 (after decreeing that the official language would return to French, for he

99

spoke very little Italian) was to have all property that had been confiscated by the revolutionary forces, which was now distributed among the former communes, hospitals and churches, made over to him, as well as revenues from all taxes and even from the manure swept up in the streets and sold as fertilizer.

On March 13, only ten days after his arrival, an English troopship was sighted sailing toward Monaco. Honoré ordered the gates of the port closed. The English officer in charge, a Colonel Burke, demanded to see him. Honoré kept him waiting for a reply before he finally agreed to allow him to enter. He greeted the Englishman from his throne in the old Throne Room ("Only a Colonel?" he was heard to comment to one of his attendants.) Burke presented him with a letter from M. d'Azorque, the King of Sardinia's representative, stating that in consequence of Napoleon's reappearance, and Honoré's admission that he had met and spoken with him, English troops had been dispatched to occupy Monaco. Honoré suspected this was a scheme of Sardinia's King, Victor Emmanuel I, to annex Monaco. But with a guard of only thirty-five or so undisciplined cadets he did not dare attempt to match swords, especially with several ships belonging to the British fleet anchored inside his territorial waters.

After several hours of negotiations the Colonel agreed to sign the following statement:

In the year 1815, on the 13th of March, at two o'clock in the afternoon, M. Burke, colonel in the English service, presented himself at the Palace of Monaco, and handed the prince a letter from M. d'Azorque, commandant at Nice, for the King of Sardinia . . . which states that the English troops have received orders to occupy Monaco. The hereditary prince has declared to Colonel Burke that the principality has been re-established in its entire independence by the Treaty of Paris, and under the protection of France; but having at the moment no garrison in the place, he finds himself debarred from offering opposition to the occupation; that he consents but through constraint, and that he protests against all inference that might be drawn from this momentary occupation against rights of sovereignty which are acknowledged.

Both the men signed the letter and Honoré added in his own hand:

> The moment the English troops entered the place Colonel Burke caused it to be garrisoned by the said troops.

Several hundred British troops immediately occupied the Principality. By now, Napoleon was back in power, and Honoré, in a direct about-face, began to petition him through the Emperor's minister for foreign affairs, the Duc de Vicence, for assistance. A week passed before Vincence finally presented the matter to Napoleon in a letter:

> SIRE
>
> From the first moment of your Majesty's return a commander of English troops, in concert with the governor of the county of Nice, has taken possession of Monaco. After the old Paris treaties [were] renewed, France alone has the right to garrison that place. The period at which this occupation took place indicated sufficiently that the commander of the English troops has acted simply on his own impulse, and that he could not then have received instructions from his government.
>
> France should demand satisfaction for this affair from the courts of London and Turin [capital of Sardinia]; she ought to insist on the evacuation of Monaco, and on her being placed under a French garrison according to the treaties; but your Majesty may perhaps judge this affair as one for explanations only, supposing that the determination of the Sardinian government, and above all, the English commander, has been accidental, and a sudden result of the uneasiness occasioned by extraordinary circumstances.

However, Napoleon had learned of Honoré's treachery in reporting his arrival in Cannes to the Sardinians, and refused him any assistance. The English troops remained well into the summer when they were eventually relieved by an Anglo-Italian regiment, maintained by England. Thus, the right of protection which for one hundred and seventy-three years had been exercised by France over Monaco ended, and the Principality fell under Sardinia's domination; the menacing, encircling hand that the Grimaldis had held off for centuries seemed to be closing in on them.

To make matters worse, Honoré had little hope of an indemnity from France for the past revenues of the duchy of Valentinois. At the Restoration a year earlier, France had agreed to a sum of four and a half million francs, but then all French rights and obligations to Monaco had been transferred to the Sardinian government. Bitterly disappointed in his first months in Monaco, bored with life on the Rock and humiliated by the presence of the English, in September Honoré decided to return to France, for "he felt himself to be more French than the French in some ways—as a persecuted Frenchman who was wrenched from his homeland." But before leaving Monaco, he issued a long list of new edicts, which placed intolerable tax burdens upon his already beleaguered subjects.

The most important produce of the Principality was fruits. The quantity grown far exceeded what could be consumed domestically, and the income derived from its foreign sale supplied the growers with their livelihoods. Honoré's new ordinances taxed oranges, lemons, grapes, figs, oils and essences so heavily that proprietors were near ruin.

Four oil mills, always privately owned, were decreed henceforth to belong to the State. Honoré also took over all other places of manufacture and proclaimed that their products— linen, gunpowder, pipes, cards and straw articles could not be purchased elsewhere. A monopoly, vermicelli, the principal food of the workers, was sold by Honoré to a Genoese for a substantial price.

A Frenchman named Chappon, formerly purveyor to the French Army, was engaged by Honoré to oversee other acquisitions. Two of the oil mills were converted into flour mills, and a law was passed prohibiting the inhabitants from providing themselves with corn, flour or bread from other sources. The profits were shared by Honoré and Chappon. An ordinance was passed on December 3, 1817, with a five-hundred-franc fine and the grain confiscated if the law was violated.

His income having risen to 320,000 francs annually, 80,000 of which went toward the upkeep of the Palace, and the salaries of civil employees and former soldiers from Genoa whose job it was to enforce his edicts, Honoré returned to France. But before he departed he appointed the Chevalier Charles Trenca, a descendant of the Chevalier de Grimaldi, as leader of the government council. The decision was, perhaps, the wisest he had or would make, for Trenca, though firm, was respected and well-liked by the people; he managed to sweeten the bitterness of their poverty by keeping crime to a minimum and was adept at settling local disputes with a calm and moderating hand.

Monaco had always been poor, but for generations the Grimaldis had contributed considerably to the well-being of the people "from what the harbor and its fleet of galleys brought in, then from the Spanish or French subsidies for the fortress, and finally [through large marriage dowries and] the [Matignon] family possessions in Normandy and the Valentinois." Louis I had used taxes for his own purposes and left enormous debts; but a sense of enterprise had always existed, and the Monégasques had been able to engage in trade with Nice and other neighbors to subsidize their incomes.

While his subjects were struggling to survive under the crushing economic burden that Honoré had imposed upon them, he set about repurchasing his former properties in Normandy and furnishing an apartment in Paris. Upon his uncle Joseph's death on June 28, 1816, he halved the monthly allowance of three thousand francs that he had agreed to pay his father, claiming "the people [of Monaco] are badly hit, frost has ruined their harvest and they are unable to pay their taxes that are in arrears." This was partially true, but with their incomes severely shrunk by his edicts the people were unable to manage when weather conditions damaged their crops. And what Honoré did not admit to his father was that his personal investments and extravagances were mostly responsible for his lack of funds.

His father's bizarre death on the evening of February 16, 1819, listed officially as an "accidental drowning in the Seine," remains an enigma. Honoré IV was almost a complete invalid. He could not have reached the Seine in freezing winter and at night without assistance, and it seems improbable that whoever helped him that far would then allow him to fall into the Seine and drown. Murder seems equally remote for he had neither power nor money. Suicide, with someone's help, is possible. He was gravely disappointed in his elder son. His last years were lonely; he suffered much pain. And when Joseph died his world had disappeared.

Honoré IV had not had much happiness from either of his sons. Seven years younger than Honoré V, Florestan was born when his parents were already on the verge of divorce. He had been briefly imprisoned with his mother during the Revolution, and his youth during those troubled times had been spent under her protective wing. He saw little of his father, and the age gap between his brother and him meant that he remained home in Normandy with his mother while Honoré was fighting with Napoleon's army. At seventeen, to his mother's fury and horror, he ran off to Paris and joined an acting company. With a dark, chiseled profile and a grand and imperious manner, he was inclined to think of himself as an Alexandre Dumas, père, hero.[5] Dumas himself—perhaps persuaded by the young man's mother, in whose home he had often been a guest—discouraged him from further seeking a life on the stage.

Threatened with disinheritance by his mother unless he adopted a worthwhile career, at twenty Florestan joined the army. He never rose above the rank of corporal, carrying out his garrison duties on the island of Oessant, at Neort, Bordeaux, and then at Toulon before being sent to fight in Russia.

Florestan was not well-suited to the army, and was even more ill-equipped to fight a war. Orders were difficult for him to take, the unaccustomed coarse food hard to digest, dirty linen and the absence of wine and women drove him into a state of agitated depression. He quickly discovered that an army was sharply divided between officers and enlisted men. His arrogance had falsely convinced him that as an aristocrat he would not remain long in the ranks of the common soldier, and by the time he was sent to Russia he was deeply resentful at his lack of advancement.

Battle horrified him—earth soaked with blood, wounded men, the dead frozen in the Russian winter, the smell of rotting flesh. Frightened, exhausted, hungry and suffering from dys-

---

[5]Florestan's stage career was later written about in *Memoirs of a Paris Doctor,* by P. de La Silboutie (Paris, 1911). French singer, writer and composer Sacha Guitry wrote an operetta, *Florestan I, Prince de Monaco* (music by W. R. Haymann, lyrics by Albert Willemetz) in 1936 which enjoyed a successful season in Paris. Both the book and the operetta portray Florestan as a vain young man. The latter continues his story into his reign in Monaco.

entery, he was taken prisoner on September 7, 1812, during the daylong siege of the small, virtually unknown village of Borodino, where thirty thousand French and forty-three thousand Russian soldiers perished. This was the second time in his life that he had been imprisoned, and the experience must have recalled the terror he had felt as a young boy. Conditions were primitive in the shed in which he was held with other prisoners, but he had at least survived where tens of thousands had not. He was transferred to a hospital and eventually freed after Napoleon's defeat.

On his return to France he had met Caroline Gilbert and spent the summer of 1815 at her family's château at Lametz. Caroline was eight years younger than he, a striking Mediterranean beauty with a strong personality. They were married on November 27, 1816. Two years later, on December 8, 1818, they had a son, Charles, who was now heir presumptive to Monaco.

Women's rights had been greatly increased during Napoleon's reign. They could control their own inheritances and were active in the world of business and finance. Caroline was a woman of her time. She set immediately to work, using her own income to better her husband's and her own financial situations—and she was good at it, quickly assuming the reins of the household, and two months after Honoré IV's mysterious death, Caroline took over the house on the rue d'Enfer. Although Honoré V was to claim his father died heavily in debt, this was only partly true. Honoré IV had left numerous uncollected assets; a legal suit for reparations of his personal losses in Monaco was still pending; an estate claim against the Brignole-Sale family was unsettled. Caroline engaged a lawyer named Adolphe Eynaud on a percentage basis and with his help succeeded in winning a settlement in both cases, appropriating the largest share for her family.

Florestan's new affluence nettled Honoré, for his position had become difficult. In 1821, the Monégasques faced complete ruin when a severe frost took all their crops and they were unable to pay their taxes. His credit overextended in France, Honoré was forced to ask the French Foreign Ministry for aid (already refused by Sardinia). He cited "the consequences of the enormous debts left by my father and the lawsuits that persist" as the reasons for his inability to help his subjects. "And as for the revenues from the Principality, the frosts in 1820 destroyed my hopes and everything had to be sacrificed for my subjects. I have given up my town apartment, dismissed my servants and am reduced to the position of an obscure person stuck in the depths of the country [his revitalized estates in Normandy]. By making innumerable sacrifices, I have saved between four and five hundred people from destitution and despair. . . ."

His list of personal concessions did not persuade the French Ministry to act on his behalf. Honoré's claim that by tightening his belt he had saved many of his subjects' lives is a travesty of the truth. In reality, his despotic edicts had taken from them any means of self-support. No money had been left in the treasury to cover a disaster like that winter's frost.

Honoré remained unmarried; and as problems in Monaco became more complex, he spent very little time there, leaving Charles Trenca in charge. Conditions did not change much for the Monégasques. They struggled merely to survive. Emigration laws imposed by Honoré made it difficult for them to go elsewhere. Surrounded by the extraordinary beauty of the area, a climate that usually was sunny and mild, possessing a port and waters that held a bounty of marine life, they were denied the rewards of a good life this should have ensured. There was unrest, even riots—quelled by Trenca and a small but well-trained regiment.

Honoré and Florestan's mother, Louise-Félicité, died in 1826, leaving what remained of her family estate (the d'Aumonts') to her younger son. The two brothers no longer spoke. Honoré spent little time in Monaco. He had never thought of himself as anything but French and his Principality as a source of income. The Monégasques blamed Honoré for much of their trouble. The name of Grimaldi was losing its luster and it would take a prince with compassion, intelligence and charisma to polish it to a point where it would once again shine.

8

IT WAS CLEARLY IN the Grimaldis' interest to maintain their sovereignty of Monaco. To lose it would be to lose the tax money that was their only way to regain their pre-Revolutionary life-style in France. In heart, allegiance and birth, the Grimaldis were Frenchmen; they saw nothing wrong with stripping Monaco to replenish their fortunes in France, and applied themselves to the task with fervor.

Through the five decades that followed Napoleon's defeat at Waterloo and the return of the Grimaldis to the Principality, Honoré V and then Florestan progressively destroyed the goodwill of the Monégasques and were demonstrably unwise in their rule. Despite the constant warning of events in France and the rest of Europe, they repeatedly implemented measures that undermined their reigns. In the end, they made rebels where there had been none.

A distinct and unsavory odor of serfdom and blatant exploitation was apparent in the way they treated the Monégasques, although there are no records of physical force having been applied to collect the dizzying plethora of harsh tax laws and decrees the Grimaldis placed upon their subjects, who were mainly a domesticated, peaceful people, not as ambitious as their French, Sardinian and Italian neighbors. The Mentonians were of a somewhat more volatile character, and it was in this town that resistance appeared at times. By nature, however, they were not fighters, they were survivors—for centuries they had labored to make the rocky earth they tilled feed and support them. All the Grimaldis had ever had to do to maintain their loyalty was to help them in this task. But the Grimaldis of this period felt responsible only to themselves.

The family values were French; their ambitions to ascend to the top of the French aristocracy. After the elderly Louis

XVIII's death in 1824, his younger brother, the Comte d'Artois, became Charles X at age sixty-seven, bringing with him the ultraroyalists who sought a return to the *ancien régime*. When they saw this was impossible to achieve, they acted instead to ensure their own social and political predominance. The appointment of an uncompromising reactionary, Jules Armand de Polignac, as chief minister led to the July Revolution of 1830 and Charles X's abdication in favor of his grandson, the Comte de Chambard. However, a descendant of Louis XIII, Louis-Philippe, Duc d'Orléans, former Lieutenant General of France, with the support of the popular Marquis de La Fayette, a leader of the moderates, was chosen to become "king of the French" and Chambard never ascended the throne.

Faced with the dramatic changes in France, Honoré, despite his aristocratic pretensions, might well have perceived his own folly at trying to turn back the clock. The world he sought no longer existed. He was a lonely and a bitter man, ignoring his responsibility to Monaco and envious of his brother's affluence. His sister-in-law, Caroline, had proved to be an astute businesswoman. With the lawyer Eynaud's help she had wisely invested Florestan's inheritance from his mother. They purchased for 277,000 francs the Hôtel de Créque in rue Saint-Guillaume, a vast mid-seventeenth century mansion with a handsome wing added in the eighteenth century. Adopting the titles the Comte and Comtesse de Grimaldi, they restored the grand town house to its former elegance and rented the wing, which contained a magnificent ballroom, to the poet and statesman Alphonse de Lamartine.

A daughter, Florestine, was born on October 22, 1833. Charles was now nearly fifteen and was the heir presumptive to the Principality. His uncle and his father still did not speak to each other and neither Charles nor Florestan had ever set foot in Monaco. The Monégasques knew little, if anything, about them. Honoré's visits to his Principality grew more infrequent with the years. He made two annual trips to go over the financial statements with his administrator and to ensure his monies were paid over to him. During these times he seldom went out among his subjects. He remained a trim, handsome man, vain and arrogant. There seemed to be no woman in his life. By the time he was fifty years old he became extremely popular with hostesses whenever an extra man was required for a dinner party or ball.

In the spring of 1840 Honoré became ill with a throat condition, which made it difficult for him to swallow. He did not allow this to stop him from making his ritual visits to Monaco, and on October 2, 1841, he choked to death while dining alone in the Palace. He was buried in the small parish church with neither his illegitimate son, Oscar, nor Florestan and his family present, nor was there much grieving in his Principality. The end of Honoré's reign was regretted by few of his subjects.

At this time another claim was placed against the right of the current ruling family of Grimaldis to remain in power in Monaco. The Marquis de Cagnes, a retired general living in Saint-Marcellin in the department of Isère, France, demanded of the Sardinian government, under whose protection Monaco had been since Honoré's return in 1815, that the Grimaldis' rights be suspended and his own claims considered. The bid failed. The Marquis Grimaldi della Pietra of Genoa then filed a similar protest in his name and even offered, should his pretensions be recognized, to cede all his rights to the King of Sardinia. This claim also failed and Florestan was assured his title.

Having never set foot in his Principality before, Florestan had no idea of what he would find. Monaco was composed of two quite disparate societies. On one hand there were the people of Menton and Roquebrune who, by the topography of their land alone, were separated from the Rock. Roads now connected the three points of the Principality, but Monaco, that is, the town that occupied the Rock and where the Palace was located, could lock its gates and enjoy total isolation. Then, too, the people who lived in Menton and Roquebrune were the farmers and workers upon whom the bulk of the taxes were levied, while the population of the Rock consisted mainly of Palace, civil and military personnel whose livelihoods were dependent upon their good relationship with the Prince (or the Princesse, as the case would be in Florestan's reign). Honoré had sequestered himself on the Rock, levying higher and higher taxes on the people of Roquebrune and Menton. What they now hoped for was a Prince who would unite the three townships and work for the benefit of all.

Florestan, Caroline, their son Charles and their daughter

109

Florestine arrived in Menton in a magnificent gilded carriage on February 9, 1842, an entry planned and orchestrated by Caroline. People ran out in the streets and crowded around the vehicle to get a good look at their new royal family. The horses were detached from the carriage, which the crowd dragged with their own hands to the governor's house. Not knowing what to expect, at first Florestan was afraid, for the crowd looked menacing, but when the carriage door was opened for him and he gingerly stepped out, shouts of "Down with monopolies!" and "Long live Florestan!" assailed him.

The people believed he would bring them better days, but their trust was to prove misguided. Caroline took over the ledgers of the Principality as she had done with the family's concerns in France. In truth, it was she who governed, writing the ordinances and coercing Florestan into signing edicts to raise taxes to even more crippling extremes. No one seems to have pointed out to the new Prince and Princesse de Monaco that reforms were badly needed. Within a matter of weeks it became clear to the Monégasques that the tough times were not over.

Monégasque historian Françoise Bernardy writes in her book *The Princes of Monaco* (1961): "Another handicap resulted from the characters and opinions of Florestan and his wife. He, born into a princely family, held democratic ideas; while she, becoming a princess after twenty-five years of married life, believed in divine right, and whenever a slice of power was wrenched from her in one sphere, she tried to win it back in another. Moreover for twenty-five years she had been used to holding the reins and having matters left to her by a husband uninterested in politics and disliking financial affairs; and so she quite sincerely believed she was doing her duty by him in not ceding an inch of power or authority, not even to their son."

Friction immediately began to set in between Princesse Caroline and her son, now a tall, sharp-featured young man of twenty-four with a trim mustache and goatee. Charles was appalled at his mother's takeover of the Principality's affairs. Realizing his father was not going to intervene, he took it into his own hands to write his mother a strong letter criticizing her actions and threatening to go to Turin, the capital and the seat of government of the Kingdom of Sardinia, and have the King

force Florestan to abdicate in his own favor. On April 3, 1842,
Princesse Caroline replied by letter:

> You've said what you think quite frankly, and I'll reply in the
> same way. To begin with, you talk about my capability, and I'll
> tell you this, that only one thing counts for me, the strictness
> with which I conscientiously carry out the obligations and duties
> I have taken on, and in my opinion that often serves better than
> intelligence. My duties, as I understand them, are above the
> ordinary. I was brought up in a simple and modest position and
> was then chosen by your father to enter one of the highest placed
> families . . . from that moment my position changed. In spite of
> my sex, I became head of a family and had to fulfill the obli-
> gations attached and get myself forgiven for this preferment.
> Your father gave me a good name and fortune, in return I
> must take care to see his position is maintained and his fortune
> looked after properly. I owe it to my children, as a compensation
> for not having brought material advantages into the family, to
> guard those belonging to their father; I owe it to my son espe-
> cially to see that he receives intact the inheritance that Providence
> has placed in his father's hands, and I owe him the fruits of my
> experience and my advice—and I will tell him this, that for six
> months now he has been in error in several instances, though I
> admit that the fresh prospects opened before him by the death
> of his uncle may have confused his mind.
> [You appear to believe] that the little aptitude your father has
> for public affairs meant that you could take charge of them
> without having received your father's permission to do so; you
> then took it upon yourself to write to some of the officials, and
> although the letters are no doubt innocuous, you did not take
> into consideration that you are weakening your father's author-
> ity, and thereby giving fresh hopes to Sardinia and increasing
> the people's uneasiness.
> You can imagine that in a very small place where people have
> been used to the strong will of one person they must have been
> greatly astonished to see a prince letting himself be manoeuvred,
> the wife poking her finger into everything, and a son apparently
> going his own particular way and often lacking in respect and
> even consideration where they are due. If only to set an example.
> I am serving your father's interests here, which will one day
> be your own, and it's not a game, it concerns a whole family's
> position. . . . So it is far better that you should have, later on, a

111

solid, well-established authority than to be putting ideas of division or opposition into minds that have been submissive until now, and which you might find yourself up against one day.

Consider the position you put yourself in if you said at Turin that you're more capable than your father and that you should take his place. I quite believe you don't want to reach that point; what you would be saying in effect is—I love and respect my mother enough to leave her some of the authority she seems to like so much, but only on condition that she leaves me the rest. Oh no, my young friend, I shall not agree to a deal like that, because my great idea is always to have your father's rights respected and keep those of my children intact. Having no rights myself, I'm under the cover of your father, who thus returns the fullness of his authority.

I feel in need of a rest after such a long letter, but I've still just enough energy to tell you that ever since you were born you have been most dear to me, and the reason for all my efforts, and that until my dying day you'll be my well-beloved.

No clearer picture of this family could be painted. Caroline's ambition streaks across the pages, illuminating Florestan's weakness and her son's resentment and fury that she has made his father weak. His self-righteousness is a saber of revenge aimed at this mother whom he loves and hates at the same time. Neither mother nor son seems concerned with the Monégasques, or with enriching the life of Monaco. This is a quintessential power struggle between members of an arrogant and, it would seem, greedy family.

Florestan considered himself much put upon. "I am an unfortunate little sovereign, crushed between two big neighbors [France and Sardinia] who only hesitate as to the sauce with which they shall devour me," he was later quoted as saying. He claimed that as the new Prince de Monaco he had been "bubbling over with ideas of liberty, progress and reforms!" If this had been the case, then Caroline must have quickly quashed his plans for there is no record of any such improvements being implemented at any time in his reign. Instead, his subjects' economic conditions grew worse and their freedom diminished as embargoes were legislated that prohibited them from selling or buying goods elsewhere.

Florestan blamed not his own callousness but his subjects'

unreasonable attitude toward him for the state of hostility that existed between them. "All my acts are criticized!" he was quoted as saying. "I go for a walk—it is found I idle my time away. I do not go for a walk—I am afraid of showing myself. I give a ball—I am accused of wild extravagance—I do not give a ball— I am mean and avaricious. I build—wastefulness. I do not build—then what about the working classes? Everything I do is proclaimed detestable, and what I do not do gives even greater offence."

But the Monégasques had little respect for a Prince who was under his wife's domination and whose son felt he was incapable of ruling. Caroline's pleas for Charles to desist from his efforts to replace Florestan as Prince de Monaco did not succeed. Charles made the trip to Turin, but what he found was not what he had sought.

The last years of Honoré V's reign had proved too much for most Monégasques. Many of them, just to earn a living wage, had joined Sardinia's armed forces and were beginning to think of Sardinia as their homeland. The Chief Magistrate in Turin (in the name of the Sardinian Kingdom) conveyed in very clear terms its willingness to acquire the sovereignty of the Principality for a fair price. The offer to Charles of a rich marriage alliance with a young woman from a Piedmont family close to the King Victor Emmanuel II of Sardinia was thrown in to sweeten the package.

Caroline was in Paris when she heard of this proposal, and went straight to the offices of the Sardinian ambassador to France. She was quoted in communiqués as having claimed she would rather Monaco go to war against Sardinia than fall meekly under its heel, and threatened to report "the conduct of his agents to the King." The ambassador was apparently won over, and the offer presented to Charles was quickly withdrawn.

This meant that Charles had to find his own bride, not too difficult a task, for not only would he one day be Prince de Monaco, he was rich and he was not unattractive. Nonetheless, it was not until four years later, on September 28, 1846 (the bride's eighteenth birthday), that he married, in Brussels, Antoinette, Comtesse de Mérode, a niece of a wealthy and powerful Belgian, Monseigneur de Mérode. Charles and his golden-haired, youthful wife returned to Monaco where, despite the many problems in the Principality, they were given a warm welcome.

Florestan's power had greatly diminished in the four years since Charles had made his appeal to Turin to replace him. In Honoré's reign the commander of the Sardinian garrison in Monaco took his orders from the Prince or his representative. Now he answered dirctly to the King of Sardinia. Princesse Caroline could well have been right when she told the Sardinian ambassador in Paris, "Your King covets our little State." Sardinian agitators moved among the people of Menton and Roquebrune, and during the winter of 1847 there was a series of riots and threats to overthrow Florestan. The Grimaldis were much alarmed, for the threat of revolution was growing in France, where dissatisfaction with King Louis-Philippe's reactionary policy led on February 23, 1848, to street fighting in Paris. Government troops fired on demonstrators and the February Revolution was set off. Within a matter of days Louis-Philippe abdicated, Princesse Caroline's Paris tenant, Alphonse de Lamartine, was made head of the provisional government and the Second Republic was declared in France. The February Revolution set off insurrections across Europe, and Monaco was not exempt.

The discontent in Roquebrune and Menton accelerated. A rebel group of about fifty men formed. After they made a serious but failed attempt to storm the gates of Monaco (which had been locked), Florestan—fearing a larger force if they should try again—agreed to Charles's meeting with the agitators at Carnolès. On December 12, almost the entire population of the two towns, including the clergy and magistrates, who headed the procession, assembled there. M. Carlès, the curé of the parish church of Menton, implored Charles to exert his influence to obtain some concessions: reform, he said, was vital, a matter of life and death. Details of the people's poverty were given. Charles promised the reforms demanded in his father's name. Days passed, but nothing was done beyond a slight modification in some of the taxes.

Florestan and Caroline remained sequestered on the Rock. Finally, to appease the rebels, Florestan issued a charter which under the appearance of liberal reforms preserved his absolute power. The key paragraph read: "The council of state, established for deliberating on the laws and ordinances for general administration, is to be composed of twelve members who have attained thirty years of age. The half of the members are to be nominated by the prince, and the other half by the electors in the following proportions: two by the electors of Monaco, three by those of Menton, and one by those of Roquebrune. Each member of the council to be chosen by the electors of the commune in which he resides."

What this meant was that Florestan could not only rely on the votes of his six nominees, but could also be assured of the two for Monaco. That left Menton and Roquebrune with only four votes, making it impossible for them to have any influence in the government. The document was a sham, and the people were further aroused by its insolent disregard for their wishes.

Peace was kept by the Sardinian garrison, but Florestan and Caroline were practically besieged in the Palace. A few days later the King of Sardinia offered to purchase the Principality for six million francs. At that crucial moment Charles arrived from Paris.

He had come well armed with a plan; whether or not he had stopped off in Turin on the way to Monaco, as it was rumored, he had already opened negotiations with Sardinia on his own. He could save the Principality for the Grimaldis only if Florestan appointed him administrator with full powers, and his parents remained acquiescent to him for the remainder of their lives. Caroline was furious, but she also feared for her own and Florestan's lives. But she did not give in until a financial settlement had been negotiated which assured them a comfortable income. This goal was achieved two days later and on March 10, 1848, they signed an agreement with Charles and accompanied by Sardinian soldiers departed Monaco for Paris.

Charles immediately organized a provisional governing body, headed by Charles Trenca. But he could not convince them to remain loyal to Monaco. On March 21, Menton and Roquebrune proclaimed their independence and two months later voted for inclusion in the Kingdom of Sardinia. This did not come to pass because France insisted that treaties made between France and Monaco should be respected by Turin; the King of Sardinia decreed that the towns would be administered by the prevailing laws until a final decision was made.

A year passed, and after several fits and starts it was decided that the towns would pay an indemnity to the Prince of Monaco to compensate him for their annexation. Negotiations were long and filled with proposals and counterproposals that went from Caroline in Paris to Charles in Monaco to Turin and the French envoy there, who happened to be the Duc de Guiche, a distant relative of the Grimaldis. Finally Charles ill-advisedly took matters into his own hands.

At two in the morning on April 6, 1849, he left Nice, where he had stayed the previous night, traveling to Menton in a six-horse carriage—the Grimaldi arms blazoned on the panels and harness and wearing the full-dress uniform of the Principality, accompanied by his doctor, Chevalet, and his aide-de-camp, Lucien Bellando. At six A.M. they arrived at the Hôtel de Turin, on the Place Napoléon, in the center of Menton, on the pretext of changing horses. Charles was at once surrounded and acclaimed by thirty to forty supporters who had been secretly alerted to his coming. They took the horses out of the traces and dragged the carriage to the town hall, waving flags of Grimaldi colors and shouting, "Long live the Prince! Long live the Grimaldis!"

Charles's idea had been to win back the breakaway towns (which, because of Sardinia's intervention, were now enjoying greatly reduced taxation and a much improved standard of living) with a nonviolent counterrevolutionary band of followers. Charles got out of the carriage; and as he stood unprotected, other townspeople who had joined the crowd turned on him. A bayonet thrust tore his coat, and he was barely rescued from a second attack by the local armed police. He was then taken by the Carabinieri to the barracks and held there. All that was required was for Charles to be escorted back to Monaco and told to remain within his own boundaries. But the governor of Nice now entered the scene and hurried to Menton to claim his prisoner. He escorted him to a fort in Villefranche, notified Turin and waited for instructions.

Five days later Charles was released after a strong communiqué had been sent from the French foreign minister to Turin. The "Affaire Monégasque" now became an international matter. Rumors even circulated that the Principality was being ceded to the United States. Princesse Caroline had the last word: "It

116

all amounts to this—that Turin should indemnify the Prince de Monaco, fairly and honorably, and remove all occasion for him to open negotiations with any other Power, which would be bound to cause embarrassment to everybody."

Florestan was much happier once he had returned to Paris where he had the theater to attend and life was less stressful. He became more gregarious, associating with playwrights and artists who appear to have regarded him as amusing and enjoyed having a Prince in their circle. As in the past, he let Caroline handle their business affairs and as before she did this exceptionally well. He died suddenly of a heart attack on June 20, 1856, at the age of seventy-one. His son was acknowledged Charles III, his Principality still an international dilemma. It would remain so for five more years, two more wars and the installation of a new Emperor in France, Napoleon III.

9

WHEN NAPOLEON I CROWNED HIMSELF Emperor in 1804, the Bonapartes became a dynasty. Three of his brothers were given crowns. Joseph was King of Naples and then Spain; Jérôme, King of Westphalia; and Louis, who had married Napoleon's stepdaughter, Hortense de Beauharnais, of Holland. For thirty years Louis's son, Louis Napoleon, had stubbornly believed that he was destined to fulfill his uncle's last dream at St. Helena, the rise of a Second Napoleonic Empire. This aspiration was realized in 1848 with the February Revolution, the abdication of King Louis-Philippe, the failure of the Provisional Government over the next nine months and the election on December 10 of Louis Napoleon as president of the French Republic, an office limited by law to one term.

A son, Albert, was born to Charles and Antoinette in Paris on November 13 of that same year. Like so many Grimaldis before him, Charles had established a home in Paris and spent much of his time there. This was still several years before Charles had managed to eject his parents from Monaco, and Princesse Caroline had taken her young Belgian daughter-in-law under her wing, schooling her in the ways of the Parisian artistocratic society. Antoinette was an adept protégé and soon was a close member of the Court of Eugénie, Louis Napoleon's wife—a position that required an expensive wardrobe, extensive staff and a handsome carriage among other costly necessities.

Charles had spent Antoinette's generous dowry in 1854 on the purchase of a magnificent estate in Marchais, whose upkeep was high. Then, after his father's death just two years later, he also acquired the responsibility of his mother's care and the

Paris mansion.[1] Despite the Princesse Caroline's business acumen, Florestan had managed to squander more than they had. His son's legacy had been encumbered in debt, and Charles struggled all through 1856 and 1857 merely to keep afloat.

He spent several months a year in Monaco but he had never lost his taste for Paris society and for ladies of the theater. Count Apponyi, an Austrian diplomat in Paris, noted in his diary on March 23, 1852: "Before entering the room [where an after-dinner theater party was being held] I stopped to have a word near the stage with the actors and actresses, especially with Mademoiselles Judith, Fix, Maquet and Rimbolt. The Duc de Valentinois [Charles] was there pinching the arm of one and the leg of another."

But such *divertissements* were not enough for Charles. His ambition was to break free of Sardinia and to reestablish the Grimaldis in the French Court, although throughout the reigns of Louis XVIII, Charles X and Louis-Philippe they had been all but ignored. Now, with a Second Empire and a Bonaparte returned to power, his hopes were high that this oversight would soon be reversed.

By 1856, when Charles succeeded as Prince de Monaco, Louis Napoleon had accomplished what Napoleon had failed to do by winning an alliance with England (after France's help in the Crimean War), reinstituting the imperial dynasty and once again bringing France to the forefront of European nations. The return of a Bonaparte with Beauharnais ancestry was good news to Charles, for, after all, his uncle Honoré V had stood loyally by the Empress Josephine when both Napoleon and France had deserted her. Early in 1857, Louis Napoleon unsuccessfully intervened with Sardinia on Monaco's behalf in an attempt to obtain the abolition of its protectorate and an award of four million francs as an indemnity. Charles and Monaco were both running out of resources. Money had to be raised to maintain the Grimaldis' life-style, but from where?

Princesse Caroline, at sixty-eight, with neither her business

---

[1]The last of the land in Normandy, together with the former Matignon home, had gone to Oscar Grimaldi, the natural son of Honoré V upon his father's death. Charles tried unsuccessfully to buy it back.

acumen nor her appetite for money diminished by age, and reconciled with her son (who was now her major means of support) shortly after her husband's death, came up with the remedy. She had once seen an official memo to Florestan that suggested turning Monaco into a spa since the climate was temperate, the sea views picturesque and, as no sewers emptied into the port, the sands free of impurities. Nice had been prospering for years from the large numbers of wealthy foreigners, mainly English, who wintered there. Villas and hotels had been built in the Croix de Marbre quarter of the town, and the new cult of sea bathing had given rise to a series of other thriving resorts along the Riviera. Cannes, which twenty years earlier had been a small fishing village without a pier or harbor, was now an established watering place with five thousand permanent residents.

Except for two problems, Monaco was perhaps even more suitable for such a development. The first was accessibility. Nice and Cannes, and of course all the towns in between, had good roads connecting them with major cities and ports. But there was only an infrequent boat service to Monaco, and an antiquated horse-drawn, eleven-passenger omnibus was scheduled to make the journey from Nice to Monaco once a day, traversing a narrow road that wove through uninhabited mountainous terrain. Uncertain weather conditions and dislodged boulders presented a constant hazard during a jolting, uncomfortable four-hour ride, at the end of which there were no decent overnight accommodations. Clearly, money was needed to make the improvements necessary if visitors were to be encouraged. The Principality's lack of funds presented the second stumbling-block.

Recalling a recent visit to Hesse-Homburg, a small sovereign state in central Germany much like Monaco, which owed its prosperity to a gambling casino in its capital, Bad-Homburg, Princesse Caroline dispatched her lawyer and good friend Adolphe Eynaud to visit Bad-Homburg and discuss with the Grand Duke von Hesse-Homburg the conditions he had granted the concessionaires and what his personal recompense was from the venture. Eynaud returned to report that the Grand Duke's share amounted to 350,000 francs a year. Additional profit came from the two hundred thousand or so annual visitors to the casino who spent money "like water." Eynaud added that a similar enterprise "would undoubtedly prove a considerable source of revenue and be of the greatest benefit to the general interest as well as to that of Your Highness." Gambling, "though in reality the main object of the scheme, should appear to be only a sideshow. . . ."

The Princesse conveyed her enthusiasm to Charles, who immediately had plans drawn up for a company to be called the Société des Bains de Mer (The Sea Bathing Society). Eynaud wanted François Blanc, who operated the casino in Bad-Homburg, to take over the gambling concession. Blanc refused, on the grounds that while Monaco was still under the protection of Sardinia, the dangers were too great, such an enterprise being against their laws. "You will be ten times more respected," Eynaud wrote to Charles, imploring him to get rid of the yoke of Sardinia, "with a few gendarmes at the doors of your palace than with a whole regiment of [Sardinian] guards; they would justly be regarded as your gaolers. You see the results of this protection in the matter of the casino. Nobody dares to come to terms."

Despite the lawyer's pessimism, he began negotiations with two Frenchmen, Albert Aubert, a writer, and a Paris businessman, Napoleon Langlois, to establish a gambling casino in Monaco. Within a few months they submitted a plan for a grand casino. "The engine that activates Monsieur Langlois's brain," Eynaud wrote to Charles, "is getting up steam. He is at work on this business day and night."

The two men were not swift in raising the necessary capital. Nonetheless, they were granted an exclusive concession "for the construction of a bathing establishment, a large hotel and a number of villas, and sea and land communications between Monaco and Nice," along with authorization to provide amusements, "notably balls, concerts, fêtes, games such as whist, écarté, piquet, faro, boston and reversi, as well as roulette with either one or two zeros, and trente-et-quarante with the *refait* or *demi-refait*, the whole being subject to the supervision of one or more inspectors or commissioners appointed by His Serene Highness."

Shortly thereafter, a prospectus was printed in the hopes of procuring the three million francs required to equip the casino, build a hotel and prepare housing sites. "The premises which the company has found are virtually ready. They consist of a large and beautiful villa commanding a magnificent view of the harbor, surrounded by a wonderful garden containing 2500 lemon and 2000 orange trees, as well as a large olive grove. A splendid mansion opposite the palace, belonging to His Highness the Prince de Monaco, has been placed at the disposal of the company [for a hotel]. Finally, it has acquired an extensive tract of land known as les Spélugues [that fanned out from the foot of the Rock and overlooked the harbor], 100,000 square metres in extent. A town of small villas in the English style could be built there, complete with orange, olive and lemon groves. This land can be bought at public auction for about 30 centimes a square metre, while that on the other side of the harbor is already worth more than ten francs the square metre."

The reality was not quite as glowing as the description. The "beautiful villa" was owned by a Monsieur Arnoux, and was quite modest, although its position, which gave it the name Villa Bellevue, was excellent. The developers would not have bought the property, which Arnoux was pleased to sell for 64,000 francs including all the land, had not Princesse Caroline (who took advantage of her son's long absences from Monaco to reestablish her power), in a hypocritical spurt of righteousness, insisted to Charles that the casino be sited outside the town of Monaco and that a law be passed that no Monégasque could place bets there. Charles seemed content to have his mother occupied with this project for it allowed him to spend more time in Paris. He appears at this time to have lost faith that a casino would be a profitable venture for he wrote to Eynaud reminding him that Monaco did not have mineral waters to draw visitors as did Bad-Homburg, nor an easily accessible location.

When news of the planned casino reached the French Court, great pressure was brought to bear on Princesse Caroline by her friends to abandon the project. Early in the seventeenth century, Louis XIII had declared that all persons who owned gambling houses were to be excluded from public office, an edict that was made more severe by Louis XVI in the mid-eighteenth century, when he banned all games of hazard and proclaimed all money won in such a manner the fruit of theft and punishable by law.

With the Revolution of 1789 this ban was lifted and the government was powerless to resist, for, as M. Pasquier—a representative to the French Senate and a tough opponent of the planned casino in Monaco—stated in an impassioned speech in the Senate when the plan for the casino in Monaco was debated, "people wished to play, and they played. The madness of gambling reached a climax. . . . When the Reign of Terror arrived, [gambling establishments were] more or less tolerated by the ruling powers who found them useful, as the police often succeeded in finding their victims who sought refuge in these dens of evil."

From 1795 to 1836, eighteen gambling houses had legally operated (with kickbacks to the government) in the rue de Thionville, the rue Saint-Denis and the rue des Lombards. When these were closed by Louis-Philippe, numerous casinos sprang up and flourished in Europe, the one in Bad-Homburg being the largest. France could do little about these, but a gambling house located as near to French territory as Monaco, Pasquier warned, presented the danger of an influx of low-lifes to France. The Senate, however, did not agree and Caroline pressed forward, with Charles now more actively involved.

The Villa Bellevue opened for business in November 1857. A small house nearby had been converted into a restaurant. The only place to stay was the former French garrison (renamed the Hôtel de Russie) opposite the Palace, where a few sparsely furnished rooms were available. In the first few days of business, counterfeit coins and forged banknotes appeared at the tables, where it was also discovered that someone had tampered with the roulette wheel in favor of the house.

Although French opinion was strongly set against Monaco's new casino, Louis Napoleon (crowned Emperor Napoleon III in 1852, when a new plebiscite overwhelmingly approved the establishment of the Second Empire) placed no pressure on Charles to close it down. Most of the Emperor's efforts at this time were exerted in maintaining the goodwill of England, whom he desired as an ally. On a recent trip there he had succeeded in winning over Queen Victoria. "From behind the vast solidity of her respectability, her conventionality," Lytton Strachey wrote of their meeting, "she peered out with a strange delicious pleasure at that unfamiliar darkly-glittering foreign

123

object, moving so meteorically before her. . . . 'There is something fascinating, melancholy and engaging, which draws you to him, in spite of any prevention you may have against him,' " she recorded in her diary. He rode "extremely well." He danced "with great dignity and spirit." Above all, he listened. The Empress Eugénie, a woman much aware of her great beauty, dressed in magnificent Parisian crinolines, "which set off to perfection her tall and willowy figure." Cool and modish, Eugénie "floated in an infinitude of flounces."

When Queen Victoria and Prince Albert paid a return visit to France in September 1855, Charles and Antoinette attended the great ball in their honor at Versailles. For Antoinette this was the greatest moment of her life; the imperial grandeur of it was to affect her for the rest of her life. From this time she conjured up the dream that her son, Albert, then only a small child, would marry into the British royal family. Meanwhile, there were serious problems to starting Monaco's new gambling enterprise, and with lessening revenues from the Principality, the future of the Grimaldis looked exceedingly grim. Once the casino opened, they faced even greater economic problems.

By the spring of 1858, Langlois and Aubert, having reached the end of their finances, came to Charles seeking aid to avoid liquidation, which could cause an appalling scandal since they did not have the resources with which to repay their stockholders. Charles was forced to raise what money he could to keep the doors open until a suitable buyer could be found. On November 30, the government commissioner reported: "Though the rooms were opened to play fourteen times during the week, gambling took place only five times [the clients lost 640 francs]. Neglected publicity and lack of communications with Nice are to blame."

A man by the name of Pierre-Auguste Daval, who was known only as a small-time entrepreneur, now appeared on the scene, claiming he could raise the capital necessary to make the casino "the most dazzling and successful enterprise on the Riviera." Langlois and Aubert, their financial situation worsening each day, swiftly signed all rights over to him, and Charles granted him permission to proceed. Within a few months it was obvious that Daval was no more competent than his predecessors.

Charles was understandably alarmed. Not only was his financial situation desperate, he had begun to lose his sight and the doctors predicted total blindness in a year, two at the most. To his relief, the wealthy Duc de Valmy, a former investor in the gambling house at Bad-Homburg, decided to buy the concession, and on May 28, 1858, it was transferred from Daval to François Lefebvre, chairman of another gambling enterprise, the Valmy syndicate.

This seeming good fortune was quickly eclipsed by the out-break of war in the spring of 1859. France had allied itself with Sardinia to expel Austria from northern Italy. Although no Monégasques went to fight, the Principality sided with France and communication between Nice and Monaco was disrupted. The casino closed but Lefebvre, over Princesse Caroline's loud objections, moved his operation up to the old garrison on The Rock. By the end of the short three-month conflict, Nice and Savoy were ceded to France for its help in defeating the Aus-trians. Travel could be resumed between Nice and Monaco. A new boat, owned by Lefebvre, the *Charles III*, which could take sixty passengers, made a daily trip to the Rock from Nice. Two small hotels were opened near the port, grandly named the Hôtel d'Angleterre and the Hôtel de Paris. All these improve-ments notwithstanding, at the end of 1860 the Société des Bains de Mer showed a loss of 80,434 francs.

The one bright spot in the year, especially for Charles, had been the withdrawal of the Sardinian troops from Monaco on July 17, 1860, and the return of the Principality to the protec-torate of France. Six months later the question of Menton and Roquebrune was at long last settled. After long negotiations that lasted several months, a treaty between France and Monaco was signed on February 2, 1861, by M. Faugère on the part of France and Count Avigdor on the part of the Prince de Monaco. Under the treaty Charles III ceded all his rights over the two towns and their adjoining territories to France on the payment of 4,100,000 francs by France, which also agreed to construct a carriage road from Nice to Monaco, by way of Villefranche and the coast (completed by 1866), and to have the projected railway between Nice and Genoa pass through Monaco (work began in 1866). Charles now endeavored to claim possession of Cap Martin and the olive wood leading from it up to Roquebrune but was unsuccessful.

Charles had lost 80 percent of his Principality, but he was finally solvent. A condition, not publicly revealed until 1918, provided that the Prince de Monaco and his heirs could not transfer or cede any of their sovereign rights over the Principality unless it was to France, nor could they request or accept a protectorate from any other country.

Four million francs appeared to be a grand sum. However, with the loss of the revenues of Menton and Roquebrune, Monaco had no other income. Within five to ten years the Grimaldis' personal expenses, the houses in Paris and Marchais, Princesse Caroline's entourage and the salaries of the Palace and the government staffs would considerably whittle down that amount; in twenty years it could be gone. Earnings were needed, and a casino, bathing facilities and transportation that would attract sufficient visitors to ensure a profit-making venture.

Charles's burden was made heavier when Antoinette, in the fall of 1862, was diagnosed as having cancer. With the onset of his poor sight, Charles seldom left Monaco and had become dependent upon Antoinette, whom he called his "Angel." And she must have seemed one, for even though mortally ill, she maintained her even temperament and appeared to be more concerned about her husband and her mother-in-law than herself, writing to Charles in Monaco, when she was in the last stages of the disease and had been moved to Marchais in the belief that the country air might help, that he must not allow his aging mother (Caroline was now seventy years old) to take on too much work on his behalf. And she requested that she be allowed to return to Monaco where she could be near to them both. She traveled to her husband's Principality by coach with a doctor and two maids, dying three months later, on February 10, 1864.

Charles—now blind—had to rely on others. He turned to Princesse Caroline for advice and assistance, and she did not let him down. She knew Lefebvre lacked the vision to transform Monaco into a thriving tourist attraction. Her thoughts turned back to François Blanc, who Adolphe Eynaud had heard was looking for a new enterprise since the closure of the casino at Bad-Homburg following a series of suicides—the direct and tragic result of large gambling losses at his tables. Eynaud met with Blanc but was unable to persuade him to come to Monaco.

Princesse Caroline then made a direct appeal to Madame Blanc, with whom she had become acquainted during her visit many years earlier to Bad-Homburg. Madame Blanc suffered from arthritis, a condition almost unknown in Monaco, Princesse Caroline assured her, because of the glorious winters when one could enjoy the fresh sea air with no more than a shawl about one's shoulders. Eynaud traveled to Bad-Homburg laden with boxes of prize citrus fruit. Finally, in March 1863, Blanc capitulated and with his attorney, M. Jagot, arrived by boat from Nice at noon on March 31. They departed two days later, Blanc having agreed to pay the Valmy syndicate 1,700,000 francs in three installments to purchase all their rights. With his mother to guide his hand, Charles signed an agreement granting Blanc the privilege of operating for fifty years the Société des Bains de Mer et du Cercle des Étrangers (the last word emphasized Princesse Caroline's wish that Monégasques not be allowed into the casino). The Prince de Monaco was to receive 50,000 francs a year, plus 10 percent of the net profits, and an additional private allowance of two thousand francs a week (making his total yearly income 154,000 francs plus the percentage of the net profits).

Within a matter of weeks, Monaco was transformed into one massive construction site. Blanc had raised enough money, with the help of James de Rothschild of the Paris-Lyon-Mediterranean Railroad and the Rothschild banking family, to build a casino, roads, hotels and villas. Soil was brought in to cover the bare rock, and trees, shrubs and exotic flowers were planted. Building sites were offered at very low prices and Blanc himself built a handsome villa, encouraging friends from Bad-Homburg to follow his lead.

While this was going on, the old casino was being used, and Blanc chartered fifty stage coaches and a flotilla of steamboats to bring gamblers to Monaco from Nice and Cannes. Despite the poor condition of the road, the casino in its first year of operation under Blanc had 27,872 recorded visitors, and the profits, although still not commensurate with the immense outlay, were 640,000 francs. With the railway line which would travel through the South of France (and eventually to Genoa) soon to reach Monaco, optimism was high on the business prospects of the Principality.

By the end of 1864, a section of the new Casino was operational and the gaming tables were moved in from their former location. The imposing gambling Casino was finished the following year, its rear terrace overlooking the Mediterranean and its grand façade staring up in all its splendor at new, pastel-toned villas.

The Hôtel de Paris, which was being rebuilt and modeled in its decoration and cuisine after the Grand Hôtel in Paris, was not yet opened, but its restaurant was. A gala had been held there on New Year's Eve, 1864, a harbinger of the grandeur to come. The table silver alone cost 200,000 francs. When the hotel was completed in July 1865, with its spectacular polychromed glass dome and magnificent wrought-iron, marble and crystal details, one Paris newspaper reported that it had been furnished "with the taste of an intelligent millionaire." The bathing establishment with its beach cabanas situated in the section of Monaco called the Condamine and managed by Dr. Gillebert d'Herbourt, was opened the following November.

Blanc had recruited the finest designers he could obtain. M. André, who was responsible for the Parc Monceau in Paris, was laying out the Casino gardens. On New Year's Day, 1865, the exotic Salle Mauresque (the gaming room in the Casino), designed by M. Dortrou, the architect of the Palais de l'Industrie, opened. And the Casino, the Hôtel de Paris and the newly constructed Café de Paris (with billiard rooms and a spectacular *al fresco* dining terrace), which occupied three sides of a handsome square, drew gasps of delight when sighted for the first time by new arrivals.

The former fields and mountainsides were rapidly taking on the look of a town. A name was needed. Charleville and Mont Charles after the Prince were suggested. On June 1, 1866, Monte Carlo (Italian for Mont Charles) was chosen in deference to Princesse Caroline, who preferred the name to be foreign-sounding.

The capital of the Société des Bains de Mer at this time was fifteen million francs and there were 30,000 shares issued, of which Blanc held 22,000 and the Prince de Monaco received 400. The remainder went to various investors, including the Rothschilds, who were negotiating the purchase of land for cutting the railway line through the Principality. (Several of the small landowners demanded such exorbitant sums that the railway company threatened to bypass Monaco and the Monégasques were forced into accepting the price they were being offered.) The Prince de Monaco also received an additional 10 percent of all revenues, which included the profits from the gambling Casino, the Hôtel de Paris, the Café de Paris and the Sporting Club, along with their annual payments agreed to in the original contract.

The first of the buildings in the square to be completed had been the Casino. An English travel writer in 1867 described it: "The building is very handsome though plain; there is a reading-room with the periodicals and journals of almost every country; a magnificent ball-room, where an Austrian band plays daily from two to four, and from eight to ten. Balls are given occasionally as well as concerts and theatricals. The grounds are delightful; the terrace alone is worth going to see. People need not set their foot inside the gambling room. This last spring an order was issued forbidding any of the inhabitants of [Monaco] from entering it,[2] much to their indignation, and they endeavored to force their way in; but the *gendarmes* appeared, and, after a harmless scuffle, they were forced to submit to the imperial decree. They are at liberty, however, to enjoy and share in all the amusements consequent on the existence of a Casino. It [the Casino] may be very immoral, very wrong, and lead to the destruction of many; but it certainly renders the place most attractive. . . ."

He adds that the Monégasques "are neither rich nor poor. Poverty, as we understand it in England, does not exist in this part of the world at all . . . [the people] are well clothed, well shod, and well fed. Hardly anyone exists that does not possess their own little plot of land. . . . Society—there is none; a few retired officers, and those who surround the prince and his family, compose the better class. Little hospitality is dispensed at the palace on account of the affliction [blindness] which Charles III suffers."

Monte Carlo was fast becoming a chic resort as well as a place to gamble. Rich and titled men from England, Russia and the

---

[2]Monaco had a population of approximately 1,200 at the time. Within three years, there were 6,000 residents as tourists from England and the Continent built homes.

Continent came with their mistresses or their wives (often both); and so the finest in jewels, gowns and flowers had to be available, the food and wines superlative, the orchestras that played for gala parties and the bands that performed in the square conducted by well-known musicians. New, stylish uniforms were designed for the gendarmerie. The sea-bathing facilities were now on a par with those of Nice and Cannes.

The Principality's new, sophisticated town had made Monaco—that is, the Rock, appear to be a bit of an oddity. "Monaco, now the capital of itself . . . is a little town with clean and straightly-built streets," an English travel writer for the London *Times* explained. "It stands on a projecting rock, 300 feet above the level of the sea, commanding magnificent views. . . . There is little of interest in the town itself beyond a few dark churches and the palace. . . . The court [of the Palais Princier, as the Palace was called] is very fine, and is entirely enclosed. On the left, on entering it, is a magnificent double staircase of white marble, by which a gallery is gained, and from thence one reaches the reception rooms. On the right of the court are some very fine frescoes [which had been restored the previous year] by Caravaggio . . . some of the apartments of the palace are really magnificently decorated, especially the one called *La grande salle Grimaldi;* the frescoes on the walls, and the ceiling, which is thirty feet in height, are executed by Horace de Ferrari; the chimney piece in this room, which is of an enormous size, is one solid piece of marble. . . . The room in which the Duke of York died is very handsomely furnished in crimson satin and gold; the ceiling is also beautifully painted. The other apartments have nothing remarkable in them." He also noted that none of the paintings were "of any real worth" but that the climate, "although not as warm as Menton," was nonetheless "exceptional."

"I have seen the whole army of Monaco on parade in the Palace courtyard," a reporter from the London *Daily News* snidely wrote in 1871. "It consists of a sergeant, a corporal and a half-a-dozen men."

Travel writers—despite scathing accusations and carping tones—were now writing about the Principality. Articles appeared in England, France and Germany. Monte Carlo had become the scandalous star of the Riviera.

130

A journalist from the *Athenaeum* noted "the constant passage through Nice of the very scum of European society on the way to and from the Monte Carlo Casino." And the *Daily Telegraph* claimed that "a few Russians—the most reckless gamblers in the world—constitute the *élite* of Monaco society. To be a Russian count, or better still a countess, is to have the homage of every croupier. Waiters fawn . . . officials salute . . . they have the best seats, the most perfect facilities for ruining themselves luxuriously. . . . Next in importance to the Russians, but separated by a long interval, come the English and Americans, the latter being held in higher esteem [for] they generally play for high stakes and they lose without grumbling. The true melodramatic gambler is either French or Italian [who] comes to Monaco to work out his destiny. He has a dream that he will ruin Blanc, and he has parted with all conscientious scruples. . . . He cannot attempt to rival Russian stolidity, or American recklessness. His whole soul goes for the fortunes of the game."

Monaco's winter guests included, along with the fortune hunters, compulsive gamblers and confidence tricksters, Russian princes, French barons, English dukes and American millionaires. The season began on New Year's Eve; throughout the next few months the cognoscenti dined at the sumptuous *table d'hôte* of the Hôtel de Paris in a salon with a gold-traced vaulted ceiling and decorated with exquisite frescoes, one of Belle France in tricolor and crown driving a team of four magnificent white horses. The salon also contained marble pillars, golden-winged serpents over the entrance and chandeliers that each held over a hundred candles. Monte Carlo came vividly to life at night when the lamps of the square and the Casino were lighted, and the gas jets glittered "like a chain of gold girding the grey rock." The sea gleamed "molten silver" from the rear terrace of the Casino; and on bright, moonlit nights one dark headland after another, stretching for more than twenty miles eastward, could be seen while the breeze carried the sound of the band playing Viennese waltzes in the square.

The romantic scenery, the chic ambience and the warm winter nights added to Monte Carlo's great attraction. However, the Casino was the flame that drew the society moths. The odds at the tables were six to four in favor of the house, but there were stories of fantastic wins. A Russian countess had confounded the croupiers by amassing immense sums daily for a fortnight. Her prodigious winnings so increased the number of players at the gaming tables, who lost even larger amounts, that there were rumors of the lady being a shill for the Casino.

Such gossip, along with tales of men who had lost their fortunes and jumped to their deaths from the terrace of the Casino, did not deter the growing hordes of visitors, many of whom were now arriving by the railway line that had opened on October 19, 1868. François Blanc had brought great prosperity to Monaco and money back into the hands of the Grimaldis, but this new affluence did not comfort the sightless, widowed Charles, whose condition and loneliness made him a bitter, reclusive man.

Money problems finally solved, Princesse Caroline brought her widowed daughter, Florestine, Duchess of Urach, to care for her brother, Charles. Princesse Caroline had one more driving ambition: to see her tall, attractive and intelligent grandson, Albert, fulfill his mother's hopes for him and marry a member of Queen Victoria's family. Two years earlier, she had attempted, through the Empress Eugénie, to introduce Albert's name to Victoria as a projected husband for her cousin, Princess Mary Adelaide of Cambridge, fifteen years his senior and of a hefty physique. Albert had not been considered a viable suitor and the Queen's cousin had married the Duke of Teck. This rebuff had not diminished Princesse Caroline's ambitions to ally the Grimaldis with the English royal family.

THE RED AND
THE BLACK

10

Aheated controversy as to whether Monaco should be allowed to be represented at the Great Exhibition to open in Paris on April 1, 1867, brought Albert into confrontation with Louis Napoleon. Inside the Exhibition's focal point, a "vast elliptical building of glass 482 metres long, set in a filigree of ironwork, not unlike London's own Crystal Palace," the nations of the world were to exhibit their finest recent achievements. Although the Emperor had never publicly condemned the Casino, he did not feel its gaming rooms should be promoted in an exposition at which England's Baron Joseph Lister introduced the principle of antisepsis, Sweden's Alfred Nobel displayed his newly invented dynamite and room had been made for Herr Krupp of Essen's new weapon, the largest cannon—an immense fifty-ton gun—the world had ever seen. Albert disagreed. In the end Monaco was given space to display a newly designed portable cabana and exotic plants from its gardens in an outside pavilion where for fifty centimes you could see the works of controversial artists like Courbet and Manet, also excluded from the inner sanctum of the main building.

Albert was a determined young man. An only child, his mother dead, his father blind, he had turned to his grandmother for understanding and affection. They were both strong-willed, opinionated, and often clashed head-on. Yet each retained a forceful hold on the other. During his mother's long illness from 1862 and 1864, Albert had boarded at the Stanislas College in Paris and then went on to continue his education at Mesmin, a Catholic university near Orléans. On the grounds there one afternoon, he threw a stone pebble that missed its mark and blinded a young man who was studying to enter the church. An acrimonious lawsuit followed, and the young man who was blinded, I. Yvonneau, was awarded 12,000 francs, costs of the suit and an annual pension for life of 1,200 francs. It was directly after this tragic episode that Princesse Caroline tried to affiance Albert to Queen Victoria's cousin. When this failed (the school incident did not seem to have a direct bearing), she suggested that he come to Monaco and oversee their business interests in the Société des Bains de Mer (now referred to as the S.B.M.), which included not only the Casino, but the Hôtel de Paris, Café de Paris, the Sporting Club and large tracts of Grimaldi-owned land that encompassed about 15 percent of the Principality and was being developed into villas. Albert at first rejected this proposal, finally agreeing after much pressure from his grandmother to do so. With Charles blind and ailing, Caroline was again in control of the Grimaldis' business interests. Her age made this a difficult burden and she hoped that Albert could be groomed to take over her responsibilities. The young man, however, had no aptitude for or interest in business.

Since his childhood Albert's abiding preoccupation had been the sea, his ambition to create a Monégasque Navy that he could command. France would never have agreed to such a warlike enterprise, but Albert pressed forward in preparation for what he thought was to be his calling. To Caroline's distress, after six months in Monaco, he entered the French naval academy at Lorient, at which he did brilliantly. In 1866, in a surprise move, he joined the Spanish Navy, presumably in rebellious pique.

His choice was ill-conceived. Spain was undergoing turbulent times. Isabella II's rule had been one of party conflicts among moderates and progressives who favored a constitutional monarchy and the extreme reactionaries who did not. The conflict culminated in armed rebellion and insurrection. Good soldiers loyal to the Crown were at a premium. Albert rose swiftly from midshipman to lieutenant, but with conditions as shaky as they were in Spain, he resigned from the navy after two years. On March 1, 1868, Isabella having been deposed and replaced by a constitutional monarchy with Amadeus, Duke of Aosta, as King, he embarked from Verona for a voyage to the United States on a "magnificent frigate" under the command of Captain Don Francisco Navarro. A former lieutenant in the Spanish Navy, Simon de Manzanos, was hired by Albert's father as equerry and watchdog. Manzanos wrote the Prince de Monaco almost daily detailed reports of his son's adventures.

Two months later, they arrived in New York, where they stayed at the Fifth Avenue Hotel, having stopped at Havana and various other ports on the way. It was not easy to elude Manzanos, but Albert managed several evenings on his own with a young Spanish officer. He saw a bit of New York's night life and met a few young, attractive American women. His whirlwind American tour included visits to Philadelphia, Washington, D.C., Baltimore, Pittsburgh, Cincinnati, St. Louis, Chicago, Louisville, Cleveland, Buffalo, Niagara Falls, Montréal, Québec, Gorham, Boston, Springfield, Westport and back to New York, where on July 2 he boarded *L'Aigle* for the return voyage. Québec and the Indian country (where he purchased "curios of Indian industry for 340 francs!") appeared to interest him the most.

Princesse Caroline had not been idle during this time. Still determined that her grandson should marry into the British royal family, she sought Louis Napoleon's aid in selecting a suitable prospective bride. The Emperor did not mince his words. The very conservative Victoria would never grant permission to a marriage between a relation of hers and the future sovereign of a state that was supported by gambling. However, Louis Napoleon had another suggestion.

He was extremely fond of the attractive young Lady Mary Victoria Douglas Hamilton, the daughter of the late 11th Duke of Hamilton and Princess Marie of Baden, who was the Emperor's second cousin. The Hamiltons were very rich and had homes in Scotland, Paris and Baden. The present 12th Duke of Hamilton, Lady Mary Victoria's older brother, was a well-liked member of the Emperor's Court. An alliance with the family would mean that the Grimaldis would be related, albeit distantly, to the Emperor. Princesse Caroline could hardly refuse such a union. Albert, just turned twenty-one, was not at all certain he wanted to marry Lady Mary Victoria, or anyone else for that matter. To his grandmother's consternation and Louis Napoleon's displeasure, he bought a small yacht named the *Isabelle,* and with his aide-de-camp, Captain de Journal, and four seamen, and acting as his own navigator, he sailed off on a three-month cruise down the coast of Africa and so was incommunicado.

Lady Mary Victoria was equally unenthusiastic about the

prospect of an alliance. Had she and Albert met, they would at least have been assured of the attractiveness of their proposed future spouses. Albert cut a striking figure in uniform—tall, broad-shouldered, his dark eyes well set in a strong, robust face. Lady Mary Victoria was a Scots-English beauty, with clear blue eyes and golden hair that fell in natural ringlets about her fair face. A lively young woman, she loved horses, clothes and dancing, and adored her bachelor brother "Willie," the Duke of Hamilton, who was six years her senior and who protected and spoiled her, and squired her to the finest homes in Paris. Willie owned a prestigious racing stable and brother and sister were often seen at the races where the press described her stylish attire in glowing prose.

Albert returned from his "runaway" voyage in July 1869, somewhat chastened. The *Isabelle* had met with severe storms and had been buffeted by high waves, unable to come into the harbor at Monaco for nearly a week and with little to eat on board except for some hard biscuits. He was greeted by Princesse Caroline and the Duc de Bassano, a representative of the Emperor. A few days later Albert was in Paris and a marriage contract was being drawn that included a dowry of 800,000 francs. Willie had presumably convinced his sister of the importance of pleasing Louis Napoleon.

With the glittering triumph of the Great Exhibition and the unprecedented lavishness of the Tuileries Balls, the Second Empire had reached a peak of splendor. Its society seemed eager to follow the paths indicated by its pleasure-loving Emperor, seeking consciously to recapture the indulgences of Louis XV. The plumed hats and gowns of that era had returned to style. Masked balls were given so frequently that the Paris *haut monde* appeared to be attending a nonstop carnival of peacock extravagance.

"A procession of four crocodiles and ten ravishing handmaidens covered in jewels preceded a chariot in which was seated Princess Korsakow *en sauvage*," Anthony Peat, an English guest at one ball reported. "Next came Africa, Mademoiselle de Sèvres mounted on a camel fresh from the deserts of the Jardin des Plantes, and accompanied by attendants in enormous black woolly wigs; finally America, a lovely blonde, reclined in a hammock swung between banana trees, each carried by negroes and escorted by Red Indians and their squaws. There were three thousand guests and it is said the cost of this one ball was four million francs."

Women at these balls "emphasized their bosoms to the limits of decency (sometimes beyond)." While the Second Empire was at its pinnacle, its morals had sunk to greater depths than in the time of Louis XV. The sixty-year-old Louis Napoleon had a ravishing nineteen-year-old mistress, the Comtesse de Castiglione, to whom he gave a 422,000-franc pearl necklace and a 50,000-franc monthly allowance. (England's Lord Hertford, "by reputation the meanest man in Paris, gave her a million for the pleasures of one night in which she promised to abandon herself to every known volupté. Afterwards, it was said, she was confined to bed for three days," Mr. Peat comments.)

The *haut monde* of Paris was overflowing with *grandes horizontales*. Prostitution and syphilis were rampant. Many of the great men of the age died of syphilis, which was then incurable, including Manet, de Maupassant, Dumas *fils* and Baudelaire. Renoir was to write that he could not be a genius because he alone had not caught the disease. As one historian noted, "The terrible disease was symptomatic of the whole Second Empire, on the surface, all gaiety and light; below, sombre purulence, decay, and ultimately death."

The premature aging of the Emperor was no doubt brought on by his debauchery. In 1869 he became painfully ill with a progressively worsening liver condition and hopelessly bewildered by foreign and domestic events. His greatest miscalculation was based on his firsthand knowledge of that "deadliest of all French diseases," *l'ennui*. He believed France had to be distracted, and so he went in pursuit of *la gloire*. At home fortunes were spent to rebuild a glorious Paris. Gigantic exhibitions were held. Money raised through high taxation had financed his excesses and his failed foreign designs and his subjects grew more and more restless.

"If [the Emperor] uses his influence to favor a reactionary clerical policy," his outspoken nephew Prince Napoleon wrote in a memo, "if he continues to employ discredited and unpopular men like the present ministry, he may secure a passing success, he may dominate the country for a time, but he will be strengthening the republic, socialist and revolutionary Opposition of the future; and this new power given to it will be terribly dangerous when any crisis occurs at home or abroad."

Louis Napoleon was not unaware of the precariousness of his reign. To save the throne for his son, he was planning to convert the regime into a "Liberal Empire" and himself into a constitutional monarch. But it was already too late. With economic conditions worsening daily, unemployment high, and inflation the highest in years, the glory of the Emperor was fast fading, and Louis Napoleon, at a loss at what to do to restore his prestige was a confused and weary man. *The Illustrated London News,* covering the drill of French troops, wrote that "the Emperor huddled in his seat, was a very minor show, whereas the Empress struck a splendid figure, straight as a dart." Eugénie's powers rose as the Emperor's declined. She had told a member of the Court that if another revolution came, "she would know how to save the crown for her son and show what it meant to be an Empress." One faithful admirer added: "There is no longer an Eugénie, there is only an Empress."

Cold, capricious and aggressive, Eugénie dominated her husband and the Court; and once she had decided that Albert and Lady Mary Victoria should wed, there was no doubt about the matter. On a warm August night, the young couple met at the Tuileries at one of the magnificent masked balls in which Eugénie excelled. The Empress was dressed as Marie Antoinette, whom she greatly admired; Lady Mary Victoria came as Juliet, and Albert, complete with patch over one eye, was Lord Nelson. Strings of electric light rimmed the gardens and the dance floor; water cascaded over stucco rocks from specially constructed fountains. Despite the romantic ambience, "Juliet" reported that "Lord Nelson" indeed danced like a sailor; and the sailor— although dazzled with Juliet's charms—found her somewhat empty-headed.

The wedding, to be solemnized at the Grimaldis' private chapel at the Château Marchais on Tuesday, September 21, was to have been attended by the Emperor and Empress. As the date approached, Louis Napoleon took ill and was confined to bed. The Duc de Bassano was once again designated to be his representative. The betrothed couple might have been disappointed at this, but the bride's gifts from the two monarchs made up for some part of it. She received a superb emerald and brilliant bracelet, a diamond brooch in the shape of a thistle (for Scotland) and a suite of sapphires—a necklace, bracelet and earrings.

From her mother the young bride received a magnificent necklace of six rows of large, fine pearls with an emerald and diamond clasp and a fringe necklace containing 1,200 brilliants, a tiara of 44 large brilliants and a diamond and pearl tiara; from the Duke of Hamilton a *rivière* of emeralds and diamonds and "matchless" pearl earrings and a large diamond pendant in the shape of a star. Albert had made himself a very rich catch. And the bride?

"The daughter of our Scotch duke will become a sovereign princess," an Edinburgh newspaper reported. "Her future kingdom, it is true, is scarcely as extensive as is one of her brother's estates, but, nevertheless, the Principality has maintained its independence for many centuries. The fair and amiable Lady Hamilton is the Emperor's cousin."

Monaco was of modest size, but the Grimaldis had greatly enhanced their wealth. The Casino at Monte Carlo had brought them a huge sum of money in the past few years, and Princesse Caroline made sure that the château at Marchais would reflect their new position. For the wedding celebrations she refurbished the guests' rooms and offered dancing, concerts, racing and shooting for entertainment. The extensive grounds were decorated with colored lanterns, streamers and flags. A pavilion was erected for the dancing and a waltz band brought all the way from Vienna. In the evening there was a magnificent display of fireworks. And the marriage feast was of unprecedented splendor, even when compared to those at the Tuileries Balls.

Albert looked exceptionally handsome in his marine-blue officer's uniform, and the bride strikingly beautiful in an elegant white satin gown, designed by Worth, a white tulle veil enveloping her figure like a gentle sea spray, her train a startling sixteen feet long. Her long, blond hair was drawn back from her face by a pearl tiara, and about her neck were the six rows of pearls her mother had given her as a wedding gift. A fortune had been spent on her wardrobe, made by the top Parisian designers; her jewels (except for the gifts of the Emperor and Empress) had all come from Queen Victoria's jewelers in London.

In the course of her wedding day she changed costumes three times. For the signing of the marriage contract she was sweet and virginal in pink *poult-de-soie,* a demi-train looped at the sides, a pink silk *pouf* added at the skirt just below the waist. After the wedding ceremony, performed by the Bishop of Soissons, she changed into a brilliant lapis-lazuli blue gown, trimmed with velvet and fringe to match.

Her wedding trousseau was described in all the leading fashion columns and magazines, including *The Queen,* which went into description of a second traveling dress "made of shot green and mauve satin. The *redingote* has a train at the back which is made up *à la réactionnaire.*" The writer went on to describe four ball gowns "in the style of the Court dresses worn during Louis XV's reign—all exceedingly original and in capital taste."

Albert had married a young woman who was not only rich but a fashion plate. The new Duchesse de Valentinois was also strong-willed and could be petulant if she did not get her way. Disappointed that the Emperor and Empress had not attended their wedding, she decided she would "rather die than miss" the grand social event of the season—the Paris Autumn Races, which had been convened six days after the wedding. And so the honeymoon was postponed.

The sun shone that day, although the weather had been bitter cold for a week. Louis Napoleon was driven up to the imperial stand and stepped out of his carriage with surprising spirit, Eugénie, elegantly attired in green and black velvet, on his arm. Albert, Mary Victoria and the Duke of Hamilton were guests in the Royal Enclosure, and from there they watched Willie's horse, Capitaliste, win the Prix de St. Cloud. In the press coverage of this event, it was noted that because of the recent death of the Grand Duke of Hesse-Homburg, the number of European sovereigns had been reduced to forty: "five Emperors, one Sultan, one Pope, ten Kings, two Queens, six Grand Dukes, five Dukes, and ten Princes [including the Prince de Monaco]." The following Sunday, the weather not nearly so bright, the newlyweds watched Capitalist run the four-mile Prix de Gladiateur and win in the Hamilton colors once again.

Unlike his father and his late uncles, Albert did not thrive on Parisian social or Court life. Nor was he attracted to the sexual promiscuity of the times. While his young wife positively glowed as she attended races and galas in her extravagant wardrobe and dazzled the crowds with her newly acquired jewels, Albert yearned to be back at sea. Attractive as Mary Victoria was, he found little to share with her and described her in a letter to his former equerry Simon de Manzanos as being "sadly deficient in even the most basic of common knowledge."

Albert was developing into something of an intellectual. During his three-month journey on the *Isabelle* his interest in the sea had broadened from the intense pleasure he gained from navigation to sea life itself, and he had recently taken up the study of oceanography in a serious way. When, finally, the newlyweds departed for a honeymoon in Baden-Baden (accompanied by the bride's mother, Princess Marie of Baden, the Dowager Duchess of Hamilton), Albert packed several heavy tomes on the subject, while Mary Victoria brought along her fabulous "Louis XV" ball gowns.

Baden-Baden, in the Black Forest, had been one of Europe's most fashionable spas ever since the Casino had been built in 1824. The Grand Duke of Baden was the Dowager Duchess's father, and the family had a magnificent castle there. Despite what promised to be an enjoyable honeymoon, difficult times developed; for during the winter of 1869, relations between France and Prussia had reached an impasse. Baden was an independent state, surrounded by thirteen Prussian provinces; and if there was war between France and Prussia, the small state had little choice but to ally itself with Prussia.

The newlyweds and the bride's mother arrived in Baden-Baden at the end of October. The weather was foul and the season nearly over. Dinner conversation was gloomily directed to the growing hostility between France and Prussia and what a war between the two great countries would mean.

For two centuries Prussia had been building a strong state by means of a disciplined army and a civil service drilled in political theory, law, economics, history and penology. So powerful did Prussia become that it survived both military defeat by Napoleon in 1807 and the revolutionary surge of 1848. Now William I, King of Prussia, and his appointed Minister-President, Otto, Count von Bismarck, were determined to unite the German states in an empire under Prussian hegemony. The Grand Duke of Baden did not relish such an eventuality, which would eclipse what little power he had. And besides, he had always remained on the best of terms with his wife's cousin, Louis Napoleon.

A heavy cloud of anxiety hung over Baden-Baden during the somber month of November. Mary Victoria discovered she was pregnant and took to her bed with a violent case of morning sickness while Albert closeted himself with his oceanic tomes.

It was decided that the young couple and the Dowager Duchess should leave for Monaco and remain there for the birth of the child, due the following summer. They arrived in Geneva by coach "with a numerous suite" on December 2 and repaired to the Hôtel des Bergues where they were to spend the night before continuing on to Nice. A fierce thunderstorm struck just as they were preparing to depart, followed by torrential rain, hailstones and heavy snow, which delayed the party another three days. They arrived in Nice just in time for a devastating mistral that ripped trees from the earth. The next day, the weather calmer, they entrained for Monaco, where they were given a tumultuous welcome. But any pleasure this may have generated was short-lived.

No one had prepared the bride for the gloom that awaited her in the Palace. Not only was her father-in-law blind and short-tempered, the Palace was in mourning. Albert's aunt Florestine, the Duchess of Urach, still mourning the recent death of her husband, dressed in flowing layers of black and wandered about the Palace like a bird of night, dominating the household. To add to the problems with which Mary Victoria was faced, Princesse Caroline arrived and there were ferocious quarrels between her and her bereaved daughter over who had the final say in the running of the Palace.

Albert's marriage difficulties reached a climax in the last week of January 1870, when the Dowager Duchess prepared to return to Baden-Baden. Mary Victoria decided that she would leave, too. Husband and wife had not had much time alone. Albert had resented his mother-in-law's constant presence and the conditions under which the bridal couple had begun married life had been stressful. Nonetheless, they did appear to be unusually ill-matched. Albert was not overly distraught when Mary Victoria departed, and he had refused to accompany her when that was proposed.

"My dear Mary," Princesse Caroline wrote on February 5,

144

1870, while the bride and her mother rested in Nice before the long journey home. "My grandson's grief has so saddened me that I'm writing direct to you to make an appeal to your heart. Can you not forgive Albert for what you reproach him with [i.e., not being attentive enough]? The tender love you have aroused in him will give him the strength to change his ways, he has assured me, and to do all he can to make you happy. . . . I'm sure that for your part, my dear Mary, you must feel that a wife is the link of her family. . . ."

Two days later, still in Nice, Mary Victoria replied: "My dear grandmother. I was greatly touched by your letter, and I thank you for all its affection for me. The best memory I have of the recent sad time is the kindness you showed towards me. I am most grateful for this memory, which eases the bitterness of the weeks I spent at Monaco. . . ." On that note she left Nice with her mother and returned to Baden-Baden to await the birth of her child.

Instead of following her and perhaps effecting a reconciliation, Albert went to Paris where he met with the Emperor and Empress. They were shocked at Mary Victoria's action but unable to do anything about it. "We should try to meet together, Mary and I, just by ourselves," Albert wrote to his father on February 20, "but that's the difficulty [implying that the Dowager Duchess never gave them any time to themselves]."

Within a few months war fever had consumed France. On Saturday, July 2, the *Gazette de France* announced that the throne of Spain, which had been vacant since 1868 and in dispute since that time, had been offered to, and accepted by, Prince Leopold of the house of Hohenzollern, with the consent of the King of Prussia. Nine days of anxious uncertainty followed. A letter was then dispatched by Louis Napoleon's foreign minister to the King of Prussia's emissary: "If the Prince of Hohenzollern's renunciation is announced in 24 or 48 hours there will be peace for the moment. If not, there will be an immediate declaration of war against Prussia."

Prince Leopold withdrew his acceptance of the Spanish Crown, but this was not enough of a guarantee for the Emperor or his foreign minister, the Duc de Gramont. They wanted direct assurance from the King of Prussia that he would not authorize the candidacy afresh. This appeared to be a ploy. "It was too late to avoid war," Eugénie was later to say. "You cannot imagine what an outburst of patriotism carried all France away at that moment. Even Paris, hitherto so hostile to the [Second] Empire, showed wonderful enthusiasm, confidence and resolution. Frantic crowds in the boulevards cried incessantly *À Berlin! À Berlin!*"

On July 19, war was officially declared by the Emperor. A week earlier, on July 12, 1870, Mary Victoria had given birth in Baden-Baden to a son who was christened Louis-Honoré-Charles-Antoine. Albert did not go to see his child, for on July 21, out of loyalty to France, he signed up with the French Navy and within two weeks was with the North Sea Fleet, ostensibly an enemy of his wife's family.

11

Louis Napoleon was faced with a war and a lack of funds with which to fight it. He turned for aid to A.&M. Heine, one of the largest banking houses in France. The concern was owned by two brothers, Armand and Michel Heine, who had made their fortunes as young men in New Orleans, Louisiana. Originally from Berlin and cousins to the great lyric poet Heinrich Heine, they had left Germany in 1840, disillusioned with its anti-Semitic and right-wing policies, for Paris, where their cousin was already established as a leading revolutionary literary figure. They went on in 1843 to New Orleans, a city dominated by Creole culture and where their second language, French, was spoken. The queen city of the Mississippi, New Orleans had been swept to fabulous heights as a port and market for cotton and slaves; and the Heine brothers, whose father had been a moneylender in Berlin, saw the opportunities.

With borrowed capital and, rumor had it, gambling winnings, they started a banking house. Within ten years they had become the most successful financiers in New Orleans and had fallen in love with the same young woman, the exotic and vivacious Amelie Miltenberger. Her father, born in New Orleans but of German heritage, was an influential cotton broker and her Creole mother had endowed her with extraordinary dark eyes and jet-black hair. Amelie, then twenty-one, chose the younger brother, Michel, who was four years her senior. Their wedding in 1853 was the great event of the city's social calendar, held in the Miltenbergers' lavish home and gardens and with a guest list that included New Orleans's most glamorous and prestigious citizens.

A few months later, Michel and Amelie departed for Paris to open a European banking house, leaving Armand in charge of the brothers' American interests. In an unusual partnership arrangement, for three months each year the brothers reversed their positions, and Amelie and Michel returned to New Orleans where they remained with Amelie's family while Armand took over in Paris. Thus, Amelie and Michel's three children, George (born in 1853), Alice (1857) and Henry (1860), were all born in New Orleans and held American citizenship. The death of the infant Henry and the advent of the Civil War sent the family back to Paris and ended the Heine brothers' exchange of residences. By 1863, A.&M. Heine was one of the most powerful financial companies in France.

Part of the company's success could be attributed to Amelie, whose Southern charm and unique beauty quickly made her a popular hostess, the belle of Louis Napoleon's Court and the intimate friend of the Empress Eugénie. The royal couple even bestowed on the Heines the honor of becoming godparents to George and Alice. A clever administrator, Michel became not only exceptionally rich but powerful at Court and Napoleon's trusted financial adviser. It was therefore not surprising that Napoleon should ask Michel Heine's firm to float a loan to finance France's war with Prussia. Amazingly, the Heines were able to raise the astronomical sum required within a matter of ten days.

The idea of war with Prussia continued to be enthusiastically received by the majority of the French population, none of whom doubted the outcome. What they overlooked was that Bismarck had succeeded in making France the aggressor, and that the southern German states would now join the north in resisting a foreign invasion. Although Monaco raised the tricolor beside the Monégasque flag in a show of support, and portraits of Albert in his French naval uniform appeared in the lobby of the Hôtel de Paris and in the windows of several shops, France had no real allies.

Thomas Carlyle in *The Times* wrote: "That noble, patient, deeply pious and solid Germany should at length be welded into a nation, and become Queen of the Continent, instead of vapouring, vainglorious, gesticulating, quarrelsome, restless and over-sensitive France seems to me the hopefullest public fact that has occurred in my time."

It took six months for Paris to fall and nearly ten until peace was declared. As far as effective fighting went, the war was virtually over in six weeks. Albert's ship, the *Savoi,* withdrew with the French fleet from the North Sea at that time. He was transferred to the *Couronne* and headed south in retreat to Calais. He had seen devastating action in the North Sea while on the *Savoi,* which had suffered heavy losses, but had come through unharmed.

The defeat of the French forces and the final surrender of Louis Napoleon to the Prussians were almost more than even Eugénie's Castilian courage could endure. On September 2, 1870, the Emperor and 60,000 of his men were captured at Sedan, in the northeast of France. Louis Napoleon wrote to his wife: "I cannot tell you what I have suffered and am suffering. We made a march contrary to all the rules and to common sense: it was bound to lead to a catastrophe, and that is complete. I would rather have died than have witnessed such a disastrous capitulation, and yet, things being as they are, it was the only way of avoiding the slaughter of 60,000 men. . . . I have just seen the King [William, of Prussia]. There were tears in his eyes when he spoke of the sorrow I must be feeling. He has put at my disposal one of his châteaux near Hesse-Cassel. But what does it matter where I go? I am in despair. . . ."

The following day Eugénie was warned by the Prefect of Police not to remain at the Tuileries lest the crowds, which were already at the gates, force her to abdicate the Regency and do her harm. She consented to leave, the specter of her idol, Marie Antoinette, no doubt before her. With her at the time were Amelie Heine and a lady-in-waiting, Madame Lebreton. Amelie left the palace and went to her husband's offices where arrangements were made for money to be transferred to England in Eugénie's name, so that she could take refuge there. Meanwhile, Eugénie made her way with Madame Lebreton through secret passages to the Louvre and then out a rear door, after which the two women, dressed in concealing outerwear and carrying only one small satchel of clothes packed in a hurry, hailed a passing taxi, directing the driver to take them to the home of a known Loyalist. When no one answered their insistent knocks, they walked through milling, angry crowds, unrecognized, to the residence of another loyal friend, with the same result. Desperate, Eugénie remembered her American dentist, Dr. Evans, who lived on the Avenue Malakoff, and flagged down a second cab.

The women spent the night in Dr. Evans's home while the good dentist, with the Heines and the Prefect of Police, made all the arrangements for Eugénie's getaway. Early the next morning, with forged passports representing Eugénie as an invalid English lady, Evans as her brother, a friend of Evans's, a Doctor Crane, as her physician and Madame Lebreton as her nurse, the four left Paris in Evans's carriage, which they soon abandoned, first in favor of a hired cab and then of the train, arriving at midnight at their destination, the French city of Deauville, on the English Channel. There they met an English friend of the Emperor's, Sir John Burgoyne, boarded his private yacht, *Gazelle,* and headed for sanctuary in England.

Within six months the badly beaten French soldiers returned, their ranks devastated, much of central Paris reduced to ashes, food so scarce that many Parisians were reduced to a diet of rats. France, despite the King of Prussia's tears, was left struggling to survive under one of the harshest peace settlements ever imposed by one European state upon another. France had to pay an indemnity to Germany of ten billion francs in a period of three years. Alsace and a large part of Lorraine were ceded to Germany, which on January 18, 1871, in the Hall of Mirrors at Versailles, had been proclaimed an empire under William I. Prussian militarism had triumphed.

On September 9, 1870, Victor Hugo, now a vigorous septuagenarian, had issued an eloquent appeal to the Prussians: "It is in Paris that the beating of Europe's heart is felt. Paris is the city of cities. Paris is the city of men. There has been an Athens, there has been a Rome, and there is a Paris . . . so the nineteenth century is to witness this frightful phenomenon? A nation fallen from polity to barbarism, abolishing the city of nations; Germans extinguishing Paris. . . . Can you give this spectacle to the world? Can you Germans become Vandals again; personifying barbarism, decapitating civilization? . . . Paris, pushed to extremities; Paris supported by all France aroused, can conquer and will conquer; and you will have tried in vain this course of action which already revolts the world."

No reply was forthcoming, and France turned to Britain and

America for help. Both countries sent ships loaded with food. Much of it was held up at Le Havre because there weren't enough men to unload the provisions. On February 26, 1870, the day the Peace Treaty was signed, 300,000 Parisians gathered in the Place de la Bastille. The temper of the crowd was ugly and one man, believed to be a spy, was nearly torn apart before being drowned in the Seine. The same day, insurgents of the growing ranks of Communards[1] forced their way into the Sainte-Pélagie Prison and released political prisoners. Revolts in provincial cities followed, and in May, a violent assault on Paris, as the Communards fought for control, was begun.

Albert was awarded the Légion d'Honneur for his services to the French Navy. He had returned to Paris to inspect the Grimaldi properties—his home and that of Princesse Caroline—which had suffered severe damage during the siege. He found a city in the grip of civil war and the new president, the ultra-right-wing Adolphe Thiers, and the National Guard overwhelmed. Thiers fled with the Guard to Versailles.

Albert remained in Paris, where a second siege of the city, led by Thiers and the National Guard, followed. Despite the desperate defense of the Communards, who constructed barricades, shot hostages (including the Archbishop of Paris), and burned the Tuileries, the Hôtel de Ville and the Palais de Justice, the siege succeeded. Severe reprisals followed, with more than 17,000 people executed, including women and children. It was impossible to know just how many people had been killed in the siege. Such bloodshed had not been equaled even in the Revolution of 1792. The stench of dead flesh was everywhere.

A year later, tens of thousands of Parisians having died, the Third Republic was proclaimed with Marie Edmé Patrice de MacMahon (who had aided Thiers in the bloody suppression) as President. A monarchist of Irish descent, he had been chosen by the National Assembly to suppress the Communards and reestablish the monarchy, but he was unwilling to go to the illegal extremes necessary to do so.

Much of Paris had been reduced to rubble, food remained

---

[1]The Communards (members of the Commune of Paris) had been formed during the Revolution of 1792 and had virtually engineered the storming of the Tuileries. The Commune re-formed in 1871, its members drawn from several political groups, including the radical republicans and the Marxist First International.

short, and most of Albert's old friends were either dead or in exile. Strongly opposed to what was happening in France, he was at a loss, not knowing what he should do and suffering from a malady shared by all heirs to a throne—monarchical unemployment. He had no real job until his father died. He had already produced his own heir, and he was not a man—like England's Edward, Prince of Wales—who enjoyed the pursuit of women.

His wife and child remained apart from him in Baden-Baden. When he returned to Monaco in the spring of 1871, the ambience in the Palace had gone from merely gloomy to positively grim. His father suffered painful gout along with his other infirmities; his aunt Florestine was a despotic shrew; and his grandmother, that strong-willed woman he had always admired, was now eighty, and terribly frail.

To add to his distress, François Blanc's power in Monaco had increased with the infirmity of Charles and Caroline and the absence of Albert. Blanc's only interest was in the increasing success of the Casino and his many other investments in Monaco. But he controlled the comfortable income on which the Grimaldis lived, for if the Casino should fail or Blanc should withdraw from the running of it, they would suffer a great financial loss. Albert found the man offensive, despite the continued success of the S.B.M. to his own enrichment. Blanc was arrogant and dismissive toward the Grimaldis and had even insisted the Carabinieri salute his wife when she appeared on the street. The army was unwilling to oblige until Blanc, who, it must be admitted, paid their wages, threatened to replace them. Marie Blanc, whom Princesse Caroline thought of disdainfully as being the daughter of a common cobbler, soon received smart salutes whenever she went for a stroll.

Blanc also had strong control over Albert's father, and in 1869 had induced Charles to abolish all taxes levied on native Monégasques. With the constantly flowing income from the S.B.M. (the Casino alone made a two million-franc profit in 1872), tax money was not actually needed. But its abolition was a master stroke, for it made the Grimaldis popular at the same time that it raised Blanc to the position of benefactor of the people.

Albert was not a gambler, nor did he like the people whom

Blanc and the Casino drew to Monaco. His happiest days had been spent at sea. In the spring of 1873, he left Paris for Toulon, where he bought a two hundred-ton boat, named *L'Hirondelle*. With a crew of fifteen seamen, he sailed in African waters for several months. When he returned, this time to Monaco, he was as much confused as to what he wished to do as he had been before. Perhaps he could have rejoined the French Navy, but it was in chaos and nearly bankrupt. He turned once again to Spain, which was engaged in a civil war, serving as a captain in the Spanish Navy for the next two years, resigning in 1875 when Alfonso XII, the son of Isabella (having been proclaimed King the previous year), entered Madrid to tumultuous cheering and restored the throne of Spain to the Bourbons. Albert returned to Monaco, where he now turned his attention to his estranged wife.

Five years had elapsed since he had even corresponded with Mary Victoria, although Princesse Caroline had kept in constant touch with her and passed on whatever news there was of his son to him. During that time, Mary Victoria had fallen passionately in love with Count Tassilo Festetics de Tolna, a dashing Hungarian, and had refused to see Albert, writing instead to ask him to apply to the Vatican for an annulment of their marriage. Rocked by this, Albert nonetheless enlisted his father's help in carrying out her wishes. Considering that there had been a child of their union, dissolution would not be easy, if indeed it was possible. There was also young Louis's position as heir presumptive, plus the problem of the boy's education. Albert insisted he must be educated in France and that his school holidays be spent in Monaco. Then there was the matter of a settlement. Albert was firm that he must retain the wedding dowry, and Mary Victoria insisted upon keeping the jewels and gifts she had received. The whole unpleasant business would take four years to resolve and would cost the Grimaldis a large share of the dowry. It created such hard feelings between the Hamiltons and the Grimaldis that they never again spoke to each other.

Albert's maiden voyage on *L'Hirondelle* had convinced him that his real vocation was in oceanographic studies. He sought out Professor Henri Milne-Edwards, one of the leading experts in the relatively new science and the author of one of the books (on crustaceans, mollusks and corals) Albert had taken on his honeymoon. Milne-Edwards was director of the Museum of Natural History in Paris, and Albert studied diligently under his tutelage for several years.

Victor Hugo's "city of cities" was undergoing massive rebuilding. The bitterness of the Franco-Prussian War and the bloody siege of Paris would endure for many years. The Emperor had died in 1873 while in exile in England, where he had gone to join Eugénie. With no Court on which to center its attention, the *haut monde* of Paris had turned to the great salons that lionized the literary, artistic and philosophical intelligentsia.

Albert became a frequent visitor to the home of the young, vivacious, provocative and exceptionally clever Duchesse de Richelieu—none other than Alice Heine, grown and married at seventeen into one of France's most distinguished families. The châtelaine of the magnificent Château de Haut-Buisson, and the leader of a young group of aristocratic intellectuals, she held brilliant salons in the de Richelieus' grand and elegant home in Paris.

Princesse Caroline, who had been almost entirely bedridden since Albert's return from Spain, died in her sleep on November 23, 1879, at the age of eighty-six. Despite the infirmities of her last years, her mind had remained sharp and she had not lost her zest for expressing her opinion. She had been a strong influence in Albert's life, and a constant force in the lives of both her son and grandson, as she had with Albert's father. With his grandmother's death, and to his father's bitterness, Albert spent most of his time in Paris.

On July 28, 1880, the Vatican finally annulled his marriage to Mary Victoria, yet declaring Louis legitimate. The previous month, Mary Victoria had married the Hungarian count in a civil service (although forbidden by Church law to do so) for she was pregnant with his child. With the Duchesse de Richelieu's encouragement, Albert pursued his oceanographic work. Recognizing that the science lacked the necessary instruments and equipment to probe the depths of the sea, he invested a large sum of his money into their development and construction. His plan was to take *L'Hirondelle* on a research voyage, which would be a pioneer excursion of its kind.

154

Partly because of the terrible state France was in after the war with Prussia, those who could afford it made their way south to the Riviera for escape. More than 140,000 people had visited Monte Carlo in 1871. François Blanc enlarged the Casino and invested in the racetrack in Nice, wisely believing that elegant devotees of prize horseflesh would eventually come to Monte Carlo since Nice had nothing to compare with the accommodations and food of the Hôtel de Paris or the many other, newer hotels.

By now, Monte Carlo was a thriving resort city that had no equal on the Riviera. There were nineteen new hotels, twenty-four grand villas, and eighty furnished apartments. The opportunity that one might, after ten years, acquire Monégasque citizenship and so live tax-exempt brought many new residents.

But Monte Carlo had been built to please a particular social group—the international nobility and the American millionaires who were fast marrying into their ranks and adopting their standards. "The Russians might be a little more barbaric, the English slightly more puritanical and philistine, but taken all in all there was a generally accepted code of taste, of manners and maybe even of morals," one commentator of the times wrote. "They [the social set of Monte Carlo] presented a solid, polished front to the world, as closely-knit as chain-mail; and perhaps greater even than that which their ancestors had found in moated bastions and armour plate. The newly-rich bourgeoisie modelled their behaviour as best they could on that of the people who were generally regarded [if erroneously] as their betters."

Blanc was well aware of the social aspirations of the *nouveaux riches*, being one of their number himself. He decided to bring culture, which that segment of society regarded as essential, to Monte Carlo. From the beginning of the enterprise, his policy had been to provide attractions for those visitors not drawn toward the tables—wives, husbands, children and mistresses who were brought along as appendages and whose restlessness and dissatisfaction could keep the players away from the gambling.

He therefore contracted with (Jean Louis) Charles Garnier, the architect and designer of the newly completed Paris Opéra, to build a smaller version, to adjoin the Casino. It was called the Salle Garnier. Splendid caryatids decorated the corners of the interior, holding up a painted ceiling and backed by "florid frescoes along the walls, gilt cherubs on the pillars, and gilded statues of Nubian slaves brandishing massive candelabra." The theater opened on January 25, 1879, with the appearance of Sarah Bernhardt who read a prologue written by the French playwright, Jean Aicard. The Divine Sarah was a compulsive gambler and had lost a large sum of money earlier that evening at the gaming tables, to which she returned after her performance, unfortunately to add to her losses. The Salle Garnier was to be François Blanc's last contribution to Monte Carlo, for he died the year it was completed. His son Camille Blanc inherited his control in the S.B.M. and a fortune of over seventy-two million francs.

Despite the Salle Garnier's new cultural contribution to life in Monaco, public opinion was strongly against Monte Carlo's main attraction—the Casino. A Committee Against Monte Carlo for the Suppression of the Gaming Tables had been organized in 1878; the petition presented in the Chamber that year was initiated by leading inhabitants of its French neighbors—Menton, Nice and Cannes—who were fearful of losing large sums in tourist money from travelers lured to Monte Carlo by the gaming tables. When the petition was denied and the Casino continued to flourish, these towns forgot their scruples and built casinos of their own. By this time Monte Carlo had acquired a reputation as the fashionable place to gamble, one reason being that Edward, Prince of Wales, using an assumed name but with a current ladyfriend, frequented during the season.

A damning book, *Monte Carlo and Public Opinion*, with contributions from European and American writers (mostly anonymous) was published in England in 1884. Its appearance followed a series of reported suicides of heavy losers at the tables and stories of ruined families and runaway husbands. "Last of its kind to be tolerated in the neighbourhood of the respectable communities of Europe, the public gambling institution of Monte Carlo, in the petty principality of Monaco, has been arraigned and found guilty at the bar of public opinion, and only now awaits the sentence and final extinction which it falls to the part of the Government of the French Republic to pronounce and inflict," the editor (credited only as "a visitor to Monte Carlo") stated in his preface. All of the book's contributors supported the closing of the Casino. (There were no essays in favor of the continuance of the gaming tables.)

The authors of this book all seemed to believe that it was up to France to prohibit gambling in the Principality "as there has always been a dependency on the court of France, which became, in the reign of Louis XIV, scarcely distinguishable from complete subjection. It has been renewed and reinforced, since the final withdrawal of the Italian garrison, by the transfer of its customs and civil rights to the French Government (convicted criminals are even incarcerated in French gaols). The present ruling family is in the male line descended from a French nobleman. . . . The claim of the Prince de Monaco's friends that he should be allowed to rank as an independent prince, with a right to pass his own laws, is one that is opposed to the facts . . . the natural position of Monaco is as an enclave of France."

An Italian by the name of Mancini wrote that "the gambling house, officially protected and surrounded by unbridled luxury, continues to add to the number of its victims, and to desolate countless families all over Europe; [the ruinous losses of Italy's Prince Orsini which had bankrupted him had been a scandal in that country]. Every day fresh suicides appall the inhabitants of [the Riviera]. The well-paid defenders of gaming say these are mere accidents. According to them every man who flings himself over a precipice, or is dashed to pieces on the rocks, or who blew his brains out with a revolver, did so quite accidentally. . . . It is hoped that the European Powers will come to an understanding to take diplomatic action on this subject."

A French detractor points out that "the only plausible objection against French interference is that France wishes to respect the independence of Monaco . . . but we maintain that Monaco is not an independent state, seeing that the management of affairs of importance in that state is in the hands of France." One good reason for France's lack of interference was the assistance of two million francs yearly that Monaco had been giving France since the war to help pay off its enormous war debt. This decision had been made by François Blanc and forced upon Charles at the time of the peace treaty with the reasoning that the newly created Germany with its powerful military force would not interfere with the gaming tables in Monte Carlo, although casinos in Germany had been outlawed, if they received sufficient compensation and it could not be traced as coming directly from Monaco and the Casino. France had also welcomed this plan, for it helped them to pay off their obligation.

Although there was a large and growing cartel in Europe and America attempting to put an end to the Casino, it continued to flourish and to fascinate and to draw to it an ever larger clientele. One American visitor gave a good description of the Casino and its ambience in 1884:

> The gaming-house stands in the midst of well-kept gardens, and there are statues and seats, palm trees and terraces everywhere. . . . We mount the steps on the north side, away from the sea, and pass through the large glass doors that are held open by an obsequious official in uniform. We find ourselves in a spacious vestibule adorned with evergreen plants; a fine reading-room on the right, where papers of every country may be found; a grand ball-room and theatre in front, and a balcony all around. Most of the visitors disappear through large doors on the left. Two guards are stationed there, who say, as we advance, "No one is admitted to the gaming-rooms without tickets." We apply at the bureau close by.
>
> "What is your nationality?" the ticket-seller asks in French.
>
> "We're American," I reply in English. Then he inscribes our names and callings in a big book and gives us tickets, which we endorse. And now, provided with tickets, the guards give way, and pushing open two pairs of swing doors, we find ourselves in the "gambling-hell" of Monte Carlo.
>
> It is a vast hall in three divisions, with a roof supported by massive pillars. The decoration is rich—gold and brilliant colors and endless mirrors intermingled in a style which may not unreasonably be compared with some of the rooms I visited at Versailles and Hampton Court. There is a murmur of many voices, the chink of gold and silver, and a click-click like the sound of billiard-balls repeatedly tapped together with the hand. The hall contains seven gaming-tables, covered with the traditional "green cloth." . . . At each end of the table there are . . . croupiers, who have rakes; another and superior official sits upon a high chair and surveys the table and the gamblers sitting and

158

standing around. The roulette is motionless now, and the banker in charge of it calls out, "Messieurs, faites vos jeux!" [Gentlemen, stake your bets!]

All around the saloon are luxurious seats and gorgeously attired lackeys in attendance. But no one sits quietly there; the people are all hot and excited, both losers and winners . . . as I come out into the peaceful gardens, and look upon the Mediterranean, bathed in sunlight, I am watched by stealthy gendarmes, ready to seize me if I should attempt to blow out my brains, as the Russian gambler did the other day. Such affairs are, unfortuantely, only too common with gamblers in Monaco.

None of the controversy over Monte Carlo appeared to have any effect upon Charles III. By 1880, now sixty-two, he was seldom seen, even by former friends who had once presented themselves at the Palace when they were in the Principality. Albert was off on his long-awaited maiden research voyage. (He was to go on twenty-six such journeys and would establish for himself a position as one of the foremost authorities on oceanography.) Charles worried a great deal about Albert and his wanderlust, not understanding what his son could find so fascinating in dredging up fossils and sea life from the bottom of the ocean. He dictated letters asking him to return home, as he was old, ill and lonely. He was also richer than he had ever dreamed. He left the running of the S.B.M. to Camille Blanc while he concerned himself mainly with decisions regarding the Palace and its staff.

Despite their annulment agreement, Albert and Mary Victoria's son, Louis, spent his holidays from 1877 until 1880, when he was ten years old, with his mother in Baden-Baden (before that time he had lived there in her care). This was mainly due to his father's occupation with the French and Spanish navies and his scientific ocean travels. Until this time Albert did not appear to bear his ex-wife ill will. His feelings toward her changed at Eastertime when they had an exchange of angry letters apparently precipitated by Mary Victoria's removal of Louis, without Albert's permission, from the school he was attending in Paris, because she thought it was too cold and disciplined. In the summer of 1880, Louis visited his father for the first time in Monaco before beginning studies at his father's former boarding school, the Collège Stanislas. "He was pleased to see you, Sir," Mary Victoria wrote to Albert, her tone now conciliatory. "[He] never makes any reference to the past. He takes everything so naturally, and we should thank God for it, and try to keep this delightful frankness intact as long as possible."

Louis entered the Collège Louis-le-Grand in 1883. But Albert, although by then more attentive, saw little of his son in the next few years, even when he was in Paris where the school was located. He made more research voyages on *L'Hirondelle,* during one of which the ship was caught in a cyclone and nearly overturned. He studied the drift of surface currents in the North Atlantic, the Gulf Stream in particular, using specially designed floats he had commissioned; and he dredged the seabed at a depth of nearly ten thousand feet, an operation that took three and a half hours to lower the special equipment, and triple that time to raise it again. He returned from each of his voyages to Paris where he continued studying with eminent oceanographic scholars. He had become obsessed with the subject but it was not the only attraction in Paris.

The Duc de Richelieu, a comparatively young man, had died suddenly and Alice was now a widow—a *very rich* widow—having been left seventeen million francs. Whenever Albert was in Paris, he spent what time he could with her, attending her lively salons in her exquisite home in the Faubourg Saint-Honoré.

12

ALICE WAS UNLIKE any other woman Albert had ever known. There could hardly have been two more contrasting personalities than Mary Victoria and the Duchesse de Richelieu. Possessing a brilliant mind and a dazzling knowledge of a variety of subjects from literature to politics to science, Alice conducted a salon that greatly appealed to France's intellectuals. As a young man of seventeen, Marcel Proust was a guest there (she was fourteen years his senior) and became one of her great admirers. Years later, he used her as model for the Princesse de Luxembourg in À la recherche du temps perdu.

Proust described the Princesse de Luxembourg as "tall, red-haired, handsome, with a rather prominent nose. . . . [I saw her] half leaning upon a parasol in such a way as to impart to her tall and wonderful form that slight inclination, to make it trace that arabesque, so dear to the women who . . . knew how, with drooping shoulders, arched backs, concave hips and taut legs to make their bodies float as softly as a silken scarf about the rigid armature of an invisible shaft which might be supposed to have transfixed it." He thought Alice very beautiful and her voice "so musical that it was as if, among the dim branches of the trees, a nightingale had begun to sing." And he referred to her as "a woman of the soundest judgment and the warmest heart." He was, perhaps, somewhat in love with her, but then so were many of the men of all ages who came to her salon.

A combination of her exotic mother and her pragmatic father, even in appearance, Alice spoke many languages—all fluently and all with a melodic American Southern accent, although she had left her native New Orleans when still a small child and had returned only twice to visit her grandparents. She introduced Creole cooking to the Parisian elite and seemed more inclined in style to Spanish than to German influences.

She drove in a stately equipage, always followed by a small black page dressed in red satin.

She was close to her family, but fiercely independent. Her brother, George, had gone into the Heine banking business; and her mother, who enjoyed being the *grande dame,* spent most of her time entertaining lavishly at her daughter's country estate, the magnificent Château de Haut-Buisson (where she now lived), for Alice preferred to be in Paris. Since childhood, Alice's daughter, Odile, and her son, Armand, had been admitted to their mother's sophisticated salon. Gay, witty, wise, iconoclastic, cultured, wealthy and a striking beauty, Alice attracted her share of fortune hunters and a succession of lovers.

She was initially drawn to Albert because of his adventurous spirit. Always ready to learn about subjects previously unknown to her, she found his knowledge of oceanography and his voyages off the coast of Africa interesting. He also had a certain masculine mystique about him, unlike the intellectual, artistic and sometimes effete men who were part of her set. Albert liked the sea, hunting and adventure, yet he was extremely intelligent. He was the heir to a throne, but he was a simple man, of simple tastes. Conscious of her height since childhood (she was about five-feet seven, tall for a woman of that time), she found that his bearlike build made her feel smaller.

When he declared his love for her in 1885, she was twenty-eight and he was thirty-seven. He wanted above all else to make her his wife, but to do so he had to have his father's permission. Charles withheld it. This was not, presumably, on religious grounds, for Alice had converted from Judaism to Catholicism when she became the Duchesse de Richelieu. She was a widow and they were both free to marry. But the old monarch considered it scandalous that a single woman would conduct a salon and was a friend to writers and artists for whom he had no tolerance. In addition, her Jewish heritage provoked a degree of snobbery in him. Despite his disapproval, Albert and Alice became lovers. On his return from his scientific explorations he would go straight to her house in Paris. At least twice they rendezvoused in Funchal, the capital of Madeira.

Charles III died at seventy-one years of age, after falling ill with pneumonia while on a visit to Marchais, on September 10, 1889, his daughter, Florestine, at his bedside. Although the

162

Palace flag was lowered to half-mast and photographs of him that were on display in public buildings draped in black, his death was unmourned by his subjects. A total recluse for the last decade of his life, when in Monaco he never left the Palace. The end of his reign had cast a pall over the Principality. It had been years since there had been a royal ball or official visits from other royals or heads of state. Festive occasions were centered in Monte Carlo, which now had become a prospering city. Charles III would be remembered as the Prince for whom the city had been named and his reign as the start and rise of the gambling Casino there. But of the Grimaldis, it had been his mother, Princesse Caroline, in conjunction with François Blanc, who had made the greatest impact on his subjects, their lives and economic well-being.

Charles and Albert had never been close and shared little in common. Their relationship had grown more difficult after Princesse Caroline's death, for Albert was seldom in Monaco and managed to visit Marchais at times when Charles was not there. During the infrequent times they were together Charles was critical of his son's scientific endeavors (which he considered a waste of effort and money) and his associations. His dictated letters to Albert reflect his dissatisfaction with almost everything his son did. He expected Albert to spend more time with him, to have greater sympathy for his blindness and ill health, and to take over more duties in Monaco. Instead, Albert involved himself more with his scientific expeditions, and when he was not at sea, he was with Alice in Paris.

He was at sea when he was informed of his father's death and altered his course back to Monaco. On October 23 he accepted the oath of loyalty in the courtyard of the Palace. The ceremony had not been performed there since 1731, when the young Honoré III had returned to succeed his mother, Louise-Hippolyte. For the first time in years there was great celebration in Monaco, but almost immediately after he became Albert I, Prince de Monaco, he departed for Paris; and on October 31, accountable now only to himself, he married Alice in a quiet service in Paris with only her family and a few close friends present. They honeymooned in Madeira, then returned to Paris, where they were the guests of honor at several large balls. On February 9, 1890, the newlyweds (the bride with twenty-seven trunks filled with her new fashionable trousseau) arrived by train in Monaco and were met by an enthusiastic crowd.

Twenty years had elapsed since Albert had brought his first bride to Monaco. In the interval, the Principality had become the cosmopolitan hub of the Riviera, a gathering place for royalty, society, heiresses, fortune hunters and gamblers out to break the bank at Monte Carlo (now called just "Monte" by the cognoscenti). What it was not, despite the Salle Garnier, was an intellectual and cultural citadel.

Once Alice was installed as châtelaine of the Palais de Princier, many members of her intellectual and artistic coterie began to visit. Monaco enjoyed a new recognition with the Princesse de Monaco's smart soirées. Alice had to contend with Albert's Aunt Florestine (more testy than ever with her position suddenly usurped), but she did so with amazing finesse. Alice saw to it that Florestine was given a larger suite of rooms, which incorporated Princesse Caroline's former apartments, and that she was drawn into the extravagant and exciting redecoration being undertaken. The former gloom of the Palace was dispelled by new and brighter upholstery and curtains. Bowls overflowing with brilliant flowers graced the rooms, and the gardens became an attraction few visitors could resist.

The parade of royal guests to the Palace began. The season officially started the week before Easter with the arrival of the Prince of Wales on his yacht *Britannia*. He much admired Alice and often came to the Palace for tea. His long alliance with the beautiful actress Lillie Langtry was over (although she retained a villa in Monte Carlo and they remained friends), and he was now usually in the company of the worldly and charming Mrs. Keppel, the spirited and attractive wife of a Gordon Highlander. Alice Keppel appeared to have cured his roving eye and would become his constant companion for the remainder of his life.

He arrived in Monaco accompanied by a small personal staff, his physician, two equerries, two menservants and a butler. Although he insisted on being called Baron Renfrew, his small canine pet, who followed him everywhere, wore a jeweled collar with the inscription: *I am Caesar. I belong to the Prince of Wales*. He went to the Casino almost every night to play baccarat but did not wager large sums that would attract comment.

The Grand Duke Michael, uncle of Czar Alexander III, led

the procession of Russian nobility to Monte Carlo. The Russians lived on a far grander scale than the Prince of Wales, who was related to many of them. Russia's Empress Maria Fëdorovna was his wife's sister, and his cousin Princess Alix of Hesse was married to another cousin, the Czarevitch Nicholas. The Russians spent fortunes, losing millions of francs in a single night at the Casino, rented whole floors at the Hôtel de Paris and the other hotels, and hired innumerable servants, dressing them in powdered wigs and livery.

King Leopold II of Belgium, whose private life was even more scandalous and dissolute than that of the Russians, also came to Monte Carlo every season, first making his way up the curving road of the Rock to pay his respects to the new Princesse de Monaco. And there were Arabian princes and the Prince of Nepal, whose religion allowed him to gamble only five days a year.

Albert's scientific sea ventures increased and he was away from Alice for longer and longer periods. Municipal decisions such as zoning and building restrictions and budgetary problems were handled by the S.B.M., with the enriching assistance of Michel Heine in financial matters.

The new Princesse de Monaco enjoyed the prestige of the noble visitors who were attracted to Monaco; but she was disdainful of their reasons for coming, and she was only too aware of the courtesans and expensive whores who flocked to Monte Carlo during the season to the delight of Monte's many jewelry concerns and fashion houses. What Alice wished was to make Monte Carlo an important cultural center, attractive to the artists and intellectuals who had been part of her salon in Paris. To accomplish this she would need to change the image of the town by constructing and developing diversions other than gambling—the arts, sports and horticulture, starting exotic gardens that would be open to the public. She wanted more charity galas to counteract the Casino's bad publicity and growing numbers of con men and desperate characters attracted by the free flow of money at the gaming tables. Also, Albert was never easy about the idea that his wealth was based on gambling losses.

"When I first knew this Princelet, he was always talking of his dislike of 'the gambling house' of Monte Carlo, which gave him his princely revenue and paid besides all the expenses of his three miles long and half a mile wide kingdom," author Frank Harris, who lived on the Riviera and was a close friend of Princesse Alice's, wrote in his autobiography, *My Life and Loves*. "Everyone staying at the palace was requested not to visit or even enter the gambling house, and the Prince was continually complaining that his father had given M. Blanc a lease of the place till [1913], or else, 'I'd shut it up tomorrow. I hate the corruptions of it . . . I loathe the place.'

"It seemed to me," Harris continues, "that the Prince protested too much; in any case, surely he need not have accepted 'the wages of sin,' had he not been so inclined."

Albert had, in fact, given his father-in-law, Michel Heine, the go-ahead to try to renegotiate François Blanc's original contract on better terms, even if it meant extending the lease, for he needed a great deal of money to construct an oceanographic museum in Monaco, to be the first of its kind and the largest and most complete in the world.

Michel Heine brought Camille Blanc to the negotiating table with threats that Alice might use her influence to close the Casino if changes were not made. Although François Blanc's original agreement had another twenty-three years to run, Heine secured a new contract with an immediate payment of 10 million francs to the state treasury and a payment of 15 million francs to be made in 1913, the year the Blancs' concession expired. A further 5 million francs was to be paid by Blanc for harbor improvements, with an equal amount to go to local charities, 2 million francs for the construction of an opera house to adjoin the Casino, and 24,000 francs for each of twenty-four operatic performances a season. The Prince de Monaco would also receive an additional 1,000 shares of stock in the S.B.M., increasing his holdings to 1,400 shares, and 125 million francs plus 3 percent of the first 25 million francs staked on the gaming tables.

Plays and operas had been presented in a concert room at the Casino before the Salle Garnier had been completed, generally by traveling companies whose main function was to provide light entertainment, with short acts and long intervals to allow time for bets to be placed on the gaming tables. Comedy and vaudeville had been the mainstays of these programs. Alice set to work, with Albert's approval, to bring complete operas with the world's leading performers to the new Monte Carlo Opera House. With a generous contract and the title of Director of the Monte Carlo Opera, she secured the services of thirty-two-year-old Raoul Gunsbourg, an impresario who had been a member of her Paris salon (and possibly a former lover).

Born in Bucharest, the grandson of a rabbi and the son of an army administrator, Gunsbourg had spent much of his childhood in China, where his father was sent on a tour of duty. A remarkably gifted pianist, he had nonetheless wanted to become a doctor and obtained a baccalaureate at the age of fifteen. His studies in Bucharest were interrupted by the Russo-Turkish War, in which he served with the Russian Army as the *chef de musique militaire*. After the war he went to Paris to continue his medical studies, but suddenly decided he wanted to work in opera or the theater. To support himself he took a job as the theater critic and then editor of a weekly publication. He met Alice in the early 1880s and she encouraged him to try his hand as a concert manager and then as an impresario. She helped him finance the staging of a theater version of Jules Verne's *Around the World in Eighty Days* and operas by Saint-Saëns, Offenbach, Mozart, Meyerbeer, Verdi and Massenet in France and Russia.

Gunsbourg was a bullish, dynamic man with an explosive temper and a hearty laugh. From the moment he stepped off the train in Monte Carlo, he swung into immediate action. During its first season, 1892–1893, the new Monte Carlo Opera presented nine operas (with Nellie Melba as leading diva), six comedies (two starring Bernhardt) and four operettas. With the success of this premier season, Alice grew more ambitious and asked Gunsbourg to include works by new composers the following year.

Enter Isidoro de Lara, formerly Isidore Cohen. Born in London in 1859, he had been a piano prodigy before he turned to voice and, finally, composition, studying at the Milan Conservatory. When he returned to London, he wrote songs and became one of the favorites of the London social set. He sang his own works in a pleasant baritone, accompanying himself on the piano in the city's finest houses.

His first opera, *The Light of Asia* was performed in March 1893 at Covent Garden to encouraging reviews. Gunsbourg had received a manuscript of the score of de Lara's new opera, *Amy Robsart,* scheduled for spring 1894 at Covent Garden, and contracted to present it the following December. De Lara came down to Monte Carlo to discuss the production. Alice was not greatly taken by him when they first met, although she thought his music displayed an unusual talent. He had a curious appearance. Under five feet tall, he had a hunched back and arms and shoulders that were overdeveloped for his size. But he had a stunningly handsome face, huge burning dark eyes, a strong Roman nose, and robust, swarthy coloring. His success had given him an aura of great self-assurance, and he exuded a seductive charm.

The opera was only moderately well received in Monte Carlo, but Alice was drawn to the strange and romantic de Lara, and insisted that Gunsbourg sign him to a six-year contract that called for two new operas and allowed him to direct two other works of his choice each season. De Lara quickly became an integral part of Monte Carlo's cultural life, and he and Alice saw each other with growing frequency, meeting—when Albert was on a scientific expedition—as secretly as was possible for the Princesse de Monaco to manage in her own small Principality.

Raoul Gunsbourg appears to have been more distressed by the growing intensity of the relationship between Alice and de Lara than Albert was. Gunsbourg simply did not appreciate being commanded to engage a particular artist. On December 20, 1895, with de Lara's *The Light of Asia* scheduled for the following spring, he had two new stipulations added to his own contract, giving him complete authority in the hiring of all personnel and the absolute right to choose his artists and the works to be presented without the approval of either the Prince or the Princesse de Monaco. This still left him with the preexisting contract with de Lara.

With the Monte Carlo Opera and Alice's glittering sequence of seasonal charity galas, the town spun dizzily into its golden age. Rich American heiresses and needy titled foreigners increasingly used it as a mating ground. To an unwed heiress, a title was worth anywhere from $200,000 to $4 million. American sewing-machine millionaire Isaac Singer paid $2 million for each title for his daughter Winnaretta. She first became a duchess and then, when divorced and remarried a year later, the Princesse de Polignac; and her sister, Isobel, became the Duchesse de Decazes.

This barter in titles seemed no more moral than that of the great courtesans who demanded jewels, clothes and carriages for their favors, and perhaps it had even less to do with the honest emotions of love and sexual attraction. The American ladies, who were the buyers in this case, were quick to adapt to their newly purchased aristocratic station. Tea at the Hôtel de Paris was *de rigueur*. (A few years earlier a British guidebook had written that the hotel "cannot be recommended as a family hotel, since so many gamblers stay here. If the rooms must be visited, the ladies of the party should be left outside.") Literary, opera, and poetry societies, sports and garden clubs and numerous charity organizations were formed and were the foundation of the season's social and cultural activities.

Alice had hoped her friendship with the Prince of Wales might influence his mother to visit Monaco during her usual springtime stay on the Riviera. Queen Victoria was adamant in her refusal to do any such thing. Her son's gambling losses and those of the Russian aristocrats in Monte Carlo were well known to her, and she would have nothing to do with the place or the Prince and Princesse de Monaco. In 1899, when she was ensconced at the Hôtel Excelsior Regina in Cimiez near Nice, her entourage related stories to her about the local Russian pawnbroker who "lends money to the miserable [Russian] wretches on their way to Monte Carlo and they are generally unable to redeem their pledges, so he acquires splendid jewels for next to nothing and can afford to sell them cheap."

When the Prince of Wales's discreet suggestions to his mother that she would enjoy meeting the Princesse de Monaco had no effect, Alice wrote a letter to the Queen, asking if she and Albert could call on her. Such a request could not be overlooked, and Queen Victoria had them to tea at her hotel. Her reception was decidedly cool and the tea hour exceptionally brief. Alice did, however, meet the Princess of Wales with whom she hit it off extremely well, and her daughters, "seedily dressed and Maud [future Queen of Norway] with garish dyed yellow hair." But she was not unaware of Queen Victoria's disapproval, or the snub of her avoidance of Monaco. Albert had bought a new and large boat to use for his scientific expeditions, which he named *Princesse Alice*. He was beginning to distance himself from his wife, his Principality and his son, as he became even more deeply immersed in his research voyages, oceanographic societies and a new interest, paleontology. When not at sea, he would explore the caves near Menton, called *Rochers Rouques,* and in his diggings, he discovered bone fragments of the Cro-Magnon period. For a number of years, while he planned the building of a museum, they were housed, along with other prehistoric remains of fossilized animals and Roman findings, in the ancient dungeons beneath the Palace.

Louis had entered L'École Corneille in Paris in 1889, the year his father had ascended as Prince de Monaco. He had none of the intellectual leanings and curiosity of Albert and did poorly in most of his courses, with the exceptions of fencing and horseback riding. The idea of a military career excited him, and at Albert's suggestion, he applied for admission to the Swedish Army, knowing he would be well received and that it might do him good to travel abroad. But on May 6, 1890, he wrote his father:

". . . I must discuss with you a very serious and urgent subject. . . . It has to do with my entering the Swedish Army, and if you remember, I begged you not to say much about it to the Prince Royal [the future Gustavus V] the day of his visit [to Monaco]. It is a question which has been bothering me for two or three months, and I didn't want to talk about it without first having thoroughly considered all its forms and consequences. Also, dear father, I cannot decide to become an expatriate in such a distant country for two years, even a country with friendly ties with us, where I don't know the language and where I would feel totally homesick, lost and sad. I felt, even beforehand, that I have lived in France too long continuously, except for the two months of vacation, to go away now. I am attached to the country, and everything French. Most of my education was in France, and I want to stay here, especially since there is nothing about Sweden to make me want to go there. My desire and my dream is to enter the Ecole Militaire of St. Cyr, as a foreigner, if there is a way. I'm sure I would be happy, and I would be close to all who are dear to me. . . ."

With Albert's mounting dedication to science came a growing

pacifism. He was not keen that Louis should go into the military at all and had suggested Sweden's army because he believed it would not be an aggressive fighting force. But Louis was determined. "To serve France is my one goal," he wrote on May 11, "and I will stick to it." Albert gave way, and Louis entered the École Militaire. Once installed, he found the restrictions (placed by the school, not his father) stifling. Permission for everything required his father's authorization, even to see his mother.

". . . I have something to ask you," he wrote to his father the following February. "My mother is going to visit me in Paris as she does every year, from about April 11–May 19, and she said that she would like in the future to visit at least once a week, because during her [last] stay there was only one Sunday [when he was allowed guests]. I had gone to Monsieur du Charmier and had asked him to get permission from the Minister of War for a leave of eight days. That was last week. Yesterday, he told me he had spoken to the minister, but that he needed your authorization. . . . I ask you, therefore, dear father, to please send him a note as soon as possible so that he can take the necessary steps in accord with all the regulations. . . ."

For part of the year Louis's mother and her husband, the Count de Tolna, lived in Hungary at his family's 200,000-acre estate (many times the area of Monaco). In the middle of a vast park was an imposing baroque château, constructed in the form of a horseshoe, a wing of which contained a famous library of over 80,000 volumes. Louis was not much interested in the books to be found there, but he loved riding his stepfather's prize horses and he was close to his mother. After he had managed to gain permission to visit twice during a short period of time, Albert reproached him with: "How little you seem to like the military."

"Nobody could possibly hurt me more than by telling me that I don't like that which is the most wonderful in all the world, the career of a soldier. . . ." Louis snapped back.

He was promoted to the rank of sublieutenant a year later and was placed in the First Foreign Regiment. Detached to the 2nd Gunners of Africa in October 1893, he was sent to a primitive town in Algeria where he found a Moorish house consisting of five small rooms and a terrace upstairs, as well as a garden and stable. With him were his orderly and a maid to care for his needs. On November 18, 1893, he wrote Albert:

". . . The town . . . is dismal and sad, but I am still happy to be here. . . . I love my work . . . the Colonel made me very happy: he considers me like any other of his subordinates, and has given me a whole squadron of recruits to instruct. . . . My new men will arrive on the 25th, and I wait impatiently. . . ." Actually, one of the chief sources of Louis's newfound contentment was not his squadron but the very pretty dark-skinned maid.

Albert would never have a close relationship with his son. Louis's grandson, Baron Christian de Massey, claims in *Palace,* "Albert despised Louis. . . . He poured upon him all of the ill-feeling he had for Lady Douglas-Hamilton, whom he never forgave for the humiliation she had caused him by fleeing in the middle of the night, nor for his doubts about his son's origins [an allusion to the possibility that Louis could have been Count de Tolna's son. Mary Victoria was rumored to have been flirting with the Hungarian count in Baden when she and Albert were on their honeymoon.] The fact that Louis did not in the least resemble Albert had never helped." A Prussian quality dominated his appearance. Square-jawed and of stolid frame, he lacked his mother's graceful looks and Albert's striking figure. He had not left Baden until the age of twelve and spoke French with a German accent.

Albert found his son to be boring, lacking intelligence and rough in manner. Although he tried not to sit in judgment, Louis seldom pleased him. Albert's world was science and the ocean. Once married to Alice, he withdrew from the intellectual and artistic circles that she enjoyed. He attended the opera reluctantly and managed to be away on an expedition or at Marchais (where he did enjoy hunting) when a charity ball was scheduled. And Monte Carlo's economic success had caused him to lose touch with Europe's many political progressions and changes. He had only one friend among Europe's royalty— Kaiser William II, a young man of thirty-one, who had succeeded to the German throne.

Albert liked and admired the Kaiser. He was bold, curious, pious and according to Albert when he spoke of the sea, "would rise to the heights of moving eloquence." On the several occasions when his imperial yacht dropped anchor outside Monaco, Albert went aboard and the two men spent the day in talk of ships and seas and the ancient mariners who had navigated them.

The one political issue in which Albert became enmeshed was the case of the Jewish Captain Alfred Dreyfus, who was condemned in November 1894 by a French military tribunal on the charge of betraying military secrets to the Germans by way of a letter, meant, it seemed, for the Kaiser's eyes. France was vehemently divided in the matter of his guilt or innocence. The Catholic press engaged in a furious anti-Semitic campaign. "How," it asked, "could the Jew be innocent? How could the Army be wrong? How could the honor of the Army be impeached which alone stands between France and the German threat? Of what account is justice to the individual when measured against the safety of the State?" With only the evidence of a letter, which, it was later discovered, was not written by him at all, Dreyfus was convicted and sentenced to life imprisonment on Devil's Island in the Caribbean off French Guiana.

Two years later, it was found that Major Esterhazy, one of the chief witnesses against Dreyfus, was the author of the letter in question. Esterhazy fled to England, where he confessed to the crime, but the French Army still loudly proclaimed Dreyfus was guilty.

Alice joined the prominent intellectuals and leading Liberals and Socialists, including the future Premier Georges Clemenceau (then a political writer for *La Justice*) and the popular author Anatole France, in a struggle to reverse the Dreyfus verdict. Émile Zola wrote his stirring treatise *J'Accuse* and was forced to flee to England to avoid arrest. France was moving toward civil war over the case; and Albert, drawn into the *cause célèbre* by Alice, went to Berlin to discuss the affair with the Kaiser, on whose behalf Dreyfus had been alleged to be spying. The Kaiser admitted that Esterhazy, not Dreyfus, was the spy; and the men agreed that in view of the threat of civil war in France, Albert should make a secret mission to Paris to transmit that message to President Félix Faure, who was strongly against a new trial for the convicted man.

Albert set off at once, and he and Faure met in private on February 16, 1899, at 5:00 P.M. for twenty minutes. At 5:50

P.M., just half an hour after Albert's departure, Faure suffered a stroke. Ten minutes later he was dead. The affair, which discredited the monarchists and reactionaries, brought Émile François Loubet to the presidency and anticlerical, moderate leftists to power. Shortly thereafter, a new trial was ordered for Dreyfus, to Albert and Alice's delight. Albert, upon learning of the trial, wrote to Madame Dreyfus:

> You have defended the honor of your husband with admirable valiance, and impartial justice is getting ready to grant you a long overdue reparation.
>
> To help all honest people to make you forget so many pains and sufferings, I herewith invite you and your husband to come and visit me at the Château de Marchais as soon as the sacred work of justice has been accomplished.
>
> The presence of a martyr, toward whom the conscience of humanity turns with anxiety, will honor my house.
>
> Among the sympathies which are going toward you, Madame, there can be no more sincere nor more respectful ones than mine.
>
> Albert, Prince de Monaco.

The press got hold of the letter, and its publication caused a sensation in both France and Monaco, in the case of the latter, mostly because of Albert's lack of interest in his own Principality's affairs. Editorials in the French press stressed Princesse Alice's Jewish heritage in an insinuating and insulting manner. Count Boniface de Castellane, a reactionary French senator and the husband of American heiress Anna Gould (daughter of railroad magnate Jay Gould), made an anti-Semitic attack on Alice in a letter to Albert: "Perhaps, Monseigneur, you are a relative by alliance of Captain Dreyfus, but in that case it is premature for you to triumph. . . . You meddle into a matter that is none of your business, Your Most Serene Highness. If you think you can influence French officers in the grave decision they will take, I beg of you to remember that the game is not equal, for none of us would ask the permission of a prince in tutelage."

Madame Dreyfus did not accept Albert's invitation, for in the retrial the army refused to retract its position. Dreyfus was again, incomprehensibly, found guilty, but this time given the lesser sentence of ten years. The fight continued, and after serving six years Dreyfus was completely exonerated, all evidence branded as forgeries, and he was reinstated in the army with the rank of major.

By the turn of the century, Alice and Albert were having serious marital problems. He suspected her of infidelity but did not know that it was de Lara who was her lover. The composer even accompanied them to the Château de Marchais, Albert's great country home on the borders of Lorraine, keeping Alice company while her husband went shooting. "So long as the Princesse Alice ruled there, the food was excellent and there was beautiful music in the evening," Frank Harris wrote in his memoirs, "or a talk in a quiet room with a member of the Institute [of Oceanography] or the Academy. . . . One met at Marchais all the literary geniuses and the leaders of French thought. [Paul] Bourget and [Pierre] Loti, Saint Saëns and Sarah Bernhardt. In Marchais, more than any other French house, one touched life at many points."

De Lara had introduced two of his new works at the Monte Carlo Opera, *Moina* in 1897 and *Messaline* in 1899. His original six-year contract with Gunsbourg was terminated, but he remained in Monte Carlo and brought down his two brothers, who opened a hotel which became successful since Alice often lunched there. It has been reported (but never verified) that when Albert returned from a voyage in 1900 the words *Ici dort de Lara* ("Here sleeps de Lara") had been scrawled in chalk on a wall of the Palace.

The end of the Prince de Monaco's second marriage came in the spring of 1902, on the night of the premiere of Jules Massenet's opera *Le Jongleur de Notre-Dame.* As Alice, on the arm of her husband, started toward the steps leading to the Royal Box, de Lara approached. Alice turned toward him and the two had a whispered exchange.

To the shock of everyone watching, the Prince completely lost control of his emotions; and when Alice turned back to him, he slapped her across the face. Alice stood frozen for a moment and then preceded him up the staircase, her aristocratic head high, while Albert left the building. A few days later, she left the Palace, and in May 1902, when an official separation was obtained, she was living at Claridge's Hotel in London, and so was de Lara. Although Alice and Albert were legally separated, they were never divorced and she remained Princesse de Monaco until her death twenty-three years later. She became a close friend of Queen Alexandra after the Prince of Wales finally ascended the throne in 1910, and was hostess to one of the most glittering salons in London, visited by Edward Elgar, Rudyard Kipling and Winston Churchill. Resident in England during World War I, she was almost the sole support of the French Hospital there and turned the Château de Haut-Boussin into an army hospital. After the war, she was presented with the Medal of French Gratitude.

The lovers prevailed, occupying two large suites on the same floor at London's Claridge's Hotel, and although de Lara survived Alice by ten years, he never wrote another published piece of music.

The Grimaldis were a handsome family and their every move was covered by the press. (*Left*) Stephanie on water skis (GAMMA) and (*below*) Grace, on a garden tour of England, not long before her tragic death

Albert on the balcony of Rex Agel

Caroline looking bemused

The early years of Rainier and
Grace's marriage were clouded
with his problems with Aristotle
Onassis (*above with Maria
Callas*). Hulton-Deutsch Collection

(*Right*) To the world the wedding
of Grace Kelly to Rainier was a
fairy-tale ending; to the bridal
couple it was "a ghastly
experience." Popperfoto

(*Below*) On holiday in Switzerland
with Albert and Stephanie in 1968
Hulton-Deutsch Collection

(*Clockwise*) Grace and Rainier in her
parents' home when the engagement was
announced to the press; at the Waldorf
Astoria a few days later during a party in
their honor; moments later — a kiss that
was thought to be private; and Grace's
arrival in Monaco, her poodle Oliver in her
arms. Temple University Libraries Urban Archives

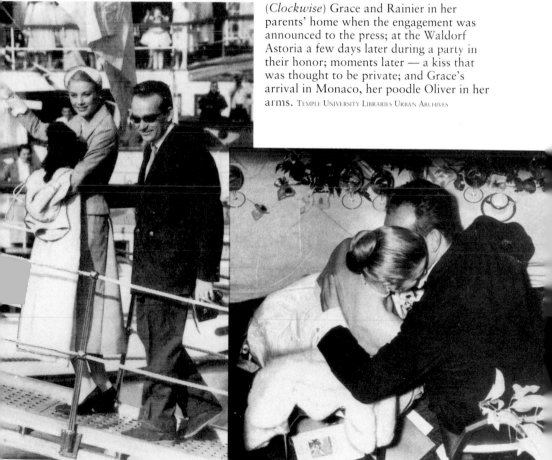

Grace Kelly giving her beloved
father, Jack, a hug when he
returned from a failed campaign
to become mayor of
Philadelphia

(*Above*) Jack Kelly was an Olympic sculling champion and he was determined
his children would be champion athletes as well. Grace desperately wanted to
please her father, but never seemed to do so. Ma Kelly can be seen in the
background wearing sunglasses.

(*Below*) The Kelly family at the New Jersey shore where they had a summer
home. *From left to right*: Lizanne, Grace, Kell, Jack and Peggy.

(*Clockwise*) Grace in the arms of William Holden, her on-screen and offscreen lover; with Clark Gable on location for *Mogambo* (she fell deeply in love with him but Gable put an end to the affair); as a successful model before she became a film star; and with Alfred Hitchcock, who directed her in *To Catch a Thief* (made in Monte Carlo) and whose love for her was unreciprocated.

French film star Gisèle Pascal was Rainier's mistress for six years. ROGER VIOLLET

During their liaison Rainier (*left and above*) served in the French Army during World War II and later bought a villa on the Riviera that he and Gisèle occupied and where he pursued his love of water sports and automobile racing.
PRIVATE COLLECTION

Rainier (*left*) was called "Fat Monaco" when he attended school in England. His older sister, Antoinette, later schemed to usurp his throne. POPPERFOTO

Louis II and his son-in-law, Rainier's father, Comte Pierre de Polignac, march together in the funeral procession for Albert I, but they hated each other and Louis soon banned Polignac from Monaco. ILLUSTRATED LONDON NEWS

Rainier's mother, Princesse Charlotte, on the battlements of the Palais Princier in Monaco with one of her many dogs. Louis adopted Charlotte, his illegitimate daughter, so that Monaco would have an heir and remain under the Grimaldis. She abdicated her rights in favor of Rainier, divorced her husband and lived at the Château de Marchais with one of France's most infamous jewel thieves.
POPPERFOTO

Prince Louis II, who
would have been happier
to remain in the army
than become Prince of
Monaco

Prince Albert with Kaiser Wilhelm II on the Kaiser's yacht
the day before Germany went to war in 1914

Prince Albert I with Buffalo Bill Cody (*right*), 1913, Cody, Wyoming. Cody acted as a guide on Albert's bear-hunting trek through the Wild West.

BUFFALO BILL HISTORICAL CENTER

Camp Monaco was set up for Albert's hunting party in rugged mountain terrain.

BUFFALO BILL HISTORICAL CENTER

Prince Albert in his officer's uniform
during his service with the Royal Spanish
Navy (1868). His first wife was an
Englishwoman. He divorced her and
married Alice Heine of New Orleans, the
widowed Duchesse de Richelieu, who
became the first American Princesse de
Monaco. She brought opera and ballet to
Monte Carlo. Her affair with a composer
caused a scandal. Albert struck her in
view of an audience at the Salle Garnier
(*upper right*). Roger Viollet

The Grimaldi
estate in Marchais
in France, where
Alice entertained
the leading artists
and intellectuals
of the time
Roger Viollet

In her days of glory, when she led the social gaieties of the Second Empire, the Empress Eugénie, consort of Napoleon III, in a Persian costume for a fancy-dress occasion ILLUSTRATED LONDON NEWS

The royal and imperial cortege in Paris, August 1855 — Prince Albert of England, Empress Eugénie of France, Queen Victoria and Napoleon III. The Grimaldis were closely aligned with the French Emperor and Empress.
HULTON-DEUTSCH COLLECTION

Françoise-Thérèse, sister-in-law of Honoré IV, was guillotined on July 26, 1794, the last victim of the Terror. She cut off a lock of her hair for her children before going to her death.

George III's brother, Edward, Duke of York, died in Monaco on his way to see his lover in Italy. He was given a proper funeral cortege (1767) by Honoré III, who was disappointed at the lack of appreciation shown him by the English king.

In 1733, Jacques de Matignon became Jacques I, Prince de Monaco, after the death of his wife, Louise-Hippolyte, ended her short one-year reign, despite her attempt to keep him off the throne. ROGER VIOLLET

ROGER VIOLLET

ROGER VIOLLET

La Ronde, Grimaldi-style. Both Antoine I's mother, Charlotte-Catherine (*upper right*), and his wife, Marie, had affairs with Louis XIV (*oval*) (MARY EVANS PICTURE LIBRARY) and were part of the Court at Versailles (*lower right*) (R.M.N.) during the latter part of the seventeenth century.

After her divorce from Junot (*above*)
(Hulton-Deutsch Collection) and her mother's
death, Caroline finds happiness with
Stefano Casiraghi. The royal wave
from the balcony of the Palace after
their wedding *(right)* Gamma

(*Left*) Casiraghi and Charlotte, the
granddaughter Grace did not live
to see Gamma

(*Right*) Caroline cut off her hair and
remained a recluse after the tragic
death of Casiraghi in a boating
accident. Sipa-Press

The Grimaldi men on the Palace
balcony — Prince Rainier III, Prince
Albert, and Princesse Caroline's two
sons — Pierre (*left*) and the elder,
Andrea   <small>GAMMA</small>

A rear view of
Monte Carlo, 1990

<small>LISETTE PRINCE</small>

INTO THE
TWENTIETH
CENTURY

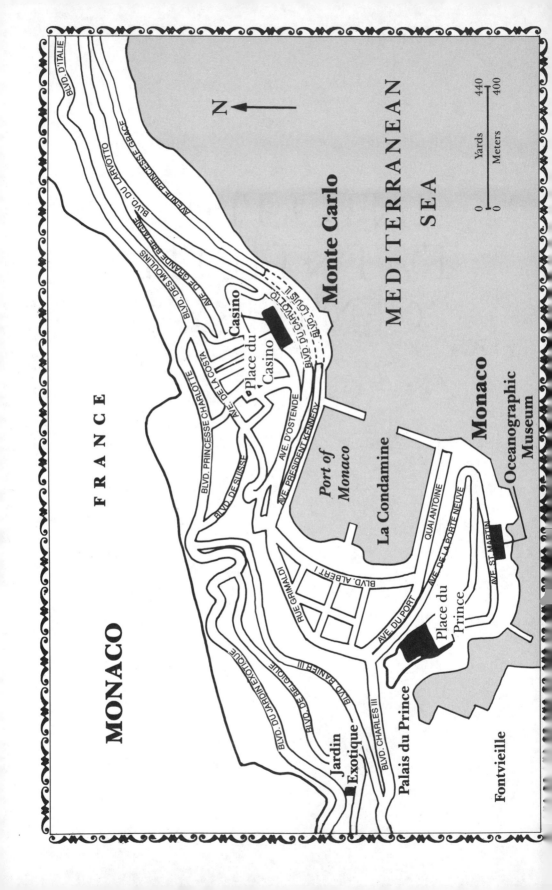

13

With Alice's departure, Monaco lost much of its luster, but Monte Carlo continued to prosper. Raoul Gunsbourg retained his hold on its cultural life (and would do so until his death) and people would soon forget that Alice had been responsible for bringing concerts, ballet and opera (as well as the greatest world artists) to the town. A concerted effort on the part of Albert to remove all evidence of the twelve years when she was officially acting as Princesse de Monaco was successful. No word of her or her whereabouts was published in the local press. Photographs and portraits were removed from display, and in the Royal Archives her papers and all photographs had been removed so that no history could record her activities or accomplishments. Almost any thing or place that had been called the Princesse Alice, including a variety of rose in the exotic gardens she had helped create, was renamed. Albert was bitter and relentlessly unforgiving.

Florestine had died in 1897 and the Palace, without any feminine hand at its helm, took on a strong, masculine aura. And with consequences far more damaging to its future, Albert was suddenly being seen as the absolute monarch that he was. Enriched beyond any of his ancestors' dreams by the flow of francs at the gaming tables and by a separation settlement with Alice in which *she* paid *him* five million francs, he gave munificently of his own money to scientific foundations in Paris and made some astute foreign investments, on the Continent and in the United States. He opened the Oceanography Museum in Monaco in 1910 at astronomical cost to the Principality's treasury. Four years later he established the Institute of Oceanography in Paris, giving it a large grant so that it would be independent of revenues from France. Then came the Institute of Human Palaeontology, which was also built in Paris. The *Princesse Alice* had been replaced in 1897 by the much larger *Princesse Alice II*, and then, after Alice's departure, by *L'Hirondelle II*, a larger vessel yet, with special equipment that reached depths of 35,000 feet and could raise up to eight tons. The acquisition of this last boat enabled Albert to extend his voyages to deeper waters. The majority of his time was spent at sea or in Paris, Marchais or at scientific conferences.

A murmur of discontent rose among the Monégasques. True, the citizens of Monaco did not pay taxes, but they had other serious financial concerns. The foreign population in 1910 numbered over 18,000 compared to fewer than 2,000 Monégasques. Outsiders were hired to work in the Casino (where 3,782 persons were employed), the hotels and the restaurants. Foreigners controlled most of the other commercial enterprises, the shipping and manufacturing interests, the banks and travel and insurance companies, and the many elegant stores like Cartier, the French jewelers, that had opened branches in Monte Carlo during the years of Alice's residence, and so constituted the richest segment of the population. Living costs were so high, and the salaries Monégasques could command—in what had become an international tourist center requiring specialists in most fields—so low, that many of them had been forced to sell their farms and vineyards at great loss as building sites for more commercial ventures controlled by the S.B.M. and lining the pockets of Albert, Camille Blanc and the other stockholders. (S.B.M. stock was now worth ten times its original value.)

The harbor had been enlarged so that great yachts could dock, but there were not sufficient educational facilities for Monégasque children, and the ill and elderly received very little civic care. Even worse, native-born citizens were not represented on the municipal council, which was dominated by resident foreign investors. While Albert gave money to his foundations and Camille Blanc lavished large amounts on tourist attractions like beauty contests, dog shows, automobile, boat and bicycle races, boxing matches, flower parades and even "the most beautiful parasol competition," the Monégasques were living threadbare lives despite their taxless income as they could find jobs only on the lowest scale, as domestic workers, hotel staff and laborers.

On April 4, 1910, about six hundred men mobilized and

marched up to the Palace, demanding to see Albert. When it appeared their protests against the foreign workers who had the majority of the better-paying jobs were to be tabled or dismissed, threats of a revolt were made.

Albert watched from a turret window as the angry mob of men descended the Rock shouting warnings. "What will this do to the coming season?" Camille Blanc cried. A rebellion had to be avoided even if violence was used to do so. French troops in Marseilles were put on alert, and three hundred British sailors on a flotilla anchored at Villefranche, about thirty-five miles away on the French Riviera, were given leave and dispatched to Monte Carlo after Albert appealed to the British Navy (to ensure the safety of British residents in Monaco). Wine cases were filled with guns and ammunition and stored in the Hôtel de Paris. If there was open hostility, orders were for the British sailors to arm and take up stations at strategic points.

No guns were fired, but the incident had sufficiently alarmed Albert to make him accede to at least one of the people's main demands—representation. With Albert's approval, on June 19, 1910, a municipal council of four Monégasque men was duly elected by the Monégasques. On October 16, after much pressure on their part, Albert, fearing a revolt might be imminent, extended his concessions to include the granting of a Constitution, which was drawn up in Paris by three French jurists and Louis, who represented his father. The four Monégasque council members joined Albert and Louis in Paris to give their views, and on January 5, 1911, a Constitution was approved. It established a public domain (ceded from Albert's holdings) and a municipal budget which included public health, educational and assistance services.

Louis accompanied his father back to Monaco, arriving by train on February 10. "The silence was broken only by the booming of the gun, firing its salute at regular intervals," the local government-controlled press reported on an unusually restrained note. "A car came along the two solid ranks of spectators. In it were the Prince and his son, and a couple of officials . . . cheering and clapping at last broke out . . . as the car passed by at a moderate speed. The Prince acknowledged [the spectators] with a motion of his head and his hand, very calmly and much at ease."

181

The Constitution, which still did not guarantee Monégasques against foreign domination in the work market, did not satisfy them. Agitators persisted but were kept under control. Albert was more concerned with Louis than with the state of unrest in his Principality. While in Paris on leave in 1897, Louis had declared his love to Marie Juliette Louvet, a hostess in a Montmartre nightclub. Marie had previously been married to a "girlie" photographer named Achille Delmaet, whose most famous pictures were of the outrageous cancan dancer of the Moulin Rouge, La Goulue, showing her nude. Louis and Marie had not met by accident. Her mother had been his laundress in Constantine, Algeria, and Madame Louvet had asked him as a favor to check on her daughter's well-being when he was in Paris.

Louis obliged, fell in love with Marie and brought her to Constantine with him. On September 30, 1898, their daughter, Charlotte, was born there. The girl was now twelve years old and in a boarding school in France, and Louis wanted to marry Marie and legitimize Charlotte. Albert would have nothing of it; he left Louis in Monaco and undertook his second journey to the United States, this time on *L'Hirondelle II*.

Hunting had always been one of his favorite forms of relaxation. Excellent shooting was to be had in the swamps of Marchais; wild geese, ducks and wild swans flocked there from the north in cold weather; and the woods were well stocked with pheasants, rabbits and hares. But Albert longed for bigger game, like bear and elk, of which he had heard much during his first trip to America.

Knowing that former President Theodore Roosevelt was a great huntsman, Albert, before he started on his journey, asked the American ambassador in Paris to write to Roosevelt on his behalf to inquire where he might find the best hunting.

"I would be very glad to see the Prince de Monaco about scientific work, but, I'm afraid there is small chance of his doing well with big game in the United States," Roosevelt replied. "For bears, he should go to Alaska."

Though disappointed, Albert did not give up on the idea and sent a letter, this time without an intermediary, to William Frederick Cody, the famous American plainsman, Indian scout, buffalo hunter and showman, better known as Buffalo Bill, who lived in Wyoming. He received an encouraging reply and an invitation to come to Cody, Wyoming, the town named for the western hero, which, as luck would have it, was not far from some oil fields owned by Albert and which he could visit at the same time.

L'Hirondelle II headed out to sea with Albert in command, first for a surveying cruise near the Azores, and then stopping by the Grand Banks of Newfoundland where, at the end of August 1913, he was the guest of Alexander Graham Bell, the American scientist and inventor of the telephone, at his estate, Beinn Bhreagh. It was here that a message from Cody reached him advising him that a hunting ground had been named Camp Monaco and tents and facilities were being installed. "I am praying for you to get a bear and elk," Cody added, signing the letter, "W. F. Cody. Shoot first and don't mis [sic]."

Albert's great steam-propelled vessel docked in New York on the night of September 9, 1913, a Tuesday. It was fifty years since he had last been in Manhattan, and during that time not only had the city skyline stretched upward amazingly but it blazed with electric light. News of Albert's impending trip to see Cody had reached New York, and the press were standing at the dockside to interview him when he came down the gangplank, this being the first visit by a reigning monarch to the United States. He confirmed that he was going to Wyoming that Saturday, adding, "I hope to have some shooting and possibly kill a grizzly or two."

The following day he went to a sporting goods store near Forty-second Street and outfitted himself for his adventure. As scheduled, he and his large, French-speaking entourage left New York by train on September 13, and arrived in the town of Cody two days later. Buffalo Bill, the mayor and assorted other western dignitaries greeted him, along with the artist A. A. Anderson. Buffalo Bill was to escort him into the mountains "with his old skill to the lair of the bear, and the haunts of the elk and deer."

Before that could happen though, Albert was obliged to be the guest of honor at a local fair where thirty Crow Indians performed their native dances. Then, in an impressive ceremony, Crow Chief Plenty Coos, in full Indian regalia, dismounted from his magnificent white steed and slowly walked

183

across an open field to where the Prince stood in wide-brimmed western hat and boots, his gift to the Chief, a rifle with both their names inscribed in silver on it, in his outstretched hands. Buffalo Bill formally introduced them and then stepped aside.

"It gives me great pleasure to meet one of the great Chiefs of one of the tribes who once controlled this great country," Albert said, in heavily accented English. "I wish to present you with this rifle, with which to kill game only—not to fire against the white man. . . ."

Camp Monaco was located in a thick forest of giant trees at the foot of the Shoshone River in rugged mountain terrain and could be reached only on horseback. Buffalo Bill had seen to it that everything was in order. One of the tents contained a kitchen and a dining hall. (This was run by a cook who became upset when Albert and his French entourage said, *"Merci! merci!"* He believed that they were crying "Mercy!" and had insulted his food.) Big game eluded the hunters in their first days of tracking, so they moved the camp to higher ground where Albert killed an enormous wapiti elk and two days later a bear, both of which he had taken down from the mountain and sent to a taxidermist so that he could transport the trophies back with him to Monaco.

Above all else, Albert thought of himself as a man of his times, forward thinking and a contributor to a new chapter in European history. There had been a great scientific revolution throughout the world. Not only was there now electricity to furnish light, heat and traction, there were new ways to communicate: the telegraph, the telephone, the cinema, inexpensive books and cheap newspapers made possible by advances in the mechanics of printing. Thinkers and writers were able to speak to wider audiences upon bolder themes.

As the twentieth century progressed into its second decade, Albert sincerely believed that there was reason to hope that Europe might expect a century of peace. The months that followed his return from the United States in October 1913 contained less stress than he had known for years, although he was concerned that Louis had not married and given Monaco a legitimate heir. There was about him an air of the aging science professor. His mind was taken up with papers, research and museums. He often digressed into long discourses on something he had just read in a scientific journal and which others did not understand. He remained on close terms with successive French presidents (Raymond Poincaré was presently in office) and with the Kaiser, believing in his ability to be a peace mediator between the two countries. In June 1914, he took *L'Hirondelle II* to Kiel Bay, an arm of the Baltic Sea in northwest Germany where the main German naval installations were based, to attend the yearly regatta as the Kaiser's guest.

The two men were on board the Kaiser's imperial yacht, the *Meteor,* "when they noticed a launch coming towards them. Standing up near the helmsman was Admiral Muller, waving a piece of paper. The launch came alongside, the Admiral put the paper into his cigarette-case and threw it up to the deck of the *Meteor*," a member of Albert's entourage reported. "When the Kaiser opened it he found a telegram inside announcing the assassination of the Archduke [Franz] Ferdinand [of Austria] at Sarajevo [Bosnia] on a visit to that country. The Kaiser went white, let the telegram flutter to the deck, and said, 'Now I must begin all over again!' [An allusion to an agreement he had made with the Archduke a few days earlier]."

The Archduke, heir to the Austrian throne, had been shot by Gavrilo Princip, a young Bosnian fanatic. His country, once part of Serbia, had been annexed by Austria-Hungary in 1908, an act that had given rise to great bitterness. The assassination was believed to have been perpetrated by a terrorist group working for the Serbian government. The Austrians demanded a full inquiry, which was not made. An ultimatum was sent to Serbia on July 23. For eleven days Europe and the world waited for Serbia's reply. When it did not come, the Kaiser stood behind Austria and declared war on Serbia. In an unprovoked violation of an innocent country, he also promptly invaded Belgium, threatening neighboring France once again with the Prussian presence and incensing other European countries.

Albert was on the high seas when the declaration of war was made, and he immediately returned to Monaco to allow his French crew to respond to the mobilization order.

DEAR FATHER [Louis wrote on August 10, from Biarritz]:
    At this hour when France is in a terrible crisis and everyone is trying to be useful or to prove his attachment to his country

185

or second country, I suppose that it would not be right for me, being a former St. Cyrian and a former trainee in two French Regiments, to remain inactive. I want, therefore, to assist in the operations which are unfolding toward the Rhine, either in the Regiment of General Joffre or as a Commander of the Corps d'Armée d'Avant Garde. I am certain that my new presence in the French colors will only tighten friendly links that unify our little Principality to France; I am writing to ask you to take the necessary step. Once my dear little girl is safe in Monaco, I can leave. I have not forgotten either that my father conducted himself valiantly in the same circumstances 44 years ago, and I hope to do as you did.

I embrace you with great affection.

Louis.

Albert sent him immediate leave to do as he wished; and on August 19, with war declared by Germany, and England and Russia allied with France, Louis was named Captain of Cavalry and attached to the Fifth Army Unit, commanded by General Louis Francet d'Esperey. Within a week he was sent to the Marne, where he was to take part in some of the bloodiest battles of the war. His daughter, Charlotte, now a young woman of sixteen, arrived in Monaco on September 1 and, without her grandfather's approval, moved into the Palace, whereupon, Albert, in an act of retaliation, took up residence on *L'Hirondelle II,* which was moored in the harbor during the length of the war for which he had declared the neutrality of the Principality.

In the first year of the war, Louis fought at Montmirail, Monceaux, Pontavert, Esternay and Berry-au-Bac. Then came Reims, where German troops, commanded by General Karl von Bülow, bombarded the city. Named liaison officer at the front lines, Louis also participated in the operations at Pompelle, Sillery, Béthany, Prunay, La Neivillette and Loivre and was given the War Cross with the Palm Branch for his courage in rescuing comrades while under fire. These were his finest hours; and for the first time in his life he received the approval of his father, who, shattered by the death and destruction of the war and disillusioned over his mistaken faith in the Kaiser, believed the Allies were engaged in "a final fight against oppression."

Nonetheless, Albert proceeded, almost as his first act after the declaration of war had been made and with much opposition from the municipal council, to rescind the Principality's Constitution, obviously to allow him to make what decisions he thought necessary, without referendum. Though ostensibly neutral, Monaco set up hospitals and convalescent homes for Allied soldiers. In the ancient way of the Grimaldis, Albert engaged in a cautious balancing act that would allow him to survive whichever side should be victorious. Although his sympathies were entirely with the Allied side, he never lost sight of his own best interests. Monaco and his subjects' welfare were not given much thought, except in connection with his holdings—property and financial—and his ability to maintain control over Monaco and his position as ruler of the Principality.

Petite, attractive, dark-haired and strong-willed, Louis's daughter, Charlotte, was an extraordinary young woman. She had been placed in an awkward position by her father. Cut off entirely from any maternal influences at Albert's insistence, she had known only the occasional kindness extended to her by sympathetic nuns at the French convent school where she had been sent at the age of five, and the affectionate visits from Louis, although these were infrequent, due to his army career. Taunted by other girls about her illegitimacy, she had hated the convent school and was often rebellious. Now here she was, only sixteen years of age, separated from the one person, her father, who had given her love, and living in a cold, vast medieval castle where most of the staff was over fifty, ignored by her grandfather, and merely tolerated by the rest of the Court.

In a sense, the horror of war was her salvation. The buildings in Monaco that had been converted to hospitals and convalescent centers were filled with injured and recuperating Allied soldiers and naval personnel. Charlotte spent much of her time as an aide, reading to them (seldom the Bible unless requested, for she had a penchant for Dumas and tales of adventure) and writing letters for those who could not. She was often witness to death and amputations as she comforted the wounded, but she enjoyed the company of the war-weary men, eager to see a pretty young girl. About thirty thousand men of the Allied forces passed through Monaco each year of the war.

Promoted to Squadron Leader on October 18, 1916, Louis remained at the French front where he had been stationed since

187

the outbreak of war. A year later he was sent to the small village of Liesse, near Reims and about a hundred miles north of Paris, which had just been recovered from the Germans. The Château de Marchais was close by, and it had been bombed and occupied for a time by German officers. After surveying the damage, Louis wrote to his father:

"A short note to tell you that I have arrived as one of the first in Marchais, while everyone was fighting in the streets of Liesse and Biencourt [a neighboring village]. The château is intact but empty and the look of the land is heart-rending. . . . Tomorrow more details. In haste, I embrace you affectionately, Louis."

"Sick at heart at what I find," he informed his father the following day. "The gardens are destroyed, the ground scorched. . . . What they did not pillage or care to take with them they burned; like for example all my memories of childhood piled up [formerly] in the closets—now burned in the fireplace . . . charred bits as evidence. . . . It must have formed an immense blaze. . . . You know how attached I am to this superb residence so full of childhood memories."

The Germans had not been entirely routed from the area around Marchais. Frequent attacks of harassing fire continued, and the roads were gashed and filled with muddy rivulets of gushing water from incessant torrential rains. Louis was moved farther up the front and was not to see Marchais again during the war. Allied losses were staggering, and the Germans proved a formidable fighting force, but the entry of America into the war on April 6, 1917, had given the Allies new hope and energy.

In Monaco, Allied flags were raised outside the windows of the Palace and there was great celebration throughout the Principality. The German population in Monaco had never been large and the Monégasques felt closely bound to the Allied countries of Italy and France. On November 17, 1917, after numerous articles appeared in the French press strongly reproaching Albert's action in rescinding the Constitution of Monaco, and perhaps in a display of confidence that the war would be won by the Allies, he reestablished it. Administrative and judiciary powers were separated, and it was agreed that only Monégasques could be elected to the general and municipal councils. It would take two more years before Albert would agree to a Finance Committee responsible for the preparation and approval of the budget, but his return to a constitutional monarchy was met joyously by his subjects and applauded by the foreign press.

Word of the Armistice reached Albert by telegram on November 11, 1918, at Marchais where he had gone to assess what damage had been done. The old hostility between father and son returned with the peace. Louis could have left the army, but for the time being he preferred to serve, a post as liaison officer having been offered to him in the Bureau of [French] Government Information at Metz.

Albert, who could no longer justify living on *L'Hirondelle II*, moved back into the Palace. A lonely man in his seventies, he believed that his son, now fifty, would most probably not have a male heir. This posed a most serious problem.

A new treaty between Monaco and France had been signed on July 17, 1918, replacing the 1861 Treaty. France guaranteed to protect the independence and sovereignty of Monaco, but it was agreed that the regency or succession could pass only to a Monégasque or a French subject, that the Principality could be ceded to no other country except France, and that should there be no heir or heiress and the line become extinct, Monaco would become a French Protectorate. At this time there was only one person in the line of succession—Louis. If he had no legitimate heir, the descendants of Albert's late sister, Florestine, Duchess of Urach, and her husband would be next in line. But because they were German, this would mean the end of the Grimaldi possession of Monaco, which would then become French.

Charlotte suddenly became Albert's hope for the future of his family. Her hospital work during the war had made her popular with the people, and despite his past fierce resistance to his son's pleas to legitimize Charlotte, Albert now saw the wisdom of doing so. The timing was more opportune, Charlotte's mother, Marie, having died. On April 18, 1919, Charlotte was legally recognized by Louis, the document signed and agreed to by Albert. To make sure that no one contested Louis's parenthood, Albert had his son legally adopt her since the French Treaty recognized an adopted child as a legitimate heir as long as the other requirements were met.

This done, Albert returned to Marchais to oversee its refurbishing, stopping en route in Paris. He had with him a list of eligible young Frenchmen who could be prospective husbands for Charlotte. The most promising name was that of the Comte de Polignac, who was from one of France's oldest aristocratic families. The Comte frequently came to Monte Carlo, usually as the houseguest of the rich and titled, and Charlotte had met him and found him attractive. Indeed, he was, which was why he was in high demand as an extra man, a necessity to any hostess who had an overabundance of single, divorced and widowed ladies as her friends. A "very delicate, very sensitive man," with clear blue eyes and a pencil-thin mustache, de Polignac possessed an Old World elegance, was fluent in several languages and had the kind of innate charm that was impossible to cultivate.

Following the peregrinations of society was de Polignac's career. He lived on a small inherited income that did not pay for much more than the fuel in his elegant automobile and the cigarettes in his silver and ebony holder. His actual living expenses appeared to be taken care of by loans from good friends and gifts from rich women. It was his uncle, the Prince de Polignac, who had been given $2 million as a dowry to marry the Singer Sewing Machine heiress twenty years earlier. But now in 1920, there was an overstock of impoverished aristocrats for an heiress to choose from.

De Polignac's personal history was of great importance, because the man who married Charlotte had to fulfill not only the definitions of the Treaty with France, but the conditions of Monaco's Bill of Accession, which stated that a female Grimaldi could inherit only if her husband was also a Grimaldi. This meant that de Polignac would have to legally change his name to Grimaldi. A deal was struck before Albert departed for Marchais, and a prenuptial agreement was drawn limiting de Polignac's power should Charlotte become the Princesse de Monaco and guaranteeing him a substantial personal income for life.

De Polignac became Prince Pierre Grimaldi, Comte de Polignac, on March 18, 1920. The following day he and Charlotte were married in a sumptuous ceremony at Marchais. Nine months later, on December 18, 1920, Charlotte gave birth in

190

Paris to a daughter, Antoinette. Albert could now relax, for even if Charlotte never bore a son, Monaco had an heir.

What was to be the culmination of Albert's life's work came in the spring of 1921 when he was invited to Washington, D.C., to receive the Alexander Agassiz and National Geographic medals from the National Academy of Sciences in recognition of his contributions to marine research. He crossed the Atlantic this time on the luxury liner *La France,* as the cost of coal was too high for the owner of a private vessel with no paying passengers. He stepped off the gangplank in New York on April 16. Attired in a natty tweed suit and a pearl-gray fedora hat, he posed for newsreel photographers, readily complying with their commands while chatting with the press.

His last research voyage had been one to determine the ocean's drift. The study proved invaluable. Because of it, mines could be more easily located and many lives, endangered by Germany's mining of the North Sea during the war, were saved. Albert's main concern, though, was the condition of marine life. "Now I shall take up a matter which is one of a really serious nature," he told the audience of his acceptance speech after a long preamble on the ocean's drift. "I mean fishing generally, the destructive effects of which are becoming greater and greater in the seas where more and more powerful and numerous implements such as steam trawlers are being used, grazing the very soil of continental plateaux, plucking off the sea-weeds and ruining the bottoms that are fittest for the breeding as well as the preservation of a great many species. So much so that in a few years' time they will be in danger of becoming extinct."

He returned to France at ease, satisfied with his achievements in science, proud that his peers had so honored him. Affairs in Monaco were in order, the Casino was doing exceptionally well, and he had made sure that, at least for one more generation, Monaco would remain in Grimaldi hands. ("My family was only interested in the money it could reap from Monaco," his future grandson would later write censoriously.)

Louis was a problem. He had been resentful of having to make Grimaldi-Polignac, a man he considered "effete" and "a society dandy," his heir. Louis had no interest in Monaco. His life remained the army, although he was now retired. He lived in Paris surrounded by memorabilia of his military career. He loathed and was jealous of his son-in-law, who, in turn, intensely disliked him.

But it was the future, not the harmony, of his family that concerned Albert. He was a scientist who saw things in pragmatic terms. He had never understood that both his wives had left him for other men because his passion, oceanography, had been his mistress throughout his life, which might have been difficult for them to accept. He was an intellectual, not a sensual man; and he seemed sincerely to care more for the creatures of the sea than for the human variety. This left him unaware of the chaotic state of Charlotte's marriage and of her growing dislike of the husband he had chosen for her.

14

W HEN THE DUST of World War I had settled, Central European nobility was almost nonexistent, and those who had survived were impoverished. The gaming tables of Monte Carlo were not affected by their demise. Monte's hotels in the 1920s were filled with North and South Americans rich from the war, the new machine age, the rise of the film industry and Prohibition. The *beau monde* was less solid, without historical references; film stars and their large entourages now occupied the royal suites, and Monte was crowded in summer, which had traditionally been considered off-season.

Princesse Alice, who was an ardent devotee of the ballet, had tried unsuccessfully during her years in Monaco to attract a major ballet company to Monte Carlo. But her dream had been realized in 1911 by Raoul Gunsbourg when Sergei Diaghilev and the Russian Ballet appeared in the Principality for the first time. That year, *Le Spectre de la Rose, Petrouchka* and *Shéhérazade* made their premieres in Monte Carlo, danced by a company that included Karsavina, Fokine and Nijinski. Performances were not given from 1914 to 1918, but with the war's end, Diaghilev had returned and at Gunsbourg's invitation had made Monte Carlo the home of his ballet company.

Princesse Alice had signed an agreement that she would never return to her former domain. Had she done so she would have found Monte Carlo even more crowded than when she left and noisier from the many shiny motor cars and their blaring horns. But the pastel nineteenth-century villas, rising tier after tier like an amphitheater above the harbor, the yachts of all sizes glittering in the sharp, bright sunlight, the formidable medieval Palace on its rugged yellow rock were the same and would have brought back the golden years of the turn of the century, which she had ushered in. The atmosphere of the place had retained

193

"an aura of Europe: 1900, the international Europe of *le grand luxe, les grands crus, le tout Paris,* and, quite often, *le bon goût.*"

Monte Carlo had survived the war, its green baize tables still supreme; and as the pea-sized ivory ball again spun dizzily around the red and black roulette wheel, the gamblers seemed more reckless. This was, after all, the start of what would be called the roaring twenties.

Albert was never able to take the research voyage to which he was so looking forward. He fell ill in the spring of 1922, and on June 10, he was operated on in Paris for intestinal trouble. The operation appeared to be successful, but he suffered a relapse two weeks later, and on June 26, while still in the private clinic, he died at the age of seventy-four.

He had wanted to be remembered first as an oceanographer, but his *New York Times* obituary called him a man "whose chief distinction it was to own the biggest, the best known, the most lucrative and the most splendiferous of gambling houses," and went on to say: "In these days of decadence and disaster for royal, princely and hereditary rulers, Prince Albert enjoyed an enviable lot. He was made secure in the possession of his eight-mile square domain by the assured protection of [France] . . . all the expenses of its upkeep were defrayed from the profits of the Monte Carlo Casino . . . and the ample income enabled the Prince to apply himself to scientific pursuits and he acquired considerable distinction along the lines toward which his researches were directed. He is said to have been one of the greatest of oceanographers and his knowledge of ocean drifts and currents was of much advantage to the Allied navies during the war in facilitating detection of German mines and guarding against submarine perils."

To the last, he and Louis did not get along. Certain that his son would not properly administer his beloved Oceanographic Institute, he left it to France with a substantial grant for its upkeep.

Louis was now Prince de Monaco. He showed little interest in his Principality, spending less than three months a year there. Charlotte remained the single most important person in his life. He insisted that she and her family live with him whether he was in Paris, Marchais or Monaco, and his loathing for his son-in-law intensified in such a familial atmosphere. Charlotte was

194

torn between two violently contrasting men and the stress began to show in her frequent emotional outbursts. Her second child, a son named Rainier-Louis-Henri-Maxence-Bertrand Grimaldi, was born on May 31, 1923, in the Palace de Princier, the first Grimaldi heir since Honoré IV, in 1758, to be a native Monégasque.

Rainier's sister, Antoinette, was only twenty-seven months older than her brother, a closeness that might have made them extremely good companions. However, Antoinette resented Rainier from the moment he was brought into the nursery and she had to share the attention of her beloved English nanny, Kathleen Wanstall. Nanny Wanstall was a cousin of Winston Churchill, a strong-minded woman who refused to learn French and whose royalist leanings encouraged her to favor the child who was heir to the throne. Both children spoke English before they learned French. Nanny Wanstall had small regard for their French tutor and ignored his pleas that his students practice their French when in her care.

At the age of five, Antoinette learned from Nanny Wanstall that her brother had supplanted her in the succession and that the Palace she visited every spring would one day belong to him. It is doubtful that she understood what becoming Prince de Monaco meant. However, she did perceive, and never forgot, that something that had once been hers had been taken away from her.

Once Grimaldi-Polignac had produced a male heir, there was no further necessity for his presence. Charlotte had been unhappy almost from the start of their marriage. She wanted her father's love and approval above all else, and she knew how much Louis disliked her husband.

"We'd only come to Monaco for about three months of the year," Rainier was to recall in an interview with biographer Jeffrey Robinson. "It was usually in the spring around Easter when the weather was good. I liked that because there was always a lot to do, the people were very welcoming. We wintered at Marchais. The Palace of Monaco was closed. My family, my grandfather's entire staff—the cooks, valets, footmen, maids, everybody—would go to Marchais for five or six months. Except the Government. They stayed in Monaco. I remember my grandfather installed a telegraph at Marchais so he could keep in touch with them. It was very exciting, something brand-new for us. I can still see a secretary tapping out messages all day long. There were also a couple of months every year when the family went shooting in Scotland. But I hated that. It never stopped raining. . . ."

Rainier was six and Antoinette eight years old in 1929 when, with their grandfather's encouragement, their parents separated and filed for a civil divorce in the French court. Ostensibly this legally ended the marriage, but an annulment was never secured from the Church. ("To make love," Charlotte said about de Polignac to a close friend, "he needs to put a crown on his head.") Once the divorce was final, Louis issued an order that his former son-in-law be prohibited from returning to Monaco and the Carabinieri were instructed to eject him bodily if he ever appeared. The children were then "shuffled around," and "never quite sure of their parents' love," according to Rainier.

"When we were with mother we were always being told, when you see your father don't say anything to him about me or your grandfather. When we were with father we were always being told, don't say anything to your mother or your grandfather about me. That wasn't easy. Like any child who is the product of divorced parents, I felt hurt by it."

Charlotte and Antoinette were never in harmony. Nothing the girl did pleased her mother, any more than Louis had satisfied his father. She was constantly putting Antoinette down; her French was impossible, her demeanor a disgrace, her looks a disaster—it would cost a fortune to buy her a husband. Antoinette "took out her childhood frustrations and isolation in her treatment of others," a family member said. "When tutors or governesses were appointed, she found fault with them. . . . She would eat enormous amounts of food for psychological reasons, bloat up, and then [eat] nothing with equal fanaticism."

Charlotte—whom the children called Mamou—was also a personality of extremes, loving one moment, distant and preoccupied the next. She had entered into an explosive affair with a mysterious Dr. Del Masso about whom little was known, almost as soon as de Polignac had left her home. When her lover told her he was leaving her for another woman, she took out a pistol she always kept by her bedside and shot at him, just missing him as he threw himself onto the floor. He crawled terrified from the room before she had a chance to aim a second time.

She had begun to collect small terrier dogs, who were allowed free run wherever they were. Eventually there were seven of them who followed her in a barking clatter and would bite the ankles of the servants and the children if they came too near.

Louis seemed as unaware of what was happening in his Principality as he was of the affairs of his family. He lived in the memories of his army years in North Africa and at the front, and was bitter that in order to take up his role as Prince de Monaco he had been obliged to forfeit his military career. Whenever he dined at the Hôtel de Paris he requested the orchestra play "The March of the Foreign Legion," and he looked forward with great joy to the Foreign Legion parade on feast days. He had been given the honorary title of Major-General, and in 1929 was awarded the Médaille Militaire, the highest French distinction for staff officers. Behind his desk in all of his residences was a full-length portrait of himself in complete, bemedaled regalia. There is little doubt that his crowning moment had not been his accession as Prince de Monaco, but his return to North Africa to preside with his former commanding officer, Marshal Francet d'Esperey, and the Governor-General of Algeria at the Centenary Celebrations of the Foreign Legion, which were held at Sidi-bel-Abbés.

With 1930 came the Depression, which was not as keenly felt in Monaco as in the United States and Great Britain. The gaming tables at Monte Carlo were crowded with men and women who were desperate for the big win that would save them from bankruptcy at home. The atmosphere of the Casino was tense, but the money that was lost at the tables by hopeful gamblers kept the Casino, Monaco and the Grimaldis financially secure.

In 1918, after the long, difficult hiatus of the First World War, Camille Blanc had asked Albert to accept a reduction in his annual payment from the Casino. Albert had refused; and Blanc, aging and ill, sold his vast holdings to the septuagenarian Sir Basil Zaharoff, a man with a mysterious past. Apparently very rich, he had lived in Monte Carlo for many years. No one knew where he had been born or when. His early formative years had been spent in Britain, but he was as much at home in France, Austria, Russia and Greece, all of whose languages he spoke like a native.

Zaharoff's considerable fortune had been made in the sale of arms. Queen Victoria had knighted him for his help in supplying guns in the Boer War. He had proved equally adroit in assisting the Allies in World War I. He understood the true aims of German militarism and throughout the conflict kept the Allies accurately informed of what he suspected the Germans were planning, gleaned from his contacts in the arms industry in Germany.

Upon acquiring control of the Casino, Zaharoff (who claimed never to set foot inside its doors) immediately had the minimum stake doubled on all bets and appointed his own managing directors. Even though profits rose dramatically, Louis loathed and distrusted Zaharoff. Whether Zaharoff's original takeover of the Casino had been an old man's whim or a desire for greater influence in Monaco, he soon lost his enthusiasm for the project when the married woman he had loved for thirty-seven years was finally widowed and they were wed. Within a year she became terminally ill and her elderly bridegroom refused to leave her side. His interest was sold in 1924 to a group of Paris bankers.

In 1933 the French government voted to allow roulette to be played in French casinos. Italy approved a similar act. Casinos began to flourish in Nice, San Remo and the Venice Lido. Monte Carlo had lost its monopoly. For a time it looked as if the Grimaldis and Monaco might slide back into their mid-nineteenth-century penury.

The S.B.M., since it controlled the Casino, prime property and much of the income of the Prince de Monaco and his family, held tremendous power. Now, in a bid to appeal to the new, short-term tourist and to increase its revenues, the S.B.M. (which was a private company in which the Prince de Monaco held title to fourteen percent of the shares) set up souvenir shops. When Monaco's postage stamps became sought after, Louis authorized a department to issue them. New, colorful, finely etched stamps were printed at an alarming rate, and sold just as fast, to become a reliable and handsome additional source of income. An automobile Grand Prix (known as "the race of a thousand turns") was founded to encourage tourism. Twenty of the world's best drivers competed in a race of one hundred circuits that twisted and curved over and around Monte Carlo's roller-coaster terrain. The number of spectators, which reached tens of thousands, startled even the organizers.

The boost to the economy of Monaco and to his own finances could not cure Louis's many other problems, not the least of them the rising unrest among native Monégasques who had found themselves, in the spring of 1930, suddenly replaced on the National Council by the Paris bankers who controlled the Casino—in direct contradiction to former agreements. A revolutionary group of Monégasques threatened to throw Louis off the throne—by force, if necessary. They held a meeting in July, at the Hôtel Negresco in Nice, fearing arrest if they gathered in the Principality. To their overwhelming surprise, Charlotte—sent by her father—appeared and made such an impassioned appeal for them to remain loyal to Louis that they agreed to wait for a sign of the new reforms she promised. These proved to be false hopes, and Charlotte herself was deceived by her father, for in December 1930, Louis, ignoring the Constitution, dissolved the National Council and ruled by decree.

When he was advised that a delegation of Monégasques was at the Palace to ask him to reinstate the National Council, the French press (who were considerably disturbed at the situation in Monaco) reported that he said, "Give them live bullets instead of a constitution." Whether or not there is any more truth in this than in Marie Antoinettes's fabled retort when told the citizens of Paris were starving, "Let them eat cake," Louis's concern for his subjects was no greater than the French Queen's had been for hers.

Under pressure from the Paris bankers, who feared violence on the part of the dissatisfied revolutionaries, in November 1931 Louis established a Monégasque Assembly, but he handpicked each member from those subjects he knew to be loyal to him. Despite these men being chosen for their royalist attitude, they refused to support his 1933 budget, which gave his personal expenses—the upkeep of his homes and the luxurious life-style of himself and his family—precedence over public needs for housing, education, health and utilities. As if this were not

199

enough for their resentful, self-centered monarch, in January of the same year Charlotte wrote to him that she wished to renounce her right to the throne, "at the risk of being a disappointment to your hopes and aspirations." She stated: "I believe I have accomplished my duty which condemned me to remain in a marriage against my wishes, in the name of political interests in which I fear I do not have the force to assume my responsibilities."

A regency council was established to rule in Rainier's name if Louis should die before the boy reached the age of twenty-one, at which time Charlotte, should she still desire to abdicate her rights, would be granted her request. Rainier was ten years old when these events took place and had been entirely taught by tutors. The authority to decide his son's education had been one right de Polignac (the name of Grimaldi now discarded), had received in the divorce. Louis wanted his grandson to attend a French school; Polignac insisted upon a private English prep school named Summer Fields, in Oxford, which was known as "the nursery for Eton." De Polignac won this round in his fight to control his son and to distance him from Charlotte and Louis.

Nothing in his previous life had prepared Rainier for Summer Fields. Chubby, spoilt, unhappy and terrified to be so far away from anything familiar, he arrived wearing the short trousers that were demanded and was quickly named "Fat Little Monaco" by the other boys. The climate and accommodations left something to be desired. Summer Fields had lost half its students because of the Depression, and sometimes two classes were held simultaneously in the same room to save electricity and heating costs.

"The icy damp of the North Oxford winter gripped us for weeks on end," Cecil Day Lewis, the well-known author who was then Rainier's English master, wrote in his autobiography, *The Buried Day*. Drafts swept the corridors. Rainier and the other boys in his room were awakened by a bell at daybreak and showered in freezing water. Summer Fields, according to Day Lewis, was "a world of bells and tattered books and football boots and crazes [crosswords, the banjo and the ukulele at this time] and blackboards and piercing screams; of ink smells, chalk-duster smells, smells of mud and mown grass and the mousey smell of little boys; of draughts, radiators, chilblains, stringy meat and steamed puddings; of catchwords endlessly repeated . . . a world of rewards and punishments, reach-me-down justice and covert partiality, of sadly unoriginal sin; a world where, under controlled conditions, the workings of the herd instinct may be observed in all their pristine innocence and mindless brutality. . . ."

The headmaster, Cyril Williams, was a stern man who ruled by fear. One of the Summer Fields boys recalled that Williams was "determined to stamp out talking after lights out. After a week or so, he announced that it would be a beating offence. Shortly afterwards, the penalty was raised to TWO [canings], then to THREE; finally . . . it was raised to SEVEN. There was an impasse which was further complicated by an incident when through a misunderstanding he flogged several boys for something of which they were not guilty. The school vibrated with protest. . . ."

Privacy was unknown. There were no doors even on the toilets, which were outside in a structure called the Vinery, so named because it had once been a grape-growing conservatory. "It consisted of a number of cubicles, each housing a rudimentary water system," a former Summer Fields boy recalled. "A stream of water would sweep down the channel under the compartments, carrying all before it at certain intervals." Like many other new boys, Rainier was disconsolate; his "morale in his boots," he would have difficulty fighting back his tears.

Even the days set apart for special occasions were not easy. Hay Rag Day was one such annual event. Boys and masters trooped down to a mowed hayfield and scrapped indiscriminately as old scores were paid off and masters were hectored. "It was the one time they could be hit or slapped or rolled in the hay with impunity," recalled a participant. Rainier was good at such contests and was on the boxing team, winning the school title for his weight. "Other than that, I hated it. . . . It was a horrible place," he later complained.

He made few friendships and never got over the bleak, oppressive horror of homesickness. Unlike the other boys, he had no parental visits. He returned after school holidays in 1935, much against his will, but at the end of that term refused—

201

threatening to run away—to go back. He was sent instead to another English school, Stowe, in Buckinghamshire, near Oxford.

On first glance, the place looked far more promising than Summer Fields. The main building, which was extraordinarily lovely with its Doric columns and wide pavilions, had been built in 1680 by Sir Richard Temple. Queen Victoria and the Prince Consort visited Stowe in 1845, which then was owned by the second Duke of Buckingham. His descendants maintained the estate until July 1921 when it was bought and converted from Stowe House to Stowe School. Rainier arrived with his father, not knowing any of the housemasters or the students. Fagging—doing menial chores for older pupils—was to be his first hard lesson and he was to learn the true meaning of being a "Stoic" (which was what the boys were called). Although he spoke perfect English, he was the only foreign boy among the five hundred Stoics, and certainly the only student also to be a hereditary prince. The other boys taunted him, and after three days he ran away, almost causing an international incident when his flight made the headlines of the newspapers in England and France.

"It turned out to be much easier than I thought it would be," he said. "I left the grounds and headed for the railway station. My plan was to buy myself a ticket to London and then make my way home from there."

The police had been notified by the school authorities as soon as he was missed and the stationmaster, seeing a young boy with a Stowe cap on his head waiting to board the London train, rang the school. "The headmaster, an ex-military man, came to fetch me in his enormous car. I thought I was in for trouble and would be severely caned," Rainier continued. "But he took me back to his study and welcomed me home with a gigantic high tea. He didn't reprimand me at all. He said, 'You must be hungry so here's something to eat.' It was the first meal I'd had all day. I thought to myself, finally someone understands. But then I was put in the school infirmary because they couldn't figure out why any child wanted to run away from this heaven."

While Rainier was at Stowe, de Polignac, in Paris, had custody for the summer of the rebellious, fifteen-year-old Antoinette. They had a violent quarrel. Antoinette telephoned Nanny Wanstall, claiming her father had abused her (it was not clear if she meant sexually); and the Englishwoman contacted Louis, who was also in Paris. Louis ordered Nanny to go to de Polignac's apartment and get Antoinette out under any pretext she could think of and bring her to him. She managed to do this, and Louis sent Antoinette to Monaco, out of her father's jurisdiction. De Polignac accused him of kidnapping her. "Under the statutes of the royal family of Monaco," Louis responded, "I have full authority over all its members." Antoinette's removal was thus an act of sovereignty, not a kidnapping, he claimed. He then canceled de Polignac's rights to see his daughter.

The girl's father sued in France for her return to his custody, but lost the case. A week later, in August 1935, Louis filed a petition in London for Rainier's custody, requesting a restraining order to stop de Polignac from taking his son out of England. The British High Court was faced with the difficult decision of possibly having to make a hereditary prince of another country a ward of their courts with his welfare their responsibility. The case was not decided until March 1936, at which time the judge ruled in favor of Louis. Rainier, after a year of insecurity, unhappiness and notoriety, joined his grandfather and Antoinette in Monaco for Easter and then was sent to Le Rosey (called "the school of kings" because so many future monarchs had attended it) in Switzerland. It resembled a luxury hotel more than a school. There was no school uniform but the dress code called for shirts tucked neatly inside trousers and the boys were expected to wear a coat and tie every night for dinner.

French was the official language of the school. However, English was spoken by the students, who came from all over the world, when they gathered socially. There was hot water for showers, doors for privacy, the food was good, rooms were shared with only one or two other boys, and there was a girls' school nearby and dances were held in the autumn.

For the first time in his short life, Rainier was happy. Le Rosey was run on a democratic, laissez-faire basis. Boys could choose what subjects they wanted to take as long as their educational requirements were covered. There were not the restrictions of Stowe, and although privileges could be revoked, no corporal punishment could be administered. Also, since it was an international school with students of many nationalities, there was much tolerance for a boy's background, no matter how exotic it might be. Rainier displayed a keen interest in the arts and joined the dramatic club, seeming to enjoy "gussying up," as he called applying makeup and dressing in costume, to appear in several of the school productions. In the winter Le Rosey moved from its main location just outside Rolle on Lac Leman to the ski resort of Gstaad so the boys could engage in winter sports while living in charming chalets that dotted the snow-covered mountainside. Despite this new, happier existence, the scars of Rainier's difficult childhood would have a lasting effect.

While Rainier was safely buffeted in the Swiss Alps and his grandfather was engaged in reclaiming sufficient land from the sea at the foot of the Rock to moor a vast sports stadium to attract yet ever more tourists, Europe was edging once again toward war. In Germany, Adolf Hitler and the Nazi party were a threatening presence that made the small countries that bordered it tremble for their lives. The new republican government of Spain was treading uneasily on shaky ground. A coup d'état had recalled King George of Greece to his throne after he had been overthrown by monarchical adversaries, but it did not look as if he had the power to remain there. Refugees were in flight everywhere: Jews from Nazi Germany, Russians from the rigor of Communist rule. Few felt that peace could be preserved.

Louis was not blind to the tempest raging about him. As Germany rearmed, the Principality quaked, together with other small nations. To maintain the continuing protection of France, Louis allowed the French to build defense installations along the coast, making it clear, however, that Monaco would remain neutral should war ensue.

Rainier graduated from Le Rosey in the summer of 1939, and arrived at Montpellier University at the end of August to begin his university studies. The medical section of the school, with its white stone buildings gleaming in the strong Mediterranean sun, dated proudly from the twelfth century when Rabelais was a student. The city of Montpellier was on a rise above the sea, the craggy peaks of the Cévennes to the north. Lush vineyards edged the city's borders. Before Louis XIII had taken the town for France in the seventeenth century, it had been the capital of the medieval kingdom of Languedoc-Roussillon. These roots remained and Montpellier was bilingual, having retained much of the Catalan language and culture.

Along with the great neoclassical waterworks, aqueduct and Arc de Triomphe built by Louis XIV in the early part of the eighteenth century, opulent mansions and elegant shops gave the city, which could also boast a superb opera house and trea-sure-filled museums, an aristocratic air. With the university and the famous medical school located there, a large, young, exu-berant population frequented the cafés that spilled out onto the pavements of its streets. Despite its more recent history as a winter retreat for sufferers from tuberculosis, Montpellier was a city of great *joie de vivre* and it would seem that Rainier had found a perfect successor to Le Rosey.

He enrolled in a general course of education with an em-phasis on French history. Unlike Albert and his dedication to oceanography, or Louis, who was a military man, Rainier had no marked leanings in any field. He enjoyed tennis and golf and loved animals. Although fellow students thought he was shy, he was simply a private person, somewhat withdrawn. He was conscious of his pudgy build and embarrassed easily. Yet, all in all, he had progressed far in his ability to make friends and was expecting a happy time at the university.

Then, on September 1, 1939, without a declaration of war, Germany invaded Poland. Two days later, Great Britain and France declared war on Germany. The ground shifted under Rainier. A week of confusion followed until Louis decided that his sixteen-year-old grandson should remain in France, a vote of confidence, it seemed, in that nation's invincibility.

15

GERMANY PROCEEDED to unveil modern war to an appalled world. World War II, as it was called almost from the first, absorbed every other topic of conversation in the cafés of Montpellier. Nine months after the war's start, a sense of shock prevailed at the sheer, technical brilliance of German arms and outrage over Hitler's invasion of peaceful Denmark and Norway on April 9, 1940. Denmark offered no resistance and Norway was conquered by June 9.

Hope had turned to France, which the Allies believed was strong enough to stand up to Germany's dazzling blitzkrieg tactics. Three million French soldiers stood ready along the Maginot Line, commonly thought to be "the most spectacular piece of military engineering of an age both military and engineering."

But on May 13 German forces had outflanked the Maginot Line after they had overrun Luxembourg and invaded the Netherlands and Belgium. Their armored columns rolled on to the English Channel, cutting off Flanders. Allied forces were evacuated from Dunkirk, and in the first weeks of June the Germans marched on France. The battle was pitifully short. On June 22, France signed an armistice with Germany and a few days later with Italy, which had entered the war on the side of the Germans on June 10. A section of France became occupied territory; the remainder (in the southwest, including Montpellier) was under the new collaborationist Vichy government, headed by Marshal Henri Pétain. Under the inspiring leadership of Winston Churchill, Britain, the only remaining Allied power, resisted the German attempt to bomb it into submission.

Monaco had remained officially neutral. However, when France fell, the Italians occupied the Principality on the premise that the defense installations along the coast meant it was allied with France. The Italian population of Monaco, having increased steadily since 1900, when they were first brought in to staff the expanding needs of the Casino, the hotels and various other enterprises, outnumbered all other nationalities by a generous margin.[1] When, on July 4, 1940, Mussolini's Blackshirts marched into Monaco for the first time to place the Principality under Italian control, they were greeted by cheering rows of their expatriate countrymen who lined the streets. A considerable number of the Italian colony collaborated with the occupying power, creating an atmosphere of bitterness and fear among Monégasques and foreign residents loyal to France and England, although most of the English and American residents had returned home as soon as war had been declared. A Fascist political bureau was set up with assistance from the Italian secret police to ferret out Monégasques and French who might be working for the Resistance or were known for their anti-Fascist sympathies. There were arrests but the Resistance continued its work, managing to hide the Jewish population until they could get them out of the area of occupation by leading them over the mountains into Switzerland.

Louis's loyalties were undeniably pro-French. He had watched with "anguished horror" as the beloved army of his youth crumbled so swiftly beneath the German Army. With France and Monaco's occupation he was torn as to what position he should take. Throughout their history the Grimaldis had survived the many wars fought on their borders and the periods of foreign occupation by carefully balancing their allegiances. Louis was not a particularly smart or clever man, but he did know that if Germany and Italy won the war, Monaco would fall to Italy, a country that he did not hold in high esteem. He allied himself with the Vichy government, a German tool in the hands of French collaborationists, and thus placed himself at cross-purposes with the Allies, which, since the bombing of Pearl Harbor on December 7, 1941, had included the United States. His thinking appears to have been that if the Germans won, Monaco might have some leverage against being taken over by the Italians. Constantly at Louis's side during this difficult

---

[1] The population in Monaco in 1939 was: 9,724 Italians, 8,540 French, 1,804 English and 1,761 Monégasques. Another 1,325 residents were of numerous other nationalities.

period was his Minister of State, Émile Roblôt, who was affiliated with the pro-Fascist elements in Vichy. Both French and Monégasque segments of the population petitioned for Louis to dismiss Roblôt, but he was adamant that his minister remain.

A coup to remove Louis from the throne was discovered and the Italian pro-Mussolini organizers were arrested before any damage was done. Louis released the guilty men after receiving Mussolini's personal assurances that he would remain as Prince de Monaco and that no one in his Principality, including resident Jews, would be forcibly removed. This last was not true, for Raoul Gunsbourg was compelled to resign his post at the Opéra and go into hiding when he was warned by a member of the Resistance that he was to be arrested and "transferred for trial" as a spy. Gunsbourg was not involved in anything of that nature and managed to escape to a friend's house nearby the morning of his planned arrest. With the help of the Resistance he finally made his way to Switzerland. Louis had always respected Gunsbourg and appreciated the cultural atmosphere he had brought to Monaco. But he had not attempted to help Gunsbourg in his plight. Louis was now a puppet prince whose strings could be yanked anytime Mussolini or Hitler wished to do so.

Rainier remained in Montpellier. The brief exhilaration he had felt at the start of his university life had been replaced by a sense of constant anxiety. The coastline was rimmed with armed defenses; barbed wire stretched along the beaches, and a blackout and a curfew were rigidly kept. Every day there were stories of the deaths and arrests of students. A professor would suddenly disappear, and there would be whispers that he had been a Jew or connected with the Resistance. Rainier lived in a twilight state in which his mind and heart were caught up in the war, and he went through his daily life by rote. Always there was fear for his family and for his own safety should anything happen to his grandfather, who, he had recently learned, had fallen in love at the age of sixty-nine with Ghislaine Dommanget (also known as Ghislaine Brullé), an actress thirty-five years younger than he. Ghislaine had moved into the Palace, to Mamou's disgust, Antoinette's fury and Nanny Wanstall's loathing.

As Rainier had matured, so had his differences with Louis. He felt his mother, who had become more and more eccentric, and his grandfather had conspired to rob him of his father's presence. Forbidden contact with de Polignac, Rainier had secretly corresponded with him and found him to be a far more compassionate man than the picture given by Mamou and his grandfather. But as the war progressed, he was not sure where de Polignac was, or if he was safe, for he could no longer be reached at his Paris address. He was, in fact, in the country, and was said to have been helping the Free French, a story which later proved to be true.

Antoinette was in Monaco, engaged in war work: rolling bandages, visiting the injured Italian and German soldiers who had been sent to Monaco's hospital for medical help. Her letters served only to irritate Rainier. They did not get on much better than they had as children, and she had inherited their mother's mercurial nature. (Her son would later say that she shifted "radically from pro-German to pro-American to pro-British sentiments with little pause between.") She fought constantly with Mamou and clung to Nanny Wanstall, who now ran the domestic life of the Palace for Louis with an iron hand.

Rainier went home for Easter, 1942. Traveling was a hardship. Trains did not run on schedule, and they were packed with German soldiers who demanded to see identity cards at every stop. Monaco was dismal. Mussolini's Blackshirts were everywhere. Shop windows displayed very little merchandise. The yachts were gone from the harbors. Food was rationed and many restaurants and hotels had closed. Streets were dark at night. Nonetheless, the Casino remained open; and during the month Rainier was home, Edith Piaf, Max Régnier and Maurice Chevalier gave concert performances in the Salle Garnier, and Claude Dauphin and the gamine actress Gisèle Pascal appeared in the comedy *Vive le Théâtre*, which Rainier attended.

Until this time, Rainier had not had a serious relationship with a woman. He was, after all, not quite nineteen. But from the moment he met Gisèle after the performance, he knew he was in love. She had dancing blue eyes, a bewitching smile, golden hair and a funny little catch in her voice that turned her laughter into music. She was a divorcée, born in Cannes (Gisèle Tallone was her real name) to a French mother and an Italian father. A few years older than Rainier (although she claimed to be younger), she had just played her first starring film role, in *L'Arlésienne,* and did not take his attentions seriously. She gave him her address in Paris, and once he had returned to Montpellier he began a correspondence with her. He received his B.A. in June 1943, and then headed straight for Paris for additional studies at the École Libre des Sciences Politiques and to look her up. She was now quite favorably inclined toward his attentions, the war having temporarily put an end to her brief film career.

In the summer of 1943, the Allies followed up their victory in Tunisia with the conquest of Sicily and the invasion of Italy, which surrendered on September 8. However, the German Army in Italy fought bloody rearguard actions and now occupied the Principality, the Nazi High Command using the Hôtel de Paris as its headquarters. There is a story (claimed to be true) that the hotel management, upon learning of the Germans' approach, gathered all its vintage wines and sealed them inside walls and the Nazis never found out they were there.

Louis might have thought of himself as a military man, but he did nothing during either the Italian or the Nazi occupation that would reveal an astute military mind. Monaco's ruling family saved its skin and its fortune by collaboration. Over three hundred Monégasque holding companies were created. They had to have the Prince de Monaco's approval, and through them Göring, Himmler and many other top Nazis and French collaborationists laundered money.

The Germans decided to turn Monaco into a furlough base, a scheme that neither Louis nor the S.B.M. opposed. Money began to stream into the Casino and the S.B.M. as German soldiers squandered their paychecks, not knowing if they would live to receive many more. Antoinette took a more active role as the war dragged on. She formed the Committee for the Assistance to Prisoners of War (Allied and Axis) and dragged food and blankets from the Palace to give to the people gathered in shelters during air attacks. Monaco had several Allied air assaults, but there were no direct hits on major buildings. Rome fell to the Allies on June 4, 1944, and the last attack on the Principality was on August 2, 1944, when Allied planes bombed the harbor, destroying several German minesweepers. On August 25, Paris was liberated and the Germans left Monaco. For a week Louis and his subjects were in limbo, not sure if the

Germans would return. Then, on September 3, a scaldingly hot day, an American jeep with a squawking horn and two GIs shouting unintelligibly entered Monte Carlo from the Menton road and screeched to a halt outside an open bar. One of the soldiers was American writer Irwin Shaw, who would always claim he had liberated Monte Carlo's Tip Top Bar, just as the author he most admired, Ernest Hemingway, always claimed he liberated the bar in the Ritz Hotel in Paris at the end of World War I. In the short time that it took Shaw and his companion to be served their drinks, the street outside became crowded with Monégasques who had heard the Americans had finally arrived.

Rainier returned home a few days later. The Germans were gone from Monaco and France, but the war was not yet over. His sympathies since the fall of France had been anti-Vichy, and he was infuriated that Roblôt remained as Minister of State. Roblôt had not only shown hostile indifference to the Allies after the final withdrawal of the Germans, he had forbidden all anti-Nazi or pro-Allied public demonstrations. Rainier confronted his grandfather about Roblôt's attitudes and begged him to dismiss the man. Louis refused. Monégasques who had accepted Roblôt's position without protest during the years of occupation (although in all fairness, they had little choice) now wanted him to leave. A petition with over three hundred names was sent to Louis asking him to remove Roblôt from office. Louis held fast to his authority in keeping Roblôt on his staff. Louis's popularity, never high, was at its lowest ebb.

Roblôt eventually left of his own accord in 1945, a little less than a year later. He returned to France, but was not tried as a collaborationist. There were no war trials in the Principality, a decision of Louis's but one that met with popular approval from his subjects. Rainier was officially made direct heir to the throne on June 2, 1944, a few days after he had celebrated his twenty-first birthday. At that time Princesse Charlotte, in full agreement with her father, renounced her rights to the succession. He enlisted in the Free French Army as a foreign volunteer under General de Monsabert the following month and was made a second lieutenant, seeing action in the Alsatian campaign that winter during the Nazi counteroffensive. Cited for bravery under fire, he was awarded the Croix de Guerre and the Bronze Star, and then, because he spoke English, he was sent to Strasbourg (which had been a stronghold for the Germans, and was the first major French city to have fallen to them), where he acted as a liaison on the general staff of the 36th Infantry Division of the Texas Rangers. He was transferred to Berlin in the Economic Section of the French Military Mission with the rank of colonel. The unconditional surrender of Germany was signed at Rheims on May 7, 1945, and was ratified at Berlin on May 8. Rainier was not decommissioned from the French Army until January 1947, when he returned home to Monaco.

The time had come for him to embark upon a career. He still had no definite aim. Cars interested him and he thought he might like to try his hand at racing. He was still very much in love with Gisèle and convinced her to join him on the Riviera.

He took a villa in Petite Afrique, a small, exclusive colony on a narrow strip of seafront extending from the port of Beaulieu-sur-Mer, about twenty miles up the coast of the French Riviera from Monaco. During the German occupation, refugees from Nazi persecution had hidden in the dozens of natural caves in the steep cliffside of the Corniche that rose sharply above Petite Afrique. There they waited until members of the Resistance felt it was safe to attempt a nighttime escape over the top of the precipitous Corniche, through a dangerous patch of enemy-infested terrain to Switzerland. This was a mode of escape that Raoul Gunsbourg, now back as director of the Monte Carlo Opéra, had taken. Rainier's villa on the water was directly below these caves.

In 1948 Gisèle made two romantic comedies, *Après l'amour* and *Mademoiselle s'amuse*. The slightly risqué tone of the films and Gisèle's humble background as the daughter of Nice flower vendors did not endear her to the women in Rainier's family.

Rainier had developed into a complex young man, forged by the bitter battles of his childhood, a family bonded by ill feeling, the loneliness of the boarding schools he had attended and his sense of always being regarded as an outsider. The war and his own part in it had greatly affected him. He was an introspective man who had learned all the superficial social refinements, but had few close friends.

Despite the fact that Antoinette had a neighboring villa in

Petite Afrique, Rainier remained distanced from his sister, who was now married to Aleco Noghes, a handsome, athletic man descended from the first Spanish commander of the Monaco Garrison (which made Antoinette the first Grimaldi to marry a Monégasque). Noghes, who had a reputation as a playboy, was a lawyer and former tennis champion, and he had been previously married. When Antoinette entered into an affair with him at the end of the war, his divorce was not yet final. This upset everyone in the family, including Rainier. The couple was married in Monaco in a civil ceremony in October 1946. Only three months earlier, on July 24, Antoinette had refused to attend the marriage of Louis to his buxom mistress, Ghislaine Dommanget, the first Grimaldi bride without a dowry. To her fury, her grandfather returned the slight.

Intense internecine rivalries enveloped the family. Neither Louis nor Rainier could abide Noghes and all family members other than her loving husband disliked Ghislaine and suspected her motives, certain that she would persuade Louis to change his will in her favor. To complicate matters further, Gisèle received the same exclusion from the family as Noghes had and was never included in their scheduled social events, which obliged Rainier to attend them without her.

Antoinette's son, Baron Christian de Massey, born in 1949, would later write in his autobiography: "I entered this bizarre family . . . inheriting a legacy of father hating son, mother hating daughter, children hating parents, sisters hating brothers, a tradition in the blood of our family of constant conflict."

For stability, Rainier turned to Gisèle. Although she tried desperately hard to help him find himself, taking an interest in animals (zoology was one of his preoccupations), the sports he enjoyed (boats, cars and spearfishing) and in his family problems, she refused to give up her career. She appeared in *La Femme Nue (The Naked Woman)*,[2] *La Chocolatière, Véronique* and *Bel Amour* over the next two years, choosing films that were made at the studio in nearby Nice and not in Paris. Rainier, never able to accept the easygoing nature of her theatrical friends, tried to persuade her to abandon her career.

---

[2] An English translation of a film title denotes the name by which it was released in English-speaking countries.

Rainier was restless. He suffered from the same ailment that had afflicted both Edward VII and Edward VIII when they were Princes of Wales. To be heir to a throne often meant years of waiting before you could take over the job that you were born to fill. During that time there seemed to be no useful position within the monarchy that the ruling sovereign was willing to give his or her heir, and since they received an income from the civil list, the heirs were restricted from pursuing an occupation in the commercial workplace. As a result, there was little for them to do that was not of a purely social nature: appearing at charity galas, cutting ribbons as a new road or building was opened, or visiting hospitals and schools.

Rainier filled his days with challenging and often dangerous sports. He turned with the seasons from downhill skiing at Saint-Moritz to spearfishing in the shark-infested Red Sea (where several times he nearly drowned as he doggedly remained underwater to retrieve his arrow from the ocean bed after a missed kill) to automobile racing around the steep, curving roads of the Corniche. Gisèle was usually there to cheer him on, and since her great love remained the theater, they attended most of the productions at the Salle Garnier (one of the few public places they were seen together).

By now Louis was a sick man, which did not alter the difficult relationship between him and his grandson. Their conflicts centered on two issues: Rainier's continuing affair with Gisèle, and the ban that remained in effect on de Polignac ever crossing the border into Monaco. De Polignac and Rainier had found each other again after the war, and theirs appears to have been the one loving father-son relationship in the Grimaldi family.

Antoinette did not help to ease Gisèle's position. She spread a rumor that Gisèle could never have children and so the Grimaldi-Matignon line would end and Monaco become French. She also made much of Gisèle's "lowly" background—which was ironic, as hers and Rainier's was even less grand: their mother had been illegitimate, their grandmother Marie a Montmartre dancer, and their great-grandmother a laundress. Nonetheless, Antoinette's rumors about Gisèle made their rounds of the various social circles in Monaco with much injury to Gisèle. To Rainier's credit, he confronted his sister about her insidious gossip (although this did not stop Antoinette) and his love for

Gisèle was open and supportive. He was never seen in public with another woman, nor she with another man.

Louis took fatally ill in April 1949. His reign was not one of any achievement and his attachment to the Vichy government during the war had lost him whatever small regard his subjects might have had for him because of his father. Now, too infirm to administer the Principality, he delegated power to Rainier. He died on May 9, 1949, three weeks before Rainier's twenty-sixth birthday. Rainier was now Prince de Monaco with all the responsibility the title brought with it, including being the new head of a warring family.

His first battle was over his grandfather's will. Louis had bequeathed half of his vast personal fortune, which ran into many millions of francs and included his inherited foreign investments, to Ghislaine, and the remaining half was divided equally among Rainier, Antoinette and Charlotte. Rainier blocked the will, using his power as absolute monarch, and then filed a court action to make it null and void on the grounds that much of the property was not personal but belonged to the Crown and was not his grandfather's to give away.[3] In the end, Ghislaine received a relatively modest annual income and was denied all the property willed to her. She kept her jewels (a handsome treasure) and whatever personal gifts Louis had given her during their marriage, and she had the right to remain in apartments in the Palace, a privilege she used even though she and Rainier did not speak to each other.

Rainier lifted the ban on his father's exclusion from Monaco and arranged a luxurious accommodation for him at the Hôtel de Paris. Additionally, he established a prestigious annual award, the Prince Pierre Prize in Literature (to be given each year to a European author chosen by a committee appointed by Rainier), in an effort to improve his father's standing in the Principality. Antoinette, her dislike of her father having increased with age, was furious. According to her son Christian, she "also hated and feared her mother," who now lived in se-

[3] The case was heard by a specially convened secret tribunal in the Court of Revision, created exclusively to settle Monaco's dynastic disputes. Ten attorneys from the French Foreign Office (whose names were not disclosed and do not even appear in the archival records of the Palais de Princier) flew clandestinely to Monaco and eventually ruled in Rainier's favor.

clusion with her dogs at Marchais and seldom visited the Principality.

Louis II was buried in Monaco on May 17, 1949, with great pageantry. A six-month period of public mourning followed; the Grimaldi standard was flown at half mast above the Palace, then raised again on November 18. The coronation of Rainier III was set for April 11, 1950, the day after Easter Monday.

The previous evening, brilliantly glittering garlands of light stretched all the way from the Rock, along the harbor, the Casino and the shoreline of Monte Carlo. A religious service was held the next morning at the Cathedral, with Rainier dressed for the first time in the full regalia of reigning Prince: the striking royal blue uniform with the red and white sash of the Order of St. Charles. After a long, celebratory lunch with Antoinette at his side (Gisèle conspicuously missing), he reviewed the guard in the Place d'Armes and presented them with the standard of Louis II with its black crêpe bow (to be placed in the Palace Museum). He then watched as his own standard was raised on the flagpole above the Palace to the sound of trumpets. The new reign had officially begun.

Once Rainier ascended the throne, he moved into the Palace and spent only his weekends with Gisèle in the Villa Iberia, a newly purchased house in Saint-Jean-Cap-Ferrat. He claims he never proposed to her, but he did insist she give up her career, and for three years she complied. This was not an easy time for either of them. Rainier had decided that not only would he make Monaco his main residence and remain there for most of the year and appear in public as frequently as required, he would take a far more active role in the affairs of his Principality than had any Prince de Monaco since the time of Honoré II in the seventeenth century. His schedule was demanding and Gisèle could participate in very little of it. He had to attend social and ceremonial occasions without her, at which he would be seated by a hostess or, as a matter of protocol, beside an attractive woman. The strain on the relationship began to tell.

Rainier has said, "We were together six years and it was fine while it lasted but I think we both felt it was long enough. It was a love affair that had to come to its own end." That is something of an oversimplification. Gisèle had been in the theater since her youth, and she was used to working hard and to the independence her success brought her. By 1953, having lived with Rainier for six years and remained in the background for most of that time, she decided to resume her career.

Although Rainier was much against her doing so, she accepted a role in *Horizons sans fin* and then was cast opposite the dynamic Raymond Pellegrin in *Marchands d'illusion (Nights of Shame)* and *Le Feu dans la peau (Fire Under Her Skin)*. She fell in love with her leading man. Pellegrin (born Pellegrini) was a Niçois of Italian descent, and they had much in common. He was a cerebral, intense man who had starred on the Paris stage and gained international recognition for his performances in *Le Fruit défendu (Forbidden Fruit)* and in the title role of *Napoléon*.

Gisèle, realizing that Pellegrin's world was the one to which she belonged, moved out of Rainier's villa a year after his coronation. A short time later, she married Pellegrin and—putting an end to Antoinette's rumor that she was infertile—had a daughter the following year.

With Gisèle out of the way, Antoinette now hatched a scheme that she hoped would remove Rainier from the throne and put her son, Christian, age six, in his place. It seemed that economic affairs in Monaco, having just taken a convoluted and scandalous turn, might work in her favor.

The year that Rainier ascended the throne, the S.B.M. suffered serious losses and there was a 75 percent decline in the number of visitors to the Casino. All of Europe, of course, was in a postwar slump, but other factors were involved. Casinos were now operating up and down the Riviera, and the Cannes Film Festival had been inaugurated. In the United States, Reno and Las Vegas, with their modern, glitzy casinos with star performers surrounded by the added lure of beautiful girls in flashy stage shows, had become hugely popular and Monte Carlo still clung to the more classical forms of entertainment—theater, ballet, concerts and opera. Competition can often be a good thing. In this case it made Monte Carlo's Old World adherence to formal dress and a stiff atmosphere seem archaic, prompting the Hollywood star Edward G. Robinson's famous observation in 1950, after losing several thousand francs at roulette in an almost deserted room in the Casino: "What this joint needs is a real crap game."

Crap tables were finally installed along with slot machines a few years later, but it was Aristotle Onassis, the Greek shipping tycoon, who was responsible for turning the S.B.M. and the Casino back into a high-rolling, big stakes business. The curious thing was that Rainier did not know Onassis was planning to become the majority stockholder of the S.B.M. until it was a *fait accompli*.

Onassis and his elegant blond wife, the Greek shipping heiress Athina "Tina" Niarchos, leased the Château de la Cröe (formerly inhabited by the Duke and Duchess of Windsor) in the spring of 1951. His yacht, *Olympic Winner*, on which most of his entertaining was done, was anchored in the harbor. The squat, middle-aged Onassis "strolled around in thickly-tinted glasses with his wife and two small children" and avoided the casino. "My whaling fleet is out and might earn or lose me $5 million within three or four months," he would say. "That's what I call gambling!"

The real estate owned by the S.B.M. included the Hôtel de Paris, the Hermitage Hôtel, and the Monte Carlo Beach Hotel (the three largest and most luxurious), the two Sporting Clubs, Winter and Summer, the Country Club and the spectacular golf course on the crest of Mont Agel. Then there was the Café de Paris, numerous villas, gardens and tourist attractions. A shrewd businessman who had come up the hard way, Onassis saw that even more money could be made from the real estate owned by the S.B.M. than by the Casino. He also envisioned expanding the harbor to accommodate oceangoing liners on luxury cruises. Working through a network of foreign companies, he bought a controlling interest in the S.B.M., leased a derelict building on the Avenue d'Ostende for his offices and moved from the Château de la Cröe to the Hôtel de Paris with his family while he awaited delivery of his mammoth new yacht, the air-conditioned *Christina* (named after his daughter) on which he planned to live.

Rainier not only had a new partner in the S.B.M., he had lost his power to influence its operations. This on its own would have been a difficult hurdle for him, but soon thereafter, the Société Monégasque de Banques et de Métaux Précieux (the Precious Metals Society or the PMS), which even more than the S.B.M. was a semi-official creation, suddenly declared itself bankrupt. Rainier's closest staff occupied positions in the PMS or its subsidiary companies, and major deposits of his own and the government's (55 percent of the state's reserves) had been made there.

Normal practice was to divide the government reserves among the thirteen existing Monégasque banks. The bankruptcy was catastrophic and the taint of corruption, graft and payoffs rubbed off on Rainier. Advised by Jean-Charles Rey, the president of the Finance and Fact-Finding Commission of Monaco's Council, Rainier reinstated in his Cabinet only two months later the men known to be guilty of these untried crimes. (This was on the premise that by doing so he would be publicly displaying his belief that the men had been unfairly admonished by the French press who covered the story and printed editorials that prejudged the men as guilty.) What Rainier did not know was that Rey and Antoinette, now separated from Noghes, were having an affair and that they were conspirators working traitorously against him.

"The bank scandal," Rainier's nephew, Christian de Massey, states in his autobiography, "had provided the breach into which [my mother] now proposed to rush. Her intention was to depose Uncle Rainier and name herself as regent on the basis of having a son [himself] she could put on the throne . . . she no doubt thought there was enough discontent with Uncle Rainier in the government and among the population to give her a chance of succeeding."

News of the proposed coup d'état leaked, giving Rainier enough time to stop Antoinette from proceeding. He now had to make the most difficult decision of his life. He could ban his sister from ever setting foot in Monaco or he could arrest her and have her and her lover face trial as traitors. Either path could prove disastrous. He did not know if Antoinette had supporters and if she did who they might be. There was always the chance that the Monégasques might side with her, in which case he would have helped her achieve her aim. Or her thwarted ambitions could have been used by some other political force to undermine his position.

There were other considerations which Rainier's unwelcome Greek partner now stressed. If Monaco was to regain its former esteem and seem attractive to investors, peace had to be made in the family, a united front displayed, the world led to believe that Antoinette had been grievously misrepresented and that the idea of her engineering a coup d'état was ridiculous. Whatever Rainier's personal feelings might have been, he was well aware that this advice made good sense and that his own position and the security of the Principality could collapse if he did not control his personal emotions. He therefore did not banish Antoinette, nor detain her. Instead he issued a statement that there was no truth in the allegations that she wished to overthrow him, and photographs were taken of the family together with his arm around his nephew's shoulders and a broad smile for Antoinette.

Clearly, though, some good public relations were desperately needed to help Monaco's economy and to enhance Rainier's image. His religious adviser was Father Francis Tucker, an American oblate priest from Baltimore, who had spent a number of years in the Archdiocese of Philadelphia. He had been assigned by the Vatican as Rainier's private chaplain. In this capacity, Tucker had become a good and trusted friend. Rainier asked him for his advice.

"My Lord Prince," Tucker replied, in his usual old-fashioned style, "perhaps it is time for you to get married."

16

In May 1955 Grace Kelly was on the Riviera as a special guest at the annual Cannes Film Festival. In the short span of four years she had established herself as a star with unique appeal: a rare beauty with unruffled elegance and flashes of an inner fire waiting to be kindled by the right man. The closest comparisons might be drawn to Katharine Hepburn, whose nervous energy made her seem more vulnerable on screen than Grace, and Ingrid Bergman, who had the added intrigue of a foreign accent. Grace had co-starred at this time in nine pictures, two of them not yet released and one, *The Country Girl,* directed by George Seaton, that had brought her an Academy Award for her performance only a month earlier. Her leading men had been Hollywood's most successful actors: Gary Cooper, Clark Gable, James Stewart, Bing Crosby, William Holden and Ray Milland. At twenty-five, she projected a mature image on screen that was reassuring to middle-aged male stars who shied away from uncomplimentary comparison with a much younger leading lady.

Cannes was crowded with film executives and performers promoting their latest efforts and the usual drumbeating crews and press representatives who helped them do so. The event was, in fact, one huge publicity pitch to help sell new films and their stars. Grace had not been interested in this aspect. She was in a state of terrible confusion, plagued with guilt over her numerous ill-chosen love affairs and unable to understand why her career, which she had fought hard to achieve, decreased in meaning for her with each new film. She wanted desperately to marry, to have a family and—perhaps even more—to please her parents, which she never seemed able to do.

John Brendan "Jack" Kelly, her father, had been one of ten

children born to poor, immigrant Irish parents in the Irish Catholic, working-class East Falls neighborhood of Philadelphia, Pennsylvania. East Falls was virtually a company town for a local carpet mill, where John Kelly senior and all of his children went to work as soon as they were old enough. In Jack's case, since he was big for his years, this was at the age of nine. His oldest brother, Patrick, had managed to break loose from mill work. Starting as a laborer with a construction firm, he had launched his own small company, and when Jack turned twelve, Patrick put him to work carting lumber and kegs of nails and wheeling barrows filled with bricks.

The Kellys stuck together to survive, but Jack's bitterly disappointed mother, Mary, who had come to America seeking a better life as had millions of other immigrants, fiercely drove her sons upward, stressing the importance of financial success. Only two other things mattered to Mary: her religion and keeping her family together. Hers was a life of hard work and drudgery, and she was married to a man who drank too much and cared too little about his wife's well-being or contentment. Home, a cramped tenement row house on the banks of the Schuylkill River, was the scene of constant angry parental quarrels. Despite Mary's tenacious tribal instincts, her children left home—but not Philadelphia—as soon as they could afford a room somewhere else.

Only one child, George (destined to become a successful playwright), had been able to escape. In 1900, at age thirteen, he had run away and for ten years no one knew his whereabouts. George had been the frailest of the Kelly boys, sensitive and introspective, which was probably why his mother had expected him to go into the church. He had, instead, joined a touring vaudeville company. When he returned to Philadelphia in 1910, he was writing vaudeville sketches and one-act plays. He did not stay long because he was heading back on the road again, hoping one day to make it to Broadway as a playwright. He gave his mother some money from his carefully managed savings and then, to her distress, convinced another brother, Walter, to try his luck in vaudeville with him, and the two of them left town.

Jack had been impressed by George's small success and envious of his independence. At the same time he suspected that his brother was what he called "womanish" and, having been too young to know him before he had left home, that his years in the theater had probably been responsible. Jack wanted desperately to *be* someone, to have people in Philadelphia look up as he passed. Always a good athlete who excelled at boxing and rowing (which he had done since childhood on the Schuylkill River), he had developed tremendous strength in his arms and legs in his years as a construction laborer. He now fostered two dreams: to compete on a rowing team in the Henley Regatta in England and to be chosen for the next Olympic Games to be held in Stockholm two years hence, in 1912, as a single sculler.[1]

The idea that he could compete in the games seemed utterly impossible. Most Olympic contenders had experience on college teams. But Jack was a determined man, and began to train himself, working on the river every day, no matter what the weather, unless it was frozen over. To everyone's amazement except his own, he tried out for the American Olympic Rowing and Sculling Team and not only was chosen but won the gold medal for single sculling.

The advent of the First World War caused the 1916 Olympics to be canceled. Jack joined the army as an enlisted man in 1917, saw very little action, but became the boxing champion of his regiment. His success at sports had brought him the recognition that he had sought. With the war's end, he returned to Philadelphia, determined to escape from the Irish ghetto. He immediately began to train for the 1920 Olympics, to be held in Antwerp, but he needed money if this dream was to be realized, for competitors now had to pay their own way. In 1919, his brother Walter returned to Philadelphia from his stint as a vaudeville performer. Though not the success George had been, Walter had accrued some savings and he agreed to help Jack, but only if he took part of the stake and started his own construction company so that he would have a business to return to after the games. Kelly for Brickwork was thus formed. An-

[1]Sculling is a variation of rowing in which the oarsman controls two oars, one in each hand; in rowing both hands are used to pull one oar through the water.

other brother, Charles, joined the firm as business manager, allowing Jack the freedom to pursue his dream.[2]

He won a second Olympic gold medal in single sculling at Antwerp and returned to Philadelphia as the conquering hero. Handsome, vital, aggressive and a promising businessman, he could have won the hand of almost any of the city's eligible young women other than the socially select Main Line debutantes, and even one of those privileged ladies might well have eloped with him despite the certainty of incurring parental wrath for marrying a Kelly from East Falls. Instead, in 1924, at the age of thirty, he married a beautiful former magazine cover model and graduate of Philadelphia's Temple University, Margaret Majer, a German Lutheran from the outer, somewhat more affluent, fringes of East Falls.

At first sight the newlyweds seemed to have much in common. Margaret was a top-class athlete and the first woman to teach physical education at the University of Pennsylvania. Her good looks, self-assurance and strength of character led the Kellys to believe that she would be able to keep Jack's roving eye and taste for high living in check; and her conversion to Catholicism placed her in good standing with the family. Her enthusiastic acceptance by her in-laws quickly soured when she began, from the start of the marriage, to assert her independence and to display an attitude of superiority.

Ma, as Margaret came to be called, was morally upright, a stickler for social propriety. She did not believe, as did her sisters-in-law, that women should stay at home while their husbands caroused and drank. Nor did she take much pride in her husband's Irish gift of the blarney, nor in the business that quickly brought a fine, large two-story brick house in the better section of Philadelphia's middle-class Germantown.

Their first child, Peggy, was born in 1925, John B., Jr. ("Kell") in 1927, Grace in 1929, and Lizanne in 1933—by which time Jack Kelly had the first of several mistresses and the marriage had turned hostile, but behind closed doors. As one close observer said: "Appearances were everything; unbecom-

---

[2]The start of Kelly for Brickwork, which was to become a multimillion-dollar business within a decade, caused much friction and bitterness within the Kelly enclave. Charles Kelly had been their brother Patrick's business manager and the backbone of his small company before he quit to join Jack.

ing emotions were to be banished or suppressed." Jack was not often at home, women, sports and politics—including an early, greatly felt loss as Democratic mayoral candidate for Philadelphia—taking a good chunk of his time. But when he was at home, Jack Kelly livened the house with his raucous sense of humor and his initiation of highly competitive family sports.

A day with their father meant the Kelly children were up at six A.M. for calisthenics and, apart from short rests during the day, not finished with their physical activities until sundown. In summer these included swimming, diving, climbing (at the age of ten Kell was expected to make it up a two-story ladder, over a slanted shingled roof and to a third-floor window of their beach cottage and beat his own record each time), touch football and tennis. Ma's rigid, cold nature was even more difficult for her children to cope with than their father's insistence on athletic excellence.

"Oh, that Ma Kelly, she's a tough one, a tough German cookie," her son Kell remarked years later in a newspaper interview. "Now I wouldn't say that Mother's a Nazi . . . but sometimes I do refer to her as, quote, 'That old Prussian mother of mine.' "

Ma Kelly was the daughter of German immigrants and had grown up speaking German at home. She had insisted that her children learn to speak the language at an early age. But in the late thirties and early forties, German was unfashionable, if not unpatriotic, for an American to speak. The children would hide their grammar books, pretend to be sick—anything to get out of their mother's hated private lessons, usually with little success. Bristling with unswerving Prussian discipline, Ma Kelly was difficult to disobey.

All three sisters adored their father, none more, perhaps, than Grace. But his favorite was Peggy—lusty, extroverted, the best sportswoman among them. He had hopes that she might one day become an Olympic swimmer. Lizanne was also a good swimmer and he pushed her to compete with the much older Peggy.

From early childhood, Grace had eye problems. Despite apparently obvious signs that she needed glasses, she went through her early youth made to feel that her squinting was "an unpleasant habit," her failing to catch a ball sheer, perverse awkwardness. A dreamer, withdrawn, she had difficulty in capturing her father's attention in the brief times when he was at home, although she desperately yearned to do so.

Kell was the center of Jack Kelly's ambitions, for he intended his son to follow in his footsteps, not only as an Olympic sculling champion but as a future entrant in the Henley Regatta, an opportunity Jack felt had been denied him in his youth because of his humble background and the snobbery of the English. He trained Kell ruthlessly from the time he was able to hold an oar in his hands. The boy resented being pushed into something not of his choice, but Jack refused to accept this. Denial was part of the Kelly family's crucial belief.

"Betrayals of weakness or unhappiness were to be swept away by wholesome activity," Lizanne recalled. "Sports were a must in our family. . . . [We] often spent Sundays [in the winter] at the Penn Athletic Club downtown." Rigorous exercise was a set part of the children's daily routine whether Jack was at home or not. Grace gamely tried to participate in sports, but always lagged behind her siblings' accomplishments.[3] The established creed in the Kelly household was "to be the best"; there was no excuse for coming in second, even in family contests.

The girls began their education at Ravenhill Academy, a strict Catholic school in East Falls. The school uniform was dour; patent-leather shoes could not be worn in case undergarments were reflected in them. The hours were long and the nuns relentless in their demands for excellence in lessons and deportment. Ma did not object to this as much as she did to the school's lack of social prestige. She had great hopes for her girls, just as Jack had for Kell. They were all to marry men from Main Line families, not an easy task since few Catholics were ever allowed into the hallowed country clubs of this elite group, and Jack would strongly resist any of his daughters marrying a non-Catholic.

When Grace was eleven the three sisters were transferred to the less regimented, secular, socially acceptable Stevens School for Girls in Germantown. The change would have been much

[3]Kell was to win an Olympic bronze medal for sculling in the 1948 Summer Olympics held in London, and to win in his category of sculling in the 1947 and 1949 Henley Regatta, while both Lizanne and Peggy won national swimming medals.

welcomed but for one thing. The school was directly across the street from the house of their father's current mistress, Ellen Frazer, a divorcée whom he deeply loved and wished to marry but for the Catholic law against divorce. Nonetheless, he spent most of his free time at his lover's house; his black limousine would be parked boldly in front for the sisters to see in the early morning, when he had not been home the previous night. Still, the façade of a happy marriage was maintained by Ma, who had adopted the Catholic approach that marriage was "till death do us part."

"There was always something a bit different, a bit withdrawn about Grace," her mother was later to say. "She was a frail little girl and sickly a good deal of the time, very susceptible to colds. She was completely self-sufficient and could amuse herself for hours by making up little plays with her dolls."

At the age of twelve, Grace had joined the East Falls Old Academy Players, her interest in theater piqued by the encouragement of her uncle George Kelly, who since 1922 had been famous in the theater for such plays as *The Torch Bearers*, *The Show Off*, and the Pulitzer Prize–winning 1925 hit, *Craig's Wife*. Almost all of his plays were psychological studies of the disintegration of neurotic characters, a theme that fell out of favor in the Depression. Kelly went to Hollywood, where, like his contemporary F. Scott Fitzgerald, he was given hack stories to adapt for the screen and, again like Fitzgerald, failed at the attempt.

Uncle George only occasionally returned to Philadelphia, where Kelly for Brickwork was a tremendous success and his brother Jack a kingpin in Democratic politics. (It has been said that there were very few public buildings built in Philadelphia from the thirties to the sixties that had not sported a Kelly for Brickwork sign during construction.) Of all his nieces and nephews, George Kelly had the greatest empathy for Grace and she admired him above all her father's other brothers.

Even this distanced Grace from her mother, who seemed to understand their daughter even less than Jack did. Ma never liked George Kelly, and was embarrassed by and contemptuous of his homosexuality. (Jack, for his part, refused to recognize it even though George lived and traveled openly with his long-time lover.) Ma also considered a career in the theater, which

Grace seemed set upon, an outrageous idea for her daughter, and believed that George Kelly's influence was mostly to blame. Over and over again she repeated to this "wayward" daughter of hers the importance of a good marriage (defined as finding a rich, socially prominent husband). Women, she insisted, did not have careers, they had hobbies, interests (especially charity or medical causes), to occupy their time until the right man came along. After all, she herself had had a college education and a teaching degree and had given that life up immediately upon marriage.

Ma Kelly did not want her daughters to settle for the first man who came along. Bitter over her own unhappy union and believing in marriage as a vow not to be broken, she wanted her girls to take their time until they found a man who was not only socially acceptable, but who would never stray and whom they loved deeply.

Finding the right husbands for her daughters was additionally important to Ma Kelly because she was now only too clearly aware that in no other way could they make it into Philadelphia's Main Line, which was even more elite than New York's Four Hundred. New money—and the war had made Jack Kelly even richer—was considered gauche in this select group where wealth had been accumulated several generations earlier. The Kellys had more marks against them than being nouveau riche. They were Catholic, their ancestors had been immigrants, not pioneers (worse, Jack and Ma were only first-generation Americans), they had been raised in East Falls, and they lived in Germantown.

Grace told her good friend Judith Balaban Quine, shortly before she attended the Cannes Film Festival, that she often fantasized about having a coming-out party at the Main Line's annual Assembly Ball for the city's debutantes, wearing an "enormous formal gown that swept the floor," and having as her escort a handsome young man from one of the leading military schools or colleges. But she, Peggy and Lizanne were never invited to attend the Assembly.

Upon her graduation from Stevens in 1947, she tried and failed the entrance exams at Bennington College, her parents' choice for her. Then, despite her parents' objections, she applied to the American Academy of Dramatic Arts in New York, with her uncle George's encouragement. She auditioned and was accepted and had finally talked her father into financing her studies for a year at the Academy, during which time she would live at the sedate and well-chaperoned Barbizon Hotel for Women.

"We hoped she'd give it up," her mother later commented, while Grace said, "I . . . went to New York to find out who I was, or who I wasn't."

Although she did not see herself as a startling beauty, the teachers at the Academy and her new friends at the Barbizon immediately recognized her as such. She now wore strong glasses for her extreme myopia, but that was only a superficial reason for her lack of self-esteem. "My sister Peggy was my father's favorite," she confided to a journalist in later years. "Then there was Kell, the only son. Then I came and then I had a baby sister, and I was terribly jealous of her. I loved the idea of a baby, but was never allowed to hold it. So I was always on my mother's knee, clinging. But I was pushed away, and I resented my sister [Lizanne] for years."

Grace was determined to remain in New York even after she received her diploma from the Academy. Her father insisted that she return to Philadelphia. More than anything Grace yearned for Jack's approval and although staying in New York was against his wishes, she believed that if she succeeded as an actress he would come to respect her ability. Jack, in anger at her defiance, withdrew some of his support, and she went to work as a photographic model. A friend had given her the courage to have pictures taken and to apply to a professional modeling agency where she was accepted. She was immediately typed as "the girl next door" because of her classic beauty, her shyness and her great sense of propriety in dress and makeup; she was highly successful, appearing in many national advertisements for leading products. But what she wanted most was to become an actress.

She was hired by the Bucks County Playhouse in Pennsylvania for the summer of 1949 and cast in two plays, George Kelly's *The Torch Bearers* (with the obvious thought that the publicity angle would do the Playhouse good) and in the title role of *The Heiress*, adapted by Ruth and Augustus Goetz from Henry James's novel, *Washington Square*. The film director Gregory

Ratoff, who was looking for a young Irish girl to co-star with another newcomer, Dan Dailey, in a low-budget film called *Taxi*, came to see her on the advice of a talent scout; he was impressed, and had her make a screen test in New York. She projected quite a different image on-screen from the one he had expected. Her near-sightedness gave her an expression of cool detachment that her pale blond beauty emphasized. But she appeared far too elegant for the role, and instead he cast Constance Smith, a young British actress who had recently made a name for herself in the critically acclaimed *Brighton Rock,* in the part.

But the summer experience at Bucks County had given Grace the boost in confidence that she needed, and she now began to make the theater rounds in earnest. She auditioned, along with twenty-five other hopefuls, for the part of the daughter in a Broadway revival of August Strindberg's *The Father,* starring Raymond Massey (who also directed the production) and Mady Christian (who had just closed in *I Remember Mama,* the successful John Van Druten adaptation of the Kathryn Forbes book). The play is about a father's obsession to control and finally destroy his daughter, who he believes is another man's child. "Grace was the third girl I auditioned," Massey recalled. "I had to see the other twenty-three before I could make my decision. She was just about the most beautiful youngster I ever saw and she gave a lovely, sensitive performance as the bewildered and brokenhearted child . . . George Jean Nathan [the critic] proclaimed my performance as the worst of my career. The play ran for seventy-nine performances. It was a slow and agonizing death."

Massey's lack of success in the play was to haunt him for years, but Grace had received kind, if not extraordinary, reviews. (Brooks Atkinson, the *New York Times* drama critic, wrote, "Grace Kelly gives a charming, pliable performance.") Now considered a professional actress, she was cast in a series of television dramas, appearing in sixty of them over the course of the next year and a half, starring in adaptations of Sinclair Lewis's *Bethel Merriday* and F. Scott Fitzgerald's *The Rich Boy,* as well as many others. This was to prove to be her training ground for films and she developed into a fine actress, unselfconscious before the camera, with a distinct persona. She exuded refinement, social position and a depth of character. In 1951, she was offered a minor part in her first movie, *Fourteen Hours*. Directed by Henry Hathaway it was a small-scale, well-crafted suspense story starring Richard Basehart, Barbara Bel Geddes and Paul Douglas, in which Grace played a woman whose husband threatens suicide by standing on a skyscraper ledge prepared to jump. She had only two scenes and received only passing mention in most reviews. But although not a major success, the film received good notices and Grace came to the attention of the top Hollywood agency, MCA. She signed a contract for them to represent her, and they assigned a young man from their New York office, Jay Kanter, as her agent. Making it on Broadway remained Grace's top priority, but she seemed to do poorly in auditions.

Ironically, it was her old stage appearance in *The Father* that won her the lead opposite Gary Cooper in *High Noon*. The film's producer, Stanley Kramer, had seen the play and vividly recalled her. "She was a very beautiful lady and I thought she had the makings of a great star. So I took a chance and offered her this part," Kramer told his biographer, Donald Spoto.

Lectured throughout her life by Ma that a lady was not fully dressed in public without white gloves and a hat, Grace came into the office to meet Kramer for the first time so dressed. He suddenly had second thoughts about his decision. "She still looked beautiful. But she also resembled a prim debutante. I thought, 'She's wrong for the part, too stiff.' I let it pass. . . . She gave a creditable performance, she was *not* right for the part."

"When I saw the picture," Grace was to comment, "I was extremely disappointed with myself. In fact, I jumped on the next plane out of Hollywood and went back to New York, begging Sandy Meisner [a famous drama coach] to give me more acting lessons!"

Grace might not have realized the full potential of her role, but the cool innocence she projected was one of the underlying reasons for the success of Cooper's performance as the aging, disheartened, tired marshal, "anxious for peace and frankly unable to comprehend the easy morality of his fellows." Played against Grace's naïve young Amy, a Quaker who deplores violence and has a strong belief in honor, Cooper's Marshal Will Kane defends his town against revengeful outlaws even though the townsfolk do nothing to help him.

Grace rushed back to New York for more intimate reasons than to hone her craft. Shortly before departing for Hollywood to film *High Noon,* she had fallen deeply in love, for the first time, with an up-and-coming Broadway actor named Gene Lyons, a decade older than herself, married but separated from his wife. He was an emotional man, bordering on alcoholism and seeming to be headed for self-destruction. Her parents had strongly disapproved of her even seeing him before she made *High Noon,* and winning back their approbation after she had defied them to remain in New York to continue in the theater meant everything to her. She was to tell one of her closest friends at the time, "I never could marry a man of whom my parents did not approve."

It is highly improbable that the Kellys believed that Grace was involved in a sexual liaison. This was a time of moral righteousness in America, and if a young, unmarried woman was believed to be having an affair, she stood a strong chance of her reputation being ruined.

Certainly Grace had a physical relationship with Lyons. But she seems to have backed away from being drawn into a sexual liaison with Cooper. Ma Kelly had drummed into all of her daughters the importance of being pure for the man they would marry. Grace's affair with Lyons—and with each of her successive lovers over the next few years—created a devastating moral dilemma for her. She not only had to conceal her deepest feelings from her friends and family, she had to convince herself that if she was physically drawn to a man she was sincerely in love with him and considering marriage. The problem was that she seemed invariably to be attracted to married men, and since she did not believe in divorce, this made the relationship so intolerable that she knew she would have to break it off.

However, affairs with married men offered alternative incentives. There was the very secrecy with which such a liaison had to be conducted. The pair could not be seen in public together, and what they meant to each other remained concealed from the world.

Grace had thought that the separation from Lyons while she filmed in Hollywood would end the affair. It almost did, except that then Grace found herself attracted to Cooper. Fifty-one at the time, married and at the end of an intense affair with actress

Patricia Neal, his career unsettled as he began to be offered only older-men roles, he was particularly vulnerable to Grace's beauty and youth. Carl Foreman, the scriptwriter on the film, was to claim that Cooper went into an emotional decline when Grace rejected him and returned to New York. Robert Rossen, who was to direct him seven years later in *They Came to Cordura,* said Cooper confided to him that, after the breakup with Neal, he had tried to rekindle a spark in Grace but had failed. He had gone to France for the Cannes Film Festival in 1951, and had met and had fallen in love with a French film star, Gisèle Pascal, Rainier's mistress. They had, he said, a brief affair (this was just before Gisèle and Rainier broke up), which she had ended. "Not because of Rainier," Cooper said. "But because she fell in love with another actor. Can you beat that?"

Grace and Lyons continued to see each other, but after a disastrous visit to Philadelphia, when he drank too much and her family asked him to leave, she came to the decision that the affair must end. She still considered New York her home and shared a simple apartment with a friend from her Barbizon days, Prudence "Prudy" Wise. Jay Kanter called to say she had been offered the second female lead in an M.G.M. remake of the 1932 film *Red Dust,* originally about an overseer (Clark Gable) on a rubber plantation in Indochina who falls in love with a stranded prostitute (Jean Harlow) and is pursued by his engineer's wife (Mary Astor). The film, renamed *Mogambo,* would be directed by John Ford and shot in East Africa. In its reincarnation it was set in Kenya, but would have Gable playing largely the same role he had played twenty years earlier, except that he was now to be a white hunter, Ava Gardner, a stranded American showgirl he falls in love with, and Grace, who falls in love with him, the wife of a British archaeologist.

Grateful at the chance to break completely from Lyons and thrilled at the idea of foreign travel and appearing with "Rhett Butler" (by her own count she had seen *Gone With the Wind* a dozen times), she hastily accepted the part even though it meant signing a seven-year contract with M.G.M. The studio gave her permission to appear in theater between films but retained the right to pre-empt her services if they had a suitable role for her ready to go before the cameras.

Gable had gained weight, and his age was evident (he was

fifty-two). His recent life had been trouble-strewn. His popularity was on the wane. His brief marriage to Lady Sylvia Ashley was being settled in the divorce courts and he was drinking so heavily that he often could not control his shakes before the camera. East Africa was unbearably hot and the film difficult to make. Ava Gardner, who became Grace's lifelong friend, was having difficulties in her marriage to Frank Sinatra, who had remained in Hollywood; she did not want to further incite a jealous husband and so was cool to Gable's off-camera overtures. Gable turned to Grace. When not shooting, the pair would take long journeys in a jeep over the rugged terrain and "[make] camp by firelight in desolate reaches." A pattern was beginning to form: Grace seemed always in pursuit of the love of an older man or father figure, as she herself recognized. They parted at London Airport, Grace sobbing, Gable insisting that he was too old and too confused to continue the affair.

Mogambo was not a box-office hit, nor did her role in it show her talents to their fullest (or even close to it); but it made Grace Kelly a star, for on-screen she projected that certain chemistry that creates sparks. She was perhaps more a creation of Ma Kelly's design than her own or Hollywood's. She was the ultimate lady, aloof but with a charitable heart and a promise of yet unplumbed depths.

"I've been at the studio for years and years. In all that time there's been nothing like it," Grace's biographer Steven Englund quotes one of M.G.M.'s publicity men as saying about Grace after the release of *Mogambo*. "What gets me is that when all the hullabaloo started, she'd only really been in one [M.G.M.] picture. We can't keep up with the demand for interviews with her. We even had somebody here from *The Saturday Review of Literature. The Saturday Review of Literature!* I've never dealt with *The Saturday Review of Literature* before!"

Next, Grace was loaned out by M.G.M. to Alfred Hitchcock to star opposite Ray Milland in *Dial M for Murder*.[4] The old pattern of an attraction to an older man was repeated but with

---

[4]Studios often made deals with other studios involving their principal players. Sometimes one star would be traded for another, or, as in Grace Kelly's case for *Dial M for Murder,* a price. M.G.M. was paid $100,000 (nearly as much as Kelly was being paid in a year at that time) for her to appear in the Hitchcock film, which the studio guessed rightly would give a great boost to her career.

a double edge. By the end of the film Hitchcock was hopelessly in love with her. She admired him greatly as a director and appreciated his faith in her, but no more, and over the years Hitchcock's continually frustrated passion would become obsessive. Ray Milland was equally mesmerized by Grace. Both men were older, both were married. She was attracted to Milland but resisted becoming as involved as she had with Gable (the memory of that relationship still caused her pain).

After the completion of *Dial M for Murder,* she returned to Philadelphia, where the preview was to be held, accompanied by Jay Kanter and his wife, Judith.[5] After the showing of the film, which was attended by all the Kellys, they and Grace and her friends went back to the house in Germantown. Somehow under the impression that Grace's family was high society, Judy Kanter was taken by surprise at the middle-class surroundings and was quick to note that Jack Kelly's eyes were focused with pride on Peggy, not on Grace. After nothing was said about their daughter's appearance in the film they had just seen, Judy Kanter asked Jack, "Isn't it exciting what's happening to Gracie's career?"

"She was a weak little thing," Jack Kelly sighed dismissively, as if Grace were not in the room. "I don't understand why she'd want to be an actress, never did, but I told her she could go to New York when she asked because I couldn't even think of anything else she could do. Not even getting into college. Oh well, I'm glad she's making a living."

"It was clear," her agent's wife later wrote in her book, *The Bridesmaids,* "that in Jack Kelly's eyes, his daughter Grace was an unprofitable and unexceptional investment. To her dad, Grace was a write-off."

Hitchcock borrowed her for a second picture, *Rear Window,* opposite James Stewart, one of the few of Grace's leading men with whom she did not dally. (Stewart was a constant and loving husband to his wife, Gloria.) Hitchcock was determined to show the world how truly talented Grace was, and he worked with her in an almost brutal fashion to bring out for the camera the sexuality he believed lay beneath that cool exterior. ("Grace is

---

[5]Judith Balaban Kanter later divorced Jay Kanter and married Don Quine. She remained a close friend to Grace Kelly throughout her life.

like a mountain covered with snow," he once told a friend, "and when the snow melts you discover it to be a smoldering volcano.") It worked, and Grace's sensuality contributed to the tremendous commercial success of *Rear Window,* which was a gripping suspense film, well produced and acted. Hitchcock began the search for yet another script suitable for Grace's talents. Meanwhile, she was loaned out again, this time to co-star with William Holden in the action thriller *The Bridges at Toko-Ri,* adapted from a novel by James Michener about jet pilots during the Korean War. This was a drama about men, war and planes, and although her role was not as strong as Holden's, she had the only woman's role of any size in the film and her elegant sexuality and her beauty helped to give the picture, and the grim drama of the story, a fuller appeal.

She appeared drawn to Holden from their first meeting. He was twelve years older than she, married to actress Brenda Marshall and drinking heavily. The director, Mark Robson, took Holden aside after the first day of shooting and warned him against involving Grace in an affair. Holden ignored the advice. The film was made in Hollywood, and his car was said to be parked outside Grace's apartment house on Sweetzer Avenue almost every night. "It was hard not to fall in love with Grace," Holden later told the press. When *The Bridges at Toko-Ri* opened at Radio City Music Hall in January 1955 her name came below Holden's in the credits. The *New York Times* critic called her "briefly bewitching," and the *New York Herald Tribune* film editor wrote, "Everyone knows how nice it is to have her around." But in Hollywood, it is the box office returns, not reviews, that are important and Grace's films were commercial hits. Grace, on the other hand, believed she could, if given the right role, have it both ways.

The part she wanted to play was that of Georgie Elgin in the planned adaptation of the Clifford Odets play *The Country Girl,* to be directed by George Seaton and to star William Holden and Bing Crosby in two of the three main roles. Georgie was the long-suffering wife and caretaker of an alcoholic actor (Bing Crosby), managed by the Holden character. She was plain, a tough, uncompromising woman. Metro-Goldwyn-Mayer refused to allow her to do the film. She threatened to break her contract and return to the stage. Finally they agreed.

The Country Girl began filming almost immediately after *The Bridges at Toko-Ri* was completed. Grace was still in love with Holden but he now decided that he had to give his marriage another chance. Grace was under tremendous tension—there were her problems with Holden, the difficulty of the role and, in the beginning, a personality clash between herself and Crosby. Midway through the film his attitude changed as he saw how hard she was working at her part and to keep Holden at a distance. Crosby now became as enamored of Grace as had the majority of her other co-stars. In his favor were his Catholicism and the fact that he was a widower. Grace did not return his feelings to the same extent, but the romance helped her to overcome her feelings for Holden.

In the short time she had been in Hollywood, Judy Balaban Quine later wrote in her autobiography, "Grace had done six of Hollywood's hottest pictures [*High Noon, Mogambo, Rear Window, Dial M for Murder, The Bridges at Toko-Ri* and *The Country Girl*] and, reputedly, four of the hottest male stars in the business [apparently referring to Cooper, Gable, Holden and Crosby]."

Grace's schedule was difficult. She still maintained her New York apartment and between films flew back to appear in short-term stage productions; in stock and off-Broadway. She thought of herself as "of the theater." She had never gone Hollywood and seemed unconcerned about her image. She seldom appeared at galas or premieres or dated for publicity, and despite her new affluence, she did not spend her money on a showy apartment or an expensive car. It seemed she might be perfectly happy to turn her back on Hollywood. But then Hitchcock sent her the script of the film he had been preparing since they had worked together on *Rear Window,* a story about a slick and very attractive cat burglar who uses his past talents *To Catch a Thief,* which would be shot on the Riviera; in fact, most scenes would take place on the Corniche above Monte Carlo. Cary Grant was to co-star. Perhaps because she had heard the Hollywood rumors about Grace's penchant for older, married men, Grant's wife, the actress Betsy Drake, accompanied him. The three became good friends, frequenting the Casino which Grace, although betting small stakes, found exciting. Rainier, who was deeply involved with the PMS bank scandal at this time, did

237

nothing to welcome the film people to his Principality. Had they met then, it is doubtful they would have had a future, for Grace was deeply in love with a man who she was convinced would be her mate for life—suave, European Oleg Cassini, a fashion designer recently divorced from actress Gene Tierney.

Cassini had an exotic background. Born in Paris of aristocratic Russian parents and raised in Florence, he had achieved success as a couturier before the war and had gone to the United States, where he immediately became the darling of cosmopolitan society. He and Grace had met through the French actor Jean-Pierre Aumont, who was appearing with Grace in a television film.

Cassini followed her to the Riviera, and their affair flourished in the warmth and beauty of the surroundings and in the company of good friends such as the Grants and the Hitchcocks and the many fascinating Europeans of Cassini's acquaintance from the art, literary and society worlds. He was unlike any of the men Grace had known. He was not just a bon vivant. He had charm and wit, spoke four languages fluently (Russian, French, Italian and English), and was well-read and well-informed. His second daughter with Gene Tierney had been born severely retarded because of a case of measles he had caught during his wife's pregnancy and had given to her. He carried this guilt with him and the tinge of sadness aroused Grace's emotions. Cassini was sixteen years older than Grace, yet she had a faintly maternal attitude toward him.

Cassini was the first eligible man with whom Grace was truly in love. They returned to the United States after the completion of *To Catch a Thief* in the spring of 1955 to be met with an avalanche of public and press interest. Grace took him home to meet her parents, which proved to be disastrous. "The mere thought of Grace marrying a divorced man was distasteful to us," Ma Kelly wrote in a newspaper piece not long after.

Cassini was unprepared for the intolerance and rudeness that greeted him. "Mr. Cassini," Ma said in a clipped, hard tone, "you're terribly charming and continental, and I can certainly understand Grace's wanting to date you, but as a marriage risk you're very poor."

Cassini refused to let Grace's mother take the upper hand. Having been told by Grace of her father's infidelities, he replied:

"You know, I've always said that before one accuses another person, it is a good idea to be sure of one's own ground."

He had dinner with the entire Kelly family. It was a ghastly evening. Neither Ma nor Jack addressed him directly, and Grace's sisters were cool, fearing their parents' wrath if they were friendly. Brother Kell, who had told a reporter that Cassini "looked like an odd ball" to him, had been threatening to "kill him when he walks through the door."

Grace's younger sister, Lizanne, had just become engaged to a young man of whom the family also did not approve, Donald Le Vine. "Donald was Jewish," Cassini commented to biographer Steven Englund, "so he, too, was in bad odor with the family, though not so bad as I. He was the only person [apart from Grace] who talked to me. We were the pariahs."

Grace was firmly told that if she married Cassini (whom her parents still considered a married man), "there would be no more Christmases at home." It may seem astonishing that a twenty-five-year-old woman who had been living away from home for seven years and was one of the most famous film stars in the world would have considered this a serious deprivation. But Grace could not bear to think of being cut out of her family's celebrations, nor could she deal with the idea that they did not find the man she loved acceptable. Cassini fought to hold them together, but he was on the losing side, far outnumbered by the Kelly family.

In April, Grace, to her amazement, won the Academy Award for her performance in *The Country Girl*. William Holden presented her with the Oscar. It was an emotional moment. Unable to control her tears, Grace could only mutter a heartfelt "Thank you for the honor." Jack Kelly, on the other hand, telephoned by a reporter for a quote, said: "There's been too much publicity about Grace. Peggy's the family extrovert. Just between us, I've always thought her the daughter who's got the most on the ball."

Within a week after Grace won the award, M.G.M. placed her on suspension for not accepting a role opposite Robert Taylor in *Quentin Durward*, a costume picture based on the novel by Sir Walter Scott. She was in a state of serious depression, not knowing what she should do next in either her career or her personal life. The affair with Cassini was all but over. The film part she had wanted in *Giant,* which was to be directed by George Stevens, had gone to Elizabeth Taylor. She had also been rejected for the role of Roxanne in a Broadway revival of *Cyrano de Bergerac.* A journalist named Rupert Allan, with whom she had become friendly, suggested she go to the Cannes Film Festival. He impressed upon her that she was currently the most popular star in Europe as well as in the United States, and that rather than sit and brood she should be in the public eye. She flew to Paris a week later and took the train to Cannes with Pierre Galante, editor of *Paris Match,* who was married to the film star Olivia de Havilland.

During the journey Galante discussed an idea he had for a photo shoot. Would she be agreeable to meeting Prince Rainier and doing a tour of the Palace gardens? Recalling Rainier's coolness to the crew of *To Catch a Thief,* Grace suggested that he might not like film stars. Galante informed her that he had lived with one for years. "Well, in that case," she laughed.

"You agree?"

"If the Prince does," she replied smiling.

17

Rainier's favorite place to escape for a few solitary moments in the Palace was his private zoo. His love of animals had awakened during his childhood visits to Marchais, and Gisèle had shared his interest in wildlife. He was particularly drawn to primates because of their intelligence. Tanagra, a chimpanzee that had been born in the jungle and raised in captivity, was the object of his fondest regard and indulgence, for she had been his first feral acquisition and the only one allowed in other parts of the Palace. He now had quite a collection of monkeys, gorillas, lions, tigers, numerous other varieties of wild cats, a retired circus elephant (Rainier was especially fond of circuses) and some uncommon breeds like a llama and an oont (a species of camel).

There was a large zoo staff, but Rainier enjoyed helping to feed the animals. He had what one family member calls "a magic touch with them" and fearlessly entered their cages even when the keepers were cautious. Never able to work up great enthusiasm for creatures of the sea, he nonetheless understood his great-grandfather Albert's zeal for nature.

With his breakup with Gisèle, he was a lonely man. He could trust no one in his family. He loved children, and despite the bitterness of his relationship with his sister, he was happiest when his two nieces and his nephew came to visit and he could be lost in their simple childhood world. One problem after the other had beset him in his six-year reign: Ghislaine, the attempted coup, economic imbroglios, the PMS scandal, and the growing animosity and power struggle between him and Aristotle Onassis.

After a serious car accident in 1953, which almost cost him his life, he no longer raced. He enjoyed his yacht but remained shy with people, which meant his cruises were often friendless journeys; and he had never been the kind of man who was at ease with casual female companionship.

Rainier was now ready to accept the advice of his spiritual adviser, Father Tucker. He was thirty-two, a good age for a man to marry. Finding the right young woman was not that easy, however. First there were the things a prospective Princesse de Monaco must be: Catholic, fertile, rich, beautiful, and someone who would be a good companion to him. And then there were the things she could *not* be: German, of questionable birth, a woman not able to devote her complete life to him, their children and the Principality. This last requirement was perhaps the most difficult to meet, for Rainier's reticent nature drew him toward lively, intelligent women whose own experiences could bring excitement into his life and who might not be pleased to give up their independence.

Father Tucker had compiled a short list of prospects, headed by England's Princess Margaret, although he doubted whether her sister, Queen Elizabeth, would agree to a marriage that meant conversion to Catholicism. The name of the actress Grace Kelly had come to his mind on this May morning on which the film festival had begun at nearby Cannes, because a request was received for permission to shoot some photographs of the actress with the Prince in the Palace gardens. Rainier seldom agreed to such requests on the grounds that it was difficult to say yes to one and refuse another. But this time Father Tucker had come to him personally and seemed most eager for him to agree.

Father Tucker was an unusual man, not liked by many members of the Palace staff, who feared he held a "Rasputin-like influence" over Rainier and believed his "red-faced, robust Friar Tuck-like charm and good humor" were a mask for a devious personality. Although in his sixties, he rode a motor scooter, "possessed tremendous energy and his bustling busybody presence was to be discovered everywhere." Now he was going to become a royal marriage broker.

The priest, who was confessor to all 104 Catholics on the Palace staff, and who made it his business to know everything that was going on in Monaco, was Rainier's closest adviser. Father Tucker also had a strong grasp of Monaco's political and economic situation. Rainier had to recapture from his subjects their ardor for the Grimaldis won by Albert and lost by Louis II; he had to bring Monaco and Monte Carlo into the international forefront as a place of culture and economic stability as Albert I (and Alice) had done; and he had to outshine Onassis if he wanted to retain his power at home. Right now the Greek was the Principality's only hope to reestablish its former success, for he had invested large sums to refurbish the Casino and the hotels controlled by the S.B.M. and his presence brought confidence to other investors. Tourism was on the rise in Europe and, as Father Tucker was quick to point out, the Royal Wedding in London eight years earlier, followed by the lavish coronation of the young queen, had made England the greatest tourist draw in the world.

He now suggested a plan that first startled, and then pleased, Rainier. With the collapse of so many European thrones during the war, few eligible royal young ladies remained. Why not then a film star—who would at least be able to play the role? If she was Catholic it would be a bonus. But conversion would also be acceptable to the Church if she had not been previously married and divorced. She must, however, not have been involved in any scandal, be independently rich (for Monaco could not afford the cost of a lavish state wedding and Rainier's own finances were at very low ebb), and yes—of course—appeal to him as a woman.

The list was regrettably short. There was the English actress Deborah Kerr, the American Eva Maria Saint, winner that year of the Academy Award for supporting actress in *On the Waterfront*, the eighteen-year-old Natalie Wood, whose new film, *Rebel Without a Cause*, was creating much excitement, and Grace Kelly.[1] Of this group, only Grace was Catholic and reputedly rich. Father Tucker knew of the family from his days in Philadelphia. And, as fate would have it, here was the lovely Miss Kelly, eager, it seemed, to meet Rainier and view his gardens.

Grace was not enthusiastic to learn that an appointment had

[1]Several stories have circulated stating Marilyn Monroe was first considered. In one version, Monroe was approached by two of Aristotle Onassis's representatives. When asked if she thought the Prince would want to marry her, Monroe reportedly replied: "Give me two days with him, and of course he'll want to marry me." In another account, Father Tucker wrote directly to Monroe on Rainier's behalf. Since the actress was divorcing her second husband, Joe DiMaggio, at the time, it is unlikely that a Catholic priest would have promoted her candidacy as future Princesse de Monaco.

been set for the following afternoon, May 6, at 4:00 P.M. by Galante and Rupert Allan, who was also in Cannes. She was expected to attend a reception for the American film delegation at 5:30, and it would be impossible to return in time from Monaco during rush-hour traffic. Allan called the Palace and the meeting, with Rainier's approval, was changed to 3:00 P.M. As Rainier had altered his schedule to suit hers, Grace resigned herself to doing the right thing and, although she did so with much reluctance (for she never enjoyed publicity appearances), accepted.

She awoke the next morning, her first in Cannes, to be informed that during the night a nationwide general labor strike had been called. There was no electricity and she had washed her hair in the shower and not bothered to have anything pressed after unpacking the previous evening. She tucked her hair back into a twist with some delicate artificial daisies that came off a badly crushed dress and pulled on the only frock that did not need pressing, a boldly flowered taffeta creation that was all wrong for an afternoon tour of a garden. At least she was relieved to learn that as an American she did not have to make a proper curtsy to the Prince, for the dress had a crinoline underskirt that would have made curtsying difficult.

Despite all his best efforts, Rainier arrived nearly an hour late for their appointment, a heated council meeting having detained him. Grace, meanwhile, had been taken on a tour of the Palace and was in the Blue Drawing Room admiring a portrait when the massive doors opened and Rainier entered, wearing sunglasses, his face flushed, his demeanor self-conscious; he was not at all the princely figure that she had expected. To her surprise, he posed effortlessly for Galante's pictures, one of him and Grace meeting and another of them standing on a balcony overlooking the courtyard, where he asked if she was ready to tour the Palace and gardens with him. She replied that she had already done that. Apologetic, he then suggested that she might like to see his private zoo. Galante, camera poised, moved to follow them but Father Tucker's ample figure barred his passage.

When Rupert Allan asked Grace later what she thought of Rainier, she said, "He's charming, quite charming—and shy." She had been shocked and impressed to see him walk fearlessly into a lion's cage, and she laughingly said he had been amusing and rather better looking than she had expected. When she returned to her hotel in Cannes, her old friend Jean-Pierre Aumont was waiting for her. A widower for the past two years, he had finally picked up the pieces of his life after the tragic heart attack and premature death, at the age of thirty-one, of his wife, the actress Maria Montez. Aumont was in Cannes promoting his current French film, *Mademoiselle de Paris*.

By the time Grace left Cannes for Paris a week later, she believed she was in love, not with Rainier as Father Tucker would have hoped but with the tall, blond, blue-eyed, charming Aumont, who was already hinting at marriage and who had a small daughter in need of a mother's immediate care.

Nor was it love at first sight for Rainier, but he was not immune to Grace Kelly's obvious charms, despite her appearance in the inappropriate flowered taffeta dress. He requested a private showing of *The Country Girl*. Disappointed in her plain appearance in it (for she was made to look dowdy for her role), he asked if he could see *To Catch a Thief*. In no other film had Grace looked more beautiful. He wrote her a polite note telling her he had enjoyed their short visit together, apologized again for having kept her waiting, and expressed a wish that they might have more time to talk the next time she was on the Riviera. Privately he did not believe anything would come of it, for the newspapers had been filled with photographs of Grace and Aumont together at the Cannes festival, lunching and dining tête-à-tête, walking hand in hand through the French countryside, and smiling into each other's eyes across a table in a Paris nightclub.

But Father Tucker had not given up; and neither, it seems, had Rainier. Shortly after Grace had left the Palace after that first meeting, Father Tucker had asked Rainier how they got along. The Prince told him he was most impressed. Within a few weeks, the priest had not only written Grace a letter ("I want to thank you for showing the Prince what an American Catholic girl can be and for the very deep impression this has left on him"), he had contacted former associates in the Archdiocese in Philadelphia and gleaned (according to Grace's friend the writer Jeffrey Robinson) "more about Grace and the

245

Kellys from his priestly intelligence network than even Grace and the Kellys might have known."

Some friends of Jack and Ma Kelly from Philadelphia, Edith and Russ Austin, arrived in Monte Carlo in August when a large gala was being held at the Sporting Club. Desperately wanting to attend and having seen the published pictures of Grace and Rainier, Russ rang up the Palace, asked to speak to Rainier's secretary and, using Grace's name, requested tickets to the event for him and his wife. An hour later Father Tucker called, and the Austins (who got their tickets) and he met. From them, he learned that Grace's romantic interest in Aumont had ended with her believing that he had used her for his own publicity needs, and that she would soon be filming *The Swan* for M.G.M. on location near Asheville, North Carolina. What neither he nor the Austins knew was that Rainier and Grace had been corresponding secretly.

Grace had returned to Philadelphia in June 1955, shortly after her unexpectedly public romance with Aumont had ended almost as quickly as it had started. Lizanne was marrying Donald Le Vine, and Grace was to be a bridesmaid. While she was at home, Ma had several long, stern talks with her about "the loose style of her life" and how it was upsetting both her parents. Peggy was married well and a mother; and now Lizzie was settled, although Ma was not comfortable with the idea of having a Jewish son-in-law. An effort was made to pair Grace off with one of Philadelphia's most eligible young bachelors, but she had absolutely nothing in common with him.

Before she left for Asheville, Father Cartin, the priest in the Kellys' diocese, requested a private meeting with her. She was surprised by this and somewhat nervous about what he might have to say, believing that her mother must have asked him to speak to her. Grace was taken aback when he inquired if she felt anything more than regard for His Serene Highness, Prince Rainier of Monaco. She had kept their correspondence secret and had not discussed their growing pen friendship with anyone.

She did not know that by the beginning of October Rainier had decided she was the woman he wanted to marry, and that royal protocol prohibited him from proposing to her if there was any chance she might refuse. Rainier had confided his dilemma to Father Tucker, who had contacted Father Cartin. Grace did not know how to reply to the question he had put to her. It was almost as if the priest were proposing to her for Rainier. She answered honestly that she had liked him when they met and that his letters were endearing. She felt comfortable writing to him about some of her deeper feelings, for she thought he understood her.

"Should he feel optimistic if he should come here to see you?" the priest asked.

Grace thought about it for a while before replying, "Yes."

Within two weeks Rainier announced that he would be making his first journey to the United States in December. Asked by a journalist if he was thinking of becoming engaged to anyone, he shook his head with embarrassment. "Give me three years," he laughed nervously. The reporter then inquired what sort of woman appealed to him. He described Grace, almost exactly. Ostensibly his trip was being made to submit to a thorough medical checkup at Johns Hopkins Hospital in Baltimore. His automobile accident two years earlier had left him with some pain down one leg.

Before he departed, Rainier had his Minister of State speak to the French Consul in Monaco about his intention to propose marriage to *une Americaine* (Grace's name supposedly was not submitted). According to the 1918 treaty between France and Monaco, all members of the Monégasque royal family ruling or in line to the throne had to have formal permission from the French Consul General to marry. The request was sent on to the proper person, and Rainier was given to believe that his marriage to an American woman would be acceptable.

He sailed with Father Tucker and his private physician, Dr. Robert Donat (no relation to the English actor of the same name), on December 8. He arrived in New York on the fifteenth, and the next day he traveled to Asheville to see Grace. The film she was doing, *The Swan,* directed by Charles Vidor and co-starring Alec Guinness and Louis Jourdan, was about an American girl whose mother is determined to marry her to a prince. Rainier was brought to her dressing room when she was in costume, wearing a magnificent ball gown and a glittering paste tiara. They had met only once before, and in view of the importance of the moment, both of them were apprehensive. After

247

a few minutes they were left alone and spoke for about half an hour. Then Rainier went out on the set with her and watched as she went through a grand ballroom scene several times with Alec Guinness, her fictional prince.

There had been no proposal, but Grace had given Rainier to understand that she might consider one if it was proffered. Rainier left for Baltimore and his medical checkup. A plan had been advanced that he visit Grace and her family in Philadelphia for the Christmas holiday. In that week, Rainier had a lot of formal matters to attend to.

Grace's name was now submitted to the French Consul General and approved. Rainier arrived at the Kellys' Henry Avenue house on Christmas Day accompanied by Father Tucker. Rainier says he did not actually propose to Grace until two days later, the twenty-seventh, when they attended a gala party in New York and he escorted her home to her apartment (a new one that she was in the throes of redecorating). He says he asked her simply, "Will you marry me?" and she replied, "Yes."

Grace told Judith Kanter the day after she accepted Rainier's proposal, "I am so much in love. So very much. . . . It isn't like any time before. . . . He is everything I've ever loved. . . . I love his eyes. I could look into them for hours. He has a beautiful voice. . . . I love him."

They drove to Philadelphia the following morning. Rainier spoke privately to his future father-in-law, and told him of his intentions. Kelly was obviously pleased that Grace would at last settle down and raise a family and that Rainier was Catholic. But he had small regard for his title. He had been brought up in the years when European titles were bought for the daughters of rich men like himself, and the idea seemed particularly un-American to him.

In fact, the idea of royalty itself seemed un-American to Jack Kelly. When first approached by Father Tucker the week before, he had shouted, "I don't want any damn broken-down Prince who is head of a pin-head country that nobody knows anything about to marry my daughter!" Now, as Rainier faced him in person, he warned, "I hope you don't run around like some princes do, because if you do you'll lose a mighty fine girl. Don't forget she has Irish blood in her veins and she knows what she wants."

Ma was more than pleased, she was ecstatic, until she learned that the wedding would have to be held in Monaco. "That's not the way it's done in America!" she complained.

Now came the tricky problem of the marriage contract. When Jack Kelly first saw the document, he was furious. Rainier and Grace were to be married under what is known in France as *séparation de biens,* which meant that each kept the property that he or she brought into the marriage but must contribute to the family ménage, and what was acquired during the marriage would belong to the husband. At first Jack Kelly was asked to give a two-million-dollar dowry and to maintain certain of the household costs of running the Palace and any other houses they might acquire. He refused point-blank to sign an open-ended agreement like that. "My daughter doesn't have to pay any man to marry her," he insisted.

He was informed that a dowry was quite normal in Europe. This cut no ice with Kelly. The contract was redrawn. He would pay two million dollars toward a large state wedding (American fathers did, after all, pay for their daughters' weddings), and he set up a trust for Grace, on which she could draw annually. On January 5, 1956, Monégasques heard the announcement that their Prince was to be married to Grace Kelly. Many were not pleased at the idea of another actress becoming the Princesse de Monaco (Princesse Ghislaine being the first); even more felt uncomfortable that she was an American. Few had seen her in a film; and since Rainier's first edict on his return was to ban the showing of her movies in the Principality (her love scenes with other men were considered unseemly), they would only see them elsewhere.

Rainier claims that Grace was never subjected to a fertility test by Dr. Donat or any other doctor, and it seems likely, despite reports to the contrary, that she was not. Fertility tests are not necessarily reliable for one thing; for another, the 1918 French-Monégasque Treaty provided for the possibility of an adopted heir (as Charlotte had been) if both countries approved. In the event that Grace did not give birth to an heir, Antoinette's son, Christian de Massey, could have been legally adopted by his uncle and become his heir. But the strongest case against this procedure having been performed was Grace's known repugnance for such a clinical approach to their proposed marriage.

It has been suggested that Dr. Donat accompanied Rainier to America in order to conduct the test, but after a week of close contact with Grace, Rainier was truly in love with her—besotted might be a better description. One has only to see the photographs of them taken during this period—the direct gaze of his eyes as he looked at her, the caressing hand on her arm, her shoulder, her back—to sense that here was a man deeply, sexually in love. It is doubtful that he could have denied her much at this stage in their relationship for fear of losing her, and Grace was not about to submit to what she considered an unsavory examination.

What had taxed Rainier's persuasive powers was to convince Grace that she must end her acting career before the marriage. He impressed upon her that, in his opinion, she would be playing the greatest role any woman could play—Her Serene Highness, Princesse de Monaco—and that she would remain in the public eye for the rest of her life.

Once again, Grace confided her deepest feelings to Judith Kanter. "I don't want to be married to someone who feels belittled by my success. . . . The Prince is not going to be 'Mr. Kelly.' What he does is far more important than what I do. I want to help him in his work. I hope I can. That's the way it should be."

Rainier had succeeded, but the problem was that Grace was under contract to M.G.M. for another four years. Her agent, Jay Kanter, was consulted and he approached the powers at the studio. Finally, an agreement was reached. Grace would make one more film, *High Society,* which would go before the cameras in a matter of weeks, and M.G.M. would have the exclusive film rights to "the wedding of the century," which Grace had already agreed would be in April, less than four months hence.

Grace and Rainier made their first public appearance together on January 6, 1956, at an extravagant gala aptly titled "A Night in Monte Carlo," held in the grand ballroom at New York's Waldorf-Astoria Hotel and attended by about two thousand people, including scores from the international press corps. When Grace entered on Rainier's arm she looked more beautiful than ever in a strapless white taffeta gown, tight at the waist, tiered with taffeta bows on the billowing skirt, two rows of pearls on her neck, long white gloves, her hair pulled back into a chignon, pearls and diamonds on her ears and a slash of color on her lips that matched the magenta red at the throats of the white orchids pinned to the bodice of her gown (which was one of her costumes from *The Swan*).

In mid-January she started work in Hollywood on *High Society,* a musical version of *The Philadelphia Story,* directed by Charles Walters and featuring songs by Cole Porter. Grace, in the original Katharine Hepburn role as Tracy Lord, the society girl, wore her official engagement ring, a magnificent twelve-carat blue-white diamond, throughout the film, but on her right hand. (Rainier had given her a "friendship" ring of diamonds and sapphires until it was ready.) Her co-stars were Frank Sinatra and Bing Crosby. Rainier and his father, Prince Pierre, joined her in Los Angeles ten days later. Grace was under tremendous pressure. This was the first musical in which she had ever appeared, and the part had been originally created by playwright Philip Barry for Hepburn. Shooting had to be completed by the end of March, and she would then have to leave for Monaco and the wedding almost immediately. In the few moments she had, she took French lessons, worked on the plans for the wedding and had fittings for her bridal gown and her trousseau. And daily there were photographers and reporters for her to face.

Sinatra has said that her calm in the midst of all this havoc was impressive. Only once did she lose her temper. One morning she awoke to find the front page of the *Los Angeles Herald Tribune* was carrying a story headed: MY DAUGHTER GRACE KELLY—HER LIFE AND ROMANCES, the first of a ten-part syndicated series by Margaret Kelly. Thinking it was some terrible mistake she telephoned her mother. Ma told her that she had written the story and sold it to the highest bidder to help her favorite charity. "Couldn't she have given a damn benefit?" Grace snapped to Judith Kanter via long-distance telephone.

Rainier returned to Monaco two weeks before Grace was finished on *High Society.* Grace made her last appearance in Hollywood at the Academy Awards ceremony, presenting Ernest Borgnine with the Oscar for Best Actor for his role in *Marty.* Then she flew to New York to be a bridesmaid at Rita Gam's wedding to publishing heir Tom Guinzberg. Rita had been a former roommate of hers in Hollywood and the two had retained a close friendship. Three days later, on April 4, in pouring rain, Grace, her beloved black poodle Oliver, and sixty-five friends and family (and friends of family) boarded the *U.S. Constitution* at Pier 84 in New York on their way to Monaco and "The Wedding of the Century."

18

On the morning of April 12, Rainier paced nervously up and down the bridge of his white yacht, the *Deo Juvante*, the Grimaldi colors flapping in a high wind. There had been the threat of a mistral the previous night, and though the rain had subsided and the wind had dropped, the Mediterranean was so choppy that his captain was having difficulty in bringing the boat alongside the *U.S. Constitution*. For the first time in Monaco's history, an ocean liner was to anchor just outside its waters. The bridal party, except for Grace, would disembark (along with two whole vanloads of her luggage) onto the launches brightly decorated with banners and flags (American and Monégasque flown side by side). Grace was to transfer from the larger ship to the yacht and then to travel with Rainier the short distance into Monaco's harbor where a crush of Monégasques, tourists, reporters and press photographers were waiting.

The disembarkation took nearly an hour, while the two vessels pitched and rolled; a half-dozen additional smaller launches worked to secure them side by side, while three helicopters (with camera crews inside) circled above. Finally the task was completed, and a flower-carpeted gangway lowered onto the deck of the yacht. Rainier positioned himself at its base. Protocol required that Grace come down the gangway to him.

Suddenly, there she was, huge sunglasses masking her eyes and half her face, holding on to a massive white cartwheel hat with one hand and grasping Oliver in the other. As she began to descend, a stream of red carnations thrown from the decks of the *U.S. Constitution* by the wedding party, passengers and crew cascaded onto the deck of the Grimaldi royal yacht, spilling over into the sea and creating swirling crimson waves. When Grace was only a few feet from him, Rainier jumped onto the gangplank and grabbed Oliver, almost knocking off Grace's hat;

placing his free arm around her waist he guided her onto the deck of the *Deo Juvante.*

As the yacht entered Monaco's waters, the cannons on the Palace ramparts fired a twenty-one gun salute, a simultaneous volley of sirens burst forth from every vessel in the bay, fireboats sent up sprays of water, and a quayside band played the popular song "Love and Marriage." From overhead, Onassis's private plane showered the harbor with many thousands more red and white carnations; and throngs of people waving both Moné-gasque and American flags crushed together to welcome the Principality's future Princesse.

Onassis stood on the deck of the *Christina* with a clear view of Grace as she stepped down from the gangplank of the royal yacht, Rainier supporting her arm. The Greek (as he was called by the royal family) turned to a friend. "A prince and a movie star. It's pure fantasy," he said.

Rainier and Grace were driven up to the Palace where the bride-to-be and the close members of her family were to remain for the length of their stay. (Rainier was chauffeured each eve-ning to his Villa Iberia in Saint-Jean-Cap-Ferrat.) A private luncheon was held in the dining room. The Kellys and the Grimaldis—except for Rainier—were meeting for the first time. The atmosphere was excruciatingly tense. Rainier had told Grace about his family and their quarrels, but she was still not prepared for the chilly greeting she received from his mother, stepmother (Princesse Ghislaine) and Antoinette, nor for the strained atmostphere between these women.

With Grace's presence, Antoinette knew her social and po-litical power in Monaco would slip. ("The marriage won't last two years," she told a friend, a trace of hopefulness in her voice. "Grimaldi marriages seldom do.")

"I don't think anyone felt comfortable," Rainier's nephew, Christian de Massey, wrote. "The expression on my grand-mother Mamou's face was something to see. . . . She was ab-solutely furious at finding herself in the presence of the groom's father, the Prince de Polignac [her ex-husband], whom she hated with a Grimaldi-like fierceness. She was also upset by the presence of Ghislaine. . . . And Mamou and my mother [An-toinette] had been estranged for so many years that Mummy's presence was also a problem for her. Mingled with all of these strains was the fact that she was compelled to receive an American movie star as her son's future bride."

Ma Kelly complained that she was rudely snubbed. And within a day, rumors spread about Jack Kelly's penchant for greeting servants and staff in his apartment in his undershorts, bare-chested, several ryes to the wind, and in a voice that echoed through the chambers. Jack was less than impressed by the powdered wigs and satin knee breeches of the footmen, whom he accused of being "an army of sneaky informers," or by his future in-laws, whom he called "a bunch of god-damned degenerates."

Even Rainier had been shocked when his mother arrived at the Palace with a notorious jewel thief, René Gigier, formerly France's Public Enemy Number One and known as "René la Canne" ("René the Walking Stick") due to a peculiarity in his gait which gave him a stiff-legged step. Looking rather startling in a tight-fitting white uniform that showed off his muscular physique, he flourished his official pass as chauffeur to Princesse Charlotte, whom he had driven down from Marchais. He had been paroled into her custody while serving a twenty-year term for armed robbery. (It did not ease the tension over Gigier's presence when Ma Kelly's and a bridesmaid's jewels were stolen.) René was now Charlotte's lover as well as her gardener-chauffeur. To her son's dismay, when René was recognized by reporters, his mother told him, "I thought the air and sun would do him good. His health is delicate after his years in prison."

For the first two days following her arrival, Grace remained sequestered in the Palace. Her M.G.M. hairstylist, Virginia Darcy, was the only member of the Kelly group apart from the family who remained at the Palace; the others were staying at various hotels.[1] The massive press corps was under tremendous pressure to get pictures of Grace any way they could, and of any kind they could, and they were (unsuccessfully) offering members of the Kelly entourage inside the Palace bribes to smuggle in a camera and secure some candid shots. On the

[1]The S.B.M. was footing the bill for the bridesmaids' accommodations and Rainier for the Kelly family members who were his guests at the Palace. Jack Kelly was responsible for the huge costs of the ocean crossing of the sixty-six-member contingent of his family and guests.

second evening Darcy came to Grace with the news that Russ Austin (the same Philadelphian who had called the Palace for tickets to a gala the previous year, using Grace's name) had approached her in the lobby of the Hôtel de Paris, pressed a miniature camera into her hand and promised her one hundred dollars for each shot of Grace she could deliver. Darcy refused. Austin then handed her a roll of bills which she pushed away.

"I'll ask her," Darcy said. "If she says okay, I'll do it." She then went to Grace and told her what had happened.

"Do you need the money?" Grace asked.

"No, Grace," she replied. "I just want you to know what a circus it's getting to be down there with everyone, not just the press."

This carnival atmosphere was not what Rainier had wanted for his wedding. His first disappointment had been the refusals on the part of the major nations to send a significant dignitary to attend the ceremony. Invitations had gone to Buckingham Palace, Winston Churchill, President Eisenhower and President de Gaulle. His family's behavior had also greatly distressed him. And he was concerned that the overwhelming press presence would diminish the joy and the solemnity of the occasion and unnerve the bride.

He underestimated Grace, who retained a calm appearance and a clear head throughout, although later she was to say that "the royal wedding day and the whole period that preceded it were among the worst ordeals [I have] ever known." She was miserably aware of the tension that existed among the Grimaldis and between Rainier's family and her own. What she seems to have done was to propel herself into the role of Princesse de Monaco the moment she entered the Principality.

It rained almost steadily for the first three days and nights and then intermittently until the morning of April 18, the day of the civil marriage ceremony (the actual wedding was on the nineteenth). The sun broke through gray skies just as Rainier and Grace entered the throne room, at eleven A.M., and sent a shaft of shimmering gold through the centuries-old windows. They stood "rather nervously" opposite the high stone chimneypiece from which hung the Grimaldi coat of arms. Eighty guests sat in gilt chairs that lined two sides of the room. The marriage contract was to be signed and witnessed by two representatives for Grace (her sister Peggy and, curiously, Princesse Antoinette) and three for Rainier (his cousin, Count Charles de Polignac; a close friend, Lieutenant Colonel Jean-Marie Ardant; and Grace's brother, Kell.)

Grace looked lovely in a champagne alençon lace dress with a chiffon turban to match, but she seemed unusually solemn. One guest noticed that she was taking short nervous breaths as if to control her anxiety. Not only did the premarriage contract she had signed make her responsible for a share of their household expenses and guarantee Rainier that the $2 million dowry paid by Jack Kelly in the form of the cost of the wedding would not be returnable should the marriage vows be broken, it also stipulated that should the marriage break down, no matter who was at fault, their children would remain with their father. If she had any doubts about the contract into which she was entering, this was the moment to speak up, and as she stood waiting for the civil ceremony to begin, Rainier by her side, she appeared visibly disturbed.

"Have I the permission of Your Highness to proceed?" asked Monsieur Marcel Portanier, the President of the State Council.

"Yes," Rainier, trim in his morning coat and striped trousers, replied.

The bride was then asked if she was willing for this marriage to take place. "Yes," she said, in a barely audible voice. Rainier made a small gesture with his right hand to touch her left hand and then withdrew it, raising it to his neck and finally lowering it to his side. She turned to him at that moment, and his face flushed. They were now legally man and wife, although Grace nervously joked a moment later that they were only half married until they exchanged their vows in the Catholic service the following day.

That evening celebratory parties were held all over Monaco. A special gala performance for the royal couple and members of their family and entourage by the brilliant ballet artists, Margot Fonteyn and Christopher Soames, was held in the Salle Garnier. Grace and Rainier sat in the Royal Box, newly engraved with an entwined R and G. Grace wore an exquisite collection of newly acquired diamonds; and the red and white Order of

257

St. Charles, the highest that could be bestowed in Monaco,[2] crossed from her right shoulder to the left side of her magnificent white Lanvin ball gown, lavishly embroidered in gold and encrusted with mother-of-pearl that caught the splintered light from the many crystal chandeliers.

After the performance the "half-married" couple and their guests returned to the Palace where a pavilion had been constructed for a reception. At one minute past midnight, all of Monaco went dark. Then, suddenly, the sky overhead was ablaze with a dazzling display of fireworks, planned and paid for by Onassis. It continued uninterrupted for an hour and ended in enormous pyrotechnic portraits of Rainier and Grace that flashed across the heavens and then dissolved into darkness before the lights of the Principality came on once again. When they did, Rainier took his last ride alone back to the Villa Iberia for the night.

At 10:35 the next morning, April 19, Rainier caught the first glimpse of his bride in her spectacular wedding gown as she started up the nave of the white stone Gothic Cathedral of St. Nicholas on the arm of her father. Protocol required that she precede him to the altar and wait for him to join her there. Her face was half hidden behind a sheer tulle veil. Her gown, of pale caramel lace, which weighed half as much as Grace herself, had an old-fashioned high neck, long skintight sleeves and a form-fitting bodice that topped a magnificent skirt that pouffed and billowed with nearly four hundred yards of combined silk and Valenciennes lace.

The Cathedral was heavily scented from the thousands of branches of white lilac (Grace's favorite flower) that hung in golden baskets from the chandeliers and the sweet-smelling wax of the candles that illuminated the high altar. When Grace and her father reached the altar to the sounds of Purcell's "Alleluia" (the six bridesmaids; the matron of honor, her sister Peggy; two ring bearers, one being young Christian de Massey, Antoinette's son; and four small flower girls following solemnly behind), Bishop Barthe of Monaco, who was performing the ceremony,

---

[2]Previously, the Order of St. Charles had not been given to a Princesse de Monaco until long after her marriage.

nodded to Jack Kelly that he could leave his daughter's side and take his seat in the bride's section, as had been rehearsed.

Kelly did not budge. The bishop nodded again. But the father of the bride refused to move and would not do so until her groom was by his daughter's side.

Rainier wore a uniform of his own design which represented Monaco's history. Elements of French, Italian and the Principality's Carabinieri officer uniforms of the eighteenth and nineteenth centuries had been incorporated in the red-and-white-sashed costume with its black and gold tunic, blue trousers with a gold stripe down their side, and a midnight blue bicorne hat with white ostrich feathers. On his tunic was a breastful of medals. The impression was a touch Napoleonic, emphasized by Rainier's short, square physique.

Preceded by Father Tucker, Father Cartin (the Kellys' priest from Philadelphia) and the Papal Legate, Monsignor Marella from Paris, Rainier walked down the nave of the Cathedral to take his place beside Grace in front of the altar. Monsignor Marella read a letter from the Pope in French and English. Then followed the actual wedding ceremony, which lasted almost sixty minutes. During this time there was a merciless battery of flashlights from television and movie cameras. Two unauthorized reporters, masquerading as cassocked priests, had to be removed with somewhat noisy authority, and a photographer, smuggled into the orchestra, almost succeeded in focusing his camera from inside a bassoon while Bishop Barthe pronounced the benediction.

Despite all the microphones and amplifiers, Grace could not be heard saying, "I do," although her lips could be seen to move when the film of the wedding was released. There was no kiss after the bishop pronounced them man and wife, but Rainier grasped his wife's hand and as they exchanged a long, lingering glance, there was a tear in her eye.

A wedding lunch in the Palace followed. At five that evening, dressed now in their going-away clothes—a dark suit for Rainier and a simple gray silk ensemble and a small white hat for Grace, who was once again holding Oliver tightly in her arms—the newlyweds boarded the *Deo Juvante* to the screeching of sirens and the flare of rockets. The sea was rough, and because Grace

259

was not a good sailor, a decision was made to anchor the boat a short distance up the coast at Villefranche before proceeding on the six-week honeymoon cruise to Majorca and around the Spanish coast.

Aristotle Onassis stood on the bow of the *Christina* and watched as the royal yacht pulled out of the harbor. He had great hopes that with a film star of Grace Kelly's magnitude and beauty as Princesse de Monaco, the Principality, and his investment in it, would burgeon. Her majestic demeanor during the difficult wedding week bolstered his confidence. Grace Kelly had been perfectly cast as the "fairy tale princess," and he was confident that the pictures of the wedding and the release of the filmed coverage were worth millions of francs in potential tourist revenue. What he had to do when she returned was to woo her over to his side, for she could help him to bring back to Monte Carlo its golden glories when it was *the* social center of Europe.

The wedding had put a temporary halt to the growing hostilities between Rainier and Onassis. The Greek was sinking large sums of the S.B.M.'s money along with his own into the building of a luxurious new Summer Sporting Club, and he had plans to remove the railway from its present site directly through the main thoroughfare, so that the dirt, noise and swarms of people using it would not interfere with the beauty of Monte Carlo's fashionable streets.

Onassis had invested over five million francs in adding four floors of luxurious new suites, and a magnificent rooftop restaurant with an electrically operated sliding roof for warm summer nights, to the Hôtel de Paris. He had a vision of Monte Carlo as a new haven for well-heeled sophisticates.

Rainier (whom he never addressed in the manner called for by his title, "Your Serene Highness," or as "Sir," but simply as "Rainier," which greatly irritated the Prince) had turned out to be a shrewder businessman than Onassis had anticipated. That would have been welcomed, except that they did not see eye to eye on Monte Carlo's future. While Onassis thought on a grand scale, Rainier, with the middle-class tourist ever in mind, was preoccupied with plans for building factories and workers' apartment blocks in the reclaimed Larvotto quarter, which was west of the Rock and a distance from Monte Carlo, and he kept reminding Onassis that "middle-income visitors, many on package tours, needed less costly hotels and *pensions,* a good stretch of beach, and more imaginative entertainment generally than the casino's fruit machines or a tour of the Oceanographic Museum."

Harsh words had passed between them. Rainier had taken offense when Onassis had told the press he had "only two toys: *Christina* and the S.B.M."; while Onassis was furious when it got back to him that Rainier had told a mutual acquaintance, "Monte Carlo is getting more like Monte Greco every day."

Onassis had contributed a large sum to help make the wedding the splendid affair it was (allowing Rainier to keep most of Grace's dowry). And he had given the new Princesse a magnificent diamond and ruby suite along with other gifts. To his mind, this entitled him to some new cooperation.

"Lucky bastard," he said to a friend as the *Deo Juvante* disappeared from sight.

"You or him?" his confidant asked.

Onassis laughed, but he didn't reply.

THE YEARS OF GRACE

19

GRACE BECAME A PRINCESS before she had a chance to understand what the term really meant. When she returned from her honeymoon in July 1956, pregnant and suffering from morning sickness, everyone familiar to her had departed for America. (To her friend Judith Kanter, she wrote: "We're preggos! Ecstatic!! Rainier will make the announcement soon . . .") Rainier had not disappointed her. He had been a kind and caring lover and an even more interesting man than she had expected, surprising her at every turn with his insight and knowledge. Yet, once back in Monaco, she was acutely aware of how far away she was from those people who had meant a great deal to her, the women friends whom she had always been able to confide in and the creative people in films and theater with whom she had worked.

To another friend she wrote that it seemed as if they had gone home and she had been left behind. For most of her life, despite her new position and eventually her own family, she held on to the past and to her old friends. And though she had given her word to Rainier that she would not act again, her letters home gave the impression that this was only a temporary situation, for she discussed films being made in the near future that she thought might have good roles for her and books that she hoped might be developed for the screen with her in mind.

The announcement of the expected birth of an heir to the throne was made by Rainier on August 2. He took the occasion as an opportunity to convey to Monégasques his position in his continuing struggle against Onassis's control and the National Council's resistance to his plans:

"The significance of this awaited event is clear to all of you. However, I find it indispensable to link this guarantee of the Principality's surviving in its independence and privileges, to the absolute necessity of establishing an era of total trust and confidence.

"The projects for economical and technological development which have received my approval are neither unreasonable, imprudent, nor opposed to the true interests of our country. They answer new needs which stem from a normal and desirable evolution of our general economy. . . . In light of this news [the imminent birth of an heir] . . . it seems impossible that we should not strengthen our trust in the future. . . . One chooses one's future and then starts building it. I ask you to trust in the choice I have made for Monaco's future, and also to remember that the Principality has endured, and will only endure, as long as its Sovereign Prince has full and complete exercise of power."

Grace had learned on her honeymoon about Monaco's domestic conflicts: the ongoing battle her husband was having with Onassis and Antoinette's envy and constant threat to his peace of mind. Grace and Rainier had returned from an almost idyllic honeymoon cruise to the realization that their wedding, which they believed would not only help Monaco's economy and bring the Principality to the attention of the world but unite Monégasques closer together—a wedding that had placed them under much stress and pressure—had been followed by infighting and accusations. Rainier was now seen as an opportunist, using the marriage as a means of publicity, not just for Monaco but for his personal financial benefit. And where Grace had previously been surrounded by a circle of warm, concerned friends and respectful associates, she now was treated as an outsider by Rainier's family and by Monaco's society matrons who were mostly French and spoke their own language in Grace's presence even though they were aware that she did not yet fully understand it.

Before World War II the non-Monégasque population had been mainly Italian. After the war there had been great prejudice toward the Italian population of the Principality and the more important Italian families—even those who had lived in Monaco for several generations—reemigrated to Italy and the French population tripled. Frenchmen took over many of the highest positions in business and government, from the directorship of the Casino to the members of Rainier's Cabinet and personal staff. There was a fair-sized English colony but they kept pretty well to themselves and were not, as a general rule, involved with the Palace, the Casino or the French society. At the time of Grace's marriage there were only forty-two Americans resident in the Principality. She would later seek her countrymen and countrywomen out. But in the beginning she tried hard to become a part of her husband's social world.

Despite her title and privileged situation, Grace began her married life as many brides have done, redecorating her husband's family home, which in this case happened to be an enormous ancient palace with antiquated plumbing, insufficient heat and furniture, and stonework and plaster that were in desperate need of repair. The royal apartments, which constituted only 5 of the Palace's 225 rooms (mostly offices and state rooms), were arranged railroad style, in a direct line, so that you had to walk through one room to get to the next.

Rainier backed her up in the changes she wished to make. Heavy curtains were soon replaced by lighter fabrics. Giant pots of flowers were much in evidence. Faded and dark wallpaper was replaced. The room adjoining their bedroom (where Rainier had formerly kept his recently born lion cubs and which had first to be fumigated)[1] was turned into a bright, cheery nursery with a Disney motif of Snow White and the Seven Dwarfs. Her child, she was told, would have to be born at home, and so the private study was converted into a modern delivery room. This left only a sitting room, dining room and master bedroom for Grace and Rainier, but plans were already being drawn for a new wing to be added. It would overlook the sea and would include a terrace and an outdoor swimming pool.

While she awaited the approach of motherhood, Grace studied French and Monégasque history. Only now did she learn that she was the second American Princesse de Monaco. Researching her predecessor became one of her most enthusiastic projects, although a difficult one because so much had been destroyed. Grace discovered that Alice had been a highly accomplished woman and a great patron of the arts, who had made Monaco a center for opera, ballet and the theater. Her

---

[1]The young lions had been banished to the Palace zoo when one of them almost devoured a happily fast-footed Chihuahua belonging to a visitor.

marriage to Albert had ended badly, it was true, but Alice's cultural influences on Monaco were not to blame. Anyone could see from reading their histories that Alice and Albert were ill matched, whereas she and Rainier had much in common. They laughed at the same things, had a strong desire for a close family life, and knew what it was to fight for privacy and to deal with difficult family members.

A sad tradition of unsuccessful marriages plagued the Grimaldis, but Grace had great faith in her love for Rainier, his for her and their ability to surmount all obstacles. Most of Rainier's predecessors had entered into marriage for dynastic and financial reasons. Grace refused to believe that her husband had married her for those purposes. Marriages to rich women had endowed the Princes de Monaco with many additional titles and estates, and they had tended to live in France rather than in their Principality, to which they paid only occasional visits. Even Albert I had most often chosen to be in Paris or at Marchais when not at sea, and this had also been true of Rainier's grandfather, Louis II.

But Rainier had come to the throne with a determination to live among his people. Marchais, of course, was still occupied by his mother, and he had little desire to visit her. The house in Paris, now his, held no happy memories for him, he had sold the house he had once shared with Gisèle, and he was, at heart, a man who loved the sun, the sea air and outdoor sports.

Although she struggled with intense loneliness at the outset, for she could not seem to win over the women in Rainier's social set and could not turn to his family for companionship, Grace enthusiastically endorsed her husband's decision to make Monaco their primary residence. A great part of Rainier's attraction for her had been his title and the idea that she would be a princess. This is not to say she did not love him for himself. But first had come the exhilarating idea that a prince desired her, and then the amazing revelation that she could become a royal highness. A distinct romantic haze had been cast over her emotions during the decision-making days of their relationship. At that time Rainier had made it clear to her that he intended to be an active monarch and that Monaco would be their home. Grace fully accepted the plan. She would not only be a princess, she would be one of the few in the world with subjects and the power to rule, or at least to be a considerable influence on her husband's reign.

She would emulate Alice's contribution in developing a Monégasque cultural life, but she was equally determined to help Rainier with his plan to bring foreign businesses to Monaco, to construct sufficient housing for workers and hotels to accommodate a larger influx of package-tour visitors and to establish a convention center.

Onassis had miscalculated. The movie-star princess would lend her glamour and public appeal to Monaco, but she would use it to help Rainier achieve his goals—which were now hers—and these were completely at odds with those of the Greek, who wished to recapture the lush sense of luxury that would be a magnet for the rich and famous and allow them to enjoy each other's company. And he was adamant in his argument that to lower Monaco's standards would be a disaster, for it would fail to attract new clientele and almost certainly drive out the old.

Because of the tremendous publicity engendered by the wedding, and the attraction of a chance to glimpse H.S.H. Princesse Grace (in full royal regalia if possible), Monaco was enjoying a new prosperity and a new group of visitors. Onassis had brought in the Greek shipowners; Grace's presence had lured Hollywood film personalities—Cary Grant, Alfred Hitchcock, David Niven, Ava Gardner and Frank Sinatra; and emigré royalty was back at the tables. Still, since Onassis controlled the Casino and the S.B.M., Rainier had to rely upon him for the major portion of his income, and he was not content to continue in this fashion.

"Onassis's seignorial view of his role in the principality was increasingly at odds with Rainier's vision of a 'new Monaco,'" states a book published in 1990 on Onassis's business affairs and written by a team of investigative reporters. "Each had the power to frustrate the other's designs. As the largest shareholder, Onassis could appoint his men to the SBM board. Rainier not only had the right to appoint two directors of his choice, he also had veto power over Onassis's appointments and did not hesitate to use this prerogative. There were frequent shifts of personnel in the company as each set of administrators failed to live up to Rainier's rising expectations.

"At Onassis's suggestion, the company acquired a special negotiator who shuttled between the palace and Onassis's head-quarters in the hope of finding common ground between the two parties. This device was a failure. By nature conspiratorial, both Onassis and Rainier attempted to secure the exclusive services of the unfortunate mediator with the result that one of them was invariably disappointed."

Rainier did, eventually, get Onassis to agree to build an artificial beach just beyond the Casino, a heliport and a new luxury hotel. But when it came to the contract stage, Onassis inserted a provision that for his own efforts Rainier would have to revoke his veto power and any interference in the management of the Casino or the S.B.M. Rainier refused and the relationship between the two men became more acrimonious. "The prince had always believed in divine right," a Palace staff member recalled, "and he now wished to apply it to corporate practices. If Monaco was to become a modern business, there should be no doubt about who was in charge." Rainier had made this clear from the day he had announced Grace's pregnancy.

Ma Kelly arrived for Christmas with an American gynecologist and obstetrician, Dr. Hervet, to await the birth of her daughter's royal child. On January 23, 1957, a day of torrential rain, Caroline-Louise-Marguerite Grimaldi was born. Informed by telephone of the arrival of his new granddaughter, Jack Kelly exclaimed, "Hell! I wanted a boy!" Rainier, on the other hand, was far more enthusiastic about having a daughter. United States citizenship is granted to any child born abroad with at least one American parent if such citizenship is claimed before the age of eighteen. When asked by the press whether the new princess would be encouraged to do so, Rainier snapped back, "She is Monégasque and nothing else." Princesse Caroline was also heir to the throne.

Fourteen months later, on March 14, 1958, Grace gave birth to a son, Albert-Alexander-Louis-Pierre, who replaced his sister in the royal succession and was now Hereditary Prince de Monaco.

Rainier proved to have a much more domestic nature than any of his predecessors. He enjoyed being with Grace and the children and gave freely of his time to them. Grace had made a definite place for herself in their small kingdom, devising new ways to help the old and the needy while adding her glamorous presence to all gala state occasions. She was also actively involved in the opera; Raoul Gunsbourg had recently died in Paris, and Grace worked closely with the several men it had taken to replace him. She was intent on establishing a theater repertory company and a school of ballet. Yet her and Rainier's life was not as idyllic as it appeared.

The Prince of Monaco is an absolute monarch with the power to change any law or the taxation of his subjects as he so wishes. However, there are eighteen members on the National Council elected by male Monégasque citizens (Monégasques were, and remain, about 17 percent of the population of the Principality) to serve a term of five years each. They convene for six weeks, twice yearly, to review the budget and any new legislation sent to them from the Prince and drawn up by his personal staff, which consists of three ministers (finance, foreign affairs and domestic issues) chosen by him. The National Council has the right only to recommend new laws or to suggest changes in old or new laws or to alter the budget. Their suggestions are returned to the Prince, but he is under no obligation to accept or incorporate them. Sometimes, however, pressures can exist which make it expedient for the Prince to compromise or to give way on certain issues to assure there will not be undue unrest in the Principality caused by one of his edicts.

In 1956 Jean-Charles Rey, who had been behind Antoinette's bid to overthrow Rainier and place her son, Christian, on the throne, was the most powerful member of the National Council. He had initiated an independent party in Monaco (which held no vote and could only apply pressure through Rey) which urged the establishment of a constitutional monarchy subject to the approval of the Council and circulated a petition for Monégasque women twenty-one years or older to have a vote and to be elected to the National Council. Not long after Albert's birth, Rainier finally became aware of his sister's long secret alliance with Rey. With the advent of a Hereditary Prince, Antoinette had lost all hope of one day placing her son on the throne. She seemed determined now to diminish the power of her brother and his heir and she worked through Rey and his growing strength on the National Council to achieve her aim.

In the spring 1957 session of the National Council Rey led the opposition, greatly increasing their numbers to a majority, in disputing every one of Rainier's new measures and his budget, including a rise in real estate taxes (Monégasques pay no personal income tax, but are assessed on real estate) and raises in the yearly monies being paid over to himself and for the running of his household. Rainier made minor adjustments in legislation dealing with education and health, but passed all his other changes into law. But Rey still had several unexpired years on his National Council term, and Rainier was concerned that he could create an atmosphere of unrest in the Principality. He feared that to remove him from the Council and from Monaco could boomerang as Rey was now open about, and even flaunting, his relationship with Antoinette and her approval of his actions on the Council.

"[Rey's] visits grew more and more frequent to our home," Christian de Massey recalls. "He was often present at lunch and dinner. As he grew more confident, he installed his own butler and chef. . . . I remember that when I was playing with the footman, Rey would appear in the kitchen or at the gardener's cottage snapping orders at the staff, screaming at them that they should not waste valuable time playing with me . . . they shared my contempt of Rey, and that gave us a common bond."

Grace had made friends with Antoinette's children, and Christian in particular adored her. Through them it was not too difficult to assess how deeply their mother was involved with Rey. By the summer of 1958, the problems between Rainier and his sister and her lover had reached an impasse. At Rainier's request (Grace not having the right to do so), Grace asked Antoinette to relinquish her rooms at the Palace. This Antoinette did, but the humiliation added fire to her resentment, and for three years her children were not permitted to see their Uncle Rainier or any member of his family, including her own father.

Within the next year, not only did Rainier's problems with Rey reach the breaking point but his difficulty with Onassis intensified into open hostility with Onassis using his controlling interest in the S.B.M. to display his power. "I am the boss here now," he remarked to Louis Vuidet, the manager of the Hôtel de Paris restaurant, when he was told that any changes in the hours ·of opening and closing (Onassis wanted to extend the closing time) had to be approved by the Palace.

The project closest to Rainier's heart at this time was an

extravagant plan to build a floating laboratory for his friend Professor Jacques Cousteau, the great oceanographer, to pursue his underwater research. It would be named after Albert I and also be a suitable tribute to the birth of his son, Albert II. Onassis would have no part in it, and the Council, under Rey's strong influence, refused to allocate any money for the "Marinarium," as it was called.

On January 29, 1959, Monégasques were startled to hear Rainier declare on the radio, "I cannot tolerate any pressure whatsoever which might undermine my complete rights." He then announced that he had suspended the Constitution, dissolved the National Council, and abrogated the rights of political assembly or demonstration. These edicts were, according to Dr. Joseph Simon, president of the National Council, "a veritable coup d'état." Both Louis II and Albert I had used the same tactics to remind their subjects that they were absolute monarchs by hereditary divine right. "The divine right of kings exists nowhere else in the world," Christian de Massey comments. "This arrangement in Monaco rendered our family absolute administrators of power. They could virtually make up the law as they went along. . ."

"For a year, the National Council has hindered the administrative and political life of the country [and] a certain Council member has been intriguing ceaselessly for many years for the purpose of furthering his own ambitions," Rainier proclaimed to the press. Grace attempted to win over disapproving foreign reporters by assuring them that "six months of princely rule would settle down Monaco's problems." She was furious when she heard from friends in the States that Rainier had been called a dictator in the American press and read articles in the French papers that repeated this accusation, but he had flagrantly disregarded the Constitution of 1911 (as had Albert I and Louis II). He claimed that he was acting on behalf of his subjects (although in what way was unclear) and that his plans were for a more prosperous Monégasque economy and to earn international respect for their small country through the work of the esteemed Cousteau. But, in fact, the progress of this scientific endeavor was greatly powered by his own self-interest.

A wave of discontent rose, stirred up whenever possible by Rey, who spoke quite freely to American and French journalists.

But after Rainier threatened to expel Rey from Monaco, his sister's lover no longer made public his views on the wrongness of Rainier's actions. His autocracy assured, Rainier established the Monaco Development Corporation with state money. He touted the climate and tax-free status of the Principality in the hope of luring major foreign investors. Work was begun on Cousteau's floating laboratory; a tunnel was excavated for a new train route to pass under Monaco and leave the streets above clean and accessible; and corporate headquarters for hundreds of foreign companies were given tax-free status. The result was a boom for Monaco, and Grace's plea for Monégasques to "trust her husband and everything would be all right" appeared to be good advice.

What Rainier had not considered was how Charles de Gaulle and the French government would react to having a tax-free state bordering their own, one in which French citizens could fairly easily establish residence to avoid paying French taxes. In October 1959, de Gaulle gave Rainier six months' notice of his intention to abrogate the convention guaranteeing friendly relations between the two countries. As the deadline approached, France installed temporary customs barriers at Monaco's frontier and threatened to cut off its gas and electricity supplies if Monaco did not accede to its demands.

During this period Rainier had the additional stress of a marital crisis, as Grace began seriously to entertain the idea of resuming her career—at least for one film. Rainier was opposed to the possiblity, and life at the Palace was a series of difficult confrontations. Grace was frankly bored with dealing with domestic issues and the role of Princess Bountiful. She could not see how appearing in a film, provided the role she play was that of a woman of good character, could have local repercussions. Rainier understood that his subjects would view the Princesse de Monaco's return to acting as a diminution of his own standing as a man and a monarch—and he desperately needed their support in his battle with de Gaulle.

Cary and Betsy Grant visited the Grimaldis at this time and returned to Hollywood bearing the secret news to Alfred Hitchcock that Grace might be agreeble to doing a movie. (Metro-Goldwyn-Mayer had recently offered her the role of the Virgin Mary in their upcoming production of *The King of Kings,* an idea which the horrified Pope Pius XII, when consulted by Rainier, declared would be sacrilegious, for Grace was obviously not a virgin.) Hitchcock sent Grace a copy of a screen adaptation of Winston Graham's novel *Marnie,* a psychodrama about a rich man who marries a kleptomaniac. The story contained scenes of violence, was sexually explicit and was played against a criminal background. It seemed to be an unsuitable choice but the idea of working with Hitchcock again and the promise that Grant would play opposite her attracted Grace.

Rainier, faced with Grace's determination, eventually agreed, although he did elicit a promise from the producers that the script would be rewritten and Grace would not appear in any scene that was even mildly offensive in language or content or contained sexual overtones. On March 16, 1960, he issued a statement that he and Her Serene Highness would spend the summer in Hollywood where the Princesse would star in *Marnie* and that they would return to Monaco in November. Monégasques reacted to this with disbelief, and in the end, they decided the matter, for there was a rush to judgment in the local and the French press. Numerous published interviews with Rainier's subjects made it perfectly clear that they could not regard a woman who was also a working Hollywood actress as Her Serene Highness. Rainier withdrew his agreement immediately, creating a cold atmosphere in his home but regaining the support of his people.

The Kellys had never been good losers, and Grace was no exception. However, she understood that her husband was under fire and that the very survival of Monaco was at stake in the confrontation he was having with de Gaulle. She therefore accepted his final mandate on her career plans and stood beside him in his decisions regarding France and the Principality.

As de Gaulle's April deadline to his ultimatum drew near, Rainier had no option but to capitulate. A pact was agreed which guaranteed that French citizens who lived in Monaco could not evade French taxation. There was a sudden exodus of capital, and two thirds of the sixteen billion francs held by Frenchmen in Monte Carlo was transferred into Swiss bank accounts. Overnight Monaco's prosperity evaporated as its escaping Frenchmen either canceled their orders for new apartments and offices or sold them at rock-bottom rates.

The National Council was reinstalled, with Rey still one of its members, in time for the spring session. But the former agitator seemed more compliant and Rainier's next budget was accepted without much contest. Rainier turned his attention to Onassis. It now became a matter of principle and expediency to get Onassis to sell his shares in the S.B.M. It was to be a test of force and not an easy one at that.

When Jack Kelly died of cancer in June 1960, at the age of seventy, Grace was inconsolable. Since her marriage she had returned home once a year, but to her great disappointment her relationship with her father did not improve. Kelly's disapproval of Rainier grew during his last year, and he was obdurate in his view that Grace's success in her career and marriage was nothing more than an accident of fate. When Grace had visited Philadelphia in the summer of 1959, she had intended to confront her father over their differences. She found him in poorer health than she had expected, and the words went unspoken.

Her frustration over this inability to talk to her father might well have been increased by thoughts of her aborted career. The years 1959 to 1960 were unhappy ones for her, and the public nature of her life at the Palace caused her to spend more and more time at the old farmhouse Rainier had purchased for them as a second home shortly after Albert's birth. Situated on the peak of Mont Agel above the Monte Carlo Golf Club, on one of the highest and most precipitous sections of the Corniche, it sprawled over the French side of Monaco's frontier. The road leading up to it curved sharply in hairpin turns and there were few guard rails. The drive terrified Grace because of her poor eyesight. Nevertheless, she fell in love with the farmhouse, its spectacular views, its privacy, the expanse of land where the children could play unobserved, the proximity of the Golf Club (golf was one of her favorite sports) and the casual life there. Whenever she could she would take the family up to the farmhouse, usually driven by Rainier or their chauffeur, to oversee the extensive alterations being made and to relax. When she had difficult personal problems, she would go up alone to the house which they called Roc Agel. A swimming pool was built, horses were installed in the stable, and a modern kitchen where Grace could do most of the cooking was added to the main building—which with its terra-cotta tile roof and large stone fireplaces resembled some of the old haciendas in Southern California.

By now the panoply of royal life, the constant public exposure (even more intense than when she had been an actress) and the tensions of her husband's reign had eclipsed the dazzling image of being a princess that she had nurtured before her marriage.

After her father's death, the fiasco of her flirtation with returning to the screen and two successive miscarriages in 1960 and 1961, she retreated to Roc Agel, which quickly became her home and refuge, the place where she could unwind and be herself. With all the attention she had received, Grace never forgot her roots. She was the daughter of an American bricklayer, a self-made man whose parents had left Ireland to escape poverty. "I wonder," she wrote to a close American friend, "what it is I might have come here to escape."

20

THE FINAL SHOWDOWN between Rainier and Onassis had all
the elements of the shootout in a Hollywood Western. These
were two men who knew they could not co-exist in the same
town: One is the stranger—the foreigner—and he is considered
dangerous; the other is the power figure—the boss—of the
invaded territory.

With Rainier's final capitulation to de Gaulle, Onassis appeared to have the upper hand; for if there were to be free
elections of candidates to the National Council, the members
he supported could act on his behalf. As in all good melodramas
of this kind, a strong, seductive woman entered the scene, dis-
tracting one of the men from his main objective and giving the
other the advantage.

During the height of Rainier's battle to maintain his divine
right, Onassis fell deeply, passionately, in love with the volatile,
darkly exotic opera diva Maria Callas, born in America of Greek
parents, who was married. He soon separated from his wife,
Tina, and was living openly on the *Christina* with his paramour.
Despite their hypocritical disapproval of this situation (for, after
all, both had had lovers and Grace several who were married
men) Rainier and Grace attended social occasions on the yacht
and did not exclude the couple from their own parties or state
affairs. To do so would have created an irreparable breach and
in 1963 Rainier was still hopeful that Onassis would support
his new plan for land reclamation from the sea, which was the
only scheme he could envision that would increase the size and
enable the potential development of the Principality. By the use
of landfill, the coastline and inlet directly to the east of the Rock
could be built up to accommodate a hotel, convention center
and large apartment project. When he saw that Onassis, still
concerned that the Principality would lose its appeal to rich

tourists if it was allowed to become more commercial, would not bend to his ideas, Rainier's attitude took a sharp turn.

His open offensive began with his 1964 New Year's address to the nation when he made a slurring reference to the shortcomings of the S.B.M. and Onassis's part in its failings. Immediately, the Greek sent an emissary to the Palace to inquire exactly what Rainier wanted. The man returned to Onassis with Rainier's refusal to reply until Onassis revealed to him precisely what *his* intentions were. The next day, Rainier sent his representative, Roger Crovetto, to Onassis to repeat his request.

"Crovetto found Onassis drinking in the Salle Empire," one witness reported. "He took a dislike to Crovetto, who announced he had been insulted and left in a fit of pique. Onassis mellowed to the extent of following Crovetto in his white Rolls-Royce on a mission of apology. . . . [He] managed to catch up with him in the square outside the palace by taking the traffic circle in the wrong direction and plowing into the fender of the minister's car. Apologies were made, [Crovetto] was promised a new car and departed shaken but to some degree mollified."

Rainier, obviously setting the scene for a confrontation, was appeased by Onassis's overture to his representative. In what could only be construed as a retaliatory countermove, he requested the resignation of Charles Audibert (known to be an Onassis man) from the Council. Next, after he had reconciled his differences with de Gaulle, he petitioned for his help in ridding Monaco of Onassis (whom de Gaulle held in low esteem), and was offered France's unconditional support. Items began to appear in the French press referring to Onassis as "an undesirable presence," and in an interview with the editors of *Le Monde* Rainier stated that Onassis was "devoid of any real concern for his adopted country," and was "above all a speculator." He concluded that "the only solution appears to be a test of force. My government and myself are resolved to it."

In a startling turn, Rainier teamed up with his old enemy Jean-Charles Rey, who had married Antoinette in a civil ceremony only a few months before, in a scheme that created 600,000 new shares in the S.B.M., to be controlled by the state, which thereby became the majority shareholder. It would seem that Rainier was now using his new brother-in-law's conspiratorial talents to his own good. When Onassis was told about the proposed legislation (pointedly described by his staff as *"loi gangster"*), he thought Rainier was merely trying him. But the decree was drawn up and passed despite Onassis's attempt to get the Supreme Court to rule the legislation unconstitutional. (If it had done so, Rainier could have vetoed the decision, anyway.)

Within a week the *Christina* lifted anchor and sailed out of Monte Carlo. Onassis was so grieved, and so certain that he would never return, that he did not remain on deck to watch the town, where he had once held so much power and that had been his primary home for ten years, slip into the distance and fade from view. In a final humiliation before his departure, Onassis had been sent a check by Rainier for 39,912,000 francs ($10 million) for the buy-out of his entire interest in the S.B.M., the figure arbitrarily set by Rey and the Council at considerably below its real value. A great percentage of the stock, at an advantageous price, he told his associates, would soon make its way into Rainier's possession. Later he was to exclaim, "I was robbed!"

To Monégasques, Onassis's departure held little personal meaning. He had never won their hearts and had always been looked upon as an outsider. Nor did they appear concerned about who had control of the S.B.M. as long as Monaco's economy was on the upswing and their own finances improved. This soon occurred with the growing realization of Rainier's plans for land reclamation, new construction and medium-priced housing. An added boon was the lowered price of international air fares and the advent of the jumbo jets which could accommodate many times the passengers of former overseas air transportation and required far less flight time. There was a huge boom in tourism, and Monte Carlo, with its superb climate and many distractions, quickly became the most popular resort on the Mediterranean.

Prices of the Principality's limited available land soared, along with the cost of apartments and office space. Rainier was fast becoming one of the richest men in Europe. Monégasques, their rising earnings free of tax, had also benefited, and their new affluence not only raised their standard of living, it caused them to seek better jobs. Labor was difficult to find within the Principality and hundreds of foreign workers, mostly from Italy, were brought in. Space became an almost nonexistent luxury as new buildings were wedged into every possible gap. For the first time the Principality had to concern itself with environmental issues. Traffic was badly congested and a complicated system of one-way streets was inaugurated.

Through it all, the pampered beauty of Monte Carlo was miraculously preserved. England's Edward VII would have easily recognized the square in the center of the town with its beautiful manicured gardens and its trio of *belle époque* buildings—the Casino, Hôtel de Paris and Café de Paris—although the café might have given him pause, for in 1962 gaming rooms, which were open night and day, had been added. To Rainier's credit (and that of his planners and architects), nowhere in Monte Carlo had the elegant avenues and tree-lined streets been allowed to deteriorate.

The major part of the restoration and redecoration of the Palace was completed by the mid-sixties, along with the royal family's private apartments (furnished by Grace with the help of American decorators in what was sometimes sniped at by critics as "California wide-screen casual" with its massive windows, huge potted palms, exotic plants and oversized, sand-colored couches, chairs and ottomans and beveled-glass cocktail tables). This enabled Rainier to open the public rooms for tours. Soon, most of the ground floors of the old buildings on the narrow, curving streets of the Rock were transformed into cafés and souvenir shops, leading to accusations that Rainier had become crassly commercial and, since he held the leases on most of the buildings, money hungry.

The family was completed when Grace gave birth to a second daughter, and third child, Stephanie-Marie-Elisabeth, on February 1, 1965, in the same room where her other children had been born. Grace's easy pregnancy had given her the confidence to drive to Nice to meet Ma Kelly's arriving plane. After their return to the Palace and lunch, Grace had gone into labor two weeks early. When the cannon shots announcing the royal birth stopped at twenty-one, seven-year-old Albert exclaimed proudly, "*I* got a hundred and one!"

The children were being raised to be bilingual in French and English—as Rainier had been—by an English nanny, a high-spirited, hefty lady from the Midlands, Maureen King, who established a rigid rule that only one language could be spoken at a time. Grace almost always communicated with the children in English, and it was due to this that they had a distinct American accent which, because it appeared to please their mother, was never discouraged. The wide age difference between the two oldest and Stephanie bonded the youngest child closer to her mother.

Caroline bore an uncanny resemblance to Princesse Charlotte in both appearance and character. With her vivid Prussian-blue eyes, brown hair and olive complexion, she was a commanding presence even as a toddler. Uninhibited, precocious, garrulous and bossy, she quickly gained the upper hand in the nursery. Albert, whom the family called Albie, was the most like his mother, with fair hair, finely chiseled features and the same myopic eyes. They also shared similar temperaments. Albie was shy, slow to accept new adults or peers, fiercely loyal once he did and tremendously sensitive to those close to him. Although he followed his father's lead in sports, he had a talent for art and shared his mother's love of the theater and ballet. Both the older children were aware at a very young age of their position and accepted the rigors it demanded: the public exposure, the control, the recognition that they were not as free as most children to be themselves and that, except for each other, their contemporaries in Monaco would view them with mixed awe and reserve.

Stephanie was the maverick. Unable to diminish the age gap between herself and her two siblings, to wedge herself into becoming a part of their close relationship or to compete with them on any level other than for parental attention, she was a disciplinary problem from the age of two, willful, stubborn, and with a temper that could erupt unexpectedly. "I could have beaten her like a gong without making her give way," her mother would later say. Yet Stephanie's recalcitrant personality created a tighter bond between the two. For Grace refused to accept the notion that she might not be able to bring her younger daughter into line and spent more time with Stephanie than she had with Albert or Caroline. Then, too, Stephanie, her coloring so darkly striking and her personality so outgoing, also possessed a great vulnerability and was the most openly affectionate of the three children.

Albert struggled to overcome his difficult position as the middle child caught between the strong personalities of his two sisters. As hereditary prince, he found that more was demanded of him than of his siblings. He desperately wanted to please his father, who expected him one day to be as great a sailor as his namesake, Albert I, but as a child, Albie had a fear of the water and a tendency toward a queasy stomach. He endured much to overcome these shortcomings. Tortuous hours were spent in the new, Italianate marble pool at the Palace practicing swimming, placing his head under water for as long as he could manage. During boating trips with his father he had to fight to control his nausea for he was inclined to uncomfortable seizures of seasickness. By the time he was nine he had a serious stutter and was immensely self-conscious, but he had succeeded in conquering his phobias.

Her royal obligations, her children, the running of a complicated household and the well-being of her husband filled Grace's life, but still there was something lacking. She had intensely wanted to play the Tzarina Alexandra in the film adaptation of Robert Massie's Pulitzer Prize–winning biography, *Nicholas and Alexandra,* but Rainier was adamant that she never return to the screen. By the early 1970s, his plans for developing Monaco were being put into action, and the royal couple were rarely together because the demands of his enterprise consumed much of his time. After her primary education on the Rock, Caroline was sent to St. Mary's, a strict convent school near Ascot in England. Although Albie attended school in Monaco, he went for the summer, at the request of his mother, to a camp in New Hampshire with some of his Kelly cousins. Family was something Grace believed in and in Rainier's family there were no children Albie's age.

Her yearly pilgrimages to Philadelphia continued, but after Jack's death, and despite her attempts to remain close, nothing ever seemed the same. Ma grew more difficult with the years and her sisters seemed to have become envious and to expect more from her than she felt they gave in return. Her family became a sore point between Rainier and her, for he felt they took advantage of her and treated her in a demeaning manner, never acknowledging her royal status. Her faith had come to mean more to her since the birth of the children, although she was never obsessive about it. But she liked to go alone to the small private chapel at the Palace, where she would sit totally absorbed for an hour or more, in silent contemplation. She would walk by herself in flat shoes on the grounds of Roc Agel, or in the Palace gardens overlooking the sea, a scarf on her head; a lonely figure, her step hesitant.

An unsettling feeling of displacement had begun to overtake her. She felt more American than when she had left home. The French and Monégasque women, wives of Rainier's friends and associates, had never opened themselves to her, and feminine bonding, which had been so much a part of her life before coming to Monaco, remained important to her and greatly missed. Her closest companions were the American author Paul Gallico and his wife, Virginia; another American, Jeanne Kelly (who, although not related, shared many of Grace's roots); and a few of the women on either her own or the S.B.M.'s staff—with whom, however, as their employer and as Princesse de Monaco, she could never truly be herself.

She became fluent in French and Italian, although her American accent was much in evidence (and often privately mocked by courtiers). Her hands were always active: with needlework, painting, modeling with clay. She never lost contact with her old friends and former bridesmaids and kept up a lively correspondence with the former Judith Kanter, who had divorced her agent husband, had married and divorced actor Tony Franciosa and was now married to Don Quine, a professional karate expert. She subscribed to *The International Herald Tribune, The New Yorker, Architectural Digest* and the Book of the Month Club. A week seldom passed in which she did not see a current or favorite Hollywood film in the Palace's private theater.

She remained close to Cary Grant and nurtured a special camaraderie with Frank Sinatra, and perhaps a small flirtation. Rainier was observed by his nephew Christian to be "often short-tempered with Grace, too frequently in the presence of others . . . she never contradicted . . . nor called him on his tone. Grace was always deeply hurt [after such a display] . . . but her brave silences seemed only to exacerbate and prolong the discomfort and embarrassment of such moments."

In Rainier's defense, he was under considerable pressure. What he had called "ocean-stealing," reclaiming land from the sea, had added nearly an entire square mile to his realm. He had been determined that Monaco would overcome its reputation for living off the Casino. Wise enough to know that a sizable portion of its livelihood (and his own) was dependent on its remaining a popular tourist resort, he had begun an active policy of economic development that balanced hotels and high-rise apartments with industrial expansion.

To achieve the proper equilibrium, Monaco was divided into three distinct areas, with the Rock (site of the old town and of the Palace) in the center separating the more aristocratic Monte Carlo from Fontvieille, where the reclaimed land was used to provide space for lower-income housing and for industrial and commercial premises. With its paucity of land, Monaco stood little chance of ever evolving into a major hub for heavy manufacturing. Nonetheless, Rainier lured cosmetic, pharmaceutical and plastics companies to his country. Unemployment became almost nonexistent and the per capita income of its thirty thousand residents one of the highest in the world. This did not satisfy his detractors, who deplored the plethora of high-rise condominiums that filled in almost every space along the roads that wound through and above Monte Carlo, calling the area a "vulgar concrete slum for *arrivistes.*"

Jet-setting visitors continued to throng the Casino, the Grand Prix, the tennis and golf tournaments and many social galas. From the time of the wedding of the century, Grace's presence had given the Principality a renewed aura of grandeur, of a time lost in history, and a fairy-tale mystique that appealed equally to the blue-blooded and the *nouveaux riches.*

Rainier's critics condemned him for pushing "into France [meaning over the border from Fontvieille] everything that isn't profitable or attractive—warehouses, cemeteries, utilities . . . and the old people's rest home." Questions were being asked publicly about the true names and nationalities of the companies that were being registered in Monaco, "subletting apartments as 'headquarters,' but never showing up, let alone doing business or constructing plants? Who [a French editorial inquired] own many of these high rises?"

Such innuendos threatened, or at least seemed to threaten, the Principality's future stability and good name. In the 1930s Somerset Maugham had labeled Monaco "a sunny place for shady people." Unquestionably, the small country's spectacular commercial growth had brought with it promoters and financial corruption. Companies had been set up as fronts for less ethical operations than they professed. Arms were being trafficked in plush offices on the Boulevard des Moulins. Scandalous press allegations were published almost weekly in France.

The postage-stamp size of Monaco with its often crass displays of luxury and wealth, the presence of the Casino and the tax-free position of the Monégasques, invited contempt and suspicion from France, which by 1970 had suddenly found itself with an irritatingly rich neighbor when times were not that good at home, unemployment being high and the value of the franc deflated.

Along with the Principality's brimming affluence came serious problems of pollution, caused by too many cars in so small an area, and crime. There had been more jewel robberies than ever before and drugs were beginning to become a problem. Rainier decided to drastically augment his police force and to detain and expel any person looking suspicious. These undemocratic practices were not well received by Grace, and became a matter of unpleasant argument at home. The Princesse de Monaco also fought to prohibit the destruction of some of the best examples of *belle époque* architecture. ("I will nail myself to the door [of one such structure] if they try to raze it," she was quoted as saying in *Le Monde*.)

Yet Rainier's love and attachment to his American princess remained evident to all those who were close to them. At public galas when restraint was dictated, he could be glimpsed reaching for her hand. At more casual gatherings his arm would fall quite naturally and protectively about her shoulders. He did not appear to comprehend why an expression of intense sadness would suddenly cloud her classically beautiful face. Whatever their differences, they shared a strong attachment to their children and a belief in the rightness of their faith. He admired her independent spirit even if he seldom gave in to her ideas (unless he had leaned toward them at the outset). The Moné-gasques had gone through periods of approving and of disapproving of their sovereign's consort, but they did feel the marriage was built on a solid foundation and it gave them a deep, abiding sense of security. Rainier had much the same feelings, and it seemed that the curse of the Grimaldis, so often written about in the past, would never apply to Grace and him.

The twenty-fifth anniversary of Rainier's reign (May 1974) was celebrated with a spectacular series of events that extended throughout April, May and June. Monaco was ablaze with flowers, red and white primulas decorating the bases of all the trees on the major boulevards. Special services were conducted in all the churches and cathedrals in the Principality. There was an extraordinary parade of flower floats and galas were held at the Monte Carlo Opera House; lavish dinners at the Hôtel de Paris (where additional crystal chandeliers were hung to add to the brilliant display) were attended by Prince Juan Carlos and Princess Sophie of Spain (Juan Carlos was designated heir to the Spanish throne, and would become King upon the death of the dictator Francisco Franco, which occurred that September) and the Begum Aga Khan, along with numerous Hollywood stars. The celebrations ended with a magnificent display of fireworks.

Albert, just turned sixteen, was co-host with his parents, the first time he had performed at an official function. He continued to spend the summers at camp in New Hampshire and with his Kelly cousins in their beach house in New Jersey, and he had become "very American in appearance, and his speech was so completely East Coast that no one could tell he had not grown up there," his Grimaldi cousin, Christian de Massey, says, adding that "he continued to be slightly handicapped by his childhood stammer. . . . Bespectacled, reserved, and self-conscious, he acted out his part with great concentration, while Caroline played hers with more effortless and authentic relaxation."

There was a majestic Te Deum for Louis II in the Cathedral, presided over by Cardinal Krol, Archbishop of Philadelphia, and the current Bishop of Monaco, Monsignor Abele, as well as by representatives from the Greek and Russian Orthodox churches and the Church of England. For the first time in many years the entire Grimaldi family were present and seated together (even Princesse Ghislaine attended), and appeared to do so in harmony. However, Rainier and his sister still exhibited great hostility toward each other within their Court and private circles and never saw one another except on public occasions.

Stephanie, still difficult and only nine years of age, required a good deal of her mother's attention. Caroline, who had only recently passed the second part of her *baccalauréat* in Paris, was living in her parents' magnificent recently acquired and refurbished home on the Avenue Foch. Nine years older than Stephanie, and a young beauty at eighteen, she was, perhaps, even more headstrong than as a child. She struggled to live what she thought was a *real* life, which meant spending her evenings whenever possible at a disco with an attractive escort. She was seldom alone, for a member of either her own or her mother's staff was always in attendance and she never left the house without a detective at her side.

Day and night found the *paparazzi* positioned outside the house on the Avenue Foch, waiting to flash their cameras as Caroline left or returned. She began to feel hounded, with good reason, for the press's relentlessness in stalking her every move and the wild speculations that were printed about her were certainly excessive. "Why do I have to be a princess? I hate it!" she would exclaim to the staff and security guard, whom she called her "keepers." She was a competent pianist, an avid reader, and an excellent linguist, but she had no idea what she could or would be allowed to do with her life.

Rainier was a devoted father, albeit often an absent one. He had also suffered greatly as a youngster growing up royal. But he knew even less of the real world than his children and he counted on the strength of his marriage and on Grace to assure the well-being and stability of their daughters. Albert was more his concern. For, after all, it was his son who would, like himself, one day be Prince de Monaco.

21

SMALL THOUGH IT WAS, Monaco demanded far more of its sovereign than Great Britain did of the Queen, who made no major decisions and had little to do with the economics, or for that matter with the political machinations, of her domain. In contrast, Rainier had the final word on almost everything of a public nature that went on within the boundaries of his realm. For, although Monaco had a Constitution, the Prince de Monaco had the right to override any article within the document or to suspend it, as he had already once done. He was an absolute monarch who, in essence, had simply given his subjects a forum to discuss and suggest changes or additions to his plans for the Principality and its budget. But his was the final word.

Prince Pierre, Rainier's father, had died in 1965, leaving him without a trusted confidant during a time of mounting economic complexities caused by the landfill project and the enormous cost of engineering and construction attached to it. Associates now found him a good deal tougher in business matters than he had previously been and they appeared to be right, for the contracts he negotiated with lessees were far more favorable to him than previously. And although he had legal representation, he made all decisions. There were members of his staff who felt he was driven by a passion to become one of the richest men in Europe (a goal which he was fast approaching). He leaned less on Grace, seldom involving her as he once had in the problems of the Principality. He had begun to look middle-aged, a paunch about the middle, his dark hair washed with gray, a noticeable double chin. But he had not lost his ability to joke, and the boyish smile that had been so beguiling could occasionally alter the growing seriousness of his expression.

He remained strongly attached to his children, took great

pride in any of Albert's accomplishments and was, by turns, both protective and overly permissive with his daughters, who he believed because of their sex should be under the control of their mother and not himself. This attitude became even more apparent as the sixties segued into the seventies and Caroline into a headstrong teenager. Grace had found it difficult to face her fortieth birthday on November 12, 1969, but she was, if more mature and a bit heavier, as strikingly beautiful as ever. Rainier and Grace were now frequently apart, for he remained in Monaco when she was in Paris with Stephanie. Unfounded rumors abounded in the gossip columns of the more abandoned press, and pictures were printed in tabloids of Rainier seated next to one beautiful lady or another at Monaco festivities (the photograph often touched up, cropped or intentionally made to create a false impression by narrowing the distance between Rainier and a dinner partner).

Rainier's interest to the world was due to his position, not his influence on international affairs. Rainier was one of a select few remaining hereditary monarchs. Of course, Queen Elizabeth still occupied Buckingham Palace; Queen Juliana remained on the throne in the Netherlands; and King Baudouin held his country together, despite Belgium's recent division into three regions with their own languages.

But as a monarch, Rainier's situation was unique. Although his power was absolute with Monaco, he was not a world-class leader. What occurred in the Principality had no bearing on European affairs, even those of the countries that bordered his. Monaco had no land, no great seaport, no oil, no products needed by other nations, nor was it an aggressive country that might pose the threat of a war. And since France was now satisfied that its citizens could not evade paying taxes by being resident in the Principality, it was content to leave Monaco to its own devices. Rainier and Monaco existed in a time warp; it was an old-fashioned princedom in a modern world, and it ironically exemplified the fast-growing materialism of the last half of the twentieth century.

His mother, Princesse Charlotte, died on November 16, 1977. Rainier had never been able to forgive his mother for her treatment of his father and had not approved of the eccentric manner in which she had lived. She had been rude to Grace (but, perhaps, even more unpleasant to her own daughter). She had continued to maintain a fairly vicious troop of dogs, nine at the time of her death, which discouraged visits from her children and grandchildren. Marchais belonged to Rainier, and with his mother's death, he and his family visited the estate more frequently. But for country gatherings, Grace—who was suffering occasional bouts of depression that had begun during the past year—preferred the ease and informality of life at Roc Agel. "There are times, you know, when the Princesse is a little melancholic—which I quite understand—about having performed a form of art very successfully, only to be cut away from it completely," Rainier had told his biographer, Peter Hawkins. He described her moods as her "nostalgia for acting."

Grace's periods of melancholy could not be brushed aside with such a casual phrase. Rainier cared deeply for his wife, and her unhappiness weighed heavily upon him. She had never found in Monaco the devoted friends she had surrounded herself with before her marriage. Her relationship with Antoinette had always been cool and she infrequently saw her own sisters and their families. Her position in the Principality forbade the kind of spontaneity she so much enjoyed. And so, with both Caroline and Stephanie in Parisian schools, she spent most of the school year in Paris at their home on the Avenue Foch. In September 1976, Albert would depart for Amherst College in Massachusetts.

Rainier was closer to his children than most of his predecessors had been to theirs. He was determined to prepare his son for his job as the next Prince de Monaco and kept him as informed of Monaco's affairs as Albert's age and ability permitted. He was concerned about Caroline, who was now of eligible age and was dating men of whom he did not approve. In fact, she was being portrayed as a disco habituée and the *paparazzi* continued to stake out the Paris town house day and night and trail her relentlessly.

"I really would shoot these people if I had my way," Rainier was quoted as saying after he observed the deleterious effect this harassment was having on his daughter, who seemed to be going out of control, maintaining late hours, smoking heavily, drinking more than he believed was becoming and doing so in public places. The constant vigilance of the press hounds only drove Caroline to invent ways to outwit them. Her friends were mostly from the disco set. She was photographed nuzzling, drinking and smoking in public, and even her lenient father was alarmed. He blamed the fish-tank life she was forced to live and threatened legal suits against the more persistent newsmen and photographers who beleaguered her. When this tactic failed, he surrounded her with bodyguards, which only added to her sense of a loss of privacy. In the winter of 1977, while she was working to obtain a bachelor's degree in psychology at the Sorbonne, Caroline announced to her parents that she wanted to marry Philippe Junot, an investment broker seventeen years her senior, who was well known in Parisian café and disco society as a playboy and ladies' man.

Despite her parents' strong objections, Caroline insisted that she loved and wished to marry Junot. Grace is reported to have said to Rainier, "Well, perhaps it's for the better. This way she'll have a successful second marriage." Such an attitude seems at odds with Grace's Catholic views on marriage. But her philosophy did encapsulate two creeds—one for herself (marriage was for life), the other (an unhappy marriage should be dissolved) for the rest of the married world. She had also recently told the Comtesse Elizabeth "Lisette" Prince de Ramel, who was caught in a difficult and distressing marriage, "Divorce [the Comte] before he wrecks your life."

Lisette was an American heiress, a child of divorce, brought up in Europe and the United States. She had been a successful photographer before her marriage to Comte Régis de Ramel. She lived part of the year in the Comte's family château in France and the rest of the time in a house in Monte Carlo. A warm, ebullient, intelligent young woman, although about twenty years younger than Grace, she became her friend. Grace insisted Lisette join the exclusive Monte Carlo Garden Club (Grace's favorite organization and the only one in Monaco that required royal patronage for membership) and enlisted her as the official photographer on the Garden Club's excursions to England and Denmark, so that they could travel together.

They had met when their mutual friend Jeanne Kelly Van Remoortel, whose husband was the conductor of the Monte Carlo Symphony Orchestra, had brought Grace to Lisette's house. It was not an official occasion, just three American women gathering for a few hours of casual conversation over lunch. Albert had also come along, and Lisette's Asian housekeeper, Chang, was making Chinese food, which was one of Grace's favorites. At one point Chang came in much concerned. "I didn't know I would have to cook for all those bodyguards," she said, worried that perhaps she had not made enough food. Grace had not known that the Palace had sent four men along as security. Albert explained that there had been a threat to his life but that Prince Rainier had not wanted Grace to be frightened by it. When she had been convinced that Albert was not in any serious danger, she told Chang, "Certainly don't feed the guards. They apparently got here on their own and they can find their own lunch," adding that one of them could go out and buy lunch for the others.

Lisette found Grace "someone used to making other people comfortable." To twist an adage a bit: You could take the girl out of America, but not America out of the girl. With Lisette and Jeanne Kelly and some of her other American friends, Grace would revert to the kind of friendships that had meant so much to her before she became Princesse de Monaco. She chose the few available women in Monaco who shared similar backgrounds and tastes and who could laugh over small, silly things. What she responded to in her companions was their ability to accept her on her own merit and *yet* respect her position—not an easy mix. Nature, the environment, food, children, ballet, theater and her newly developed passion for forming pictures from pressed flowers were some of her interests. She loved "a good gossip" and freely gave advice. More of a disciplinarian than Rainier, she was stricter with Stephanie than she had been with Caroline, hoping to avoid the problems she was now having with her elder daughter. Until Albert's departure for Amherst, she saw as much of him as was possible in the six months or so that she was in Monaco, and mother and son had a close rapport that continued in the form of frequent letters and telephone calls once he was away at college.

The only times Lisette recalled Grace displaying any ill feelings ("flushing red with anger") were when she related stories about how she had felt belittled by members of the English royal family. Princess Margaret had once looked her up and down in icy appraisal and said rudely, "Well, you don't *look* like a movie star."

"Well, I wasn't *born* a movie star," Grace had hotly replied. Another time she had overheard one of the British royals referring to her as "definitely not one of us."

She traveled quite frequently during the late seventies. Ireland had become one of her favorite places to visit and she was researching her Kelly-Irish roots, the area that had once been home to Jack Kelly's parents before they had emigrated to the United States and the distant relations who had remained behind. Irish literature also became a compelling interest. She had recently inaugurated the Princesse Grace Library on the Rock and was speedily building up a research center for Irish scholars, with many rare books and the manuscripts of James Joyce and several other famous Irish writers. And there were her trips to England and Denmark to open garden shows as guest of honor. Lisette accompanied her on these journeys, and the women spent time together in Paris as well as in Monaco.

"Did you take a good look at those books?" Grace once grinned when they were together in the library of the house on the Avenue Foch (which Grace described as "a retreat within a fortress"). Lisette stepped closer. One shelf held leather-covered books (blank inside) which were humorously inscribed with titles that applied to her good friends (e.g., *The Perils of Jeanne* for Jeanne Kelly Van Remoortel, who seemed always to be in and out of great dramas).

Caroline lived at the Paris house until her wedding to Junot. Since she could not be persuaded to wait or to break off with him, her parents (Rainier giving in first) had finally agreed to the marriage, fearing she might run off with him. ("When it comes to something Caroline wants badly enough, you just know her father will permit it," Grace complained to Judith Balaban Quine, adding: "This man [Junot] . . . doesn't do anything. Oh, he's in investments or something, but it doesn't sound very real to me. Mainly what he seems to do and Caroline does with him is go to nightclubs and parties. . . .")

Although not the international extravaganza that her parents' wedding had been, Caroline's marriage to Philippe Junot in June 1978 was not a simple affair. Six hundred guests were to attend and all of the surviving Kelly relatives and close Philadelphia friends were included. Rainier still had a difficult time dealing with the Kelly family, and when Lisette asked Grace what she could do for the wedding celebrations, Grace suggested she host a dinner at her home for the American contingent—which she did, and at which neither Grace nor Rainier was present. (Jeanne Kelly Van Remoortel also gave a party for the American guests. This meant Rainier was spared two evenings of unwelcome confrontations.)

Caroline's marriage to Junot began on an acrimonious note when he permitted a photographer to take pictures of them on their honeymoon in the South Pacific without first seeking Caroline's agreement. This was followed by extravagant trips he arranged for them to take to the United States, the West Indies and England and Scotland. They did not return to Paris and the luxurious penthouse Rainier and Grace had taken for them on the Avenue Bosquet until November, having been traveling almost continuously for five months.

Caroline wanted to start a family, but Junot was not pleased with the idea. Before he had met Caroline, Junot had told friends that "staying single was the natural condition for a man and marriage was a social convention." Within a matter of weeks of their return to Paris, Junot began the first of a series of extramarital affairs, conducted quite openly for he was photographed at parties, nightclubs and on a deserted beach with his lovers. This continued for eighteen months, Caroline's attempts to make a go of the marriage finally failing completely after a photographer caught a picture of Junot dancing with Countess Agneta von Furstenberg, a woman friend from his premarital days, at Studio 54, a popular New York discotheque, when he had told his wife he was in Montreal on business.

Despite the problems with the Church that a divorce would cause, Grace and Rainier, who had never liked their son-in-law and had felt great anger at his ill-treatment of Caroline, did nothing to help reunite the couple once Caroline had ordered him to leave their Paris apartment. On August 8, 1980, Caroline issued a statement that the marriage was over and that she would file for divorce.

Monaco was the "family firm," and when the Grimaldis were viewed badly by the press, it affected business. Caroline did not wait long after her separation from Junot to be seen with a parade of good-looking young men. The effect was to give the world the impression that at least one member of the Grimaldis cared little about her Catholic vows or her privileged position as a role model.

(Many years later Caroline would say: "When you're young you make mistakes of course, but if you're anybody else [other than a princess] you have time to sort it out for yourself. . . . I would rather have done things differently. I would rather have lived somewhere else and been left alone. . . . I'm fundamentally a lucky person without the littlest right to complain. But always in the back of my mind I had plans and other ideas. . . .")

Feeling she had failed Caroline in some way, Grace now became almost obsessive in her tight control of Stephanie, who had blossomed into a beautiful fifteen-year-old. Stephanie and her mother were inseparable, a situation that was disturbing to Rainier who could see how terribly dependent the girl was upon Grace. Albert had grown into a handsome young man and was attending Amherst, where he had been very quickly accepted by his fellow students. But the press hounded him, and Albert was frequently photographed with different girls.

Rainier was known to be homophobic, and there are many reports of his sharp, disapproving comments about gay rights at dinner parties and social gatherings, and his rudeness to certain friends of Grace's who were known to be homosexual. He was not entirely displeased that his son was attractive to and attracted by good-looking women. "He pushed Albert into sports and manly pastimes all through the boy's youth," one friend comments. But he was increasingly concerned that the public perception of his children could discourage the family tourist trade and investors and so affect the enterprising climate that had given the Principality the highest per capita income on the Continent.

Rainier did not approve of Grace's driving a car. Her eyesight had grown weaker over the years, and he did not think she was a good driver to begin with. There was, in fact, little necessity for her ever to get behind the wheel of a car, for she had her own chauffeur, and if he was not available there was always someone on the Palace or her personal staff who could take his place. She also claimed that she hated driving. Nonetheless, from time to time she would set out alone in one of their cars, always with the explanation that it was less bother and more convenient at that moment. In truth, much as she disliked driving, it offered one of the few times that she could be by herself.

She owned a series of curious vehicles for a princess. During the late seventies her favorite private mode of transportation was a converted black London taxi that was big and commodious in the passenger compartment but had room only for the driver up front. She disposed of it when it was severely damaged after she hit another car broadside at the intersection that led up the hill to the Palace. No one was hurt but the accident unnerved her. "I'll never drive again," she told friends. "That should make Rainier very happy."

A used 1971 metallic-green Land Rover (similar to a jeep) replaced the London taxi. From the time of the collision, Grace did not drive except on the vast private property at Marchais or Roc Agel. This gave many friends and members of the press the false impression that she had allowed her license to lapse and that she no longer *ever* drove a car, which would later create much confusion in the press.

On the morning of Friday, September 10, 1982, Stephanie returned to Monaco from a vacation in Antigua where she had suffered a serious water-skiing accident that had required fifteen stitches in her head. The chauffeur brought her up to Roc Agel from Nice Airport, and Grace immediately began hovering over her. Although Stephanie insisted she was all right, Grace wanted further X rays to be taken.

The weekend proved to be stressful. Business detained Rainier at the Palace on Saturday. Grace was preparing for a trip in ten days to England and then to the United States, where she would embark on a three-week tour of poetry readings (Irish poets mainly, with some of Shakespeare's sonnets included), her newest involvement, the proceeds to go to charity. The project was finally approved by Rainier after several weeks of trying to get Grace to change her mind, his objection being more to the difficulties of such a trip in terms of security and of Grace's comfort than to the project itself.

Albert was in Italy for a soccer match and would not return until late Sunday night. Caroline was departing for London on

Sunday and Stephanie for Paris on Monday night to start her school term that following Wednesday. Grace was to accompany her, but with the news of Stephanie's accident it was feared that the *paparazzi* would be out in full force and there would be no peace on the Avenue Foch. Arrangements had been made for them to stay for two nights at the Hôtel Meurice in Paris to outwit the press. The plan would make things easier in one way, more complicated in another. Extra clothes had to be taken because the press would be watching the house on the Avenue Foch to see if anyone came in or out who might give a clue to where Grace and Stephanie might be.

But Grace's main concern was Stephanie's well-being. She remained adamant in her wish to have further X rays taken, and she was not at all sure that it was advisable for Stephanie to fly to Paris or to begin school so soon after the accident. At ten A.M. on Monday morning, September 13, the chauffeur drove the Land Rover from the garage to the front of the house. Although not yet old enough to have a license, Stephanie was permitted to drive through the grounds of Roc Agel. Normally she would have brought the car around, but because of her head wound, Grace did not think it was wise for her to do so. And Rainier, who was spending a few short hours at Roc Agel on Monday to relax, agreed.

The plan was for the chauffeur to drive them down to the Palace and then later to a doctor's office for X rays. But after Grace had placed all the additional clothes they needed across the backseat of the Land Rover, she decided it would make matters simpler, since the car ride took only about fifteen minutes, if she drove. The chauffeur suggested he take them and then return for the clothes, but Grace insisted that she and Stephanie go alone and then he could bring Rainier down later. Grace's insistence indicated that she might want some time alone with Stephanie to discuss something personal. Mother and daughter set off a few moments later, Princesse Grace, wearing her glasses, behind the wheel of the car.

The sun was glaring, making the precipitous road difficult to navigate. Stephanie later told doctors that about five minutes down the steep incline from Roc Agel her mother complained of a sudden pain in her head and then slumped over the wheel of the car just as she was about to negotiate a particularly sharp, steep hairpin turn which, Stephanie said, required her "to brake very hard and fight with the steering wheel to follow the road 150 degrees to the right." Stephanie, seeing Grace was not in control, tried to apply the hand brake but was unable to do so. The car careened straight toward the edge of the cliff where a small safety barrier about a foot high separated the road from a sheer drop of 120 feet. The Land Rover crashed through the barrier and plunged over the side of the mountain.

The car came to rest in the field of a farm at the foot of the cliff. Neither Grace nor Stephanie had fastened her seat belt. In the downhill fall Grace had been thrown into the backseat, Stephanie onto the floor under the glove compartment of the front seat. She managed to get the door open by kicking at it with both her legs. Already half off its hinges, it fell to the ground and Stephanie stumbled out on the passenger side. Smoke was coming from the car. A woman who lived on the property was standing nearby, too stunned to move. "Please get help! Call the Palace! I'm Princesse Stephanie, call my father and get help," Stephanie screamed. "My mother's in the car! Call my father!" The farmer who owned the property had now joined her and asked who her father was. Stephanie explained and began to sob, "Call my father at the Palace."

The woman ran back into the house to call an ambulance and the fire department while the man led Stephanie away from the Land Rover, which all of them feared was about to blow up. Before the ambulance came to take them to Princesse Grace Hospital, Stephanie collapsed. Her head wound had opened and she had suffered spinal injuries. Stephanie had either been too upset to remember or had not known that her father had remained at Roc Agel, and by the time he was notified, Grace and Stephanie were on their way to the hospital, where he arrived not long after.

The Princesse Grace Hospital had recently undergone minor refurbishment and the installation of new equipment. Even so, it was not up to the standard of a modern institution. Not long before, Lisette de Ramel had been scheduled to have her twin sons in the hospital and had gone to look at the facilities. "It was so dirty and ill-kept that I decided I would do anything rather than have my children there," she says. "After they were born, I told [Princesse Grace] that I had gone to a small Communist town in France to have the twins because I would not go to her hospital. 'Well, we're taking care of that right now,' she assured me, and I knew she really cared and work *had* begun."

Grace was brought into the emergency department unconscious, a thin trickle of blood seeping from her mouth—the ominous sign of a brain hemorrhage. While a team of two assistant surgeons, a radiologist, a neurologist and four nurses attended to her wounds, the doctor in charge, Professor Charles Chatelin, telephoned one of France's leading neurosurgeons, Professor Jean Duplay, at Pasteur Hospital in Nice. Duplay arrived by helicopter half an hour later. He instantly requested that a brain scan be done to ascertain the extent of the damage— but Princesse Grace Hospital did not have the equipment, and the only brain scanner in Monaco was in the private clinic of Dr. Michael Moreau.

In deep shock, Grace could have died if she was moved. The doctors agreed that first her general condition had to be stabilized. Eight hours later the short ambulance journey was undertaken. The diagnosis following the scan was that her brain response was totally and irreparably damaged. The first reports of the tragic accident did not reveal the gravity of Princesse Grace's condition. Until the brain scan could be conducted, the medical team that attended her could not be sure how badly her brain had been damaged. However, they did know that she was in far more critical condition than was reported. Members of the Palace staff say the secrecy was necessary because Princess Caroline, who was on her way back to Monaco from England, had to be told first.

The following evening Caroline, Rainier and Albert were at Grace's bedside in the hospital where she had been returned after the scan. They had been told that her brain had ceased to function. The family had gathered earlier in Stephanie's hospital room and Rainier and the three children "agreed that there was no point in continuing life artificially." Grace was moved to a white-walled room filled with flowers; and at 10:10 P.M., September 14, 1982, each member of the family having said a last farewell, the life-support system was switched off.

22

WHEN RAINIER had inherited the throne thirty-three years earlier, Monaco was viewed by many as "an exotic backwater of stucco villas, multimillionaires, of Aristotle Onassis, of fortunes made and thrown away on the gambling tables." In looking back, Monégasques could date the Principality's history in the twentieth century as Before Grace and After Grace. Her marriage to Rainier had been the turning point in Monaco's esteem. She had brought dignity and international celebrity to the Principality, giving it a recognition factor apart from the gaming tables at Monte Carlo.

While Grace gave her adopted country a sense of pride, Rainier had turned Monaco into a thriving business concern, reclaiming land from the sea and creating an all-season international conference center and playground, "not only for the wealthy but for the not-so-rich, though far from impoverished tourist." In truth, his accomplishments far outstripped hers. He had managed to keep out the vultures—the cutthroat gamblers and building contractors, the mass tourist industry and the mafia. He had emerged somewhat bruised in 1963 from his encounter with President Charles de Gaulle, but he had won in his power struggle with Onassis. But it had still been Grace who held the Principality together as a community. The doyens of Monégasque society (those women who had inherited, or who married men who had inherited, the fortunes that had been made in Monte Carlo during the golden years at the turn of the century, or who were members of European aristocracy resident there since that time), had not made life easy for her. Despite her status, they had been snobbish toward her and Grace had felt that they constantly stood in judgment of her, criticizing the way she spoke French, decorated her apartments in the Palace, her family's lace-curtain Irish background, and her own career as a film star.

But upon her death it was plain to see that *the people* had held her in very special regard. She was mourned as no reigning monarch in Monaco's recent history had been. When the bulletin saying she had died was released on Radio Monte Carlo, many Monégasques and residents pulled their cars to the side of the road and could be seen crying, and people on the street openly wept. The years of Grace's reign as Princesse de Monaco had brought pride to the average Monégasque for her elegance, beauty and charm and they had loved her because of her compassion for the elderly, the young and the ill. She had helped set up senior-citizen groups, convalescent homes and a ballet school for children. She was only fifty-three years old at the time of her death, and without a history of any serious illness; no one was prepared for the suddenness of it.

They looked to Rainier for strength and leadership, but for many weeks after Grace's death he appeared a broken man. Their fears mounted. A deep rift existed between President Mitterrand's Socialist France and the anachronistic Principality of Monaco, and some old-timers still feared a French takeover, prompted by resentment of tax-free millionaires living on their back doorstep.

There was also concern that the Princesse de Monaco's death would cause the stream of transatlantic visitors she attracted to Monaco, and upon whom the Monégasques largely relied for their prosperity, to dry up. To add to their consternation, the press published an unsubstantiated story that Rainier's grief was so overwhelming that he was contemplating abdicating in favor of Albert, whom everyone believed to be too young and inexperienced for the job of Prince de Monaco.

The royal funeral service was held on Saturday, September 18, in the Byzantine Cathedral where Grace and Rainier had been married twenty-six years earlier. On a dais by the altar, under the glare of television lights, Rainier, dazed and unable to control his grief, sat slumped in a chair between Caroline (swathed in black, a mantilla covering her face) and Albert (Stephanie remained hospitalized with her injuries), and directly behind them sat Grace's brother Kell and her sisters, Lizanne

302

and Peggy. Grace's coffin, draped in the red and white Monégasque flag, was close by.

She was not snubbed in death as she believed she had been
in life. The Princess of Wales was there to represent Great
Britain; Madame Danielle Mitterrand, the wife of the French
President, and Mrs. Nancy Reagan on behalf of the American
government sat side by side in the front row of the congregation,
along with King Baudouin and Queen Fabiola of Belgium, ex-
Queen Anne Marie of Greece, Prince Philip of Liechtenstein,
Prince Fuad of Egypt, Prince Albert of Belgium, Princess Feriad
of Jordan, Prince Karim Aga Khan and Begum Salima, Princess
Bénédicte of Denmark, Prince Bertil of Sweden, Prince Bern-
hardt of Holland, Princess Paola of Liège, Grand Duchess Jo-
séphine-Charlotte of Luxembourg, ex-Empress Farah Diba of
Iran, and Madame Claude Pompidou, widow of the former
President of France.

Seated behind the royals were four of Grace's bridesmaids,
Judith (Kanter) Quine, Maree Frisby, Rita Gam and Bettina
Thompson Gray; Grace's former Hollywood agent, Jay Kanter;
Cary Grant and the many other Hollywood friends Grace had
maintained from her former life. The mourners' list gave strong
proof of just how important Grace Kelly Grimaldi, Princesse de
Monaco, had been to the rise in stature of her husband's Prin-
cipality.

The suddenness of her mother's death, the shock of seeing
her father—who had always seemed the strong member of the
family—so visibly shaken, the sight of her usually exuberant
sister in a deep state of depression brought out all of Caroline's
better instincts. Within a matter of weeks she appeared to have
stepped—however lightly—into her mother's shoes. "It was in-
credible," one close observer noted. "Caroline seemed to carry
herself differently—with undeniable regal bearing. She looked
more mature. She spoke more confidently. Her sadness was
evident but it was controlled."

For many months to follow, Rainier was seldom seen in public
without Caroline at his side. Occasionally, one could glimpse
his hand touch hers as though to draw strength from her for-
titude. And as time progressed, Caroline became Monaco's official hostess, greeting important visitors and attending,

sometimes with her father, sometimes alone, galas, dedications, inaugurations, always with regal bearing. But she could not help realizing that her position by her father's side could only be temporary.

Eventually—and with Albert now of marriageable age it seemed sooner rather than later—Albert's wife would supersede Caroline in position. Then there was always the possibility that Rainier would remarry. Her aunt Antoinette, who had divorced Jean-Charles Rey and married ballet dancer John Gilpin of the Royal Festival Ballet in London (who was to die of a heart attack just forty days later) was an example of what Caroline did not want her life to become—a royal appendage who did little worthwhile with her life, and was consumed by ambition and frustrated by envy and resentment. Caroline longed for a home and family of her own. She also tried her hand at writing, beginning with a series of articles for French magazines. In one, she gave a clear picture of the problem she thought was most felt by her father's subjects—the invading army of visitors that occupied so much space in the tiny Principality.

"The rules are simple," she wrote. "If you're part of the jet-set . . . you have dinner on your terrace of the Hôtel de Paris and fiddle with your caviar on your plate. The buses drive by endlessly. The people in them stare and point. . . . So on one hand there are groups who stagger out of hot, smelly buses. On the other there are people trying to be beautiful and desperately cool, swelling with pride at the mere thought of showing off. Where do the Monégasques fit into this social jigsaw? Quite frankly, I don't think we do. . . ."

After Stephanie recovered from her injuries, she returned to school in Paris, and was soon spending most of her time away from Monaco, either in France or in California. She had some of her mother's artistic leanings and, to Rainier's disappointment (for he would rather have seen her embark on a less public vocation), only recently envisioned a stage career, preferably in music, although her pleasant voice was professionally untrained. She, perhaps even more than her siblings, missed her mother, and she turned to Caroline for the support that she had lost. But her life could never be the same. And, for a long time, she not only had to deal with constant false accusations in the press about her degree of culpability in the accident but with her own sense of failure in not turning the wheel or pulling the hand brake in time to avert the tragedy.

"There was a lot of pressure on me because everyone was saying that I had been driving the car . . . that I'd killed my mother. It's not easy when you're 17 to live with that," she told her mother's friend and biographer, Jeffrey Robinson. "After a while you can't help feeling guilty. Everybody looks at you and you know they're thinking, how come she's still around and Grace is dead? . . . I needed my mother a lot when I lost her. And my dad was so lost without her. I felt so alone. I just went off and did my own thing."

Within a year of her mother's death Caroline married twenty-seven-year-old Stefano Casiraghi. A tall, blond, intelligent Milanese, the son of a wealthy Italian industrialist, Casiraghi was, according to one of his good friends, Mauro Ravenna, "arrogant but shy. A born manager, an indisputable professional [in business dealings and in his hobby of power-boat racing], demanding and always well prepared. [Racing] was a passion with him. . . . He had thousands of ideas for ventures—a sharp mind for business. . . ." Another friend called him "an intense, fervent kind of man." There is no doubt that his electric personality had a strong effect on Caroline. Many of her former café society friends were dropped, and her life quickly revolved around Casiraghi.

Caroline had divorced Junot and in the spring of 1984 been wed in Monaco in a quiet ceremony outside the Church when she was four months pregnant with Casiraghi's child, a fact that was well-publicized in the press and did not help her public image. The choice of a civil divorce and marriage had not been easy. Since her mother's death Caroline had become the most overtly religious member of the Grimaldis; and it greatly disturbed her that without an annulment of her first marriage, she could not take communion. But shortly before Caroline had separated from Junot, Grace had told her (as she had once told Lisette Prince de Ramel about *her* difficult marriage) that she must divorce Junot or her life would be destroyed.

Her mother had seemed to imply that things would be worked out with the Vatican and an annulment would be forthcoming. That had not yet happened, but Caroline was deeply in love with Casiraghi and he with her. They settled in a house on the Rock; Stefano went into real estate and boat building. A son, Andrea, was born in 1984, a daughter, Charlotte, in 1986, and another son, Pierre, in 1987. The children were being brought up to speak French, Italian and English, and as the Casiraghis lived most of the year in Monaco (they also spent time in Paris), the children saw Rainier often and were a great source of happiness to him.

Caroline took over most of Grace's work—the president's chair at the Monaco Arts Festival, the directorship of the Monaco branch of the Princesse Grace Foundation and the Princesse Grace Dance Academy (for young ballet dancers) and the formation of a professional ballet company for the Monte Carlo Opera. Then there were the Garden Club, the Girl Guides and the Princesse Grace Irish Library.

"It's because I'm here. I have a family and I'm here," Caroline told Robinson, who then asked, what about "all those stories about wanting to take over the throne?"

"You mean the ones that say that I'm manoeuvering in dark corridors in the Palace? All that intrigue and counter-intrigue. Richelieu and Mazarin look like kids compared to what I'm apparently doing. . . . Frankly I can't wait for Albert to get married. . . . Of course he keeps telling me he has to find the right girl. Well at this stage . . . I think I'd settle for Joan Collins."

Albert had served six months with the French Navy after his graduation from Amherst, and then he had spent five months with the New York office of the Morgan Guaranty Trust Company as a management trainee. After that there had been short stays of employment with Wells, Rich and Green Advertising in New York (his idea, for he thought he would like the profession) and in the marketing department at the champagne makers Moët et Chandon (Rainier's suggestion so that Albert could "get a feel for the way a major French conglomerate operated").

In 1986 Albert returned to Monaco, and his father involved him as much as possible in the running of the Principality. Rainier had regained his equilibrium. He had friendships, and perhaps romantic liaisons (associates say this is the case), with some suitable women—one a close friend of Grace's, another a member of the international set. But remarriage was never discussed. He had truly loved Grace. Her death had wounded him deeply and he seemed unable, or unwilling, to let go of the pain or to distance himself from her by marrying again.

He threw himself wholeheartedly into his business ventures and the further development of Monaco. When Rainier began the work of reclaiming land from the sea for his Principality, there had been strong objection to the project by France, which was concerned that the air and sea rights on their border, set forth in the treaty Albert I had made with France, might be infringed upon. In January 1984, President Mitterrand of France paid Rainier an official visit. The two men were seen smiling in a relaxed manner together. Shortly after their meeting a new treaty with France was ratified by Rainier that better defined Monaco's air and sea rights so that there would be no question that land he was reclaiming from the sea belonged to the Principality.

Monégasques breathed easier. Rainier appeared to be his old self again, confident and an excellent diplomat. He had, after all, brought Monaco from being a "sunny place for shady people" to a nation, however small, that was no longer solely dependent upon a Casino for survival. With a permanent population of only 30,000 (of which only 4,700 were Monégasques), the Principality had an embassy, consulate, or full-time representative in fifty-one countries, including the United States, Canada, Great Britain, France, Italy, West Germany and Spain. That it did not have a seat in the United Nations rankled. Rainier had tried to obtain a seat with an independent vote from that of France; but the 1919 Treaty of Versailles between France and Monaco states that in return for France's undertaking to defend the independence and sovereignty of the Principality, its reigning monarch undertook to exercise its rights in conformity with French interests. The United Nations, therefore, refused to agree that the Principality's vote could be independent of France, and Rainier abandoned the idea.

With a police force of 450 (about three times the police-to-population ratio of other Western countries because of Rainier's determination to keep down the crime rate), he has been accused of playing "Big Brother." "This isn't a police state," he insists. "I've heard that comment but I don't agree with it at all. Come on, what is a police state? A place where the police interfere with your life, with whom you see, with what you say, with what you think. That isn't the case here." Nonetheless, privileges such as residency or business interests in the Principality have been denied or removed by royal edict from time to time without contest because, despite the Principality having a Constitution, it is an absolute monarchy.

Monaco's present Constitution is based on the one originally drawn by Albert I in 1911, revised by him in 1917 and given a more liberal character by Rainier on December 17, 1962. But the first chapter of the Constitution stipulates that the executive power derives from the high authority of the reigning Prince, who not only represents Monaco in all its dealings with foreign powers but signs and ratifies all treaties and appoints his own Minister of State and three Governmental Councillors, responsible for Finance and the Economy, the Interior, and Public Works and Social Affairs.

Even the judicial powers belong to the Sovereign, who delegates all exercise of them to the courts and tribunals, but the Constitution guarantees the independence of the judges and their rulings. Although Monaco is a Roman Catholic country, freedom for other religious denominations is guaranteed, as well as public education for all children from six to sixteen years of age. The Constitution also established the National Council. Still, the Council shares legislative power with the Sovereign, who can override or veto their suggestions or decisions. Monaco's eighty-five man army is composed entirely of French nationals seconded from the French Army (an arrangement inaugurated in 1861 by Prince Charles) to eliminate the possibility of a military coup d'état. (This had not stopped Antoinette from plotting to overthrow Rainier.)

By 1990 the Grimaldis appeared as solid as the Rock they ruled over. There had been serious rivalries between Caroline and Albert before her second marriage, with Caroline threatening to leave Monaco completely if he married and his wife became First Lady. Rainier had entered the fray and there was talk about changing Monaco's Constitution to allow her to inherit. Casiraghi's death ended the discussions. Rainier and his immediate family were a closed, tight circle, each drawing strength from the others. Stephanie, who had become a model-cum-entrepreneur-cum-punk-singer-cum-pop-singer, was difficult for Rainier to control. He had left the raising and disci-

ficult for Rainier to control. He had left the raising and discipline of his daughters to Grace and seemed to be at a loss as to how to cope with Stephanie's rebellious nature. He felt her romantic affairs were entirely too public and the men she saw unsuitable for a young princess. But Stephanie still suffered emotional depression from the effects of the car crash that had killed her mother and despite her world travels and Rainier's disapproval of her life-style, she remained close to him, warm and loving, and he treated her with considerable tolerance.

Only thirty-three years old in 1990 when she was widowed, Caroline could hardly be called the matriarch of the Grimaldis, but she began to take on the mantle. Grace's impact on Monaco was everywhere one looked, her name carved in stone, her beauty and glamour remembered by all. The Monégasques would recall her ever more radiantly each year. In fact, an unsuccessful attempt was made to have her made a saint.

Caroline did not rebound from the loss of her husband with the same resilience that she had shown upon her mother's death. In the early days of her widowhood she had learned not only that her husband had a mistress all along, but that he was deeply in debt. To protect the investments he had left her, she put up $2 million of her jewels as collateral to the banks and worked successfully to rescue her inheritance from his creditors. Rainier once again became the mainspring of his family. He was undeniably not only a vigorous Prince de Monaco, but the strong head of his family. He had been the one to break the news of Stefano's death to his grandchildren and he remains a potent presence in their lives and in Caroline's as well, dining with her at her home two or three times a week, and spending weekends at Roc Agel with the young widow and her children.

A year after her husband's death Caroline showed no sign of emerging from the strict mourning she had imposed upon herself. In a ritualistic gesture she had cut off her formerly luxuriant hair, had not taken to wearing makeup again and dressed in an austere fashion that was diametrically opposed to her once flamboyant image. More vital to the Monégasques, she displayed no inclination to return to her role as the Principality's First Lady. When photographed surreptitiously by the press, she presented a somber figure, the radiant smile gone. But during this time she developed a close relationship with the French actor Vincent Lindon.

Monégasques were hopeful that Caroline had finally put aside her public mourning when they read that she had appeared in December 1991 with Prince Rainier and Albert and Stephanie at a benefit held at the Louvre Museum in Paris to honor her mother and Georges Pompidou, the late president of France. Elegantly dressed in a floor-length black velvet gown, she had entered the room on the arm of her father, smiled cordially at the five hundred guests, and spoken easily to many of them.

After this one public appearance, she withdrew once again into seclusion, having now to face rumors that Casiraghi had been murdered. His co-pilot, Patrice Innocenti, claimed that "Stefano had many enemies. Some of them drank to his death with champagne that day in Monte Carlo." However, a police investigation concluded that his death was a tragic accident. ("Everything was going well," Innocenti stated in a press interview a year after the investigation. "Then, in a fraction of a second, I felt the boat rising up and flipping over. . . . We had been the victims of a [huge] wave. . . . The boat was raised up two or three metres, flipped over and then hit the sea on Stefano's side. I felt the thud, it was tremendous.") The investigation had been hard for Caroline to bear.

Albert stepped into the breach that Caroline's withdrawal from public life created and took on a higher profile. Constantly described in the press as "Europe's most eligible bachelor," he refuses to be rushed into making the wrong choice of a bride. The loss of Grace's glamorous presence and Caroline's prolonged mourning has cast a pall over Monaco. Whomever Albert marries will be expected to assume the roles his older sister and his mother have played so brilliantly as hostess for visiting celebrities and at the Principality's festivities; and then as Princesse de Monaco when he ascends the throne. Finding the right wife is not an easy task. Meanwhile, Albert remains an heir-in-waiting, and the only male in the direct Grimaldi line who, as things stand at present, can inherit the throne. Caroline has petitioned her father for permission to marry Lindon. The conditions are not easy. Lindon would have to convert from Judaism to Catholicism and sign a contract that would deny him any title or custody of the children in the event of a divorce. He will also have to adopt the name of Grimaldi and make his home with Caroline in Monaco. The Vatican finally granted Caroline an annulment from Junot on February 26, 1992. The decision was confirmed by a second commission on June 20, clearing the way for her to marry in the Catholic Church. With their father dead, the children's illegitimate status remains, but Lindon (or whoever Caroline does marry) could adopt her three children and thus legitimize their position.

Caroline's problems now seem resolved and the Grimaldi line more secure. But Monaco has now to face a minor scandal with Stephanie, unmarried and about to deliver a child by a live-in lover who was a former Palace guard and whom she claims she will marry after the birth of her child. But the Grimaldis have survived nearly eight hundred years in their position of power. While other nations crumble around them, political parties disappear, and economic despair is on the rise, Monaco and the Monégasques prosper under the ruling hand of the man, Prince Rainier III, who remains the only absolute monarch in Europe. The Grimaldis are the oldest ruling dynasty in the world despite the miniature size of the country, which might easily have roused a large nation to seize it. They are a family of survivors of legendary stature.

The Grimaldis and Monaco—inseparable and one.

SOURCES AND NOTES

Money: The *livre* (twenty *sous*) was equal to approximately one pound (U.S. $1.80), 1991 figures.

The *écu* was equal to three *livres*.

The *pistole* (or *louis d'or*) was equal to ten *livres*.

The *franc* became the main denomination of money during the Revolution. Its value fluctuated wildly until the mid-nineteenth century.

Full bibliographic information for sources cited will be found in the Bibliography.

CHAPTER 1

For Princess Caroline and the death of Stefano Casiraghi, personal interviews and contemporary newspaper reports and obituaries in France, Monaco, Great Britain and the United States.

CHAPTER 2

Where the town of Monaco now stands was formerly the temple of Hercules Monoecus, which gave the Principality its name. "The father-in-law coming down from the rampart of the Alps and the Citadel of Monoecus" (Virgil OEN6). For the early history of the Grimaldis: the Monégasque Collection in the Manchester Central Reference Library; *Historical Documents of the Rulers of Monaco and the House of Grimaldi Before the Fifteenth Century* (Monaco, 1905); *Princes of Monaco: The Remarkable History of the Grimaldi Family,* Françoise de Bernardy, translator Len Ortzen (1961); and H. Pemberton's *History of Monaco* (1867).

Hercule's death is recorded in the Monaco Parish Registry, November 21, 1604. "The most noble and worthy seigneur Hercule Grimaldi seigneur of Monaco, Marquis of Campagna, called to a better life at the age of about 42. Attacked by five or six in the Grand-Rue, in front of the house of the *podesera* master, Bartholomies Dadino, he at once delivered up his soul to God." Hercule's body was found washed up on the rocks at the shoreline of Monaco and was buried in the St. Sebastian Chapel of the Church of St. Nicholas.

Honoré II's sister, Jeanne, married Théodore Trivulce. She died in childbirth in 1620. Her distraught husband took holy orders and eventually became Cardinal Trivulce, a very powerful figure in the Church.

In January 1643, the title of Comte de Carladez in Auvergne was added to the honors received by Honoré II from Louis XIII.

Antoine, Duc de Gramont, was colonel of the regiment of the French Guard, governor of Bayonne, of Béarn and of Basse-Navarre (the Pyrenees). He was married in 1534 to Charlotte-Catherine's mother, Françoise-Marguerite du Plessis-Chivre, niece of Cardinal Richelieu.

A portrait of Charlotte-Catherine was sent to Honoré II before it was decided that his son should marry the Duc de Gramont's daughter. On March 22, 1659, he wrote to the genealogist Pierre d'Hozier, who had been charged with establishing the family tree of the Gramonts: "I cannot thank you enough . . . for the lengths you went to to derive this excellent portrait . . . which is quite good. Everyone likes it, especially the Duc de Valentinois, my grandson, who keeps it over his bed. And therefore, I would appreciate it at your convenience if you sent me the full family chart. . . ." [Archives du Palais Princier]

CHAPTER 3

Pau was the capital of the province of Béarn. The château there was chosen for the wedding because it was where ancestors of the Gramont family had married for more than a century. It is believed that Jean du Haut de Salies, Bishop of Lescar and a good friend of the Gramonts, officiated at the wedding service, but there is no name inscribed on the marriage certificate to substantiate this.

For Louis XIV and his Court: *Louis XIV,* Vincent Cronin (1964) and *The Sun King,* Nancy Mitford (1968). For European history: *Europe in the Seventeenth Century,* David Ogg (1959). The descriptions of the Comte de Guiche: *Assault on Olympus,* W. H. Lewis (1958). For Philippe, Duc d'Orléans: *The Letters of Madame,* translated by G. S. Stevenson (1924). For Louis and Antoine's marital relations: Monégasque Archives, Manchester Central Reference Library; *Mémoires du Comte de Gramont* (1866); *Letters from Marshal de Tessi to Prince Antoine I of Monaco* (1911); *The Letters of Mme. Marie de Sévigné* (1862) and her *Mémoire de*

Saint-Simon (1926); *The Courts of Europe,* edited by A. G. Dickens (1977).

Louis XIV often asked the Maréchal de Gramont's opinion on literature and art. One morning he handed a madrigal to the Maréchal. "Here is a poor piece of work" he said, and asked if he agreed.

Gramont read the madrigal. "Your Majesty judges divinely well in everything. It is true that this is the most idiotic and ridiculous madrigal I have ever read."

"Would you describe its author as a conceited ass?"

"Sire, there is no other word for him."

"I wrote it," the King laughed.

Gramont looked horrified. "Sire . . . I've been guilty of treason. I read it hastily: If your Majesty would let me see it again . . ."

"No, Monsieur le Maréchal," the King replied. "First impressions are always true." [Cronin]

CHAPTER 4

For information on Louise-Hippolyte, Antoine I and Jacques de Matignon: *Mémoires de Saint-Simon; Annales Monégasques,* Nos. 3, 7 and 12; *Jacques Grimaldi: Comte de Torigny, Duc de Valentinois, Prince de Monaco,* Léon-Honoré LaBande (Paris: Editions Picard, 1939); *Mémoires sur la cour de Louis XV,* Vol. VIII, Duc de Luynes (Paris: Didot, 1895); *Anecdotes secrètes du règne de Louis XV,* ed. Roger de Parnes (Paris: Rouveyre & Blond, 1882).

The War of the Spanish Succession lasted for a decade. Louis XIV might be said to have emerged victorious, for his grandson Philip V was to remain King of Spain. Moreover, from 1705 to 1709 the French King had virtually ruled Spain from Versailles, instituting reforms and curtailing the powers of the Church and grandees in order to strengthen central government reforms that brought Spain new prosperity.

Antoine's recognized children were: (by Marguerite Renée, a dancer in the Paris Opéra) Antoine, Chevalier de Grimaldi, b. Oct. 2, 1697, Paris, d. Nov. 28, 1784, Monaco; Antoinette, called Mlle. de Saint-Rémy, b. 1699, Paris, d. unknown; and Louise-Marie Grimaldi, b. June 2, 1705, d. Sept. 21, 1723, Sospel. Antoine I also had two other known illegitimate children, one (1697) by Victoire Vertu, also a dancer at the Paris Opéra, and one by an unknown Provençal woman after he returned to Monaco in 1702. Dates from *Burke's Peerage.*

The report of the visitor to Monaco in 1705 is recorded in the Manchester Archives. For the correspondence between the Comte d'Armagnac and Antoine I: Archives du Palais, Monaco. Other historical information relating to Monaco was either contained in papers in the Archives du Palais, Monaco, or culled from *Histoire de la Principauté de Monaco,* Léon-Honoré LaBande (1934); *Monaco et Ses Princes,* Henri Metiver (1865); *Histoire de Monaco,* J. B. Robert (1973); *Monaco: Ses Origines et Son Histoire,* Gustave Saige (1988). Bernardy and Pemberton were also used as sources.

The story of the visit of the future Louis XV to the bedside of his grandfather, the dying Louis XIV: Cronin.

Letters of the Duc de Valentinois: Archives du Palais, Monaco, and Bernardy.

CHAPTER 5

For the history of Monaco and the Princes de Monaco, the same French histories as listed for Chapter 4. Letters from the Palace Archives and Bernardy. Story of the arrival of Honoré II's bride in Monaco as above. The claims against the Grimaldis in 1761, 1764 and 1841 are on record.

For Versailles and life at the French Court: *The King's Memoirs,* edited by C. Dreyss (1860); *Mémoires de Saint-Simon,* edited by A. de Boislisle (1879); *Louis XIV: An Informal Portrait,* W. H. Lewis (1959); *The Sunset of the Splendid Century,* W. H. Lewis (1955); *Louis XIV,* C. Petrie (1938); and *Louis XIV,* Vincent Cronin (1964).

The reports on the death of the Duke of York are in the Manchester Archives.

CHAPTER 6

The story of Louis XVI on his return from Cherbourg is from *Louis and Antoinette,* Vincent Cronin (1974).

The Treaty of Péronne was made in 1468 during the reign of Claudine and Lambert Grimaldi when Charles the Bold of Burgundy, ally of Edward IV of England (and the Grimaldis), humiliatingly defeated and imprisoned Louis XI of France, who was forced to sign a treaty granting his captors important concessions.

Thomas Paine (1737–1809) and the Revolution: *The Writings of Thomas Paine,* edited by M. D. Conway (1894–96, reprinted 1969); *Thomas Paine: His Life, Work and Times,* Aubrey Williamson (1973). Paine was born in Norfolk, England, the son of a Quaker. He emigrated to America in 1774 and became swiftly involved in its conflicts with England. His published pamphlet *Common Sense* (January 1776), in which he advocated independence, was an instant success in the colonies. He returned to England in 1787 and while there wrote *The Rights of Man* (two parts, 1791 and 1792) defending the French Revolution. The antimonarchical attacks in it led to his prosecution for treason and to his subsequent flight to Paris where he was made a member of the National Convention. He was imprisoned during the Reign of Terror from December 1793 to November 1794, during which time he wrote *The Age of Reason*. He returned to the United States in 1802, and died in poverty seven years later.

Louis XVII, eight years old when his mother went to the guillotine, remained in solitary confinement in Temple Prison. His food was passed to him through a barred slit in the door, the window of his cell was sealed, his clothes and bedclothes never changed, nor his excrement removed. For six months no one was allowed to speak to him. He developed tuberculosis of the bones. There were rumors of several attempts to rescue him, but it is fairly certain that he died in the Temple on June 8, 1795, although stories did circulate (all unproven) that he had escaped and a deaf-mute child had been substituted in his place.

The Comte de Provence—Louis XVIII—was the younger brother of Louis XVI. He fled in 1791 to Koblenz and intrigued to bring about foreign intervention against the revolutionaries. After his nephew's death, he was recognized as King by other nobles who had escaped and lived abroad. He returned to France as a moderate in 1814, taking a conciliatory approach to the Revolution; and with the support of Talleyrand, he was restored to the French throne following Napoleon's defeat at Waterloo. In 1820 his son, the Comte d'Artois, was murdered by the ultraroyalists, who then took control of the government. This thoroughly reactionary ministry headed by the Comte de Ville was replaced by the even more reactionary reign of Charles X (1824–1830), Louis XVIII's younger brother.

CHAPTER 7

For information on Napoleon, Josephine and the Court: *At the Court of Napoleon,* the memoirs of the Duchesse d'Abrantès; also the memoirs of Prince Napoleon, biographies of Napoleon by J. M. Thompson and Georges Lefebvre and of Josephine by R. M. Wilson and André Castelot.

The Kingdom of Sardinia included not only the island of Sardinia but lands given to Duke Victor Amadeus II of Savoy in 1720 to compensate him for the loss of Sicily to Austria. The Kingdom also included Savoy, Piedmont (now a section of Italy with Turin as its major city) and Nice.

France 1789–1815, by D.M.G. Sutherland (1985), gives a complete picture of France's expansionist years following the Revolution.

For additional background on France during the Revolution: *The Diary of Fanny Burney,* ed. L. Gibbs (1940); *The English Traveller in France, 1698–1815,* C. Maxwell (1932); *Patriots and Liberators,* S. Schama (1977); *Citizens,* S. Schama (1989).

Honoré IV and his physical and mental condition during his army days are fully documented in letters in the Archives du Palais, Monaco, and in *Annales Monégasques,* Nos. 6 and 9.

CHAPTER 8

Florestan's stage career: *Memoirs of a Paris Doctor,* P. de La Silboutie (1911). Correspondence of Princesse Caroline, Florestan and others: Archives du Palais, Monaco. Other information regarding Honoré V, Florestan and Princesse Caroline: Bernardy, Pemberton, Metiver and Saige. For Menton and its secession: Archives de Menton, Librairie Menton. For Florestan's army career: *Annales Monégasques.*

For Charles X, "a fallen, shattered structure": *The March of Folly,* Barbara Tuchman (1989).

CHAPTER 9

For the founding of Monte Carlo and the Casino: *The Money Spinner,* Xan Fielding (1977); *The Big Wheel,* George W. Herald and Edward D. Radin (1963); *The Little Tour,* Giles and Constantine Fitzgibbon (1953); publications and archives of the Société des Bains de Mer.

All quoted correspondence of Adolphe Eynaud to Princesse Caroline and Charles reposes in the Archives du Palais, Monaco.

Travel quotes from Pemberton and the various English newspapers (Monégasque Collection, Manchester Archives): *Pall Mall Gazette,* the *Times, Daily News, Standard, Athenaeum, Illustrated London News* and the *Daily Telegraph* for 1869–1870.

Princess Mary Adelaide, Duchess of Teck, was the mother of Victoria Mary of Teck, who became Queen Mary, Consort of George V of England.

CHAPTER 10

Descriptions of the Great Exhibition: *Illustrated London News*, April, 1867. America, just recovering from the Civil War, sent a complete ambulance service, representing the best of contemporary military medicine. But it was its patented new piece of furniture, described as a "rocking chair," that was the hit of the show. Britain not only had Lister, it sent locomotives and heavy railway machinery as well as the new Victorian oak furniture, which did not meet with much approval. A lightweight "wonder metal," "aluminum," and a substance called "petroleum" were introduced in the science section. Additional information: *The Fall of Paris*, Alistair Horne (1965).

Lady Mary Victoria Douglas Hamilton's ancestors, the famous house of Douglas, was intricately connected with Scottish history and was world famous. There had been "Black Douglas," an infamous pirate, and Good Sir James Douglas, who assisted Robert the Bruce in establishing Scotland's independence and who, after the death of King Robert, was entrusted with the conveyance of the royal heart to the Holy Sepulchre. (During the journey he was murdered.) A Douglas led the forces of Scotland against the Otterbourne in 1388. Sir Walter Scott immortalized the family in *Castle Dangerous* and other works.

The Douglas family was awarded the dukedom of Hamilton in 1643 and that of Brandon (England) in 1711 (the latter bringing the family into the peerage of England). The first Duke of Hamilton, Lady Mary Victoria's ancestor, led the Scottish army that invaded England in 1644. Defeated at Preston, he was captured, tried by the same court that condemned Charles I, and executed. His brother, the 2nd Duke of Hamilton, fled to Holland from Preston, returned in 1650 with Charles II and died of wounds received at the battle of Worcester (1651). The family was only distantly related to Sir William Hamilton, the diplomat who was the husband of Lady Emma Hamilton.

Lady Mary Victoria's cousin Malcolm Avondale, son of the 13th Duke of Hamilton, in 1931 married Clodagh Bowes-Lyon, a first cousin of Queen Elizabeth, consort of King George VI.

Princess Marie of Baden was the daughter of the Grand Duke Charles and the Grand Duchess Stéphanie Beauharnais, a niece of the Empress Josephine and the adopted daughter of Napoleon I.

Albert's voyage to the United States is covered in the letters in *Annales Monégasques*, No. 8.

Detailed description of the wedding of Lady Mary Victoria to Albert, Duc de Valentinois, was reported in all the major newspapers and magazines of the time. They can be found in the Monégasque

Collection in the Manchester Archives, along with information concerning their honeymoon journey to Baden-Baden and return via Geneva to Nice and then Monaco. Princesse Caroline's correspondence is in the Archives at Monaco.

CHAPTER 11

There are numerous articles, correspondence and records of the Heine-Miltenberger families in the Celeste and Christian Louis Miltenberger Archives at the University of North Carolina. Further material can be found in the New Orleans Library local history and old newspaper archives and the New Orleans Historical Society. The social activities in Paris of both Amelie Miltenberger-Heine and Alice Heine (as Duchesse de Richelieu and Princesse de Monaco) were frequently reported in the New Orleans daily newspaper, *The Picayune*. Additional information from private interviews with members of the Miltenberger family in New Orleans.

For Louis Napoleon: *Napoleon III*, Albert Guérard (1962) and *Memoirs of Prince Napoleon*, ed. d'Hauterive (1925). For the morals in Paris during Napoleon III's reign: Anthony B. North Peat's *Gossip from Paris During the Second Empire* (1903) and *The Amberley Papers*, ed. Bertrand and Patricia Russell (1937). For an understanding of the Franco-Prussian War: *Cassell's History of the War Between France and Germany, 1870–1871* (1894). *Queen Victoria, Letters* Second Series contain numerous entries about her meetings with Napoleon III.

Both American doctors who accompanied the Empress Eugénie on her escape to England wrote books about the siege, but the most useful information on their flight from Paris is in E. A. Crane's *Memoirs: Recollections of the Second French Empire* (1905). References are also made to it in *History of the American Ambulance Establishment in Paris During the Siege of 1870–1871*, Thomas W. Evans (1873).

The growth of Monte Carlo and that of the Casino is well covered in the books previously listed on the subject. Albert's studies in oceanography have been documented in his many speeches, articles and books.

CHAPTER 12

Descriptions of the Princesse de Luxembourg ("tall, red-haired . . .") can be found in Marcel Proust, *Remembrance of Things Past*, Vol. II: *Within a Budding Grove* (New York: Random House, 1981), p. 710.

Upon the death of the Duc de Richelieu, his and Alice's son inherited the title. Their daughter, Odile, married Gabriel, Duc de Rochefoucauld, and became the Duchesse de Rochefoucauld.

For Edward VII: *King Edward the Seventh*, Sir Philip Magnus (1964) and *Edward VII, Prince and King*, The Hon. Giles St. Aubyn (1979). Caesar, Edward VII's dog, survived his master. A short book was published in 1911 called *Where's Master? by Caesar The King's Dog.* Lillie Langtry had a daughter, who, it was rumored, was Edward's child. The girl was educated and raised in Paris under his auspices, but little is known of her after she left school.

Leopold II, King of the Belgians, was infamous for his many liaisons and his extravagant life-style. He amassed a fortune by exploiting the Congo, using forced labor, frequently under barbarous conditions, until the international scandal his methods evoked compelled him to turn over his rights in the Congo in 1908 to the Belgian government.

"When I first knew . . .": *My Life and Loves*, Frank Harris (1963).

Fifteen million francs in the years between 1890 and 1914 was about twelve million pounds. The franc was devalued at the end of World War I to one-fifth that value.

For Raoul Gunsbourg: *Annales Monégasques*, No. 8, Archives du Palais, Monaco, and the Menton and Monte Carlo papers. Letters between Prince Albert and Louis: *Annales Monégasques*, No. 9.

"Albert despised . . .": *Palace*, Baron Christian de Massy with Charles Higham.

There are many books on the Dreyfus Affair. I used *The Dreyfus Case*, Alfred and Pierre Dreyfus (1937) and newspapers of the time for the publication of Prince Albert's letter to Madame Dreyfus.

For Albert and the Kaiser: Archives du Palais, Monaco.

Frank Harris has some good descriptions of the Château de Marchais and of Alice. *Life with Queen Victoria: Marie Mallet's Letters from Court, 1887–1901*, edited by Victor Mallet (1968), contains the material on Queen Victoria's visit to the Riviera in 1899.

CHAPTER 13

For the details on Princesse Alice and her financial settlement I was fortunate in having the cooperation of surviving members of her family and access to letters exchanged between Alice and relatives on this, and other, intimate matters.

"What will this do to the coming season?": This quote of Camille Blanc's has been repeated in several books on the Blancs, father and son, and on Monte Carlo.

The letter from Theodore Roosevelt is in the Palace Archives. All the facts and quoted material (newspapers, articles and letters) about Prince Albert's trip to Cody, Wyoming, his meeting with Buffalo Bill and the hunting expedition at Camp Monaco were drawn from the archives of the Buffalo Bill Museum at Cody and the Cody Library. Other newspaper quotes and descriptions on the arrival of Albert in various other cities on this tour, if not noted in the text, are to be found at the New York Public Library, Old Newspaper Division.

All World War I correspondence between Louis and Albert has been published in *Annales Monégasques*, No. 12.

"My family was only interested . . .": De Massey.

CHAPTER 14

To re-create Monte Carlo and Monaco during the early part of the twentieth century, I used numerous guide and travel books of the period.

"An aura of Europe . . .": *The Little Tour*, Constantine and Giles Fitzgibbon.

"We'd only come to Monaco . . ." and "When we were with Mother . . .": *Rainier and Grace*, Jeffrey Robinson.

"To make love . . ." and "took out her childhood frustrations . . .": De Massey.

Correspondence of Princesse Charlotte: Archives du Palais, Monaco.

"The icy damp . . ." *The Buried Day*, Cecil Day Lewis. The other quotes about Rainier's schools and education can be found in the archives of Stowe, Le Rosey and Summerfields. "Other than that . . ."; "It was a beautiful setting . . ." to ". . . from this heaven": Robinson.

CHAPTER 15

"the most spectacular . . .": *A History of Europe*, H.A.L. Fisher, Volume II.

"radically from pro-German to pro-American . . .": De Massey.

I was fortunate in having interviews with close witnesses to the affair between Rainier and Gisèle Pascal and conversations many years ago with Irwin Shaw about his "liberation" of the Tip Top Bar.

"We were together . . .": Robinson.

"strolled around . . ." and "My whaling fleet . . .": *Onassis*, Willi Frischauer. There are many good books about Onassis from which I drew material: *Ari*, Peter Evans (1986); *Aristotle Onassis*, N. Fraser et al. (1977); and *Onassis*, Frank Brady (1978). Wherever I could, I went to primary sources. I was granted two long and patient interviews with associates of Onassis who requested anonymity but explained in finely remembered detail Onassis's takeover of the S.B.M., the PMS scandal and their observations on the relationship between Onassis and Rainier. Much helpful information was also learned from Stanley Jackson's *Inside Monte Carlo* (1975) and Steven Englund's *Princess Grace* (1984).

"The bank scandal . . .": De Massey.

CHAPTER 16

Information on the Kelly family background can be found in: *Those Philadelphia Kellys,* Arthur H. Lewis (1976); *Princess Grace,* Gwen Robyns (1976); *Princess Grace,* Steven Englund (1985); and *The Bridesmaids,* Judith Balaban Quine (1989). In addition, many articles about and interviews with members of the Kelly family have been published. Particularly helpful are the archives of the Philadelphia Public Library and the Philadelphia Historical Society.

"Oh, that Ma Kelly . . ."; "Betrayals of weakness . . .": Englund. Other quotes by John Brendan Kelly, Jr., and Lizanne Kelly Le Vine are from a *Time* cover article on Grace Kelly, January 31, 1955.

"There was always something . . ." and all of Margaret Majer Kelly's quotes in this chapter are from: *My Daughter, Grace Kelly* as told to Richard Gehman (*Los Angeles Examiner,* January 15–24, 1956).

"My sister Peggy . . .": *Collier's,* Evelyn Harvey (June 24, 1955).

"Grace was the third girl . . .": *100 Different Lives,* Raymond Massey (1979).

"She was a very beautiful lady . . .": *Stanley Kramer, Film Maker,* Donald Spoto (1978) and all subsequent quotes about *High Noon.*

"I've been at the studio for years . . .": Englund.

"Isn't it exciting . . .": Quine.

"Grace had done . . .": Ibid.

Grace Kelly won the Academy Award for 1954 over Dorothy Dandridge (*Carmen Jones*), Judy Garland (*A Star Is Born*), Audrey Hepburn (*Sabrina*) and Jane Wyman (*Magnificent Obsession*).

Additional information was drawn from Englund (all quotes by Cassini); *The Dark Side of Genius,* Donald Spoto (1983); *Sun and Shadow,* Jean-Pierre Aumont (1977); *Golden Boy,* Bob Thomas (1983); and numerous magazine and newspaper articles. Among the best: *Grace Kelly: Her Biggest Gamble,* Maurice Zolotow, *American Weekly,* April 29, 1956; *The Other Princess Grace, Ladies Home Journal,* May 1977; *That Special Grace,* Rita Gam, *McCall's,* January 1983; *Grace Kelly; Most Wanted*

Woman, Look (cover story), June 15, 1954; *Hollywood's Queen Becomes a Princess,* Martha Weinman, *Collier's,* March 2, 1956.

A video cassette, *Grace Kelly: The American Princess* (Brighton Video, New York), is available for home showing and contains some excellent commentary by Grace Kelly's close family members, associates and friends.

CHAPTER 17

Published literature on Prince Rainier is limited. One book, *Prince Rainier of Monaco: His Authorised and Exclusive Story,* Peter Hawkins (1966), was helpful. Other sources for this chapter were Englund and Quine and personal interviews. Although at first prohibited from making the sea voyage on the *U.S. Constitution* with the bridal party, members of the press persisted and were given accommodations. Some coverage therefore appeared in the press.

CHAPTER 18

For this chapter on "the wedding of the century" I was fortunate to have the counsel and comments of several of those who were involved in the plans and culmination of the wedding and of invited guests. M.G.M. filmed the ceremony and copies are available for viewing, for documented scholars, from the archives of the Motion Picture Academy of Arts and Sciences and the Museum of the Film. Other sources were *Palace,* Baron Christian de Massey with Charles Higham; *Princess Grace,* Steven Englund, and *Bridesmaids,* Judith Balaban Quine—the last-named being the most definitive book on the wedding and of Grace Kelly's transition from actress to Princesse de Monaco. It is an invaluable source.

Deo Juvante is the Latin motto of Monaco and means "With God's Help."

"I thought the air and sun . . .": Englund.

"I'll ask her . . .": Quine.

For Onassis and his relationship to Prince Rainier, Princesse Grace and Monaco, the following books were the most helpful: *Onassis,* Willi Frischauer; *Aristotle Onassis* by the London *Sunday Times* team: Nicholas Fraser et al.; *The Fabulous Onassis,* Christian Cafarakis (1972); *The Greek,* Pierre Ray (1974); *Ari,* Peter Evans; *Onassis,* Frank Brady.

I was also fortunate in being able to talk to members of Onassis's staff and of the S.B.M. during the late 1950s and early 1960s.

CHAPTER 19

"We're preggos!": Quine.

The Grimaldi town house in Paris, previously occupied by Albert I and Louis II, was given over entirely to the Monaco Legation shortly after Rainier's marriage to Grace Kelly.

"Onassis's seignorial view . . .": Fraser et al.

"Hell! I wanted a boy.": Englund.

Later in his life Baron Christian de Massey recorded a conversation (in his book *Palace*) he had with Princesse Grace regarding the domineering personality of his mother, Princesse Antoinette. "She was deprived of the right of succession to the throne by her own mother . . . who hated her," he claimed she replied, adding: "Knowing that she would never rule, she was deeply insecure. . . . And naturally, with this broken home and no family life to speak of, she would likely try to overcontrol, overdiscipline her own family. It is typical of people who have had no security early on that they try to dominate and rule over their children." This retort would seem to indicate that at least Princesse Grace believed that Antoinette had a substantial claim to the throne. Since the laws of succession have not been amended, as the firstborn child, Princesse Caroline would appear to have a claim to the throne. Nonetheless, Prince Albert has been accepted as the rightful heir since his birth.

"I am the boss here . . .": Fraser et al.

"Overnight . . .": London *Financial Times* survey on Monaco, 1989.

"I wonder . . .": Private papers.

CHAPTER 20

"Crovetto found Onassis . . .": Fraser et al.

"I was robbed!": Ibid.

"vulgar concrete slum . . .": London *Financial Times*.

"into France . . .": Ibid.

"subletting . . .": Ibid.

"very American . . .": De Massey.

This chapter has been helped considerably by several firsthand witnesses (domestic staff and friends and family) to the childhoods and education of Princesse Caroline, Prince Albert and Princesse Stephanie.

CHAPTER 21

Sweeping constitutional reform in 1971 federalized Belgium by creating three fairly autonomous regions—Flanders, Wallonia, and Brussels. A further division was caused by language since some Belgians speak French, others Flemish or Walloon.

"There are times, you know . . .": Hawkins.

"Caroline's experience . . .": De Massey.

"I really would shoot . . .": Ibid.

"Well, perhaps it's for the better . . .": Englund.

For the information on Princesse Grace's relationship with her friends in Monaco and her relations with the royal family of Great Britain, I have used personal interviews.

Although six hundred guests were invited to celebrate Princesse Caroline's wedding to Philippe Junot, only fifty people were present to see the couple exchange vows. These included only members of the intimate family and their closest associates.

"When you're young . . .": Interview with Princesse Caroline, *London Times.*

Rainier's homophobic views and "He pushed Albert . . .": Personal interviews.

"I'll never drive again . . .": Ibid.

Reliable coverage on Princesse Grace's last weekend at Roc Agel is to be found in Robinson. This has been embellished and verified through numerous personal interviews. Much controversy has appeared in the press regarding who was driving the vehicle at the time of Princesse Grace's fatal accident. It has been substantiated to my satisfaction that Princesse Grace put on her glasses and slid behind the wheel of the Rover for the ride. Medical reports taken from the brain scan that was given her state that she had a second brain lesion at either the point of the impact of the accident or shortly thereafter.

"To brake very hard and fight . . .": Robinson.

"Agreed there was no point . . .": Ibid. This last decision was not in keeping with Catholic doctrine. Nonetheless, the family believed sincerely that this would have been Princesse Grace's choice, although it has never been revealed if, indeed, she stated this in a last will and testament (which in any case is not available at this time to the public).

CHAPTER 22

I relied mainly on personal interviews for the information and subjective conclusions in this chapter.

BIBLIOGRAPHY

Two treasure troves of archival material on Monaco and the Grimaldis exist. Foremost: Les Archives du Palais Princier, Monaco, where all the papers, letters, documents, photographs and studies of the Princes de Monaco and their reigns are reposited. The Monégasque Collection in the Manchester Central Reference Library contains thirty-nine volumes and original documents and letters of various branches of the Grimaldi family and studies in their history and was given to the library in the early part of the nineteenth century by Alfred Beaufort Grimaldi.

Indispensable to any author of Monégasque history are the *Annales Monégasques*, Numbers 1–12. Another great source is found in the *Menton and Monte Carlo* newspaper published weekly in English from the end of the nineteenth century until the advent of World War II (after 1934 published as *Riviera News*).

Abrantès, Duchesse d'. *At the Court of Napoleon,* ed. Olivier Bernier. Gloucestershire: The Windrush Press, 1991.

Aga Khan. *World Enough and Time.* London: Cassell, 1954.

Aldridge, Nicholas. *Time to Spare? A History of Summerfields,* Oxford: David Talboys, 1989.

Amberley, Lord and Lady. *The Amberley Papers: The Letters and Diaries of Lord and Lady Amberley,* eds. Bertrand and Patricia Russell, 2 vols. London: Hogarth Press, 1937.

Aronson, Theo. *The Fall of the Third Napoleon.* London: Cassell, 1970.

Astraudo, Amedeo Eugenio Prospero Massimino, Duca. *Les petits états d'Europe,* Vol. III, *Monaco,* 2nd edition. Nice: L'éclaireur de Nice, 1933.

Aumont, Jean-Pierre. *Sun and Shadow.* New York: W. W. Norton, 1977.

Baedeker, Karl. *The Riviera.* London: Allen and Unwin, 1931.

Baring-Gould, Sabine. *Book of the Riviera.* London: Allen and Unwin, 1931.

Bell, Quentin. *The Legend of the Grimaldis. History Today,* April 1952.

Beresford, Hon. S. R. *Beresford's Monte-Carlo.* Nice: J. Beresford, 1926.

Bernardy, Françoise de. *Princes of Monaco: The Remarkable History of the Grimaldi Family,* trans. Len Ortzen. London: Arthur Baker, 1961.

Brady, Frank. *Onassis: An Extravagant Life.* London: Futura, 1978.

Brittain, Vera. *Testament of Experience.* London: Gollancz, 1956.

———. *Testament of Friendship.* London: Macmillan, 1940.

———, and Geoffrey Handley-Taylor. *Selected Letters of Winifred Holtby and Vera Brittain.* London: A. Brown and Sons Ltd., 1960.

Buckle, Richard. *Diaghilev.* London: Weidenfeld and Nicolson, 1979.

Bülow, Prince von. *Mémoires, 1894–1919,* trans. F. A. Voigt and G. Dunlop, 4 vols. New York: Putnam, 1931.

Burney, Fanny. *The Diary of Fanny Burney,* ed. L. Gibbs. London: 1940.

Butterworth, Michael. *The Man Who Broke the Bank at Monte Carlo.* London: William Collins and Son, 1983.

Cafarakis, Christian. *The Fabulous Onassis: His Life and Loves.* New York: Morrow, 1972.

Casimir, Philippe. *Monaco, Monte-Carlo et les environs: le passé et le présent.* Nice: Guides des Pays d'Azur, 1903.

Chevalier, Jules. *Mémoires pour servir à l'histoire des comtes de Valentinois,* Vol. II. Paris: 1906.

Cholvy, G. *Histoire de Montpellier.* Montpellier, France: Edition Privat, 1985.

Combet, Joseph. *La Révolution dans le comté de Nice et la Principauté de Monaco, 1792–1800.* Paris: F. Alcan, 1925.

Corte, Egon Caesar. *The Wizard of Monte Carlo.* New York: Dutton, 1935.

Crane, E. A. *Memoirs: Recollections of the Second French Empire.* London: 1905.

Crankshaw, Edward. *Maria Theresa.* London: Constable, 1983.

Croly, Elizabeth. *Round About Monte Carlo.* London: Mills and Boon, 1925.

Cronin, Vincent. *Louis and Antoinette.* London: William Collins, 1974.

———. *Louis XIV*. London: William Collins, 1964.

Crump, Susan, and Patricia Burstan. *Caroline and Stephanie: The Lives of the Princesses of Monaco*. London: Sidgwick & Jackson, 1988.

Damien, Raymond. *Albert 1er: Prince Souverain de Monaco*. Paris: Institut de Valois, 1964.

Day Lewis, Cecil. *The Buried Day*. New York: Harper, 1960.

De Massey, Baron Christian, with Charles Higham. *Palace*. London: Atheneum, 1986.

Dempster, Charlotte Louise. *The Grimaldis of Monaco*. London: Longmans, Green, 1885.

Dent, Edward. *Annals of Opera, 1597–1940*. Cambridge, Eng.: W. Heffer & Sons Ltd.

Dickens, A. G. *The Courts of Europe*. London: 1977.

Dilke, Sir Charles. *The Fall of Prince Florestan of Monaco*. London: Macmillan, 1874.

Dolin, Anton. *Autobiography*. London: Oldbourne, 1960.

Dreyfus, Alfred, and Pierre Dreyfus. *The Dreyfus Case*. London: 1937.

———. *Five Years of My Life*. London: George Newnes Ltd., 1901.

Dryess, C. *The King's Memoirs*. London: 1860.

Duff, David. *Victoria Travels: Journals of Queen Victoria Between 1830 and 1900 with Extracts from the Journals*. London: Frederick Muller Ltd., 1970.

Duparty, Abbé. *Travels Through Italy*, Vols. 3–6. 1788.

Du Seigneur, Maurice. *Le Théâtre de Monte-Carlo*. Paris: Rouveyre, 1880.

Edwards, Anne. *Matriarch*. London: Hodder and Stoughton, 1984.

Englund, Steven. *Princess Grace*. New York: Viking-Penguin, 1984.

Evans, Peter. *Ari: The Life and Times of Aristotle Socrates Onassis*. London: Jonathan Cape, 1986.

Evans, Thomas W. *History of the American Ambulance Establishment in Paris During the Siege of 1870–1871*. London: 1873.

Fielding, Xan. *The Money Spinner: Monte Carlo Casino*. London: Weidenfeld and Nicolson, 1977.

Fisher, H.A.L. *A History of Europe,* Vol. II. London: Fontana Library, 1960.

Fitzgibbon, Constantine, and Giles Fitzgibbon. *The Little Tour.* London: Playfair, 1953.

Fraser, N., with P. Jacobson, M. Ottaway and L. Chester. *Aristotle Onassis.* London: Weidenfeld and Nicolson, 1977.

Frischauer, Willi. *Onassis.* London: Bodley Head Ltd., 1968.

Goldberg, W. F., and G. Chaplin Piesse. *Monte Carlo and How to Do It.* London: J. W. Arrowsmith, 1891.

Gramont, Comte de. *Mémoires.* Paris: 1866.

Graves, Charles. *The Big Gamble: The Story of Monte Carlo.* London: Hutchinson, 1951.

———. *None but the Rich: The Life and Times of the Greek Syndicate.* London: Cassell, 1963.

———. *Royal Riviera.* London: Heinemann, 1957.

Green, John R. *Sketches in Sunshine: Two Towns of the Riviera.* London: Macmillan, 1976.

Grigoriev, S. L. *The Diaghilev Ballet, 1909–1929,* trans. Vera Bowen. London: Constable, 1953.

Grimaldi, Alexander Beaufort. Collection of mss. and printed extracts, letters, leaflets, portraits, etc., relating to Monaco and the name of Grimaldi, 1869–1913, 35 vols. In Monégasque Collection of Manchester Central Reference Library.

———. Scrapbooks of cuttings, engravings, photographs, portraits relating to the Grimaldi family and Monaco, 4 vols. In Monégasque Collection.

———. Collection of original documents, dispatches, letters by Princes of Monaco, Cardinals Grimaldi, Marquesses Grimaldi, etc., 1498–1907. In Monégasque Collection.

Grimaldi, Mary Beaufort. As above.

Guérard, Albert. *Napoleon III: Louis Napoleon and the Second Empire.* New York: Knopf, 1958.

Handley-Taylor, Geoffrey. *Bibliography of Monaco.* London: St. James Press, 1968.

329

————. *Winifred Holtby: A Concise and Selected Bibliography.* London: A. Brown & Sons, 1955.

Hare, Augustus J. C. *The Rivieras.* London: George Allen, 1897.

————. *South-Eastern France.* London: George Allen, 1890.

————. *A Winter at Mentone.* Wertheim: Macintosh & Hunt, 1862.

Harris, Frank. *My Life and Loves,* 5 vols. New York: Grove Press, 1963.

Haskell, Arnold. *Diaghileff.* London: Gollancz, 1935.

Hawkins, Peter. *Prince Rainier of Monaco: His Authorised and Exclusive Story,* London: Kimber, 1966.

Herald, George William, and Edward David Radin. *The Big Wheel: Monte Carlo's Opulent Century.* New York: Morrow, 1963.

Horne, Alistair. *The Fall of Paris.* London: Macmillan, 1965.

Howarth, Patrick. *When the Riviera Was Ours.* London: Routledge & Kegan Paul, 1977.

Ilchester, Countess of, see Lennox, Lady Sarah.

Jackson, Stanley. *Inside Monte Carlo.* New York: Stein and Day, 1975.

Katherin, John. *The Prince Imperial.* London: Putnam, 1939.

Kurtz, Harold. *The Empress Eugénie, 1826–1920.* London: Hamish Hamilton, 1964.

LaBande, Léon-Honoré. *Histoire de la Principauté de Monaco,* 2nd ed. Archives de la Principauté de Monaco, 1934.

La Fayette, Madame de. *Mémoires.* Paris: 1839.

Lennox, Lady Sarah. *The Life and Letters of Lady Sarah Lennox, 1745–1826,* ed. the Countess of Ilchester and Lord Stavordale, 2 vols. London: John Murray, 1901.

Lewis, Arthur H. *Those Philadelphia Kellys.* New York: Morrow, 1976.

Lewis, W. H. *Assault on Olympus.* London: Andre Deutsch, 1958.

————. *Louis XIV: An Informal Portrait.* London: Andre Deutsch, 1959.

————. *The Sunset of the Splendid Century.* London: 1959.

Lynham, Deryck. *Ballet Then and Now.* London: Sylvan Press, 1947.

McCormic, Donald. *Pedlar of Death: The Life of Sir Basil Zaharoff.* London: Macdonald, 1965.

Macdonald, Alasdair. *Stowe School*. London: Dalton Watson Ltd., 1977.

Magnus, Sir Philip. *King Edward the Seventh*. London: J. Murray, 1964.

Mallet, Marie. *Life with Queen Victoria: Maria Mallet's Letters from Court, 1887–1901*, ed. Victor Mallet. London: John Murray, 1968.

Massey, Raymond. *100 Different Lives*. Boston: Little, Brown, 1979.

Maxim, Hiram. *Monte Carlo: Facts and Fallacies*. London: Grant Richards, 1904.

Maxwell, C. *The English Traveller in France, 1698–1815*. London: 1932.

Maxwell, Elsa. *The Celebrity Circus*. London: W. H. Allen, 1964.

Metiver, Henri. *Monaco et Ses Princes*, 2nd ed. La Flèche, Jordain, 1865.

Mitford, Nancy. *The Sun King*. London: The Bodley Head, 1968.

Monaco. *Monaco: Archives du Palais*. Paris: Auguste Picard.

Monte-Carlo and Public Opinion: A Visitor to the Riviera. London: Rivertons, 1884.

Napoleon, Prince. *Memoirs*, ed. d'Hauterive. Paris: 1925.

Ogg, David. *Europe in the Seventeenth Century*. London: 1959.

Pastorelli, Jean. *Histoire de Monaco*, Vol. II. Monaco: Ministère d'État, 1986.

Peat, Anthony B. North. *Gossip from Paris During the Second Empire—Correspondence (1864–1869)*, ed. A. R. Waller. London: 1903.

Pemberton, H. *History of Monaco*. London: 1867.

Petrie, Sir Charles. *Louis XIV*. London: Thornton, Butterworth, 1938.

Plessis, Alain. *The Rise and Fall of the Second Empire, 1852–1871*. New York: Cambridge University Press, 1979.

Polovtsoff, General Pierre. *Monte Carlo Casino*. London: Stanley Paul, 1937.

Proust, Marcel. *Remembrance of Things Past*, Vol. II, *Within a Budding Grove*. New York: Random House, 1981.

Quine, Judith Balaban. *The Bridesmaids: Grace Kelly, Princess of Monaco, and Six Intimate Friends*. London: Weidenfeld and Nicolson, 1989.

Ray, Pierre. *The Greek*. New York: G. P. Putnam, 1974.

Robert, J. B. *Histoire de Monaco*. Paris: Presses Universitaires de France, 1973.

———, with J. Freu and R. Novella. *Histoire de Monaco,* Vol. I. Monaco: Ministère d'État, 1986.

Robinson, Jeffrey. *Rainier and Grace*. New York: Simon & Schuster, 1989.

Robyns, Gwen. *Princess Grace* London: W. H. Allen, 1976.

Saige, Gustave. *Monaco: Ses Origines et Son Histoire*. Monaco: Éditions des Archives du Palais Princier, 1988.

St. Aubyn, Giles. *Edward VII, Prince and King*. New York: Athenaeum, 1979.

Schama, S. *Citizens*. New York: Knopf, 1989.

———. *Patriots and Liberators*. New York: Knopf, 1977.

Saint-Simon, Louis de Rouvroy, duc de. *Mémoires,* ed. A. de Boislisle. Paris: 1879.

Sévigné, Marie, Marquise de. *Letters,* ed. M. Mommerque. Paris: 1862–1866.

———. *Mémoire de Saint-Simon*. Paris: 1926.

Sherlock, Rev. Martin. *Letters from an English Traveller*. London: John Nichols, 1802.

Slater, Leonard. *Aly: A Biography of the Late Aga Khan*. London: W. H. Allen, 1966.

Smith, Adolphe. *Monaco and Monte Carlo*. Philadelphia: J. B. Lippincott, 1912.

Smollett, Tobias. *Travels Through France and Italy*. London: 1766.

Sokolova, Lydia. *Dancing for Diaghilev,* ed. Richard Buckle. London: John Murray, 1960.

Spoto, Donald. *The Dark Side of Genius: The Life of Alfred Hitchcock*. Boston: Little, Brown, 1983.

———. *Stanley Kramer, Film Maker*. New York: Putnam, 1978.

Stevenson, G. S. *The Letters of Madame*. London: 1924.

Sutherland, D.M.G. *France, 1789–1815*. London: Oxford University Press, 1985.

Tessi, Marshal de. *Letters from Marshal de Tessi to Prince Antoine I of Monaco.* London: 1911.

Thomas, Bob. *Golden Boy: The Untold Story of William Holden.* New York: St. Martin's Press, 1983.

Thompson, J. M. *Louis Napoleon and the Second Empire.* Oxford: Basil Blackwell, 1954.

Thomson, David. *Europe Since Napoleon.* London: Penguin Books, 1990.

Victoria, Queen. *Letters, Second Series,* ed. Lytton Strachey.

Walsh, I. J. *Monte Carlo Opera, 1910–1951.* Kilkenny, Ireland: Boethius Books, 1986.

Wheatcroft, Andrew. *Dolin: Friends and Memories.* London: Routledge & Kegan Paul, 1982.

Williams, E. N. *The Ancien Régime in Europe.* London: Penguin Books, 1988.

Williamson, Audrey. *Thomas Paine: His Life, Work and Times.* London: George Allen, 1973.

Young, Arthur. *Travels in France During the Years 1787, 1788 and 1789.* Cambridge, Eng.: Cambridge University Press, 1950.

OTHER SOURCES

Periodicals: *Annales Monégasques* Numbers 1–12 (Archives du Palais Princier, Monaco). *Le Monde Illustré,* Paris.

Newspapers: *The Times, Sunday Times, Financial Times, The Daily Express, The Daily Telegraph,* and *The Evening Standard* (London, Archives, British Library); *Nice Matin, Paris Match.*

British Film Institute Library Archives, London.

Hulton Picture Library, London.

APPENDICES

Law Report, Mar. 22

HIGH COURT OF JUSTICE CHANCERY DIVISION

PRINCE OF MONACO'S CLAIM TO CUSTODY OF GRANDSON: JUDGMENT MONACO V. MONACO

Before MR. JUSTICE LUXMOORE

His Lordship gave judgment for the plaintiff in the action by the reigning Prince of Monaco against Prince Pierre of Monaco (otherwise known as Prince Pierre de Polignac) relating to the custody of the plaintiff's grandson, Prince Rainier of Monaco, who is at school in this country.

The plaintiff claimed an injunction restraining the defendant from removing the young Prince out of the United Kingdom except with his (the reigning Prince's) consent. He also asked for an order for the delivery up of the Prince to him or to such person as he should authorize.

The defendant denied that the plaintiff was entitled to the relief for which he asked.

Mr. Vaughan Williams, K.C., Mr. H. O. Danckwerts, and Mr. Acland-Hood appeared for the plaintiff; Mr. Wynn Parry, K.C., Mr. Raymond Jennings, and Mr. V. Idelson for the defendant.

JUDGMENT

His Lordship, in a written judgment, said that the plaintiff claimed in the action a declaration that he was the lawful guardian of Prince Rainier of Monaco, the only son of the marriage of Princess Charlotte (the plaintiff's daughter) with the defendant. The plaintiff also asked for an injunction to restrain the defendant from removing Prince Rainier out of the jurisdiction of that Court, except with his (the plaintiff's) consent, and an order for the immediate delivery of the Prince Rainier to him, or to such other person as he might authorize.

Prince Rainier was at the present time at school in this country. Both he and his father, the defendant, were of Monégasque nationality. Prince Rainier was not a ward of that Court. The defendant had raised a number of defences.

The first question to be determined was one of fact, whether the plaintiff was the guardian, and as such entitled to the custody of the infant Prince. It was necessary to consider and ascertain the position of the parties, having regard to Monégasque law.

The material facts appeared to be as follows:—In matters of personal status, such as guardianship and custody of infants, the law administered in Monaco was the national law of the persons concerned. That applied to the members of the Sovereign Family as well as to other persons. The Monégasque law relating to the Sovereign Family was laid down in an ordinance dated May 15, 1882, promulgated by Prince Charles III of Monaco. That ordinance had the force of law in Monaco. So far as material, it provided by article I that the sovereignty of the Principality of Monaco continued to be hereditary in the direct and legitimate succession of the Princes of Monaco.

Article III provided that no member of the Sovereign Family might marry without the authorization of the reigning Prince. Any petition for annulment of a marriage, or any difficulty arising out of a marriage properly contracted by a member of the Sovereign Family, was to be brought before a Council of State, and the decision would become final and enforceable by a Sovereign ordinance passed by the reigning Prince after hearing the Council of State. The reigning Prince had full authority over all the members of the Sovereign Family. He regulated their duties and their obligations by statutes or ordinances having the force of law.

NAME AND ARMS OF GRIMALDI

On March 18, 1920, Prince Albert I of Monaco, by an ordinance of that date, ordered that the defendant, who had been granted Monégasque naturalization by an order of February 29, 1920, should take for himself and his descendants the name and arms of Grimaldi, being the name and arms of the Sovereign Family. On March 19, 1920, the defendant was, with the consent of the same prince, married to the Hereditary Princess Charlotte of Monaco, the daughter of the plaintiff. There had been two children of that marriage—namely, Princess Antoinette and Prince Rainier. The latter was born on May 31, 1923.

On February 8, 1930, the plaintiff promulgated a Sovereign ordinance authorizing a temporary separation between the Hereditary Princess and the defendant. Article II of the same ordinance was in these terms:—

> We entrust to ourselves, Head of the Sovereign Family and of the Dynasty, and to our personal custody until this matter is finally decided, the princely children, Princess Antoinette and the Prince Rainier.

On February 10, 1930, a Council of State was convened to consider the question whether the reigning Prince was competent to decide on the application of the Hereditary Princess for a separation of herself and her property from the defendant.

The Council of State expressed the opinion that the reigning Prince had full authority and full jurisdiction over members of the Sovereign Family, and accordingly that he had full power to settle all questions relating to their civil status and their property. The Council of State also expressed the opinion that the reigning Prince had full power to delegate all or any of his rights to whatever jurisdiction he thought fit, requesting him to make use in the then present circumstances of his right of delegation.

As the result of that advice the plaintiff, on February 15, 1920, promulgated a Sovereign ordinance. Article I of that ordinance provided:—

> In cases where the statutes of the Sovereign Family defer family jurisdiction in the reigning Prince, the latter may relinquish the same, either in favor of the Supreme Court of Monaco or in favor of the *Cour de Revision* according to the nature of the litigation, or delegate his powers to them.

A FAMILY PACT

Following that ordinance a family pact was proposed to regulate the terms of separation between the Hereditary Princess and the defendant. The parties, being unwilling to agree to all of the terms proposed, agreed to submit the outstanding questions to the sole arbitration of M. Poincaré. Among the matters included in the submission were the conditions concerning the custody and education of Princess Antoinette and Prince Rainier. That submission to arbitration was signed by the Hereditary Princess and the defendant.

M. Poincaré duly made his award on March 18, 1930. It dealt, among other matters, with the custody and education of the Princess Antoinette and Prince Rainier. A family pact was entered into to give effect to the award on March 18, 1930. On March 20 the *Cour de Revision* of Monaco decreed the personal separation and separation of property between the Hereditary Princess and the defendant. The decree contained a recital of the fact that certain points had been settled by the award of M. Poincaré, and that there was no reason to give any judgment concerning the same.

On January 7, 1933, the Hereditary Princess Charlotte petitioned the plaintiff for the dissolution of her marriage with the defendant. The plaintiff submitted to the Council of State whether, being Judge as of right, he should delegate his authority in the matter of the petition to the *Cour de Revision*. The Council of State on January 13, 1933, advised that owing to the final character of the decision sought and its gravity as affecting the Dynasty, it was necessary that the plaintiff should decide, in full exercise of his family jurisdiction, on the request for the dissolution of the marriage, subject to his delegating to the *Cour de Revision*, in accordance with the ordinance of February 15, 1930, the settlement of the pecuniary interests of the parties.

On January 14, 1933, the plaintiff, by a Sovereign ordinance, decreed by article III that he would retain the hearing of, and the decision on, all matters arising out of the petition of the Hereditary Princess which concerned matters of personal status. Article III of the ordinance was in these terms:—

> As from this day and as Head of the Royal Family and its Dynasty we take over the personal custody of the princely children, Prince Rainier and Princess Antoinette. We reserve the settlement of the right of access of the parents until after the hearing of the action.

On February 18, 1933, the plaintiff, by a Sovereign ordinance of that date, dissolved the marriage of the Hereditary Princess with the defendant. On July 8, 1933, the plaintiff, by a further Sovereign ordinance, approved certain modifications in the family pact of March 18, 1930, contained in an agreement of May 5, 1933, and delegated to the *Cour de Revision* all necessary powers to ratify the agreements. On July 11, 1933, the *Cour de Revision* ratified these agreements. There was some discussion before him (his Lordship) as to the precise ambit of that order. The word used with regard to it in the order of the Court was "*enterine*." It seemed to him that the most suitable English equivalent of the word was the phrase "made the agreements a rule of Court," but in substance he saw no objection to construing the word "*enterine*" by the English word "ratified."

Questions subsequently arose between the Hereditary Princess and the defendant and there was an attempted submission to arbitration which was abortive owing to the failure of the two arbitrators to agree, and their subsequent failure to appoint an umpire. Ultimately on March 8, 1936, the plaintiff promulgated a Sovereign ordinance. Article I of that ordinance stated:—

> "We assume again as from this day as Head of the Sovereign Family and of the Dynasty the personal custody of the princely children Prince Rainier and Princess Antoinette."

It was upon this ordinance that the plaintiff based his claim in the action.

"THE FORCE OF LAW"

Maitre Jioffredy stated that under the ordinance of 1882 the plaintiff had, according to Monégasque law, the right to the guardianship and custody of any infant member of the Royal House, and that that right was enforceable by ordinances which had the force of law, and that the ordinance of March 8, 1936, was such an ordinance. He further stated that under the ordinance of February 15, 1930, the plaintiff was entitled to delegate his Sovereign rights in any case to the Monégasque Courts of Law in such manner as he might determine. But as he (his Lordship) understood that witness's evidence, the plaintiff was unable to delegate his rights so as to amount to a renunciation of them in respect of the custody and guardianship of any particular member of the Sovereign Family in such a manner as to preclude himself from resuming his rights when change of circumstances made it expedient or desirable for him so to do. So that, admitting that the plaintiff had delegated his rights with regard to the custody and guardianship of the Princess Antoinette and Prince Rainier in the circumstances existing at the date of submission to the arbitration of M. Poincaré, yet, in the altered circumstances of the dissolution of the marriage of their parents and the consequences flowing therefrom, the plaintiff was still legally entitled by Sovereign ordinance to resume the guardianship and custody at his will and pleasure, and that nothing which was recorded in the ordinances made before or subsequent to the divorce, or the orders of the *Cour de Revision* with regard thereto, precluded the plaintiff from exercising that right.

Consequently, in Maitre Jioffredy's opinion, the Sovereign ordinance of March 8, 1936, was, according to Monégasque law, enforceable in the Monégasque Courts. As he (his Lordship) understood Mr. Wynn Parry's argument he admitted that, according to Monégasque law, the plaintiff had the absolute right to the guardianship and custody of the infants if he exercised it by Sovereign ordinance, but he argued that the plaintiff had once and for all delegated his rights in respect of the guardianship and custody of those infants by the submission to the arbitration of M. Poincaré, or, alternatively, by the subsequent submission of the family pact of May 5, 1933, for the variation of the pact of March 18, 1930, to the *Cour de Revision* for its approval, and the order of that Court of July 11, 1933, ratifying it.

Mr. Wynn Parry had argued that the plaintiff had renounced for all time his right of making any further ordinance with regard to the guardianship and custody of the particular infants. Maitre Jioffredy said that the decisions in family matters, and particularly with regard to the guardianship and custody of infants, were never final and could always be amended or superseded by the reigning Prince if he determined to resume his Sovereign rights, and that the plaintiff had done so by the ordinance of March 8, 1936.

His Lordship said that in his judgment the plaintiff had established that he was entitled under and by virtue of the ordinance of March 8, 1936, to the guardianship and custody of Prince Rainier, and he held as a fact that he was so entitled. In the result, unless the defendant was in a position to satisfy him that the plaintiff was not entitled to ask that Court to assist him in respect of his legal rights, the plaintiff would be entitled to the relief which he sought. It seemed to him (his Lordship) that, the legal rights having been established, it was not open to the defendant to resist the relief sought by attempting to prove that the plaintiff was actuated by some personal motive in promulgating the ordinance of March 8, 1936.

If however, Mr. Wynn Parry desired to address further argument on that aspect of the case he (his Lordship) would give him an opportunity of so doing. Any such argument ought, he thought, to be heard *in camera*, for it must obviously be founded on matters which, having regard to the fact that the guardianship and custody of an infant was involved, would in the case of a British infant not be discussed in an open Court. The same practice ought to be applied to the hearing of an application to prevent the person legally entitled to the guardianship and custody of an infant who was the subject of the Sovereign of a foreign State from exercising his rights.

He understood that the defendant might desire to take the opinion of a higher Court with regard to the conclusion at which he (his Lordship) had arrived, and if the party thought it desirable to deal with that question first, he was willing to allow the further questions to stand over until that opinion had been taken. Or if it was preferred, he would make the declaration sought, and order the defendant to deliver the infant prince to the plaintiff or to some person authorized by him to take the delivery, and he would grant injunction in the terms of the second paragraph of the prayer in the statement of claim.

His Lordship granted a declaration that the plaintiff was the lawful guardian and was entitled to the custody of Prince Rainier; an order that the defendant was to deliver Prince Rainier to the plaintiff or to such person as he (the Prince of Monaco) should authorize to receive him; and an injunction restraining the defendant from removing Prince Rainier out of the United Kingdom except with the plaintiff's consent.

Mr. Wynn Parry submitted that it was the rule that the English Court "would not disparage the dignity of a foreign Sovereign by giving him costs."

"There is no decision," his Lordship said, "which prevents the Sovereign of an independent State claiming costs if he desires to obtain them."

Judgment was entered accordingly, for costs.

Solicitors.—Messrs. Parker, Garrett and Co.; Messrs. Lewis and Lewis.

From *The Times* of London, March 23, 1937

LETTER FROM E. K. BARBER, HEADMASTER SUMMERFIELDS, TO J. F. ROXBURGH, HEADMASTER, STOWE, JULY 12, 1936

I am probably asking you to do the impossible, but must hope for the best. You may possibly remember some years ago a visit from Prince Pierre de Monaco, who unfortunately did *not* put his son Rainier's name down for Stowe. Is there the slightest possibility of your finding a place for him next term?

He is 13½ and has been with us for a year. He came knowing nothing, except of course, spoken French, and although he is not up to C.E.E. standard, I think I can honestly say that he has learnt a considerable amount and he certainly has become a very nice boy with the most charming manners. I should not have the impertinance to ask you to take him were it not for the fact that I am certain that an English public school education would be the making if not the saving of the boy. You may possibly have seen in the English papers that there is trouble between the father and mother and also the grand-father (the reigning Prince). The father sent the boy here, and is most anxious to keep him away from the unsuitable atmosphere of Monaco for his education. Prince Pierre is in London and would bring Rainier down to see you this week if there is any possibility of your taking him. I *can't* have him back next term as there is not an empty bed. Even my dressing room is full. I hope you will forgive my making the suggestion, but it would give you the chance of seeing the boy for yourself, and possibly of asking him a few questions about his work. Would you very kindly send a line direct to S.A.S. Prince Pierre de Monaco, The Dorchester Hotel, Park Lane, London. He is a very charming man, but obviously of a disposition entirely incompatible with that of the Princess!

TABLEAU GENEALOGIQUE DE LA FAMILLE GRIMALDI

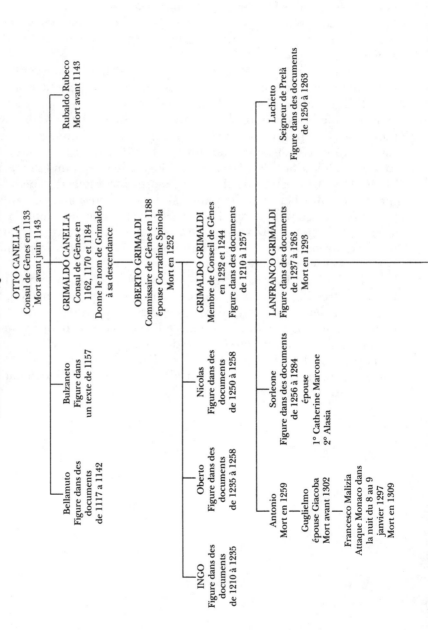

OTTO CANELLA
Consul de Gênes en 1133
Mort avant juin 1143

Bellamuto
Figure des
documents
de 1117 a 1142

Bulzaneto
Figure dans
un texte de 1157

GRIMALDO CANELLA
Consul de Gênes en
1162, 1170 et 1184
Donne le nom de Grimaldo
à sa descendance

Rubaldo Rubeco
Mort avant 1143

OBERTO GRIMALDI
Commissaire de Gênes en 1188
épouse Corradine Spinola
Mort en 1252

INGO
Figure dans des
documents
de 1210 à 1235

Oberto
Figure dans des
documents
de 1235 à 1258

Nicolas
Figure dans des
documents
de 1250 à 1258

GRIMALDO GRIMALDI
Membre de Conseil de Gênes
en 1232 et 1244
Figure dans des documents
de 1210 à 1257

Antonio
Mort en 1259

Sorleone
Figure dans des documents
de 1256 à 1284
épouse
1° Catherine Marcone
2° Alasia

LANFRANCO GRIMALDI
Figure dans des documents
de 1237 à 1263
Mort en 1293

Luchetto
Seigneur de Prelà
Figure dans des documents
de 1250 à 1263

Guglielmo
épouse Giacoba
Mort avant 1302

Francesco Malizia
Attaque Monaco dans
la nuit du 8 au 9
janvier 1297
Mort en 1309

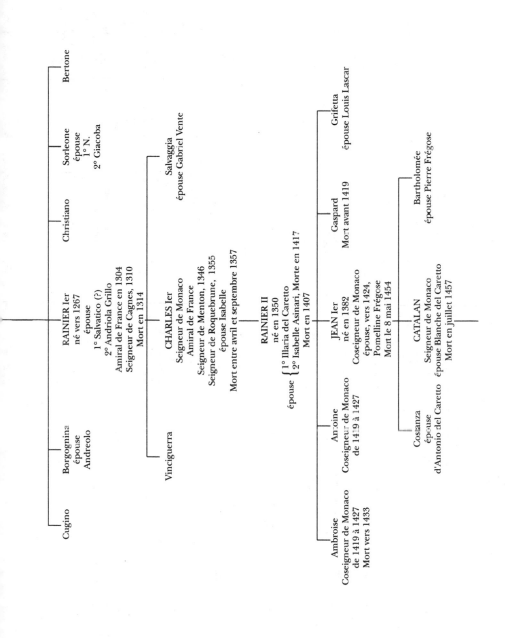

Cugino

Borgognina
épouse
Andreolo

RAINIER Ier
né vers 1267
épouse
1° Salvatico (?)
2° Andriola Grillo
Amiral de France en 1304
Seigneur de Cagnes, 1310
Mort en 1314

Christiano

Sorleone
épouse
1° N.
2° Giacoba

Bertone

Vinciguerra

CHARLES Ier
Seigneur de Monaco
Amiral de France
Seigneur de Menton, 1346
Seigneur de Roquebrune, 1355
épouse Isabelle
Mort entre avril et septembre 1357

Salvaggia
épouse Gabriel Vente

RAINIER II
né en 1350
épouse { 1° Illaria del Caretto
        2° Isabelle Asinari, Morte en 1417
Mort en 1407

Ambroise
Coseigneur de Monaco
de 1419 à 1427
Mort vers 1433

Antoine
Coseigneur de Monaco
de 1419 à 1427

JEAN Ier
né en 1382
Coseigneur de Monaco
épouse, vers 1424,
Pomelline Frégose
Mort le 8 mai 1454

Gaspard
Mort avant 1419

Grifetta
épouse Louis Lascar

Costanza
épouse
d'Antonio del Caretto

CATALAN
Seigneur de Monaco
épouse Blanche del Caretto
Mort en juillet 1457

Bartholomée
épouse Pierre Frégose

CLAUDINE
née en 1451
Dame de Monaco de 1457 à 1458
Morte en 1515
épouse en août 1465 son cousin
LAMBERT GRIMALDI
né en 1420
exerce la souveraineté de Monaco à partir de 1458
Mort le 15 mars 1494

Césarine
épouse
Charles
Marquis
de Ceva

Isabelle
épouse, en 1519
Antoine de
Châteauneuf-Randon

JEAN II
Seigneur de Monaco
en 1494
épouse en 1487
Anoinette
fille naturelle de
Philippe
duc de Savoie
Mort le
11 octobre 1505

LUCIEN
Seigneur de Monaco
en 1505
épouse le
25 septembre 1514
Jeanne de Pontevès
Mort le
22 août 1523

AUGUSTIN
Evêque de Grasse
Seigneur de Monaco
en 1523
Mort le
12 avril 1532

Blanche
épouse le
10 octobre 1501
Honoré de
Villeneuve
Baron de Tourettes

Philibert
Prévôt de
l'église de
Nice

Françoise
épouse
Luc Doria

Louis
Chevalier
de Malte

François
Mort en
1527

Claude

Lambert

Rainier

HONORE Ier
Seigneur de Monaco
né en 1522
épouse
le 8 juin 1545
Isabelle Grimaldi
Morte le 27 février 1583
Meurt le 7 octobre 1581

Marie
épouse
1° Jérome de La Rovère
2° Renaud de Villeneuve
Baron deVence

Ginevra
née le 24
octobre 1548
épouse
Etienne
Grillo

Claudia
née le
8 octobre 1552
Morte le
20 novembre 1598

Eleonore
née le 10
décembre 1556
épouse
Nicolas Interiano

Horace
né le
5 novembre 1558
Mort le
16 juillet 1559

Fabrice
né le
1er décembre 1560
Mort le
20 avril 1569

Virginie
née le
12 juillet 1564
religieuse

Horace
né le
5 septembre 1567
Echanson de
Philippe III
roi d'Espagne
Mort en 1620

Benedeta
née le
3 mai 1550

CHARLES II
né le
26 janvier 1555
Seigneur de Monaco
en 1581
non marié
Mort le 18 mai 1589

François
né le
13 novembre 1557
Mort le
4 octobre 1586

Hippolyte
née le
29 novembre 1559
Morte le
24 septembre 1562

HERCULE Ier
né le
24 septembre 1562
épouse le
15 décembre 1595
Marie-Landi de Valdetare
Morte en 1599
Mort assassiné
le 21 novembre 1604

Aurélie
née le
13 novembre 1565
épouse
Augustin de Franco

Jean-Baptiste
né le
24 mars 1571
Mort le
18 mars 1572

Honoré (Don Honorato)
Illégitime
Abbé mitré de Terlizzo
Mort assassiné
le 3 octobre 1639

Jeanne
née le
29 septembre 1596
épouse le
10 octobre 1615
le Comte Théodore Trivulce
Morte en décembre 1620

HONORE II
né le
24 décembre 1597
épouse le
13 février 1616
Hippolyte Trivulce
Morte en 1638
Prend, en 1612, le titre de
PRINCE DE MONACO
Mort le 10 janvier 1662

Marie-Claude
née le
19 janvier 1599
Carmélite à Gênes

HERCULE
né le
26 décembre 1623
Marquis de Campagna
puis des Baux
épouse le
4 juillet 1641
Aurelia Spinola
Mort le 2 août 1651

LOUIS Ier
né le
25 juillet 1642
épouse le
30 mars 1660
Marie-Charlotte-Catherine
de Gramont (1639–1678)
Mort le 3 janvier 1701

Jeanne-Marie
née le
4 juin 1645
épouse le
23 octobre 1659
Charles-Emmanuel
Philibert de Simiane
Marquis de Pianezze
et de Livourne
Morte le
8 octobre 1674

Luc-François-Marie-Charles
né le 3 novembre 1648
Mort le
17 novembre 1652

Marie-Pelline
née le
12 mars 1651
épouse
1° André Impériale
Prince de Franqueville
2° Ambroise, marquis Doria
Morte le
24 septembre 1724

Hippolyte-Marie
née le
8 mai 1644
en religion
Soeur Thérèse-Marie
Religieuse à Gênes
Morte le 24 juillet 1722

Dévote-Marie-Renée
dite Mademoiselle
des Baux
née le
4 septembre 1646
Religieuse à Gênes
(Soeur Thérèse-Marguerite)
Morte le 3 décembre 1722

Marie-Thérèse
(Mademoiselle de Carladez)
née le 19 février 1650
épouse
Sigismond-François d'Este
marquis de Lanzo
en 1678

ANTOINE Ier
né le 25 janvier 1661
épouse le 13 juin 1688
Marie de Lorraine
née le 2 août 1674
Meurt le 20 février 1731

Jeanne-Marie-Dévote
née le 14 janvier 1662
en religion
Soeur Louise-Marie-Thérèse
Religieuse à la Visitation
de Monaco, à San Remo
et, en 1726, à Royalieu
Morte le 21 avril 1741

Thérèse-Marie-Aurélie
dite
Mademoiselle des Baux
née le 20 mai 1663
Morte le 15 février 1675

Anne-Hippolyte
née le 26 juillet 1664
épouse le 18 janvier 1696
Jacques-Charles de Crussol
duc d'Uzès
Morte le 3 juillet 1700

François-Honoré
né le 21 décembre 1669
abbé de Monaco
Archevêque de Besançon
Mort le 16 février 1748

Catherine-Charlotte
née le 7 octobre 1690
Morte le 18 juin 1696

Elisabeth-Charlotte
née le 3 novembre 1698
Morte le 25 août 1702

Marguerite-Camille
née le
1er mai 1700
épouse le
16 avril 1720
Louis de Gand de Mérode,
de Montmorency
Prince d'Isenghien
Morte le 27 avril 1758
dite Mademoiselle de
Carladez

Marie-Dévote
née le
15 mars 1702
Morte le 24
octobre 1703

Marie-Pelline
dite Mademoiselle
de Chabeuil
née le
23 octobre 1708
Morte le
20 mai 1726

Louise-Marie-Thérèse
née le 2 juin 1705
Morte le 21 septembre
1723

LOUISE-HIPPOLYTE
née le
10 novembre 1697
épouse le
20 octobre 1715
Jacques-François-Léonor
de Goyon, Sire de Matignon
Prince de Monaco
du 29 décembre 1731
au 8 novembre 1733
Morte le 29 décembre 1731

Chevalier Grimaldi
né le 2 octobre 1697
Mort le
28 novembre 1784

illégitimes

Antoinette
dite
Mademoiselle
de Saint-Rémy

Charles-Maurice
Chevalier de Monaco
Comte de Valentinois,
né à Paris le 14 mai 1727
épouse le 10 novembre 1749
Marie-Christine-Chrétienne
de Saint-Simon
Mort le 18 janvier 1798
à Maury (Suisse)

Louise-Françoise-Thérèse
(Mademoiselle d'Estouteville)
née le 20 juillet 1728
Morte le 20 juin 1743

Louise-Françoise
dite Mademoiselle
des Baux
née le
15 juillet 1724
Morte le
15 septembre 1724

François-Charles
Comte de Torigni
né à Paris
le 4 février 1726
Mort le
9 décembre 1743

HONORE III
(Honoré-Camille-Léonor)
né le 10 septembre 1720
épouse le 15 juin 1757
Marie-Catherine
de Brignole-Sale
(1739–1813)
Mort le 12 mai 1795

Charles-Marie-Auguste
né le 1er janvier 1722
Comte de Carladez
Mort le 24 août 1749

Antoine-Charles-Marie
né le 16 décembre 1717
Marquis des Baux
Mort le 24 février 1718

Charlotte
dite Mademoiselle
de Monaco
née le 19 mars 1719
Religieuse à la
Visitation de Paris

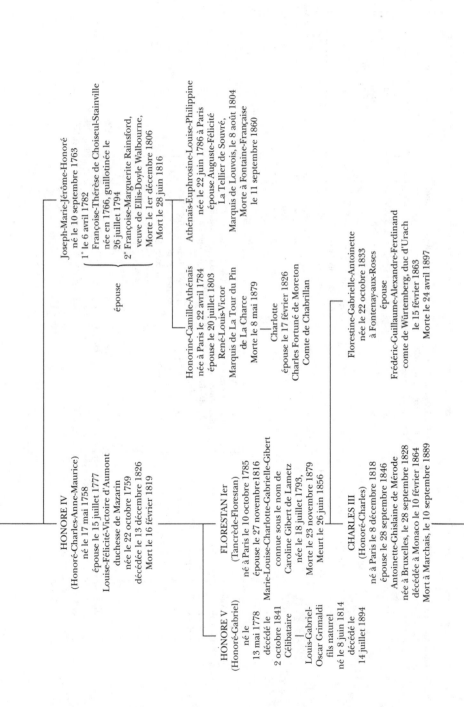

HONORÉ IV
(Honoré-Charles-Anne-Maurice)
né le 17 mai 1758
épouse le 15 juillet 1777
Louise-Félicité-Victoire d'Aumont
duchesse de Mazarin
née le 22 octobre 1759
décédée le 13 décembre 1826
Mort le 16 février 1819

épouse

Joseph-Marie-Jérôme-Honoré
né le 10 septembre 1763
1° le 6 avril 1782
Françoise-Thérèse de Choiseul-Stainville
née en 1766, guillotinée le
26 juillet 1794
2° Françoise-Marguerite Rainsford,
veuve de Ellis-Doyle Walbourne,
Morte le 1er décembre 1806
Mort le 28 juin 1816

Honorine-Camille-Athénaïs
née à Paris le 22 avril 1784
épouse le 20 juillet 1803
René-Louis-Victor
Marquis de La Tour du Pin
de La Charce
Morte le 8 mai 1879

Charlotte
épouse le 17 février 1826
Charles Fortuné de Moreton
Comte de Chabrillan

Athénaïs-Euphrosine-Louise-Philippine
née le 22 juin 1786 à Paris
épouse Auguste-Félicité
Le Tellier de Souvré,
Marquis de Louvois, le 8 août 1804
Morte à Fontaine-Française
le 11 septembre 1860

HONORÉ V
(Honoré-Gabriel)
né le
13 mai 1778
décédé le
2 octobre 1841
Célibataire

Louis-Gabriel-
Oscar Grimaldi
fils naturel
né le 8 juin 1814
décédé le
14 juillet 1894

FLORESTAN Ier
(Tancrède-Florestan)
né à Paris le 10 octobre 1785
épouse le 27 novembre 1816
Marie-Louise-Charlotte-Gabrielle-Gibert
connue sous le nom de
Caroline Gibert de Lametz
née le 18 juillet 1793,
Morte le 23 novembre 1879
Meurt le 26 juin 1856

CHARLES III
(Honoré-Charles)
né à Paris le 8 décembre 1818
épouse le 28 septembre 1846
Antoinette-Ghislaine de Mérode
née à Bruxelles, le 28 septembre 1828
décédée à Monaco le 10 février 1864
Mort à Marchais, le 10 septembre 1889

Florestine-Gabrielle-Antoinette
née le 22 octobre 1833
à Fontenay-aux-Roses
épouse
Frédéric-Guillaume-Alexandre-Ferdinand
comte de Würtemberg, duc d'Urach
le 15 février 1863
Morte le 24 avril 1897

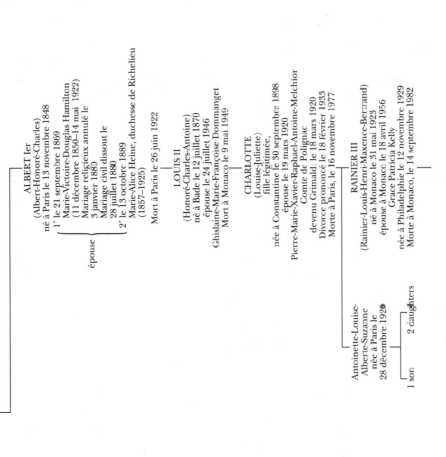

ALBERT Ier
(Albert-Honoré-Charles)
né à Paris le 13 novembre 1848
1° le 21 septembre 1869
Marie-Victoire-Douglas Hamilton
(11 décembre 1850–14 mai 1922)
Mariage religieux annulé le
3 janvier 1880
Mariage civil dissout le
28 juillet 1880
2° le 13 octobre 1889
Marie-Alice Heine, duchesse de Richelieu
(1857–1925)

Mort à Paris le 26 juin 1922

épouse

LOUIS II
(Honoré-Charles-Antoine)
né à Bade le 12 juillet 1870
épouse le 24 juillet 1946
Ghislaine-Marie-Françoise Dommanget
Mort à Monaco le 9 mai 1949

CHARLOTTE
(Louise-Juliette)
fille légitimée,
née à Constantine le 30 septembre 1898
épouse le 19 mars 1920
Pierre-Marie-Xavier-Raphael-Antoine-Melchior
Comte de Polignac
devenu Grimaldi le 18 mars 1920
Divorce prononcé le 18 février 1933
Morte à Paris, le 16 novembre 1977

RAINIER III
(Rainier-Louis-Henri-Maxence-Bertrand)
né à Monaco le 31 mai 1923
épouse à Monaco le 18 avril 1956
Grace Patricia Kelly
née à Philadelphie le 12 novembre 1929
Morte à Monaco, le 14 septembre 1982

Antoinette-Louise-
Alberte-Suzanne
née à Paris le
28 décembre 1920

1 son   2 daughters

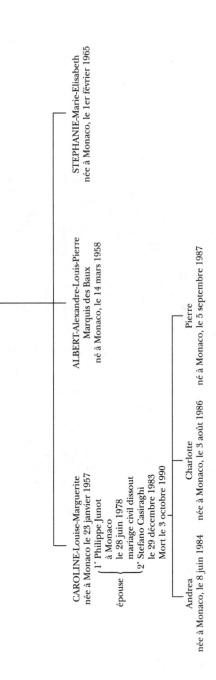

CAROLINE-Louise-Marguerite
née à Monaco le 23 janvier 1957
épouse { 1° Philippe Junot
à Monaco
le 28 juin 1978
mariage civil dissout
2° Stefano Casiraghi
le 29 décembre 1983
Mort le 3 octobre 1990

ALBERT-Alexandre-Louis-Pierre
Marquis des Baux
né à Monaco, le 14 mars 1958

STEPHANIE-Marie-Elisabeth
née à Monaco, le 1er février 1965

Andrea
née à Monaco, le 8 juin 1984

Charlotte
née à Monaco, le 3 août 1986

Pierre
né à Monaco, le 5 septembre 1987

THE FAMILY OF LOUIS XIV

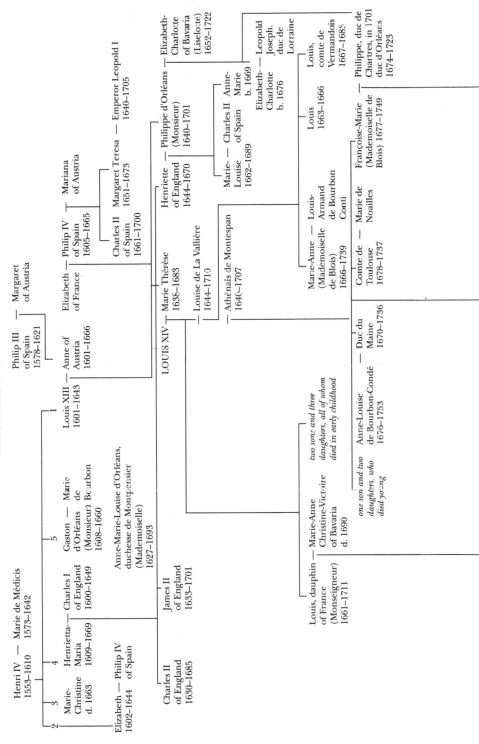

Louis, duc de Bourbon-Condé
1668–1710

Louise-Françoise (Mademoiselle de Nantes) 1673–1743 — Marie-Louise-Elizabeth d'Orléans 1695–1715

Louis, duc de Bourgogne 1682–1712 — Marie-Adélaïde de Savoie 1685–1712

Duc de Bretagne 1704–1705

Second Duc de Bretagne 1707–1712

Duc d'Anjou, in 1700 Philip V of Spain 1683–1746

Duc de Berry 1686–1714

three children who died young

LOUIS XV 1710–1774 — Marie Leczinska 1708–1768

Louis, Dauphin of France 1729–1765 — 1 Marie Raphaëlle of Spain 1726–1746
— 2 Marie Josèphe of Saxony 1731–1767

Philippe de Bourbon Parma 1720–1765 — Louise Elizabeth 1727–1759

Anne Henriette 1727–1752

Marie Adélaïde 1732–1800

Victoire 1733–1799

Sophie 1734–1782

Louise 1737–1787 (Carmelite)

Comte de Provence (later LOUIS XVIII) 1755–1824 — Joséphine Louise of Savoy

Comte d'Artois (later CHARLES X) 1757–1836 — Marie Thérèse of Savoy

Clotilde 1759–1802 — Charles Emmanuel IV of Sardinia

Elisabeth 1764–1794

Duc de Bourgogne 1751–1761

Duc d'Aquitaine 1753–1754

Duc de Berry (later LOUIS XVI) 1754–1793 — ANTOINETTE of Austria 1755–1793

Louis Antoine Duc d'Angoulême 1775–1844

Charles Ferdinand Duc de Berry 1778–1820

Marie Thérèse Charlotte 1778–1851

Duc d'Angoulême, son of Comte d'Artois 1775–1844

Louis Joseph 1781–1789

Louis Charles (LOUIS XVII) 1785–1795

Sophie Hélène Béatrice 1786–1787

INDEX

Abrantès, Duchesse d', 92
Albert, Prince de Monaco, 15, 19,
    270, 271, 273, 276, 281–283,
    297, 300, 302, 308, 310, 324
  appearance and personality of,
    282, 283, 287, 296
  education of, 283, 291, 296, 306
  father's relationship with, 283,
    288, 289–290, 306
  prospective bride of, 304, 306,
    310
Albert I, Prince de Monaco, 92n,
    118, 124, 132, 135–176,
    179–192, 196, 197, 215, 241,
    243, 267–268, 273, 307, 308,
    320
  accession of, 163
  appearance and personality of,
    135, 136, 138, 141, 162, 184–
    185
  Casino as viewed by, 165–166
  death of, 194
  Dreyfus case and, 173–175
  early years of, 135–136
  father's relationship with, 163
  first marriage of, see Douglas-
    Hamilton, Lady Mary Victo-
    ria, Princesse de Monaco
  hunting by, 172, 182–184
  Monégasques' unrest and, 180–
    182
  naval interests of, 136–138, 143,
    146, 148, 149, 151, 153, 159,
    172–173, 185
  oceanographic research of, 143,
    144, 153–154, 159, 160, 162,
    163, 165, 166, 168, 169–170,
    172, 179–180, 183, 191, 192,
    194, 205, 283
  paleontological research of, 170

scientific institutions supported
  by, 179, 180
second marriage of, see Heine,
  Alice, Duchesse de Richelieu,
  Princesse de Monaco
son of, see Louis II, Prince de
  Monaco
U.S. visited by, 136–137, 182–
  184, 191, 320–321
in World War I, 185–189, 191
Albert of Saxe-Coburg-Gotha,
  Prince, 124, 202
Alexandra, Queen of England, 169,
  176
Alfonso XII, King of Spain, 153
Allan, Rupert, 244
American Academy of Dramatic
  Arts, 228–229
American Revolution, 82n
Anderson, A. A., 183
Anne-Hippolyte de Monaco, Duchesse d'Uzès, 41
Anne Marie, Queen of Greece, 303
Antoine I, Prince de Monaco, 36,
  43–56, 59, 65, 70, 313
  accession of, 48
  appearance and personality of,
    45, 46, 50, 54, 58
  children of, 46, 48, 49, 50, 53,
    314; see also Louise-Hippo-
    lyte, Princesse de Monaco
  death of, 56
  as Duc de Valentinois, 41, 43–47
  marriage of, see Lorraine, Marie
    de, Princesse de Monaco
  military career of, 45, 46, 50
  mistresses of, 43, 45, 46, 48, 50,
    314
  musical interests of, 43, 45, 50
  regime of, 45, 48, 49–50, 62